On the far western front

MANCHESTER
1824
Manchester University Press

On the far western front

Britain's First World War in South America

Phillip Dehne

Manchester University Press

Manchester and New York

distributed in the United States exclusively by Palgrave Macmillan

Published by Manchester University Press
Oxford Road, Manchester M13 9NR, UK
and Room 400, 175 Fifth Avenue, New York, NY 10010, USA
www.manchesteruniversitypress.co.uk

Distributed in the United States exclusively by
Palgrave Macmillan, 175 Fifth Avenue, New York,
NY 10010, USA

Distributed in Canada exclusively by
UBC Press, University of British Columbia, 2029 West Mall,
Vancouver, BC, Canada V6T 1Z2

British Library Cataloguing-in-Publication Data
A catalogue record for this book is available from the British Library

Library of Congress Cataloging-in-Publication Data applied for

ISBN   978 0 7190 8005 0   *hardback*

First published 2009

18 17 16 15 14 13 12 11 10 09   10 9 8 7 6 5 4 3 2 1

The publisher has no responsibility for the persistence or accuracy of URLs for any
external or third-party internet websites referred to in this book, and does not guarantee
that any content on such websites is, or will remain, accurate or appropriate.

Typeset
by SNP Best-set Typesetter Ltd., Hong Kong
Printed in Great Britain
by TJ International Ltd, Padstow

For Tanuja

Contents

Acknowledgments

Since I began work on this topic, I have accrued more debts than I can fully acknowledge here. Peter Marsh was there at the start and his support has been critical throughout. At various stages, Michael Miller provided trenchant and wise criticism. I found very useful the comments of my friends Eric Reed and Jana Lipman, particularly in helping me to cull out excesses. I also appreciated earlier comments from (among others) Karin Rosemblatt, Fred Marquardt, Sudipta Sen, and the late Jack Cell. Syracuse University was very supportive with fellowships in the early stages of this project, and St Joseph's College has continued helping with various faculty grants to fund my research. I have particularly appreciated the assistance of Joe Glancey and Monica Brennan of the St Joseph's History Department. My great friends Megan Hickerson and Zan Fancelli have both hosted me during a number of enjoyable research trips to London, and I cannot thank them enough.

The open and helpful nature of so many the libraries and archives of the world is one of the great things about being a historian. I thank the librarians and staff at the British National Archives in Kew, the British Library, the New York Public Library, the Bodleian Library, and the libraries and archives of University College London, the University of London, Cambridge University, Guildhall, Hatfield House, the University of Pennsylvania, Princeton University, and the House of Lords. I would especially like to thank the Cámara de Comercio Argentino-Británica, particularly Jorgelina Capaccio and the director Mónica Mesz, for welcoming me into their offices during a particularly useful research trip. I am happy to acknowledge the Controller of Her Majesty's Stationery Office for permission to reproduce Map 1 from *The Merchant* Navy, by Archibald Hurd, and the Map Collection of the University of Chicago Library for supplying me with the template for Map 2. I also thank the *Journal of British Studies* for publishing an article, "From 'Business as Usual' to a More Global War," that helped me in building the early sections of this book.

My greatest debts are to my family. I appreciate the unconditional support that I have always received from my parents. Jack, Maceo, and Usha have all lived their entire lives with this project, and I treasure both their patience with me when I needed to work and their persistence in routinely luring me away from that work. Most importantly, I thank my wife for everything, and I dedicate this book to her.

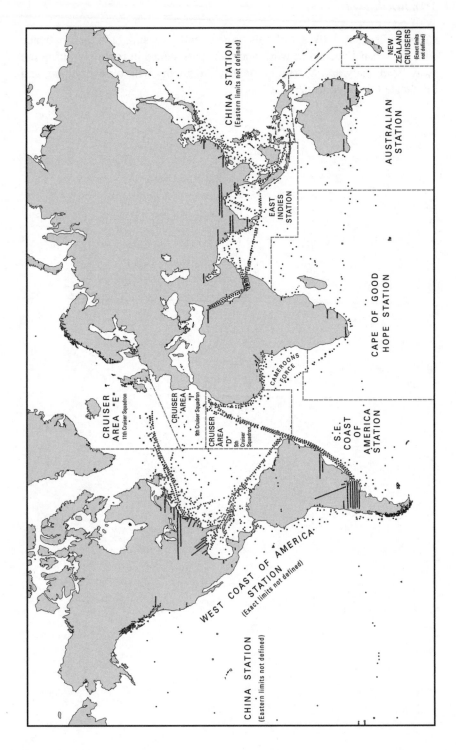

Map 1: *British global shipping in 1912*

Each dot represents the approximate position of all British-flagged merchant vessels on 1 January 1912. The striking predominance of the South American route, particularly the ports of the River Plate, dwarfed traffic to all other destinations around the world including New York and Calcutta, and even European ports like Antwerp and Hamburg, as seen in an inset map not pictured here. Tight, thick sinews of globalization bound together Britain and South America.

From Archibald Hurd, The *Merchant Navy*, vol. I

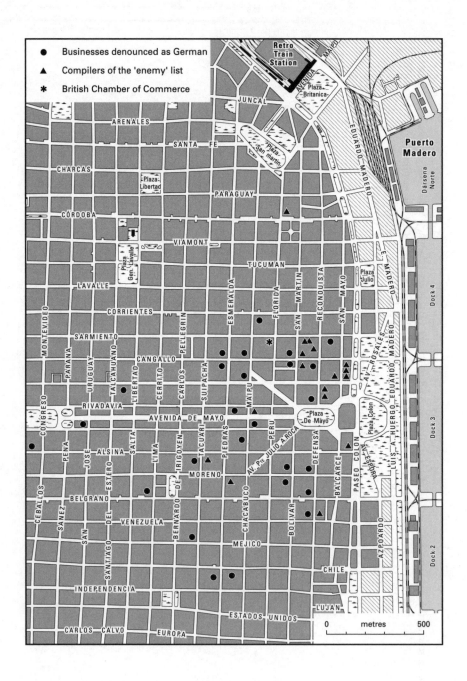

Map 2: *The Centro, Buenos Aires, in 1916*

As indicated by this snapshot of the decisions of the Council of the British Chamber of Commerce on 23 February 1916, in Buenos Aires and other South American cities the economic war pitted neighbor against neighbor. Unlike the jagged linearity of the trenches of the western front, this far western front was geographically pointillist. Including all of the hundreds of German companies in Buenos Aires eventually targeted by the British economic war through 1919 would cover much of this map with dots.

From an early blacklist sent to the Foreign Trade Department on 23 February 1916 (FO 118/390)

Abbreviations

ADM	Admiralty
BT	Board of Trade
CIB	Commercial Intelligence Branch of the Board of Trade
CID	Committee of Imperial Defence
DOT	Department of Overseas Trade
FO	Foreign Office
FBI	Federation of British Industries
FTD	Foreign Trade Department
GBLC	General Blacklist Committee
IAC	Inter Ally Committee
TCH	Trade Clearing House
WTAC	War Trade Advisory Committee
WTD	War Trade Department
WTID	War Trade Intelligence Department

Introduction

A powerful, unprecedented, even total war raged in Europe between 1914 and 1918, with millions slaughtered, billions spent, all efforts proven fruitless by the ensuing dark 1930s and the Second World War. Yet when it comes to the First World War, one cannot help wondering why it has obtained this title of 'World.' Skeptics might argue that the globalization of the war reflects a tendency among westerners to magnify the importance of their own travails throughout history, but in many objective and obvious ways it ranks as a true global war. Armed combatants battled in regions beyond the European theatre, both in heavily colonized Africa and on the high seas. Governments on all sides relied on their ability to mobilize the resources, men and material, from their global empires. The international economy trembled to its core, as the war redirected cross-border flows of trade, capital, and labor. The actions and diplomacy of European combatants eventually persuaded faraway states to enter the conflict, most notably when the United States declared war against Germany in April 1917.

Obviously, there are a variety of ways to measure the breadth of this first true "total war."[1] But despite the constant publication of works on the First World War, the battle for dominance in South America has been completely ignored. Various excellent recent surveys of the First World War, such as those by Keegan, Strachan, and Stevenson, make no mention of Argentina or Brazil.[2] Yet the war took place in South America as well as in Europe. In particular, Britain waged war against the significant German economic presence in those countries. This book uncovers this unknown front of the much commemorated 'Great War,' a campaign that even the men deeply involved, in both South America and the United Kingdom, seem to have written out of their minds after the armistice. There have been histories of how the world war affected South America, but this is the first to show why and how the Great War was fought in a handful of independent states far across the ocean.[3]

Historians of the economic war against Germany during the First World War have focused their attentions squarely on the so-called blockade. Most have been interested in measures taken by Britain, as their command of world shipping, naval dominance in the Atlantic, and financial power gave their economic war more punch than any of the combatants. Those who have written about the blockade have examined the actions undertaken by the British Admiralty to stop ships and cargoes traveling to and from German-controlled territory, the efforts of British regulators to stop trade between the United Kingdom and Germany, and the attempts of British diplomats to cajole and coerce European neutrals into curtailing their own trade with Germany. Debates swirl over what motivated the British government to install the blockade,[4] whether the blockade was conducted in the most effective and efficient manner possible,[5] if it shortened the war,[6] whether the economic war caused the Germans to capitulate more easily to Allied peace terms,[7] and if it should be judged as a legitimate tool of war or overly cruel to neutrals or the German populace.[8] The way that historians have defined and answered questions about the British economic war has been limited geographically to the territory and seas controlled by, or adjacent to, the central powers. Attempts to hurt Germans who lived and worked far across the seas have been largely ignored, apparently under the assumption that such efforts were no more than adjuncts to the blockade, merely aiming to stop supplies to Germany at their source.[9] Moving away from this consistently European focus, this book describes the local roots of the war against Germans in South America.

Bringing South America into the war inevitably entails some explanation of the way that historians have described the continent during the fin-de-siècle. Over the past fifty years, the northern hemisphere's historical relationship with South America has been regularly described through the twin paradigms of imperialism and dependency. South America has long stood as the test case of whether the powerful influence of the British over the economies of sovereign states made such countries a real, if yet informal, part of the British empire. The idea that early twentieth-century South America should fit into the British imperialist project was spurred by John Gallagher and Ronald Robinson and their concept of the "imperialism of free trade."[10] They believed that, unlike in Africa, the expansionist British state had no need to formally intervene in – not to mention annex parts of – South America, where elites in the republics collaborated with the British free trade mantra by opening their lucrative markets to foreign capital and commerce.

D.C.M. Platt, in contrast, argued that imperialist relations only exist where the imperial nation is consciously coercive. According to Platt, this never occurred in Latin America between the middle of the nineteenth century and the First World War. The Foreign Office never considered intervening to help British traders penetrate the continent's marketplaces or to assist bondholders in getting their debts repaid. Britain's foreign trade policy was simple: Foreign Office personnel, who despised questions of commerce, were merely obliged "to ensure that British trade received at least equal treatment" with that given to other powers.[11] More recently, P.J. Cain and A.G. Hopkins reasserted the relevance of the concept of informal empire to South America. According to Cain and Hopkins, British imperialism in South America followed the lead of the City of London, the center of global finance. Close ties between the "gentlemen capitalists" of the City, members of Parliament, and British officials, allowed financial interests to determine policy toward the faraway continent.[12] By regulating the flow of loans to governments and other enterprises in South America, financiers and the British government could guide the republics' fiscal policies, particularly during periods of financial crisis.[13] Although the free market generally reigned, the options available to the republics were "shaped by the major power, in this case Britain."[14] Relations were interdependent, but they were also unequal.[15] To Cain and Hopkins, British imperialism in South America was stronger than ever on the eve of the First World War.

Unfortunately, most major studies of British political and economic relations with South America – most tellingly those of Platt – run only up to August 1914. There has been little attempt to explain the commercial, financial, and administrative changes wrought by war after that date. The work that exists on the First World War is mostly infused by the concept of dependency, which assumes that long-term economic imbalance existed between the South American republics and Britain, and that this imbalance favored Britain. Roger Gravil considered the First World War to be a period when Argentina's subservient position in the world economy, when their reliance on the "metropolitan countries" grew ever more apparent, as Britain manipulated the marketplace to the detriment of Argentina.[16] Bill Albert wrote that the war highlighted not the power of any given foreign country within South America, but rather the problems of South America's abject reliance on primary exports and foreign capital. The way the world economy functioned allowed the Allies, and Britain in particular, to subject South America:

> to a greater degree of open and direct external economic coercion than ever before as the Allied governments sought to monopolize supplies, keep down prices, and with an eye to the postwar situation, destroy the substantial base of economic power established by Germany in Latin America before 1914. The process was to demonstrate that while all countries were interdependent, some were clearly more dependent than others.[17]

Rory Miller followed Gravil and Albert in arguing that the war was a period of unprecedented South American dependence on Britain, which used the leverage provided by its coal, its shipping supplies and its monopsonistic position as purchaser of many South American commodities to wield a heavy hand over the South American economies throughout the war.[18]

In short, imperialism and dependency have enveloped all discussions of the relationship between Britain and South America during the early twentieth century. Obviously, any treatment of the war in South America must take into account imperialism-focused descriptions of the long-term political and, especially, economic relationship, but to do so means entering the divisive debate over whether informal power should be labeled "imperialism." And even those historians of South America who have no qualms in placing the imperial moniker on Argentina or Uruguay are silent on the First World War, which was more than a moment of unequal commercial or financial relations, being instead the open and vociferous conflict of Britain versus Germany.[19] The framework of inequality and the consequences and outcomes of the war for South America have unfortunately often appeared more important than the war actually lived by the trade warriors and their putative victims. Looking at this situation in South America pushes one to attempt to draw together the domestic and imperial history of this era, while resisting but not rejecting the London-centric, top-down focus of much of that imperial historiography.

Perhaps it is time for a new framework of analysis for early twentieth-century South America. A meaningful direction beyond imperialism to describe this confusion of war is the idea of globalization, a historical concept critical to understanding the late nineteenth and early twentieth-century world.[20] The prophets of informal imperialism, Cain and Hopkins, have suggested that imperial history might be simply the keystone of a new, broader history of globalization.[21] The First World War took place during a period of intense global interaction and integration that was probably more economically integrated than that of a century later.[22] Markets had in many ways slipped beyond the control of the nation state, with large-scale migration of labor and communications networks enabling competition on a worldwide scale, leaving the entire world prey to global economic cycles. Some aspects of globalization might still be controlled by the global core. For example, Avner Offer has shown that Britain's ability to mobilize food resources across the Anglophone world undoubtedly proved crucial to Allied victory.[23]

But, unlike dependency or imperialism, theories of globalization allow for the possibility that global integration could work both in favor of, and against, a dominant power. Not just the story of international economic and demographic integration, globalization also encompasses the political decisions and social tendencies supporting global disintegration that certainly coexisted with the general movement toward integration in the early twentieth century.[24] Globalization allows us to see the commercial war in South America not solely as a temporary offshoot of a European conflict, but also as an intensification of the conflict-ridden transnationalism that defined the fin-de-siècle world. Likewise the concept of globalization opens new ways of analyzing the relationship between imperialism and the late nineteenth-century nationalism that helped to breed the Great War. As C.A. Bayly has explained, the states of Europe grew more militarized and warlike in a reflection of, and spur to, upsurges of nationalism among their own people. The late nineteenth century "scramble for empire" was both instigated and intensified by popular and state-supported nationalism at home in Europe – a process which fertilized and transformed the existing nationalisms of local imperialized populations, contributing to new identities that ultimately destabilized imperial rule.[25] Such transnational history recognizes that nations were not merely transcended by globalization, but were also the products of the global process.[26] Bayly's erudition spans a nearly global range of historiographies, but he is conscious of leaving out Latin America and finishes his story at 1914. This book attempts to remedy this by examining wartime South American national identities bred in transnational integration and conflict, and steeped in economic and cultural imperialism.

The growing consciousness that intricate linkages brought unprecedented unity to economic, political, and cultural relations between countries transformed many aspects of early twentieth-century life. It brought new fervor to long-contested global issues such as the meaning of international law and, particularly, the definition of neutrality during wartime. The new understanding of globalization also threatened to transform the traditionally conservative attitude that the British government held towards business. Furthermore, globalization shaped the identities of the Britons who waged economic war against the Germans in South America. Historians focusing on the creation of a late nineteenth-century "Greater Britain" (to use the best of a variety of possible terms for the late nineteenth-century globalization of British identities) have consistently examined only the Empire and the Dominions.[27] However, South America was not without its Britons, and more broadly, Britons were not oblivious to South America. This book attempts to determine just what sense of British identity immigrant and business populations had in South America, and what South America meant for British nationalism, by examining the place of South America, its individual republics, and its economic sectors within the mentality of various British trade warriors. At the same time, it analyzes how globalized Britishness interacted with broader and stronger countervailing forces in South America, contributing to the rising power of nationalist and anti-globalization politics and economics that have long been recognized as significantly marking these countries in the decades after the First World War.

In short, this book globalizes a war that took place in what has been recognized as an early era of globalization. In doing so, it integrates the hitherto disparate histories of the First World War, particularly the economic war, with those of imperialism, dependency, and national identity. Manipulating the sinews of world trade could hold incredible allure for the dominant central power, yet even hegemonic powers had difficulty controlling its forces. This war inevitably brings into question the possibility of success in enforcing trade wars, sanctions, and boycotts in a globalized economy. It may be instructive to look back a century to an earlier era of globalization to examine the potential problems existing in the present early twenty-first-century order, or disorder. As in the early 1900s, certain states, companies, and communities now hold global economic, political, and cultural powers, both hard and soft, that are undoubtedly imbalanced but rarely absolute. This war utilized all types of British power to accomplish a variety of goals, yet the outcome proved truly unpredictable. Undoubtedly, the lessons from Britain's Great War in South America might be useful, either as guidelines or warnings, for the dominant power of the present globalized age.

This book is concerned with British power and perceptions. Focusing on British warfare inevitably means examining a wide variety of records. Other historians have already tackled the inside story of their German opponents.[28] Instead, this book describes the actions and attitudes of the Britons engaged in the attack. In the British National Archives (formerly the Public Record Office), ministries including the Foreign Office, Admiralty, and Board of Trade have deposited many relevant records of committee meetings, inter- and intra-departmental discussions, and correspondence with diplomats, businessmen, and self-styled patriots at home and abroad. The British people of South America come alive through their letters and accounts of their discussions and complaints in the records of British diplomats and consuls, in their local newspapers, and in the records of individual British companies and banks established in South America. Along with such business archives, this book utilizes for the first time the wartime records of the British Chamber of Commerce in Argentina, allowing a unique view of how transatlantic economic war was waged on the local level. In this wide variety of sources appear many aspects of the German response, for example, describing how some Germans were hurt by the British war while others repelled the attack. But the overall aim of this book is to recover the lives and decisions of the British who fought this war.

While examining a war against Germans across South America, this book focuses particular attention upon the countries stretched along the continent's Atlantic coast – Argentina, Uruguay, and Brazil. The British campaign began in these three republics and eventually spread across the continent, and indeed across the Americas. Throughout the First World War, the most lusty trade warriors, and their most loathed targets, operated in the eastern republics. The centrality of Buenos Aires in instigating and leading the war makes the story of Britons there particularly crucial to describing the war in South America. Although countries such as Chile, Peru, and Venezuela, held significant British and German interests, Britain's most pronounced war against Germans occurred along the Atlantic, where the British communities quickly united against an undoubtedly formidable German commercial presence. German-identified companies nearly monopolized trade in Argentine grain, Uruguayan wool, and Brazilian coffee – the most crucial commodities in these thriving export-driven economies. By contrast, in pre-war Chile, German firms held merely 15 percent of the nitrate trade.[29] The haunting threat from German trade was most pronounced in the eastern republics, whereas along the western coast British merchants and entrepreneurs tended to worry more about competitors from the United States.[30] As shown in this book, largely satisfied British merchants in Santiago jettisoned free trade and refocused themselves on national community with far less urgency than their highly agitated brethren in Buenos Aires, Montevideo, and Rio de Janeiro. As the British commercial war was devised with the possibility of attenuation or enhancement according to local circumstances, it is significant that this unique war stabbed most sharply in Argentina, Brazil, and Uruguay. It was in these countries that the overall success or failure of Britain's war in South America must be measured.

1

The rise of the Anglo-German antagonism in South America, 1900–14

In his yearly report on the trade of the Brazilian state of Rio Grande do Sul for the year 1900, Percy Staniforth, the local British Consul, explained that in years past local British merchants had dominated the thriving port. British goods poured in, transported on a regularly scheduled parade of steamships flying the Union Jack. But when the "prosperous era showed signs of waning," British merchants and steamship owners "withdrew with a competence from a field which no longer offered sufficient scope for (their) enterprise." Staniforth noted that since then, the local economy had indeed somewhat slumped. Perhaps the British merchants and shippers – pioneers in southern Brazil – showed their legendary commercial wisdom in leaving when they did.

Or perhaps not. Staniforth continued:

> I have been informed that when it was understood that a prominent steamship line, which has the practical monopoly of the shipping of Rio Grande, was about to abandon the port, serious representations were made to them, pointing out that the trade would inevitably fall into German hands. I understand that their reply was to the effect that, as the trade no longer suited them, such a result was immaterial to them. These forebodings have been fulfilled, and a steamship trade, of which British owners had abandoned the practical monopoly, because their capital and enterprise could be better employed elsewhere, has indeed been taken up by German steamship companies.[1]

Similarly, in Santos, Brazil, Consul Francis W. Mark declared that Britain's declining share of imports such as woolens, linens, china, silk, glass, and paper, indicated that there was "something fundamentally wrong" with British business.[2] In Buenos Aires, the British Consul Arthur Grenfell complained that the British percentage of Argentine imports and exports had declined over the previous year, while the German percentages increased markedly. He believed the trend might be reversed if British merchants worked hard, "but unless this energy is shown, Germany's trade with this country will increase to the detriment of British trade."[3] All of these British consuls, and many others across the continent, feared that the Germans were taking over the economic life of the region, and expressed bitterness that the British ceded these markets without a fight.

As the nineteenth century ended, the British in South America worried about Britain's declining share of the continent's trade. Diplomats based in Argentina, Brazil, and Uruguay, along with local British newspapers and certain businessmen, called for resistance against an apparently expansionist Germany. In the fifteen years before the First World War, these Britons developed ideas about the national commercial characteristics of South America's main trading partners. Generally unimpressed with the potential for competition from the United States, these British officials and their merchant allies in South America derided increasingly ineffective British methods of conducting trade, in sharp contrast to the devious but successful German model.

Most historians have downplayed as misguided or unrealistic such perceptions that German trade threatened British dominance. They point to myriad illustrations of British power in South America. British capital certainly ruled everywhere.[4] In 1913, British investors held 60 percent of all foreign investments in Argentina.[5] Far from wilting in the face of competition, British investors had actually appeared to increase their hegemony over the previous decade. After the passage of the Mitre Law in 1907 simplified rules and regulations on railway investment and operations, railroads entered their "golden era" in Argentina, as the country's largely British-owned rail network spread its tentacles into the pampas.[6] The London money market loaned vast sums to the governments of republics, provinces, and cities across the continent. Britain likewise controlled the overwhelming share of the steamship services that traveled across the oceans to the continent's ports. In 1910, 56.4 percent of the tonnage entering Argentina's ports from overseas flew the Union Jack.[7]

In commerce and trade Britain likewise held primary importance through 1914. Statistically, the United Kingdom was the main import and export partner of Argentina and Uruguay. If not for the coffee addictions of United States consumers, Britain would likewise have held the same primary trading roles with Brazil. Through the nineteenth century, British merchant houses in the port cities handled most of South America's foreign trade, helping to give the British a special influence over the local people and governments. In Brazil, British merchants held tremendous power within the economic and political system and also influenced Brazilian intellectual culture by stimulating the activities of free traders, entrepreneurs, and abolitionists.[8] Similarly, in Argentina, the British community reigned as the most economically and socially important expatriate group in a country peopled with immigrants from across Europe. In the bustling port city of Buenos Aires, British traders reaped the greatest profits, benefiting from their connections to exporters, manufacturers, and shipowners in Britain who valued their knowledge of the Argentine market, government and society.[9]

Yet, at the turn of the century, many British observers worried about their own relative decline. Relentlessly pessimistic, they consistently overlooked the continued dominance of British shipping, insurance, and merchant banking. Instead, British officials lamented that Britain's share of the three republics' overall foreign trade sagged while Germany's share ballooned. German manufacturers supplied ever-larger percentages of the continent's needs in such goods as woolens, electrical supplies, and hardware. In part, the decline of British trade went hand in hand with the deterioration of the system of trading through merchant houses, as manufacturers sold more directly to their customers in South America.[10] But enhanced competition from entrepreneurs of German background painfully exacerbated such troubles for British houses. In the eyes of many local Britons, German merchant houses had effectively grasped control of many of the goods shipped to and from South America, including exports of coffee, wool, and grain, and imports of drugs, chemicals, and consumer goods. Germans seemed to control the sectors that had propelled South America's economic expansion since the 1880s. Ultimately, this chapter suggests that just as the Great War had roots in the "worldwide confrontation between Britain and Germany," in places like Mesopotamia, Algeria, and Tanganyika, it also had roots in the River Plate and Rio de Janeiro.[11]

Imports into South America

As the twentieth century entered its second decade, producers in the United Kingdom still commanded the lion's share of the import markets of Brazil, Argentina and Uruguay.[12] As could have been reported from most regions of these countries, a British official in São Paulo in 1912 explained that "the United Kingdom continues, as hitherto, to occupy first position in respect of imports into the State." However, he continued warily, the British "may have a close competitor in Germany by the end of 1914."[13] The British and Germans competed at each link of the chain of business transactions that marked all import trades. While downplaying the power inherent in bastions of British dominance like banking and merchant shipping, or complaining about the lack of coordination between British businesses, observers like Sir Reginald Tower, the British minister at Buenos Aires, concluded that British trade had shrunk in the face of competition. In Tower's opinion, "It would be supposed that every branch of trade would be studied and successfully developed, but the reverse seems to be sometimes the case."[14]

In the eyes of such pessimists, there were plenty of culprits. They rained blame down on the conservative, non-nationalistic lending practices of British bankers; on the rigidity and blindness of manufacturers in Britain as to the need for new marketing methods and types of goods; and on the changing British merchant communities in the South American ports. As the market-place of South America transformed, British businessmen struggled to keep up. German innovations exposed a variety of weaknesses in how the British conducted foreign trade. "The means employed in such competition are not in accordance with the business principles they (the British) are accustomed to," wrote one official.[15] The British commercial banks that handled the exchange and credit operations for many buyers of imports in South America had a reputation for trustworthiness and solidity. Unfortunately, this reputation largely resulted from their conservative practices. Banks failed to undertake new types of business and seemed content to maintain their traditional roles in exchange transactions and as a safe place for locals to deposit funds. Their policies of extending nothing but short-term credits, and even those only to businessmen deemed to be extremely safe credit risks, meant that the British banks left much potential business untouched.[16] In comparison, recently established German merchants and banks were known for more freewheeling credit terms and, as a result, quickly expanded their operations. German import houses gave more financial assistance to Brazilian buyers than the British.[17] German firms allowed long terms of credit to local buyers of imported goods: "Six and nine months are the usual periods . . . and there is, too, a readiness to extend the credit to 12 months if desired." British firms refused to grant such loans for periods longer than three months.[18] British bankers scoffed that such loans simply highlighted the desperate inexperience of German banks in Brazil, yet critics of British bankers recognized that these liberal lending practices won the Germans market share at the expense of the risk averse British.

Resolutely free-market and laissez-faire in their attitudes, British banks operating in South America repeatedly rejected proposals to tie the bestowal of credit to purchases of British-made goods. This incensed those British in South America who believed in national competition against Germany. On the eve of the First World War, the vigilant and opinionated Minister to Uruguay, Alfred Mitchell Innes, explained to the Foreign Office that a British construction company had just won a tender to pave roads in Montevideo, but had done so with money from a local German bank in Buenos Aires. The contractor went to the Germans, Mitchell Innes contended, only after the London and River Plate Bank refused to give them an advance. "It is one of the duties of our banks to support English companies," he proclaimed to his superiors.[19] But the banks did not agree.

Others traced the weaknesses in the British hold over the import trade to the practices of British shipping lines. As of January 1912, the River Plate was the main destination for British ships, far eclipsing even New York and Calcutta (see map 1).[20] Despite the dominance of British-flagged shipping, critics complained that it was not used in a nationalist manner, as lines gave rebates to all firms that shipped large amounts, regardless of their nationality. In recently established ports, British imports were hampered by the lack of a steamer service from England. In São Francisco do Sul, Brazil, the regularity of sailings by German lines meant that 64 percent of the city's direct imports came from Germany, while only 4 percent arrived from Great Britain. As Vice-Consul Addison noted, "the want of a similar (steamship) service from home for British exporters, even at less frequent intervals, helps to cripple importation from the United Kingdom."[21] Owen Philipps, the chairman of the Royal Mail Steam Packet Company, recognized the problem, explaining to the *Daily Mail* just months before the start of the war that Germany was the only rival to British shipping in Brazil and Argentina.[22] British steamship owners sniveled that corrupt local officials in Argentina and Brazil gave berthing and customs preferences to ships flying the German flag; but drawing on the reports of his diplomats in the field, Sir Edward Grey, the Foreign Secretary, publicly repudiated this complaint.[23]

The British of South America also blamed industrialists at home, accusing factory owners in the Midlands and Lancashire of ignoring South American consumers and incorrectly marketing their goods. Consuls and diplomats lamented that the few traveling salesmen sent by manufacturers rarely knew the local language. These travelers neglected newer marketplaces. During 1910, twenty-five German commercial travelers visited Cuyaba, as compared to only three British salesmen.[24] Sir Reginald Tower constantly fielded complaints about the way that British manufacturers labeled boxes and crates " 'This side up' or 'Not to be left in the sun,' regardless of the fact that the cases will be handled by persons knowing only the Spanish language."[25] The Germans, on the other hand, always sent their goods marked in the local language, with metric weights and measurements. Such complaints about anglocentrism in language, weights, and measures coexisted with criticism of a lack of anglocentrism in local hiring. Many Germans held the agencies of companies based in the United Kingdom, but critics claimed that German agents pushed sales of the German products they represented harder than British ones. British manufacturers should use only British-run agencies concentrating on national products, argued the British consul at Santa Catharina, or else they would never obtain a foothold in that newly populated southern Brazilian market.[26]

Such British representatives might help home manufacturers to respond to changes in demand, by recognizing that South Americans needed different types of goods than Europeans. The consul in Santos believed that British industry too often exhibited a snobbish disdain for South American consumers who valued low cost over high quality: "If there is a market for a lower class of goods, why not cater for it?"[27] Others lectured that South Americans preferred "cheap and showy" goods to those coming from English factories. Manufacturers should copy German brands, for instance, by packaging soap and perfume in attractive boxes with ribbons.[28] Most imports from the United Kingdom were of goods that they had long dominated, particularly textiles and coal.[29] British produce from new industries such as chemicals and electrical goods failed to penetrate South America. Sir Reginald Tower worried about the lack of electrical goods coming from Britain to Argentina, as South American cities were shifting to electric lighting, Tower speculated that the market for such goods was potentially vast. Unfortunately, this blossoming market had apparently escaped the notice of British manufacturers who, in Tower's eyes, had made no effort to sell such British products in Argentina. He quoted figures from the prime electrical trade journal, which showed that German electrical exports to the eastern republics of South America swamped those from Britain or the United States. Tower concluded that South America would soon be one of the most important export markets for the powerful German electrical industry.[30]

British consuls grew to assume that their reports went unread by businessmen in Britain, as British firms continued to repeat mistakes that previous reports had warned against, such as sending merchandise marked in the English language rather than Spanish or Portuguese.[31] But most firms doing business in the republics would have seen the readily available reports, and they also had plentiful information about their failings from their own sources. Reports commissioned by industrial interest groups in the United Kingdom took their members to task. After completing a two-year study of Argentina, in 1908, N.L. Watson reported back to British manufacturers that they had their heads in the sand when it came to that market. "It is pleasant to be told not to bother about British Trade, that 'British trade is all right.' But it is not entirely reassuring when such lessons as can be derived from statistics and the opinions of less successful men are largely opposed to this view."[32] Watson was quite certain that "at the present moment Germany is firmly established in the country, and its trade is continually increasing." As "perhaps the most important factor in international trade is the nationality of the importers," the almost complete disappearance of British merchant houses from Buenos Aires constituted a tremendous problem for British manufacturing, but the ultimate blame rested on the manufacturers themselves. Watson concluded "that although German (importing) firms have a natural preference for dealing with their own country, they are always ready to do business with English houses provided that the latter make it profitable for them to do so." He implored British manufacturers to innovate their sales techniques, particularly in granting credit to purchasers in South America. Exporters and manufacturers in Great Britain could not have failed to hear such blunt critiques of their practices in the South American markets. The City of London likewise acknowledged problems responding to changes in the local credit markets, as Germans undermined the established British firms of Argentina by selling directly from manufacturers to the customers, with only a well-trained, active German agent as intermediary.[33]

Their reluctance to change, despite recognizing their own deficiencies, meant that British industrialists, exporters, shipowners, and bankers deserved much of the blame for the relative decline in the British share of South America's imports.[34] Yet they all pointed the finger elsewhere. Some complained that the poor schooling of men in the United Kingdom made it impossible to improve their sales force abroad. At the 1912 annual meeting of the Anglo-South American Bank, a shareholder who knew the continent at first hand told of the desperate need for qualified Englishmen. "The young Englishman has only to learn the language, go out and play the game, and you will find he will prosper more rapidly in South America than he ever would in Cornhill or Threadneedle Street. Apart from this, if he lives the life of a gentleman over there, he will unconsciously become a maker of Empire." "The only thing I think our countrymen are lacking is a little of the element of push," he explained.[35]

By contrast, the motivated, ambitious Germans were capable of pushing themselves. "I have seen Germans chosen as Managers to British, French, and Brazilian houses," wrote another British subject about his experience in the Santos coffee trade, "because, quite apart from the aggressive and detestable policy of their Government, the individual German possesses thoroughness, industry and an educational equipment which is unequaled by other nationalities."[36] They knew the local languages, understood the way that local markets ran, and worked hard to succeed. "If we are to hold our own against the well-equipped and well-organised German competition and the many inborn and sterling qualities of that race," he explained, then the British must copy Germany's proven formula for success. James Bryce, the former British Ambassador to the United States, agreed. His book on South America quoted favorably the American discoverer of Machu Picchu, Hiram Bingham, who stated that "the well-educated young German who is being sent out to capture South America commercially is a power to be reckoned with . . . He is going to damage England more truly than dreadnoughts or airships."[37]

Exports from South America

After the 1890s, merchant houses owned or operated by Germans became the main exporters of many lucrative commodities including Brazilian coffee, Uruguayan hides and wool, and Argentine wheat and other grains. German houses dominated throughout the chain of exchanges sending primary goods from producer to customer. Consul Daniel O'Sullivan-Beare in Bahia, Brazil, tellingly described the tobacco industry of his district in 1907:

> The export trade of tobacco from Bahia is controlled by a number of German firms, who exhibit much enterprise in connection with that business. They finance the planters; they despatch their agents into all parts of the interior of the State to buy on the spot; and, usually, they purchase, for cash down, the tobacco crops when barely above ground. Such a method of trading obviously entails heavy risks; but, on the other hand, large profits are frequently made; and the fact that the German firms continue year after year to conduct business on the same lines would tend to prove that their methods work out satisfactorily for them on the whole.[38]

O'Sullivan-Beare noted that a small number of German-owned firms controlled local cigar manufacturing in a similar manner. As a result, most Bahian tobacco traveled to Europe through the German ports of Bremen and Hamburg rather than London.

Of course, tobacco was of minor importance to Brazil when compared to coffee. Brazil controlled 60 percent of world trade in coffee by 1913, and the bean accounted for more than half of the value of Brazil's exports between the 1870s and 1911.[39] German syndicates were considered the prime foreign owners of coffee *fazendas* – the largest planter in the state of São Paulo was a man named Schmidt, a naturalized Brazilian with German parents who, by 1916, owned approximately ten million coffee plants. However, the more significant form of control came from the German middlemen, the exporters headquartered in the Brazilian ports. The largest shipper from the burgeoning coffee port of Santos was the German firm Theodore Wille & Co., "one of whose local partners is always German Consul," according to a British competitor.[40] In 1911 the government of the state of São Paulo appointed Theodore Wille to run its valorization scheme.[41] Through Wille, the government bought coffee from planters at set prices and stockpiled it in warehouses in European and Brazilian ports, thus stopping exporters from continuing their own purchases of beans from planters at prices that assumed a low demand, and then stockpiling it themselves for sale abroad when world prices rose.[42] By taking some coffee out of the marketplace, the valorization purchases drove up world coffee prices. Such German exporters controlled the shipping and sale of Brazilian coffee overseas through the start of the war.

Despite their long-held reputation as a nation of merchants, the British found it difficult to compete in Brazilian coffee. British bankers in Brazil believed that financing coffee was too risky. The *fazendeiros* in the interior, who grew the coffee, ran up debts to the *commissarios* who bought the beans from them. These inland agents tried to obtain credit directly from British banks in the cities, but the London & Brazilian Bank preferred to deal with the large exporters such as Theodore Wille or Naumann Gepp rather than bypassing them to become direct creditors of the *commissarios*.[43] In the Brazilian coffee trade, only two of the top seven shippers were British, and they handled only 20 percent of the total exports. Even the largest supposedly British firm, Naumann Gepp & Co. Ltd, was founded by a German and employed German managers. The nationality of the exporters had proved to be important to the destination of the coffee. In 1908, Germany imported 1.93 million bags of coffee from Santos, while the United Kingdom only imported 0.21 million.[44] "It seems a pity," Consul Francis Mark lamented, "that the once important transit and distributing trade in coffee, once centred in London, has been transferred to Hamburg."[45] He and other British in Brazil refused to believe that just because British drinkers preferred tea, their businessmen should abdicate their position in the European coffee trade.

Germans held even tighter control of Argentine grain exports. In the 1880s, wheat and other grains came under intensive cultivation across the pampas. European-based commercial partnerships erected large establishments in Buenos Aires and Rosario, branches which usually became the center of the company.[46] At the turn of the century, the so-called 'Big Four' firms commanded the entire structure of the wheat trade by holding credit over the heads of agents and farmers in the pampas.[47] Although there has been some disagreement as to their nationality, the Big Four were definitely not British.[48] For example, the largest company, Bunge & Born, appeared to be international in management and partnership, with large contingents of both Belgian and German capital, headquartered in Belgium but with tremendous powers held by the flagship Buenos Aires branch. All of the Big Four grain companies were managed by men who identified themselves as Germans, appearing regularly at the Club Alemán and other local German institutions. As Sir Reginald Tower insisted repeatedly, with obvious prejudice, most of these men were German Jews. Britons accused these big firms of collusion in the international marketplace, in the grain options markets of Rosario and Buenos Aires, and in purchasing from farmers along the railway lines. According to Tower, the Big Four "constitute practically a trust."[49] It was a trust without British members; on the eve of war, British firms controlled merely 9 percent of the grain exports from Argentina.

Market share of Argentine exports (as % of Argentine total)

German companies	
Bunge & Born	23
Huni & Wormser	10.5
Weil Brothers	10
General Mercantile Co.	9.5
Hardy & Mühlenkamp	7
German total	*60*

British companies	
Sanday & Co.	6
Procter, Garrett, Marston, & Co.	3
British total	*9*

Note: These statistics result from amalgamating the lists of suspected enemy firms and solidly British firms given by British Consul General Mackie to Tower (Tower to FO No. 356 of 7 Nov. 1915, FO No. 185729 of 6 Dec. 1915. FO 368/1203) with the percentages of the pre-war grain market held by each firm in a letter from Harold Ford of Ford & Co. to Tower on 27 Oct. 1915 (Tower to FO No. 345 of 27 Oct. 1915, F.O. 181525 of 30 Nov. 1915. FO 368/1207).

Not a few observers saw this as unfortunate, especially considering the fact that the vast bulk of these grains went to the United Kingdom. Tower warned the Foreign Office in 1913 that the Big Four had a potential stranglehold over these goods vital to feeding the United Kingdom. Yet other British-owned businesses refused to help nurture British exporters in Argentina. The British-owned railways in Argentina continued to tie themselves to large German firms by granting rebates to companies willing to ship exclusively with their line. British merchant shipowners followed similar practices.[50] To British banks, life without the German-run grain export firms in the ports became unimaginable, and they fretted whenever it appeared that they might lose any of the Big Four as customers. In early 1914, the head of the London and River Plate Bank in Buenos Aires explained to a colleague that if Bunge & Born asked for facilities to exchange more than £150,000 at a time, the conservative practices pushed by their home office in London might lead the bank to refuse the business. The bank's manager, Harry Scott, feared that this would offend Bunge & Born and that that they would no longer decide to utilize the bank for any transactions.[51]

Like coffee and wheat, wool flowed almost exclusively through non-British firms. Wool was big business in Argentina and Uruguay, two countries endowed with vast pasturelands. The River Plate region produced 25–30 percent of the world's wool.[52] As the region around Buenos Aires and Rosario became dominated by beef and wheat farming, sheep-rearing shifted southward. From the southern port of Galleagos, the British consular agent described massive growth in local wool exports, but complained that the only wool-buying agencies in the territory were German, and the only ships that called regularly were coastal steamers owned by the Hamburg-South American shipping line.[53] Every year, Germany received about one-third of its raw wool from Argentina and Uruguay. These shipments from the River Plate to Germany bypassed London financial facilities, with the business transacted by German banks utilizing drafts in French francs or German marks.[54] The largest firms in the trade, Engelbert, Hardt & Co. and Staudt & Co., ran large and prosperous businesses out of both Montevideo and Buenos Aires, led by German partners and managers.

British national commercial character and the German threat

Should the evaporation of the British presence in the South American ports and marketplaces be attributed to the good sense of British businessmen? The historian D.C.M. Platt argues that British manufacturers and traders made a tactical withdrawal from South America to more lucrative, less competitive markets in the British empire. Recognizing that their worldwide market share was certain to decline relative to Germany and the United States, British industrialists and merchants pulled back from South America, where further healthy returns appeared less than certain.[55]

However, many of the British in South America would have derided Platt as defeatist, just as they derided the British bankers and shippers of their own day. The annual reports of British consuls and diplomats exhibited profound anti-German feelings among British officials and merchants. Command of the "Export-Import Complex" had long given Britain influence in the economic and political affairs of Brazil, Argentina, and Uruguay.[56] The fact that German business increasingly ruled the foreign trade of the republics struck many of the local British as ominous and terrible. These men wanted their nation, Great Britain, to repel German economic and political incursions into South America. They believed that British trade had lost control of profitable sectors due to German competition. To remedy the problem, they hoped that traders, industrialists, and all other commercial interests of their country would struggle to reassert their national identity by considering themselves part of a "Greater Britain," fighting in league with their fellow countrymen against Germany and *Deutschtum*.

British commercial nationalists recognized that such changes would transform the self-image of the British in the republics. The British in Argentina,

Brazil, and Uruguay believed simply that British businessmen conducted themselves more ethically than their competitors. The phrase '*palabra de Inglés*', the word of an Englishman, exemplified to South Americans an ideal of trustworthiness. British merchants refused to renege on contracts, promptly repaid debts, and refused to bribe customs officials and government purchasing departments. Correct practices were based on the dogmas of laissez-faire and free trade. Self-reliance was traditionally a moral imperative to British businessmen, who rejected government aid or mutual assistance. They judged the Germans as immoral because they worked together and because their government aided their trade expansion.

In other words, these Britons adhered to a specific and traditional commercial morality. But at the start of the twentieth century, attitudes began to change. British businessmen and officials in South America debated among themselves, and with their counterparts in the United Kingdom, whether it was worthwhile to maintain morally correct commercial practices even if it damaged their overall trade. A rift grew within the global British business community in regard to the South American marketplace. Shipping lines and banks resolutely refused to change any practices merely to benefit their countrymen abroad. This exasperated those officials and British merchants established in South America who believed that increasing their links with British business at home would reverse their downfall. As their presence in the local economy waned, British businessmen and diplomats in South America began to see themselves as a part of a larger British nation, imagining themselves as a community that must oppose the Germans, in league with their British brothers across the Atlantic.

The British already held a significant nationally oriented presence in South America. The English language press in South American towns helped to nurture local British communities.[57] Aided in geographic scope and immediacy of their coverage after 1876 by the transatlantic cable, papers such as the *Standard* and the *Herald* in Buenos Aires focused on British news from around the world, and also on news of the local Anglo-Porteño community, such as cricket and football matches. The advent of passenger steam liner traffic likewise enhanced interaction between the British in South America and at home, especially those of the merchant classes. Undoubtedly, a number of Britons did not see themselves as real immigrants, always recognizing "the possibility of return."[58] As Sir David Kelly, a young diplomat appointed to Argentina in 1919, later explained in his autobiography,

Young English immigrants came in without impediment, employed English lawyers, doctors and architects, shopped at Harrod's great local branch in Buenos Aires and Thompson's furniture stores, etc., and if they wished, retired to England either with their whole capital or with the (as it seemed then)

certainty of having their incomes or pensions remitted to them as though they
had merely moved from Birmingham to London.[59]

Globalization of labor and capital could appear no more complete.

Yet despite the option of return, most British immigrants appeared ready
to stay in South America forever. By building up a number of local British
institutions over the course of the nineteenth century, they did not need to
return to live a fully British life. In Buenos Aires, these included the Anglican
churches, the Scottish Presbyterian church, a variety of missions for seamen,
the British Hospital, the British Society in the Argentine, the British Club,
the Masonic Lodge, the Royal Colonial Institute, the Hurlingham Club, the
Belgrano Athletic Club, the British and American Benevolent Society, some
childrens' homes and sailors' homes, the Salvation Army, St George's
College, and more than twenty English schools.[60] "Golf clubs, lawn tennis
clubs, etc., in and about Buenos Ayres spring up like mushrooms, money
being apparently always available for benevolent or athletic objects affecting
the British community," explained Sir Reginald Tower, who in his duties as
British minister often appeared at the functions of such groups.[61] In the three
years before the war, the British people of Buenos Aires began to construct
a £40,000 clock tower, a virtual replica of Big Ben to commemorate the
centenary of Argentina's independence.[62] Like other large, assertively British
buildings, such as the Harrods department store on Calle Florida and the
Retiro train station, the memorial tower arose as a grand physical embodiment
of British power and economic successes in Argentina over the previous
century. Even while celebrating Argentine independence, these Anglo-
Argentines spared no expense to assert their Britishness.

In many ways, British diplomats and an increasing number of *soi-disant*
Britons in South America saw themselves as part of a global cultural community of "Greater Britain."[63] Since Dilke coined the term, "Greater Britain"
has ordinarily referred to the cultural connections that have been maintained
between Great Britain and white settler colonies overseas, ones that have
often been thought to have geostrategic consequences for the Empire.
Such analyses, whether they utilize the term "Greater Britain" or not, always
include Canada, Australia, New Zealand, and often South Africa and the
United States. The cultural nationalism of the numerically puny but economically dominant British groups in the South American cities should fall
under this umbrella, as these people, despite being far away from home
at times for generations, if anything increasingly identified themselves as
British. They considered themselves quite British, living largely within
English-speaking communities with their own local newspapers, churches,
garden suburbs and football clubs. They were slow to assimilate, did not
take the learning of Spanish very seriously, and "rarely regarded themselves

as immigrants," instead considering themselves expatriates.[64] But the new sense of Britishness that arose after 1900 could not be measured merely by the rising circulation of English-language newspapers, or by their willingness to donate generous sums to build nostalgic monuments like the clock tower in Buenos Aires. It must also be seen commercially, in the mentality and methods of the powerful British business communities of the republics.

And among such businessmen, fear increasingly permeated their self-identity as Britons. The new British nationalism in South America rested on many of the same beliefs as those held by the politicians and journalists in the United Kingdom interested in "national efficiency." Like these activists at home, pessimists in South America recognized only relative decline, and blamed the *laissez-faire* liberalism embodied in the British state and economic system.[65] For the new commercial nationalists, to be British meant to feel embattled by the Germans in a struggle between nations where only the fittest would survive.

Worries about decline rested upon the assumption that the continent would always be controlled, at least economically and possibly politically, by foreigners. Displaying an acutely fin-de-siècle sense of social Darwinism, British diplomats in South America consistently generalized that the peoples of Argentina, Uruguay and Brazil were inept, corrupt, and irrational. William Haggard, the minister to Brazil from 1906 to 1913, vociferously and consistently ridiculed the native politicians, whose "venal greed" led them to neglect the good of their country. In an extraordinarily lengthy and voluble appendix to his annual report for 1912, Haggard scoffed that the Brazilian people lived "practically in a state of nature," lacking a belief in law and order or any sense of public or private morality. In notably undiplomatic terms, Haggard lamented that "there is absolutely no dependence to be placed upon the word of a Brazilian, nor is it possible to appeal to him in any of the ordinary ways or on any of the ordinary motives." Officials in the government lacked discipline and acted only when bribed. Brazil could theoretically escape its dependence on imports, Haggard argued, but the laziness of its people made the production of even rudimentary finished goods impossible.[66] Many of the British believed that race was an important factor in the failures of local governments and in their potential manipulability. The so-called 'natives', tainted both by the blood of former slaves and the migrant flood from the Mediterranean, were considered incapable of fending off domination by stronger northern Europeans. The seasonal migration from Italy of *golondrinas*, 'the swallows' who labored in the grain fields and returned home each year, supported the prejudice of some Britons that southern Europeans were fit solely for labor in the service of British capital and international trade in South America.

German immigrants, on the other hand, were different. While disparaging the general population of Brazil, Haggard noted that the southern states of Santa Catharina and Rio Grande do Sul "must be judged in a different and more favourable manner" due to the Germans who settled there, bringing with them competent schooling and a work ethic.[67] The few members of the local ruling elite whom the British respected were those with German roots. Men such as Lauro Müller, the Foreign Minster in Brazil from 1913 until early 1917, supposedly exhibited far less venality than other Brazilians. Indeed, the German communities in Buenos Aires and Rio Grande do Sul believed the same about themselves, exhibiting their own beliefs in their superiority over the *criollos* and diligently maintaining their Germanic culture at a distance from the locals.[68]

Such beliefs about racial characteristics flourished among whites, blacks and *criollos* throughout Latin America in the late nineteenth and early twentieth centuries. According to Richard Graham, race was a "hegemonic ideology" in Latin America, as the pseudo-scientific ideas about race circulating in Europe were adopted by local elites and accepted by much of the South American population, helping the dominant classes to justify their rule. These prevailing racial ideas also justified "the economic and political power exercised by some nations over others."[69] The British considered themselves, and were largely considered by the local elites, as racially superior over virtually everyone else except, perhaps, Germans and North Americans.[70] The British sense of superiority was only enhanced by the efforts of South American elites to "whiten" their populations with supposedly inferior Italians and Spanish.[71]

These racist assumptions fed British worries about the consequences of Germans rising to dominance in the republics. British diplomats and consuls believed that the Germans more successfully organized themselves into an effective transnational community.[72] The Germans of South America appeared to work together to aid German commerce.[73] They proved a learned and flexible sales force for their manufacturers, and their immigrant communities avidly and loyally consumed German imports. Heavily populated German immigrant farming communities dominated the Brazilian states of Parana and Rio Grande do Sul politically and socially. Their clubs and associations (*Vereine*) drew together German businessmen in the big cities and helped to unite all classes of Germans.[74] Immigrants to rural South America formed concentrated settlements of German culture and in such places as Santa Catharina in southern Brazil, German import and export houses flourished without any British competition. As the local British consul wrote, it was a reflex for the owners and managers of such houses to purchase goods from Germany.[75]

When combined with the well-known and unsated imperialist passions of the Kaiser and others in Germany, the growing German economic influence in the republics led some of the British to consider whether Germany held greater plans for the continent. The most extreme fear of the Britons of South America was that the Reich would formally colonize a piece of the continent. Southern Brazil, where by 1900 at least 350,000 Germans had migrated since the middle of the nineteenth century, looked like the most likely place.[76] The German population in Rio Grande do Sul and Santa Catharina failed to assimilate with the non-German locals, instead maintaining separate Lutheran churches, German clubs and societies, and a German-language press.[77] This concentrated settlement of Germans dwarfed all British communities in South America.[78] The German government at times appeared anxious to seed colonies in South America. The Delbrück Law, passed by the Reichstag in July 1913, allowed Germans to keep their German citizenship even after becoming naturalized in a foreign state.[79]

In Montevideo, R.J. Kennedy worried about the successes of the German government in keeping its subjects abroad united and patriotic. Over a few generations, the Germans might lose some of their national characteristics but in general "they will maintain a close connection with their original country, and will be active and patriotic centres upon which Germany may base itself, should the day ever come in which she will find herself engaged in a struggle with the United States for extending Teutonic influence in South America." According to Kennedy, "an old German diplomatist" had recently told an American newspaper correspondent that no one in Germany believed that the writ of the Monroe Doctrine held south of Panama. Since 1823, this cornerstone of US foreign policy declared the firm opposition of the United States to any attempt by European powers to interfere in the "destiny" of the independent states of the western hemisphere. But the German diplomat believed that his country's growing navy made Brazil a potential target for German expansion: "Some day an incident will occur there which will give the German Government an excuse for interfering, and then it will only be a question of how much land Germany chooses to take."[80] He doubted that the United States would care.

In Britain as well, commentators assumed that the racial inferiority of the South American population meant that an outside empire must dominate there. As the *Saturday Review* put it:

> the Latin races have not yet evolved or assimilated the best methods of conduct-
> ing representative institutions. Though they would resent the deduction, there
> is little doubt that the form of government most likely to ensure their prosperity
> would be the consolidation of all into one empire under the direction of some
> strong will.[81]

The anti-German journalist F.W. Wile reported that German syndicates had purchased much land in Brazil and looked to bring in "immigrants willing to be 'kept German' – a race of transplanted men and women who will find themselves amid conditions deliberately designed to perpetuate 'Deutschthum' [*sic*], which means the German language, German customs and unyielding loyalty to German economic hopes." In the states of Rio Grande do Sul and Santa Catharina, German immigrants inevitably would rule. Wile concluded that the Germans planned to colonize south Brazil, expand German economic activity throughout the region, and force the United States to abandon the Monroe Doctrine.[82] Any perceived intervention by the German government to foster its foreign trade and to maintain its communities abroad was easily interpreted as underhanded and conspiratorial *Weltpolitik* aiming to dominate South America economically and politically.

Other Britons disagreed, and rejected excessive fearmongering. In his annual report for 1911, Haggard explained that the Germans of Brazil lost their "Vaterland patriotism" within a generation, just like immigrants from other countries. Lauro Müller, the Brazilian Minister of Foreign Affairs, exemplified this transformation. Müller, in Haggard's opinion, was "as un-German as a man could well be, both in appearance and, I should think, in sympathy."[83] In early 1914, Haggard's successor Malcolm Robertson noted that German emigration had diminished over the previous few years and appeared far from menacing. Furthermore, many of the Germans who emigrated to southern Brazil did so to escape the militarism of Germany. "They have become nationalised" as Brazilians in mind and body, Robertson argued, "and would be the first to resist invasion."[84] Whichever side was correct, the existence of this debate over the intentions of the Germans illustrated how some Britons believed that Germany might be pining for land across the Atlantic, in a place everyone considered ripe for domination by a racially strong imperial nation.

After all, everyone assumed that Germans were already cobbling together an informal empire. Many British businessmen and government officials in South America alleged that the German government subsidized German manufacturers and contractors, allowing them to charge below-market prices for certain goods and services. In the early 1900s, German contractors for the first time regularly underbid their British counterparts for public works projects and other large public tenders in the republics. To some, this proved that German firms were more meticulous than their British counterparts in their contract offers, but others saw the trend as indicative of a sinister plot.[85] In his report for 1911, British Minister Kennedy described the progress of a tender by the Uruguayan government for port cranes. The lowest British bid almost doubled that of the winning German firm. The situation "gives occasion for much reflection," Kennedy felt, "not only upon German commercial methods, but also upon the extent to which German merchants stand in with each other, and may be perhaps supported by their Government."[86]

Kennedy was far from alone in believing that the German government and German merchants colluded to circumvent the supposed freedom of the South American markets. The assignment of military advisers to the republics exemplified the way that the interests of the German government converged with those of its exporting industries. "The cannon followed the instructor," as those Latin American governments employing German instructors began to purchase their armaments from German manufacturers.[87] Historians of the German foreign ministry and armed forces have argued that the primary mission of the German armed forces in Argentina was to support such German economic interests.[88] At the time, British diplomats came to the same conclusion.[89]

British diplomats and consuls appeared particularly interested in action, belying their reputation as scornful of commerce.[90] They proposed fundamental changes to all aspects of British trade. Some must come from British manufacturers. "It is high time," Tower proclaimed, "that she (Britain) took a leaf out of the Germans' book, and paid more scrupulous attention to the requirements, manners, and customs, and particularly the language of this South American continent." Others must come from the banks. To boost British exports to the republics, British banks should copy their German counterparts, linking together industry, banking and the export trade apparatus of the country. These British representatives abroad challenged their government to do more. Tower noted jealously that in Argentina, the staff of the German legation and consulates far outnumbered their British counterparts, embodying the commitment of their government to national commerce.[91] Tower believed that the inactivity of British officials at home exacerbated understaffing on the periphery. The German government paid attention to South American traders and vacationers who visited Germany, giving them access to high government officials who extolled the power of German industries and the high quality of their products. Such propaganda work appeared to reap dividends.

Proselytizers for a new Britishness in South America believed that the British government should mimic the German state by putting money into efforts to support the building of the local British community. In 1912, Minister Haggard reported that in the German community "the propaganda by means of schools, churches, and music goes on steadily."[92] Similarly, in Montevideo and Argentina, German schools exemplified "the public spirit and patriotism of individual Germans" in the region, who thought it worth "great personal sacrifice" to set up these institutions "calculated to maintain interest in and encourage devotion to the motherland."[93] The sum allotted by the German government to these schools in the River Plate region was "relatively insignificant," approximately £4,200, but as one of Tower's advisers suggested, "the moral support thus ensured cannot be measured intrinsically."[94] The German government also utilized the church to maintain its influence, passing a law in 1900 that gave the Prussian state church control over congregations in other countries in return for government subsidies. Although hitherto independent, most congregations in Brazil jumped at the offer, illustrating not only their desire for money but also their yearning to enhance direct ties with Germany.[95]

The new British nationalists, however, did not aim merely to maintain cultural links to the old country. They hoped that the British in the republics could become the exclusive local representatives of the trade interests of Greater Britain, working at one with manufacturers, exporters, importers, shippers and bankers to help the cause of British commerce. At the start of the twentieth century, the creation of nationality-based chambers of commerce became a paramount goal of British diplomats and consuls hoping to make a difference on the ground in South America. In the 1890s, such nationally exclusive trade organizations began to develop among other nationalities, including the Germans, in the port cities. While at one time the foreigners conducting business in these cities held an affinity for each other and a disdain for natives, they lost their transnational cohesiveness as changes in world capitalism and local governments placed a premium on specialization and larger-scale operations.[96] Nationality-based organizations had existed a half-century earlier, at least in Buenos Aires, but had long since disintegrated.[97] In 1912, Sir Reginald Tower began to lead efforts to form a British Chamber of Commerce. "In these days of severe trade competition," he argued, such organizations are "indispensable if we are to progress or even to maintain our present position."[98] Although he was happy that local Britons in July 1913 followed his admonitions to create a Chamber, Tower fretted that the local British community gelled too slowly and half-heartedly. He attributed their reticence to their historic individualism; they had always competed with each other and feared sharing commercial information. Tower hoped that a Chamber would destroy such antiquated, nostalgic views by benefiting "British trade in general."[99]

By any objective standard, Tower was obviously reasonable to assume that bolstering British power in his own city, Buenos Aires, should rank as the most critical issue for British policy makers interested in Latin America. In 1914, Buenos Aires was the largest city in Latin America and the capital of one of the world's most dynamic economies. Argentina's overall population had doubled to 8 million over the previous twenty years, with this growth centered in the bustling metropolis where, by the start of the war, a quarter of Argentines were living. Situated on the southern side of the Rio de la Plata delta, facing the vast Atlantic on one side and the vast pampas on the other, Buenos Aires had developed since the sixteenth century into a true "embodiment of advanced civilization," a bastion of western values and successes.[100] Considered by some, particularly the proud Argentines, to be the Paris of the southern hemisphere, perhaps a more apt European comparison was to London's overwhelming centrality to both its country's economy and government.

Yet it was certainly unique, far different in its population from old European states, in that approximately three of every four adults in Buenos Aires were born abroad, mostly from Italy and Spain.[101] In 1914, the British-born population across all Argentina consisted of 19,519 men and 8,781 women.[102] However, the number who identified as British, which included many of the heirs of previous generations of British immigrants, was significantly greater, particularly in the capital. Although undoubtedly a small minority in the republic's overall population, the British of Buenos Aires probably had a slightly greater numbers than the Germans, of whom there were perhaps 30,000 locally, including around 11,000 born in Germany.[103] Buenos Aires had always been a city of immigrants at all levels of society.

Throughout most of the nineteenth century, the city's business community exemplified what Charles Jones has aptly described as a "cosmopolitan bourgeoisie," businessmen from various nations in Europe, particularly Spain, Britain, and Germany, integrated through intermarriage, ideology, and lucrative links to the global trade system centered on London.[104] Although these businessmen increasingly identified with their home nation at the turn of the century, businessmen of all identities lived and worked similarly. The homes, mansions, and clubs of both upper classes sprawled through the north of the city. The British businessmen preferred to live in the near suburbs of Palermo, while the Germans ensconced themselves further north in Belgrano. But all of their businesses congregated in the barrio of Buenos Aires known as the *centro*, an inelegant and aptly businesslike name for what was essentially the square mile of the City of London transported across the south Atlantic, the core of the nation's banking, insurance, shipping, import and export business (see map 2). Virtually all the international business of Argentina was conducted within the half a dozen blocks south and north of the Avenida de Mayo, and a dozen blocks west of Puerto Madero, the bustling terminal for transatlantic shipping. The British-owned railroads of Argentina converged on the city, and the agricultural produce of the pampas poured through its always inadequate ports.

A litany of barriers faced those Britons in Buenos Aires who wished to build a Chamber of Commerce, including the question of how to define Britishness. Businessmen and companies with English, Scottish, and Welsh roots all entered, as early members included names like Macdonald, Mackintosh, and Lloyd Davie. Their first meeting, on 1 July 1913, occurred in "St Andrew's Hall" on Calle Perú, a place colloquially known as "Scotch Hall." A point of more contention was whether a Chamber should include non-British subjects along with companies headquartered in the United Kingdom. "Anglo-Argentine houses which have taken many generations to build" were not technically British, even though the families who owned them identified themselves as British.[105] Whether such venerable "British" firms would want to cooperate with upstart importers and salesmen sent from United Kingdom manufacturers had proved a decisive stumbling block thwarting attempts of businessmen to create a Chamber before 1913.

Sir Reginald Tower dominated the founding of the Chamber of Commerce in Argentina, and provides us with a paradigm of the new commercial activist British diplomat. He called the first meeting of British businessmen together in July 1913 and chaired its proceedings, delivering a lengthy opening speech outlining the purposes of the Chamber and his hopes for the future.[106] "We have not yet outlived the character given to us as a nation of shopkeepers," Tower proclaimed. Britons in Argentina had always been there to make money. However, "our people are no longer alone in the field to supply manufactured articles to this Republic, nor are we the only nation to take the bounteous crops and products of the earth with which Providence has endowed the Argentine Republic." Creation of a Chamber would allow the "important business houses which have risen with the progress of the country on the prosperity they now enjoy" to help "their less fortunate brethren," with the resulting growth in trade helping both individual houses and "our British commercial community in general." Tower declared that he and his staff would help, and noted that the Legation had recently engaged as First Secretary Mr Hugh Gaisford, a man who had recently helped set up a British Chamber of Commerce in Lisbon.

Over the next few months, an executive committee of prominent British businessmen began to create the Chamber. After hiring a secretary and setting up offices they filed for incorporation in England, hired a permanent representative in London, and sent a circular to companies and Chambers of Commerce in the United Kingdom, explaining the benefits of membership.[107] These leaders resolved that although "the main purpose of the Chamber is to assist British firms established or having resident British representation in the Argentine Republic," they would also accumulate and supply general information about local conditions of trade in any way that would help British commerce.[108] By August 1914 the "British Chamber of Commerce in the Argentine Republic" had 85 active members and nine associates, a full-time staff and new offices, and the unprecedented attention of the local British legation and consulate.[109]

Similar efforts in 1913 and 1914 by British officials likewise nurtured new nationality-based commercial organizations in São Paulo, Montevideo, and Rosario. British business leaders increasingly recognized that they lived at a time and place where national identity largely determined business opportunities. They suppressed their various qualms about collective action and government involvement in trade, believing that change must occur for Greater Britain to maintain and perhaps even enhance its primacy in the economies of the South American republics.

What about the United States?

British worries about Germans in the early 1900s seem misplaced from the vantage of many decades later, when the subsequent growth of the United States supremacy in South American trade can appear nearly inevitable. In describing the many ways that United States businesses looked abroad for opportunities before 1914, the great historian of American business Mira Wilkins argues that "in 1914 US trade and investment in South America seemed destined to grow."[110] Of course, some Britons did worry about the United States. But British apprehension differed in form and paled in intensity when compared to fears of German infiltration into South American markets. US and British businessmen and officials in South America "feared the Germans far more than they feared one another."[111]

Some Britons praised certain characteristics of pre-1914 United States trade. The United States government followed the German example by appointing men to their legation staffs to help their nation's traders. Groups of businessmen from the United States also made excursions to South America to stir up possible trade, such as junkets of businessmen from Boston and Illinois in 1914, who aimed to learn some things about the local markets. There was, however, much disagreement among the British of South America as to whether such tours were of any benefit to their participants.[112]

In fact, British observers who fretted over German gains tended to denigrate the chances of US business in South America. 'Gringo' mannerisms were thought improper for dealing with the highly style-conscious businessmen of South America. The British viewed traders from the United States as amateurish in their commercial methods and as overly gruff and loutish as individuals. British Minister R.J. Kennedy mocked "the noisy and flashy procedure" of United States commerce in Uruguay. He contrasted this with more favorable "German methods," which "steadily, slowly, and unostentatiously" allowed German trade with Uruguay to balloon over the preceding five years.[113]

The United States, many suggested, held too many investment opportunities within its borders for its bankers to seriously consider southward expansion. If they wanted to move abroad, they could look to the Caribbean, a region in which Britain had virtually ceded political and economic dominance to the North American power.[114] At the start of January 1914, an editorial in the *Buenos Aires Herald* explained that the New York financial community had no interest in competing with either the London or European money markets for South American business. "Any intelligent American having business relations with this country has long ago sized up for himself the small prospects of success that such an institution (as a branch of the National City Bank of New York) would have in this part of the world."[115]

In Argentina and Uruguay, the prime United States threat to British interests appeared to be in the meat packing business. In a region lacking anti-trust laws, where foreign capital held tremendous importance, it appeared that Chicago-based firms might gain control of the beef business. The Argentine share of the British meat market increased by 15 percent between 1909 and 1910 – a jump prompting Horatio Mackie, the Consul-General in Buenos Aires, to suggest that British capitalists must "secure their legitimate share in the meat industry of this country before its resources become absorbed by American trusts."[116] However, Mackie was optimistic that the British-owned River Plate Fresh Meat Company and the locally-owned Sansinena Company offered US firms ample competition. In early 1914, the formation of a British trust, pulling together the River Plate Fresh Meat Company and Nelson & Sons, was seen by both the *Buenos Aires Herald* and the London-based *Financial Times* as an effective rebuttal of the expansion of United States beef interests.[117] Furthermore, British diplomats and businessmen called on local politicians to take anti-trust action against American firms, ensuring that any moves by US firms would be monitored by Argentine and Uruguayan politicians. Unlike wheat, another commodity from the River Plate vital to the well-being of the United Kingdom, it seemed unlikely that non-British firms could gain control of beef or mutton exports.

Other rumored US schemes met with even less success. The activities of the so-called 'Farquhar Syndicate' of North American investors raised some British eyebrows in 1912. The group supposedly aimed to take over a number of railways in the South American republics. Tower reported that the goal of this syndicate, headed by Percival Farquhar of New York, was "to bring the grain and wheat industries (of Argentina) into a comprehensive trust" by controlling the rail links that made possible the movement of grains. Tower also presumed that Farquhar was already in touch with the US meat companies and intended to erect meat freezing establishments, or *frigoríficos*, along the railway lines. He worried that if the United States Steel Trust and Standard Oil Trust were in league with the Farquhar group, as was rumored, "serious damage is likely to be experienced by British trade in Argentina in the future."[118] However, by 1914, the threat from Farquhar had passed.[119] Like the missions of US businessmen, the Farquhar scheme appeared more as Yankee bluster than useful action.

The debate over whether to fear Germany or the United States played itself out in the thoughts and writings of Sir Reginald Tower, the minister to

Argentina from the middle of 1911 through 1919. Of all the diplomats and consuls in the decade before war, no one expressed more fears of the United States. His apprehension about US trusts may have reflected his experiences with US business in his previous post as British envoy to Mexico. Yet Tower believed that "Germany is certainly the chief rival of Great Britain in Argentine trade." He expressed surprise that Germans had not yet entered railroads to any great degree. It was a business that had brought many profits to Britain, Tower noted, "and it is notorious that, wherever British enterprise is shown to be profitable, the German competitor promptly appears."[120] Sir Reginald felt that none of the bastions of British trade in Argentina were impermeable to German advances, and thus even the threat of trusts and monopolies pouring southward through the Americas caused him less stress than the Germans, who already dominated so many aspects of Argentine economic life.

Perhaps most surprisingly, the British both at home and in South America did not fear the Monroe Doctrine.[121] If anything, its existence pushed the fiercely proud people and governments of the republics towards Britain and Europe. In a speech to the Argentine Chamber of Deputies in 1913, Theodore Roosevelt explained that Argentina had grown into a strong country and no longer needed the "special guardianship" provided by the Monroe Doctrine. Instead, Argentina should make the Monroe Doctrine its own, working with the United States to keep the "Old World" European powers out. Such calls for a pan-American understanding and the creation of a joint policy towards the European-based empires met with a tepid response from the republics, appearing in South America as merely an updated form of the Monroe Doctrine.[122] As the First World War began in August 1914, there seemed little likelihood that any real hemispheric unity would result from the US efforts.

The official mind in London

Few British politicians appeared interested in Brazil, Uruguay, or Argentina. They rarely noted the region even when debating the possibility of installing protectionist trade policies. After Joseph Chamberlain began his campaign to overturn free trade in 1903, the issue would dominate the British political landscape for the next decade, and by 1907 tariff reform had been accepted into the Unionist platform.[123] The opponents of free trade did have in common with the British of South America a fear of German economic expansionism, but their focus on the Empire invariably separated United Kingdom reformers from their compatriots in Buenos Aires and Montevideo.

In the face of apathy and indecision from politicians and the public, the Foreign Office, Board of Trade, and Admiralty were left to determine the shape of any official imperial rivalry with Germany in South America.

Historians have consistently argued that the Foreign Office lacked interest in
South America, that diplomats and consuls who worked in South American
countries did not have the ear of the British government and were largely left
to do as they pleased because the region lacked strategic value to Britain. The
Foreign Office had no goals for South America beyond maintaining most
favored nation status for Britain, which gave Britain tariff parity with other
trading partners of the republics.[124] According to Platt, *laissez-faire* reigned
within the Foreign Office through the 1920s, and any reforms since the 1880s
amounted to little more than a slight refinement in the collection of commercial intelligence. British diplomacy only came to the aid of British holders
of foreign bonds if help was merited under the terms of international law; for
example, if British investors were repaid later than investors from another
country on an investment with the equivalent terms, or if a British subject
was not getting full and fair use of local courts in attempts to iron out the
settlement of a disputed contract.[125] The Foreign Office only rarely called for
forceful intervention in the internal affairs of a South American country, the
only notable example being in Venezuela in 1902–3, and then only when
chaos endangered the lives and property of British citizens.[126] Others have
agreed that the official mind of Whitehall simply looked to maintain a "fair
field and no favour" for British trade and finance overseas, and opposed any
government assistance for trade.[127]

This perspective underrates the effect of South America on the actions of
the Foreign Office. The fervently anti-German attitude expressed in reports
from diplomats such as Tower, Staniforth, Haggard and O'Sullivan-Beare
could only have fertilized the biases against Germany held by many in the
Foreign Office, including the Foreign Secretary Edward Grey himself.[128] The
Foreign Office began to act on these worries about Germans in South America
even before the start of the war. In April 1914 the Consul General at Rio de
Janeiro, Daniel O'Sullivan-Beare, sent a despatch to the Commercial Department outlining the present situation of Brazilian politics and the country's
economic needs. The British Minister to Brazil, Malcolm Robertson, wrote
to the Foreign Office agreeing with the consul's recommendations, but noted
that as O'Sullivan-Beare went beyond the subjects ordinarily thought of as
within the consular sphere, Robertson had instructed the consul to cease
writing this type of report. The Foreign Office immediately asked Robertson
to rescind his order. Algernon Law, the head of the Commercial Department,
explained that the Foreign Office should support all their representatives in
South America who decided to work beyond their traditional mandate to aid
British trade.[129]

Was the Foreign Office alone in the government in considering new efforts
on behalf of British trade? The Board of Trade, traditionally responsible for
the relationship between the British state and British business, claimed that

it was seeking a more active role in promoting foreign trade. In 1914, the Board asked for full command of the experimental commercial attaché program, which they had run jointly with the Foreign Office since 1899, arguing that the Foreign Office showed no inclination to utilize it to benefit British trade.[130] Yet by 1910, the Foreign Office, fiercely advocating the extension of the commercial attaché program beyond its initially Eurocentric focus, met with Board of Trade obstructionism. Victor Wellesley, one of the first commercial attachés and an important clerk at the Foreign Office, spearheaded his ministry's drive to grasp full authority over these attachés. Wellesley envisioned the commercial attachés as a new segment of the overseas services of the Foreign Office, falling in rank between consuls and diplomats and acting "as the focus of commercial intelligence and as a link between the mercantile community in the United Kingdom and abroad."[131] Wellesley also looked to subsidize British Chambers of Commerce abroad, like their French and German counterparts. These Chambers would in return become the intelligence gatherers for their commercial attachés and thus, indirectly, for their nation. The proposed attaché system would not merely enhance the amount and quality of commercial information flowing to the United Kingdom, but would also have the added benefit of tying the local British more tightly to their homeland, thereby helping to make them a more active part of Greater Britain.

The Board of Trade rejected Wellesley's suggestions, partly in the hope of eventually commanding the attachés itself, but also for ideological reasons. Eager to maintain a gap between government and business, Board of Trade officials argued that attachés should never answer specific queries from individual merchants and manufacturers in Britain about openings for trade in foreign markets. Instead, attachés should simply report the general market conditions to business groups in Britain. The Board regularly sent commercial enquiries from United Kingdom companies to the local consulates without listing the firms' names. British consuls and businessmen in Argentina complained that this anonymity, while ensuring the British government stayed out of legitimate competition between United Kingdom firms, also made it impossible for British companies in South America to judge whether it was worth while to answer the enquiry.[132] Likewise, the Board of Trade felt that "on principle," British Chambers of Commerce abroad should not receive grants from the British government. Wellesley rebutted acidly that the Commercial Intelligence Branch (CIB) of the Board of Trade , the prime contact between the government and businessmen in the United Kingdom, had proved itself incompetent and out of touch with the needs of British businessmen for information about foreign markets.[133] The gulf between the two ministries remained unbridged before the war. Discussions within the government and among businessmen about whether to create a new type of trade-oriented diplomatic corps, to subsidize British Chambers of Commerce abroad, or to undertake other initiatives to promote trade between Britain and South America remained unresolved when guns began to fire in August 1914.

Perhaps the most important way to judge British attitudes towards the competition with Germans in South America before the war is to examine Britain's war planning between 1900 and 1914. The assumption that a future war would target Germany underlay virtually all official and secret British preparations for a future war, as Asquith's Liberal government believed that Britain held a greater antagonism towards Germany than any other foreign state.[134] But few aspects of these plans addressed South America, as no British planner anticipated participating in an armed conflict on that distant continent, or believed that the region would be of consequence to any war effort Britain might undertake.

There existed a huge divide over which military strategy should be followed if a war began. Some backed a maritime policy, in which the paramount concern was the defense of the British empire. Others, the so-called continentalists, assumed that the British army must intervene in any European war.[135] At no time before August 1914 did politicians and bureaucrats holding these divergent views come together to form a political consensus behind a broad military strategy.

The diversity of views on the military aspects of war were mirrored in, and influenced by, a similar disagreement over economic warfare. They wondered what stance a belligerent Britain should take towards nonbelligerent states if war did break out. Pacifists, for whom planning for war was unpalatable, tended to back neutral rights, while others contemplated greater efforts to redirect the trade of neutrals. Dissent among the political classes over the question of war on trade appeared openly during the contentious debate about the Declaration of London in 1909. Talks at the London Naval Conference lasted many grueling months, but in the end, German and British negotiators agreed on rules of blockade, specific lists of contraband and free goods, and the abandonment of the doctrine of continuous voyage for contraband, under which cargoes on any ship anywhere could be seized if it could be proved that they were headed for enemy territory.[136] Yet a frosty reception in the House of Commons and rejection by the House of Lords meant that Britain would never ratify the Declaration. International law remained uncodified, the rights of belligerents to attack economic targets uncertain.[137]

As the primary war planning body, with members from all the main government ministries and the armed services, the Committee of Imperial Defence (CID) created the economic warfare program that would be initiated at the commencement of war.[138] Most members of the CID assumed that a naval blockade of Europe would constitute a sufficiently effective economic war.

None of the committee members foresaw the possibility of conflict with the Germans of South America, nor indeed with the Germans of any neutral countries. In 1911, Maurice Hankey, the secretary of the CID and a strong proponent of British economic warfare as a decisive weapon, doubted that the British government would ever decide to interfere with neutral trade.[139] Those members of the CID who planned for economic war concerned themselves solely with keeping raw materials from entering Germany and did not contemplate any attempts to halt trade between the United Kingdom and anyone in South America.[140]

South America was rarely mentioned in the meetings of the CID subcommittee on trade with the enemy, which met between January 1911 and April 1912 and was chaired by Lord Desart, the leader of the British delegation at the London Naval Conference two years earlier. The continent arose in a discussion of whether Germany could obtain wool from Argentina and Uruguay during a war. Lord Esher (who had been a founder of the CID in 1902 and was aligned with those favoring a navy-centered military strategy) asked whether the Germans in South America might ship bales of wool to Germany aboard neutral vessels. C.J.B. Hurst, the legal adviser to the Foreign Office, replied that simply prohibiting British vessels from accepting such cargoes would stop the flow of wool from the Plate to Germany.[141] Owing to a lack of neutral transatlantic ships, German freight rates would spiral upwards, and market pressure would stop Germany from purchasing and receiving wool from the Plate. However, Hurst recognized that such a prohibition on British ships loading German goods might not ever occur.

The mood of the committee was guided by the Board of Trade, which issued a report explaining that sufficient pressure would be applied to the German woolens industry by persuading (not forcing) imperial producers in Australia and New Zealand to stop their exports to Germany. This would force Germany to waste its money paying excessive prices for all the South American wool presently going to France, Belgium, the United Kingdom and the United States.[142] The committee also refused to recommend a blanket prohibition on British ships carrying non-contraband goods such as cotton, wool and rubber from the western hemisphere to Germany, fearing that such a prohibition might arouse "the susceptibilities of neutral countries."[143]

In short, the Desart committee clearly showed great trepidation about the possibilities of regulating British trade. Even among representatives from the rather interventionist-leaning Foreign Office, the possibility that Britain would undertake any extensive economic war touching even European neutrals seemed remote.[144] The committee did foresee the need to set up a body that could deal with such questions as they arose during a war, declaring in their final April 1912 report that at the outbreak of a war, an interdepartmental group chaired by the Treasury would be created to issue licenses to businesses and to answer any questions from neutral states about restrictions on British commerce. Each ministry represented on this committee would hold certain duties. The Treasury would monitor the effect of any laws against enemy trade on the financial interests of Britain, while the Admiralty prepared lists of contraband goods and of "warlike stores," which should not be exported from the British Isles, and the Board of Customs and Excise ensured that British ships did not carry goods whose export was prohibited.

Desart tasked the Board of Trade with formulating a 'Trade with the Enemy' proclamation to be enacted at the beginning of war. During wartime, the Board would be responsible for any modifications in enemy trade policy, while the Foreign Office acted merely as a messenger, relaying the dictates of the Board of Trade to diplomats and consuls abroad.[145] Overall, the Committee of Imperial Defence did not believe that war would necessitate the removal of foreign trade policy from the hands of the Board of Trade. Predictably, after the war broke out, arguments over this division of labor caused tremendous friction between the Foreign Office and Board of Trade.

Aside from possibly barring the shipment to Germany of some United Kingdom products, depending on how British contraband and blockade regulations unfolded, the main way that the British expected a war to impact South America was as a venue for naval action between the two great powers. The building of a massive German fleet under Admiral Tirpitz and the response this generated among British politicians and the public could not be ignored by British war planners.[146] In planning to counter German forces on the high seas, the CID left the Admiralty largely on its own. In fact, the subcommittee chaired by Lord Desart worked under the assumption that the Admiralty would turn the economic screws on Germany by blockading the North Sea ports as soon as war began.[147]

Like the CID, war planners in the Admiralty after 1905 expected that any future war would be against Germany.[148] Until August 1914 they anticipated that British naval power would quickly annihilate the German fleet at the start of war, making the seas safe for trade thereafter.[149] At that point, a blockade would encircle Germany, cutting off supplies and proving decisive for a British victory.[150] There was, however, some question as to what a blockade of Germany might look like. Many assumed that it would be a "close" blockade of the coastline, as was traditional, but Admiralty strategists foggily speculated that submarines might annihilate any British fleet attempting to envelop German shores. Among those who recognized that a close blockade would be beyond British naval capabilities, there arose the issue of what to do with neutral ships carrying goods that were most likely bound for Germany. Admiralty officials approved of the Declaration of London, which stated that a blockading force could not halt neutral ships on the high seas carrying 'conditional contraband' such as foodstuffs. However, the Admiralty's leaders before the war, particularly Admiral 'Jacky' Fisher, had a Machiavel-lian take on international law and saw the Declaration of London restrictions on contraband as idealistic and untenable with the realities of warfare. Admiral Fisher recognized that a war might demand that British forces intercept even food bound for civilians within enemy territory.[151] The Admiralty thus remained open to the possibility that their blockade plans might need revision once a war began.

Some Admiralty war plans were prescient. To the dismay of Admiral Edmond Slade, the former Director of Naval Intelligence, the Admiralty Trade Division disbanded in October 1909, but a trade branch was formed in late 1913 with the mandate to plan how to protect British trade while destroying that of Germany.[152] Men in the trade branch contemplated the creation of new methods of gathering quasi-military intelligence. It was thought that Lloyds, shipowners, shipmasters, and consuls overseas could all be enlisted in an effort to chart where German merchant ships (a.k.a. potential belligerent cruisers) lay at any given moment.[153] Utilizing the new technology of long-distance wireless communication, the Admiralty might learn of the movements of enemy ships and be able to communicate with British mer-chant ships, thus saving them from capture.[154] In short, Admiralty staffers recognized wisely that a future war would necessitate increased cooperation between shipowners and the government.

The Admiralty understood that Germany planned to attack British shipping in the South Atlantic. An estimated 40 percent of the meat and wheat require-ments of the United Kingdom passed along the route from the Rio de la Plata, along the Brazilian coast, through the Atlantic islands of San Vincent and Las Palmas, then on to Britain (see map 1). At the Hague Conference of 1907 and in subsequent talks leading to the Declaration of London in 1909, the German government refused to guarantee that its commercial ships would not be turned into commerce destroyers. As a result, the British assumed that at the start of a war, German merchant ships would mount guns on their decks and be transformed into cruisers that would attack British vessels.[155] There was no doubt that such retro-fitted ships could easily prey on the South American routes. In 1912, Admiral Slade argued that the threat posed there by German merchant cruisers meant that the Admiralty must build more cruisers to be stationed on patrol there.[156] However, standing orders a year later continued to decree only that two cruisers would be despatched from Britain to South America at the start of hostilities.[157] The Admiralty war staff recognized that this would take at least two weeks and that even after the cruisers reached their station, "it is difficult to consider this provision ade-quate," as the 2,600 miles of this route provided "the main food artery of the United Kingdom." "If any of the German steamers which habitually use the route are equipped to attack trade at short notice," the war staff reported, "this ocean area must be regarded as the worst protected point in the whole system of Imperial defence relatively to the importance of the interests it contains."[158]

Instead of repositioning the cruiser fleet, the Admiralty looked to solve the German threat by mounting arms on British merchant liners. The Royal Mail Steam Packet Company (RMSP), deeply involved in River Plate trade, was the first line the Admiralty approached to take part in the armament program in November 1912. The chairman of the RMSP, Sir Owen Philipps, agreed, and other lines trawling South American routes followed. Over the fifteen months before the war broke out, the Admiralty armed thirty-nine ships, mostly meat liners circling the English ports and the River Plate and Australia, with two 4.7-inch guns pointed backwards in a defensive posture.[159] The meat trade was manned by ships built for speed. Improved freezing technology and faster ships had opened up the transatlantic meat trade only in 1901, when quick voyages led British consumers to begin considering meat from Argentina as reasonably fresh.[160] When analyzed in conjunction with the reticence of the Admiralty to assign more cruisers to South American routes, the armament program shows that Admiralty strategists relied on the hope that British food supplies could outrun German pursuers. Obviously, the worries about being outgunned by Germany in the South Atlantic would not ease when war commenced. The Admiralty had closed its eyes to South America, following the example of the CID, the House of Commons, and the rest of the United Kingdom.

Conclusion

In supporting their arguments that Britain maintained economic dominance in South America before 1914, historians have long relied on statistics indicating that the British maintained commercial supremacy over their competitors. For example, Paul Kennedy wrote that in countries such as Argentina and Brazil, "exports from Britain had a distinct advantage" before the First World War, as their long-held commercial ties and massive investments ensured that goods from Lancashire and the Midlands continued to flow to Rio and the River Plate. Questioning the notion that British trade had declined in the face of German competition, Kennedy asked, "Was it so important that German imports to Argentina rose from £2.3 million in 1902 to £11.7 million in 1912, when British imports rose in the same period from £7.8 million to £21.3 million?"[161] To Kennedy, such statistics proved that the British held their own and even thrived in these countries.

Yet to many British people in South America such differing rates of growth did matter. The statistics, however flawed they might be, illuminated worrying trends.[162] And these Britons knew that the recital of such statistics overlooked important facets of German penetration into local commercial networks. By 1914, German-run houses controlled the flow of many vital goods in and out of Brazil, Uruguay and Argentina. German traders conducted themselves in a manner that was very different from that of the free-trade, *laissez-faire* oriented British merchants who had long dominated commerce in South America. Believing that British business was failing to meet competition from Germany, diplomats and consuls attempted to solve the problems by cajoling British businessmen and by unifying the local British communities. The focus of the British in South America on the growth of German interests there coincided with talk among policy makers and the press in Britain of a "German threat" to British industrial output and thus to the well-being and harmony of the British people.[163]

Britain's lack of competitiveness in South America particularly troubled many in the Foreign Office who called for significant changes to their ministry's mission. They struggled against British banks and shipping and also against a long-held belief about the immorality of such cooperation. Many of the British in South America judged as evil and corrupt the German system that linked the German people and government in a nefarious plot to dominate South America. Yet despite deep trepidation, the lessons of German growth were not lost on merchants who called on the British government to copy the German successes. As the Germans moved "in mass formation," the British must immediately organize in a similar fashion, even while attempting to avoid "turning themselves into Prussians."[164] For the British traders and diplomats in South America, as for people in the United Kingdom concerned with the "national efficiency" of Great Britain, "Germany assumed the dual role of model and enemy."[165]

The way that British diplomats, consuls, journalists, and merchants in South America perceived and reported on the Germans before August 1914 would shape the British attack against those Germans during the war. Wartime attacks on German trade in South America were the consequence of the pre-war atmosphere. After August 1914, the British would utilize and even abuse the wartime situation to promote British trade. The concerns voiced before the war by British diplomats and consular officials toward German competition in South America helped give these men, and the local British communities they led, a dominant voice in determining the evolution of Britain's economic war. Before the First World War exploded into the world, diplomats like Sir Reginald Tower in Buenos Aires desperately wanted to repel *Deutschtum* from South America. It took the war to galvanize the British government to act, but even then the impetus came not from London, but instead from across the Atlantic.

2

"What sort of patriotism is this?" Demanding changes to the British war, August 1914–December 1915

South Americans reacted immediately to the outbreak of war. The news at the start of August drove crowds to form and mill about Buenos Aires, propelled by a "wild anxiety to know who was at war and what fighting had taken place." After an evening of uncertainty, most people settled down, but the persistent demand for news left the streets around the buildings of the newspapers *La Prensa* and *La Nación* crowded with men reading the news stories posted outside. For most in immigrant-laden Buenos Aires, and in similar cities across the continent, the news had immediacy – it came from their homelands. Austrian and German men of military age began "leaving literally in shoals, a fact of course altogether creditable to them," wrote one local British newspaper. Similar contingents of Britons and Frenchmen similarly sailed home. The existence of cable telegraphy led one journalist to write in the second week of August that "the imminence of the dreadful presence is daily more plainly felt even at the distance of 7,000 miles from the actual scenes of conflict."[1] From the start, the horrors of war touched the lives of many people in South America.

For local Britons it also signaled new opportunities. British diplomats and commercial men in Brazil, Uruguay, and Argentina anticipated the outbreak of war as an opportunity to inflict permanent damage on German businesses. Rather than waiting for orders, British diplomats and consuls took the initiative, arguing to their superiors in London that the war must aim to eradicate Germany's foothold in the western hemisphere. While destroying German trade locally, Anglo-South Americans looked to utilize the wartime situation to construct a new British presence that would ensure Britain's long-term commercial domination in the region. They hoped to create a foreign trade apparatus linking British merchants overseas to manufacturers and importers in the United Kingdom in a mutually supportive relationship, benefiting the British nation around the world. In this effort to destroy Germans and construct a new British commercial nationalism, the British of South America received frustratingly little help from home.

The war begins?

When Britain declared war in August 1914, the official war plans lumbered into effect. No one in the British government contemplated actively extending war to the Germans of South America. The British government fell back on its long-held practice of defining its enemies by domicile, rather than by race, nationality, or any other criteria. As Attorney General Sir John Simon defined it on 9 September, for the purpose of trade, an enemy "means a person, firm, or company resident or carrying on business in hostile territory, and the test in this connection is not the nationality of the person with whom you are dealing."[2] Those bound by British enemy trade regulations were likewise geographically limited. Only British traders in the United Kingdom had to follow the laws, and no restrictions impinged upon the trade of the British overseas who lived under foreign laws. Initial extensions of the enemy trade laws continued merely to attempt to ensure that German-owned businesses based in the United Kingdom could not aid the German war machine. Through 1915, British 'Trade with the Enemy' laws completely neglected the wishes of people around the world who considered themselves British by continuing to legitimize commerce with Germans overseas. It was a truism among British parliamentarians and most bureaucrats that such restrictions could only be administered in British-controlled territory and thus passing such restrictions was futile.

To be fair, the men in London had other things to think about, with shell shortages and stalemated battles drawing the lion's share of attention. But these were failures of existing plans, underestimations of the terror of the western front. For much of the remainder of the war effort that soon developed, there had been no plans at all. In fact, the evolution within Whitehall of Britain's economic war provides a singular case study in how Britain muddled through the first year of this very new type of world war. A CID memo of January 1915 on coordinating "the war arrangements for trade restrictions" describes that the planned-for committee headed by the Treasury was up and running, but its members were consumed solely with the immense task of issuing export licenses for goods that were on the British lists of prohibited or restricted exports. The writer of the memo, most likely Maurice Hankey, noted that the main departments working to restrict exports and contraband were the Board of Customs and Excise and the Admiralty, which sent some ships intercepted in the North Sea into British ports for inspection.[3] An "Advisory Committee on the Restriction of Enemy Supplies," under the chairmanship of Sir Francis Hopwood had begun fashioning war trade policy. Hopwood had long been a Board of Trade functionary, and two years before the war had been made an additional civil lord of the Admiralty; his background epitomized the fact that the

CID expected the Board of Trade and Admiralty to determine war trade policy.

Yet reports of British goods continuing to flow into Germany exposed obvious flaws in the economic war. The CID blamed the problems on the Treasury-led "Licensing Committee," which had become overworked, often granted licenses "without full knowledge," and aimed too frequently to keep British trade flowing rather than to hurt Germans. To resolve the problems, the CID recommended that the Treasury committee should be provided with a secretariat with three internal divisions – one for the neutrals contiguous to Germany, one for the United States alone, and one for "all other countries." As a result of the CID report, by the end of January 1915 the War Trade Department (WTD) and Trade Clearing House (TCH) were formed. The TCH collected information from various departments and ministries, then redistributed it to the relevant officials. Cable, wireless, and postal censorship had been established at the start of war to prevent communications with Germany, and by January 1915 it was recognized that the information gleaned from such transmissions could help to detect attempts to evade trade with the enemy and contraband restrictions. Traders thus identified could be placed by the TCH on a blacklist of people who should not get licenses for transactions by the British government. The WTD replaced the Licencing Committee in granting export licenses for certain restricted goods, and also coordinating the myriad blacklists that had arisen since the start of war. The WTD asked for copies of the blacklists compiled by ministries including the Board of Customs and Excise, Board of Trade, Foreign Office, and the Admiralty, as well as blacklists drawn up by British consuls abroad.[4]

Historians have long argued that owing to the lack of realistic and consistent planning, the British blockade on German-controlled Europe was ad hoc and initially ineffective.[5] Avner Offer has effectively saved war planners from this derision, helping to disclose a once-secret history of high-level planning for economic warfare in the Admiralty and CID.[6] Yet certainly the campaign that eventually developed against Germans in South America was as unplanned as anything could possibly be. The proliferation of departments and committees created a true alphabet soup of authorities, which allowed long neglected South America to remain relegated to the sidelines. Official London only thought to utilize British people overseas to extend the economic war against Germans after an enduring lobbying effort by British diplomats and businessmen in South America.

"Sinister apparitions" in the South Atlantic

Unbeknown to overwhelmed British authorities at home, the war sent shock waves through all aspects of the South American economy. Fear that the war would trigger a run on the banks led governments across the continent to declare compulsory bank holidays. Although people were quite cash starved by its end, the measure succeeded. When the ten-day bank holiday in Buenos Aires lapsed, no banks faced catastrophic mass withdrawals by their depositors.[7] Authorities also feared that British restrictions on coal exports would bring railways, steamships, and electrical plants to a halt. Lacking local coal deposits of their own, all of these depended on British coal to generate electricity, to fill the engines of the locomotives crossing the pampas, and the bunkers of the steamships visiting their harbors – in short, to run the machinery of foreign trade which had made the republics such an integral part of the fin-de-siècle globalized economy. Argentina and Uruguay acted on 6 August 1914, to conserve stocks by prohibiting the export of coal, allowing ships only enough to reach the next port on their voyage. However, both countries rescinded these restrictions when Britain gave assurances that coal would continue to flow from Welsh pits to the River Plate.

Everyone recognized the need for British merchant ships to continue to ply the seas. From the beginning of the war, the Admiralty worked to rid the oceans of German cruisers, which were considered a greater threat to shipping than untested U-boats.[8] Even before the United Kingdom had declared war, the Admiralty telegraphed legations in South America asking whether locally berthed German merchant ships were being fitted out with weapons. The Admiralty claimed in a mid-August press release that it already had twenty-four cruisers in the Atlantic combing the seas for German ships doing "mischief," and planned to send more to the hunt soon.[9]

Despite such public bravado, cracks immediately appeared in the Admiralty war plans. Having armed British merchant ships, the Admiralty failed to supply these liners with ammunition. Notification of British ships on the high seas that war had broken out was painfully slow. The German cruiser *Dresden* informed the British SS *Drumcliffe* of the outbreak of hostilities by boarding the British merchant ship off the mouth of the Amazon. The *Dresden* ripped out the *Drumcliffe*'s apparently unused wireless equipment and (in the gentlemanly fashion of the early days of the naval war) forced the entire crew of the British merchant ship to sign a declaration that they would never "take service against Germany during the war." The ship was then allowed to proceed on its way.[10]

The German navy soon realized the folly of allowing British ships to pass so relatively unmolested. German cruisers began to supply themselves from the British vessels that they attacked, transferring the crews of the captured merchant ship to waiting tenders, and then scuttling the British ships. In an extraordinarily successful run before its own sinking at the end of October 1914, the German cruiser *Karlsruhe* took 20,000 tons of coal from the eighteen ships it captured – fifteen of which it then sank.[11]

As a result of such German successes, the British Admiralty gained a reputation for ineptitude among British people in the South American ports. Shipping agents and crews felt that they had been thrown to the wolves as rumors of German fleets swirled around the ports, causing masters to delay their journeys. The Trade Division of the Admiralty anxiously urged shipmasters and agents in Argentina to resume their scheduled transatlantic voyages, citing a tripling of their cruiser patrols along South American trade routes, claiming that "traders with Great Britain of all nations should therefore continue confidently and boldly to despatch their ships and send their cargoes to sea in British or neutral ships . . . with almost the same certainty as in times of Peace."[12]

The British government offered incentives to keep trade moving. State-sponsored war-risk insurance, planned before the war and implemented by the Board of Trade in August 1914, aimed to ensure that trade continued by making voyages across unknown seas financially safe for shipowners.[13] Under this reinsurance scheme, the government guaranteed 80 percent of the risks undertaken by the three primary war-risk insurers. The official historians of the merchant navy and wartime shipping industry later claimed triumphantly that from the first day of hostilities, this insurance allowed British ships to continue sailing "with almost the same freedom as under the conditions of peace."[14] But in the Atlantic, off the South American coast, the insurance scheme was insufficient to lure ships out of the safety of ports until the very end of 1914. British newspapers faithfully and fearfully reported on merchant vessels being followed or chased by German cruisers. As in many British accounts of German businessmen, stories of the Reich's cruisers portrayed the German ships as sneaky and sly, always a step ahead of the British. The crew of the Lamport & Holt Line's SS *Tennyson* claimed that on a misty, squall-filled early September morning off the Brazilian coast, a "sinister apparition" chased them for two hours. The British ship eluded capture only by opening the throttle and steaming full speed into the comparatively "friendly folds" of a dangerous rainstorm. Another rumor circulated in Bahia Blanca, Argentina, that a German cruiser hid just beyond the lightship marking the outer boundary of the port, preparing to pounce on the British grain ships. As a result, ships cowered in port, equipped to steam off but afraid to do so.[15]

It was widely believed that the Reich's navy were at an advantage because of the efforts of local German partisans. In November, Minister Sir Reginald Tower and Consul-General Mackie reported to their superiors that it was "of public notoriety" that German merchant ships had utilized Argentine, Brazilian and Chilean ports "as bases of supply for German cruisers," which then steamed to sea unhindered by British warships. Although the British naval intelligence center had been immediately informed about the departure of the German merchant ship *Pontos* from Buenos Aires, the ship subsequently evaded capture by British cruisers and successfully supplied several German warships.[16] Virtually all of the crews of British merchant ships captured by enemy cruisers witnessed similar scenes.[17] Rich German businesses such as Brauss, Mahn & Co. and Theodor Wille & Co. were notorious among Anglo-South Americans as "the most dangerous of enemy firms" for plowing their profits into assistance for the elusive German cruisers.[18] H.H. Slater, a member of the Council of the British Chamber of Commerce in Buenos Aires, denounced Julio Hosmann, the agent for a number of London-based insurance companies, for being a member of a local German committee that supplied German cruisers.[19] Germans were said to benefit from secret wireless stations along the Brazilian coast, which relayed information about the whereabouts of British cruiser squadrons, allowing the German warships to evade destruction and safely to receive supplies ferried from ports by German steamers. "Where is the British squadron?" wailed one English-language newspaper headline.[20]

Where the Admiralty failed, British diplomats acted. Local British officials pestered the governments of Brazil, Argentina and Uruguay to crack down on the German merchant ships, claiming that those ships supplying German cruisers were violating the neutrality of the republics by supplying warships. According to their argument, local authorities should have interned the ships, and refused to allow them to leave port. Differing ideas about neutrality, however, made for a variety of reactions from the republics. Malcolm Robertson, the British Minister in Brazil through the spring of 1915, explained that Brazilian Foreign Minister Lauro Müller allowed eight German ships to leave port during the first month of war because he "was feeling his way" and "was not quite certain how far he could go in preventing these ships from sailing." After some complaints, the Brazilian government issued restrictions that "no belligerent merchantman may leave a Brazilian port without a written declaration from her consul that her voyage is undertaken for commercial purposes only, and that she will not supply or coal belligerent cruisers 'en route'." Any companies whose ships contravened this would have all their vessels interned. Although a few German boats slipped out of Pernambuco and Rio de Janeiro in December and January, the Brazilian government did not sanction these departures and censured the port and naval officials. Robertson was satisfied with the attitude taken by Brazilian authorities, believing that it significantly diminished the capabilities of German warships in the region.[21]

The Argentine government posed different difficulties for the British. At least one German ship in a Brazilian port steamed to Buenos Aires under the assumption that its movements from there would be free from interference by local authorities. From the start of the war, Sir Reginald Tower complained to the Argentine Minister of Foreign Affairs that the fitting out of merchant ships for military purposes in Argentine harbors made it appear that Argentina was less than neutral, perhaps even siding with Germany.[22] Tower sent "unimpeachable corroboration" of rumors of armaments on the *Cap Trafalgar*, a Hamburg-Süd Amerika liner in port in Buenos Aires capable of turning into a merchant cruiser. He succeeded in getting the Argentine authorities to search the ship on 6 August, but they found no weaponry. Tower doubted the seriousness of the search.[23] The Argentine government, quoting the Hague Convention, claimed they could take no action against German ships that might be supplying cruisers offshore.[24] Tower believed that Foreign Minister Murature willfully ignored proof that German merchant vessels were carrying explosives bound for German warships, thereby violating Argentina's neutrality. He reminded Murature of the importance of British commerce to Argentine development, trying "to impress upon (him) the necessity of finding some means of cooperating with Great Britain in keeping open the trade routes." But Tower failed to persuade the Argentines that ships supplying German cruisers with non-military supplies were violating Argentina's proclamation of neutrality.[25] Murature felt that rather than relying on Argentina to act, the British should fight fire with fire by capturing and sinking German merchant ships like the German cruisers were doing to the British. Argentina did not want to break its own definition of neutrality or upset the Germans.[26] The attitude of the Argentine government proved a boon to the ability of Germany to conduct cruiser warfare.

But Tower found other ways to help change Argentine shipping policy. He reported confidentially to the Foreign Office in October 1914 of one success in getting the Argentine government to enforce its own laws. Fearing a shortage of coal, the Argentines passed laws prohibiting merchant ships from taking aboard more coal than was needed to reach the next port of call. Tower learned that some German ships were loading far more coal than they could possibly need for themselves, coal likely bound for German cruisers offshore. By leaking to "two independent journalists, one in Buenos Aires, and one in Tucuman, certain salient facts about the doings of German merchant vessels in Argentine ports since the outbreak of war," Tower hoped to cause an outcry among the generally pro-British public that would force the government to enforce its own rules. A story subsequently ran in the *Buenos Aires Herald* and other papers that the *Eleanore Woermann* was loading substantial amounts of coal.[27] This ship had recently ferried to port sailors from the *Cap Trafalgar* after the latter was sunk by a British cruiser, and before that had worked as a scout for the German warship. Tower's tactic succeeded. Once the newspapers broke the story, Foreign Minister Murature declared that such over-coaling must stop.[28] Inspectors from the Argentine Ministry of Marine soon searched the *Eleanore Woermann*, and subsequently ordered the ship to discharge its surplus 800 tons of coal.[29]

In all, commerce raiders in the South Atlantic sank thirty-six British ships, searched and released seven others, and utilized one as a tender.[30] The heart of the German southern cruiser squadron was destroyed by a small British fleet at the Battle of the Falkland Islands in December, but German cruisers plagued the trade lanes until April 1915, when the *Kronprinz Wilhelm* limped into port, and internment, at Newport News. After more than six months of continuous sailing, the commander of that German warship saw no possibility of further evading British cruisers.[31] However, during the preceding eight months, the German cruiser war against Britain and her allies limited trade between Britain and South America by sinking tonnage and by causing fear among businessmen in the republics.

Improvising war on the periphery

The mysterious German cruisers dismayed the British in the republics, yet at least as upsetting was the fact that local German companies seemed to experience few problems in continuing to operate. And while the threat from cruisers dissipated over time, anger about the German businesses only grew. The local British also complained that London-based companies continued to employ Germans. Such issues drew the ire of many Britons in Brazil, Uruguay and Argentina, who focused their blame on London. During this period, their distant government appeared either inept or unpatriotic in failing to address and solve the difficulties posed by *Deutschtum* in South America.

The continuation of German business was epitomized by the great export industries of wheat, wool and coffee. Before the war, the Big Four grain firms were heavily associated with German commercial extension into Argentina. A pre-existing British desire to overturn German dominance in the grain trade was consistently augmented by analyses of trade flows since the start of the war. From August 1914, grain shipments to Scandinavia from Bunge & Born and Weil Hermanos expanded unprecedentedly. Before 1914, Sweden and Denmark imported insignificant amounts of grain from the breadbox around Rosario. But as the British naval blockade halted the wheat, corn and linseed headed directly to German ports, shipments to the neutral nations surrounding Germany ballooned. The British Chamber of Commerce in Buenos Aires reported that in the seven weeks before 28 October, at least 22 ships with over 100,000 tons of cereals had exited for Scandinavian ports. Over the same period in the previous year, there had been no such shipments.[32] Once in Stockholm or Copenhagen, this grain was easily trans-shipped to Germany, as the minimal presence in the Baltic Sea of the submarine-fearing British navy comprised far less than an effective blockade.

Observers in Uruguay and Argentina noted similar changes in the flow of wool to neutral Sweden and Italy. During the season of 1914–15, the wool shipments to German ports which ordinarily took more than a third of the republics' wool had declined to zero. However, shipments to Genoa had mushroomed; from Argentina, the 6,120 bales in 1913–14 had multiplied to 47,672 during the following season, while from Uruguay, the shipments grew from 2,981 bales to 44,767, an amount well over half of the total exported from Uruguay that year.[33] Beginning in October 1914, there were reports that large shipments of sheepskins were being loaded to Sweden, which normally did not import such goods. Of course, its neighbor to the south, Germany, ordinarily did, taking 420,324 dozen of the 431,138 dozen sheepskins exported from Argentina between 1908 and 1912.[34] As for coffee, over a year after the start of war, Vice-Consul Robinson at Santos, Brazil, voiced his frustration that Eugen Urban, a German coffee exporter, continued to "boast openly that he ships for Germany."[35]

Most gallingly, British ships often carried these suspect goods. On 28 August, Minister Tower noted ruefully that the sinking of the British steamship *Hyades* was not without its positive side, as 4,000 tons of maize sent by Weil Hermanos to a German firm at Rotterdam sank to the bottom aboard the British vessel.[36] Consul-General Mackie estimated that local German grain firms held contracts controlling 85 percent of the British tonnage available in Buenos Aires. Arguing that local agents of the British lines failed to act "up to the spirit" of the 'Trading with the enemy' laws, Mackie lamented the overcompetitiveness of British shipowners and agents, who believed that spurning such trade would lead one of their compatriot competitors to grab it up.[37]

Proposals to remedy the problems of British shipping flowed in from all quarters. The British Chamber of Commerce in Argentina suggested that the British government should withhold war-risk insurance from shipowners who carried goods for German firms.[38] There was also a flurry of calls to ban the practice, common in the grain trade, of shipping 'for orders' to St Vincent or Las Palmas. Under this practice, vessels would steam to one of these mid-Atlantic island destinations. By the time they arrived, the owners of the cargo would know where in Europe they wanted to send the goods, send a telegram, and the ships would head forth where they were directed. 'For orders' increasingly meant for Germany, via Scandinavia. Consul-General Mackie suggested that the British government try to control cargoes transported aboard British shipping by making shipmasters present their bills of lading and insurance documents for the endorsement of British consuls at each port they stopped at.[39] Spencer Dickson, the consul at Rosario, agreed that the information garnered from such document inspections would help the government to trace transactions from departure to destination.[40] Controlling British-flag shipping was seen by the British of South America as a potentially effective way to cripple local German merchant houses. It could also be used to aid British firms whose access to the increasingly scarce space in merchant ship bottoms could constitute a significant competitive advantage over the Germans.

Yet British shipowners resisted these proposals. Despite their dominance in ports across the continent, they feared losing market share to neutral lines if their activities were restricted. The head of the Harrison steamship line explained to the Admiralty in December 1914 that "British ships would have to abandon the whole of the Brazilian trade if they refused to carry for such German firms . . . Certainly if it is abandoned, it will not be recovered."[41] The Admiralty, although generally favoring anything that could augment their blockade, worried that new regulations on shipowners already annoyed by the low rates the government paid for requisitioned ships might lead British steamship lines to transfer their ships to neutral flags.[42] But the Board of Trade proved by far the greatest supporter of intransigent British shipowners. The Board's Marine Department stated that because it was largely a tramp trade, on boats running without precise long-term schedules or announced ports of call, the amount of tonnage and the freight rates charged for the haulage of grain from Argentina were best regulated by market forces. "There is no likelihood" that the government would step into this market by chartering ships to bring grain to Britain from Argentina.[43] The Board of Trade rejected any measures against the Big Four grain firms, fearing that such regulations would interrupt supplies bound for the United Kingdom.

A similar debate raged over Germans in the Brazilian coffee trade. Malcolm Robertson, the British envoy to Brazil, suggested cooperation: "Unless Banks, Shipping Companies and Merchants consult and work together at this moment there will be no possibility of our capturing German trade in Brazil." Yet in the Foreign Office, Basil Newton and G.H. Villiers explained that British enemy trade laws at present allowed such British trade with Germans overseas, and to ban it would lead to protests from the Brazilian government.[44] Even after a new "Retaliation" Order in Council in March 1915, Foreign Office legal adviser C.J.B. Hurst explained that British ships could still carry goods from Germans in South America as long as the ships were not going to Germany.[45] Sir Hubert Llewellyn-Smith of the Board of Trade preferred to accept the pledge of Sir Owen Philipps, off the record, that his Royal Mail line would not carry coffee for German firms, particularly not for Theodore Wille & Co.[46] The Foreign Office acknowledged that the Board of Trade controlled the policy to be taken toward Germans in South America, and their decisions must be accepted "however much we may regret it."[47] The Board still had complete control of the official economic warfare effort in South America – what little there was of it.

As a result of the failures of home authorities to regulate British shipping, the British in the republics worked to change the practices of these shipping companies themselves. Informal lobbying of British firms occurred in Brazil, where Sir Arthur Peel urged shipping agents as "a matter of patriotism" to refuse to haul goods for local firms known to be German.[48] Some complained that men of German nationality ran the Brazilian agencies of a number of these British lines, surreptitiously aiding German exporters and using their access to important information about the movements and cargoes of British merchant ships to alert German cruisers offshore.[49] At the end of October, Mitchell Innes telegraphed the Foreign Office to complain that three Liverpool-based lines employed a German as their agent in Montevideo.[50] On receiving a letter from the Foreign Office, two of the lines said that they did not know whether the man in question was German but that they would sack him in any case.[51] But David MacIver, Sons & Co. refused to fire the agent, a man suspiciously named Schwartz, before seeing proof that he was an "alien enemy." MacIver explained that Schwartz was an Uruguayan subject whose late father, an immigrant to the River Plate region from Germany, had been the line's first agent in Montevideo.[52] Mitchell Innes acknowledged that Schwartz was Uruguayan born and bred, but argued that "this makes no practical difference. His sympathies are understood to be entirely German, and I cannot give him confidential instructions."[53] MacIver finally sacked Schwartz early in December 1914.[54] Responding to this reticence of shipping firms and to the success of the policy instituted by Mitchell Innes, at the start of January 1915 the Foreign Office issued a blanket order to its South American diplomats to "invite British shipping firms to not employ German agents."[55] Firms refusing to do so should be reported by telegraph to the Foreign Office, which would then put pressure on their home offices in the United Kingdom.

Public attention in the South American ports could also be harnessed to persuade shipping lines to toe the line against Germans. From the opening days of war, rumors swirled that the German Coal Company depots in Montevideo and Buenos Aires were hoarding coal to supply a German cruiser squadron steaming in from the Pacific.[56] Consul General Mackie in Buenos Aires employed informants to uncover those German ships anchored in the port of Buenos Aires that held coal supplies, and found that the British steamships *Clivegrove* and *Bengrove* were unloading coal to a German firm. Mackie sent a warning to the masters of those ships that they would be "liable to heavy penalties" unless they ceased such operations immediately.[57] Because the coal might go to fuel German cruisers, Mackie believed such trade constituted treason under British law.[58] However, Mackie's superiors at the Foreign Office hastened to explain that there were in fact no laws against British ships transferring coal to German firms in Argentina. Although the Foreign Office wanted "to impede and restrict German commerce as much as possible," Mackie was told that many in the government feared that changes in coal marketing in South America would unsettle the practices of the British coal industry, or disrupt shipments of food from the River Plate to Britain. The Foreign Office suggested, however, that Mackie should "use his influence" to get British ships in South America to cease such trade voluntarily.[59] Thus waffling, the Foreign Office decided to leave the question of coal supplies for German firms to the discretion of their consul.[60] He then tried another tactic. What finally stopped the masters of the *Bengrove* and *Clivegrove* from continuing to unload their coal was the public opprobrium heaped upon them after articles appeared in local British newspapers lambasting the conduct of the two ships.[61]

Tower supported Mackie, saying that the Consul-General's actions had been motivated "solely by considerations of patriotism" and followed "the only course consistent with British interests." The Foreign Office agreed to pay any legal bills that Mackie might incur in the Argentine courts as a result of his actions against the British ships, but was surprised and infuriated when the shipping company which owned the vessels, Hoult & Co. of Liverpool, billed the Foreign Office for £495 14s 2d to cover their losses for what they claimed was an illegal detention.[62] Irate at Hoult's attitude, members of the Foreign Office suggested to the Admiralty that the masters of the ships should have their certificates of competency suspended. The Admiralty agreed, but the Board of Trade refused to penalize the masters of the ships, explaining that their conduct did not breach the Merchant Shipping Act of 1894 under which such certificates were issued.[63] Mackie and his allies in the English-language press had changed the actions of the British ships and brought an end to the unloading of the coal, but had done so with very uncertain support from home.

Things only slowly began to look up for the would-be commercial warriors. In December 1914, the British government proposed that consuls in South America should compile a list of local coal importers suspected of supplying coal to German cruisers.[64] Their names would be placed on a secret blacklist, which British suppliers would have to check before exporting any coal. The Foreign Office received a prompt reply the next day from Mitchell Innes in Montevideo, who eagerly explained that the Deutsches Kohlen Depot, true to its name, was the prime untrustworthy local firm.[65] The promised blacklist was slow to appear, however. Only on 29 April 1915, did the Foreign Office send Mitchell Innes a copy of the 'List of coal importers to which shipments of British coal should not be permitted'. To his annoyance, the German firm was not included on it.[66] Other British blacklists were likewise slow to have an impact on South America. For example, the Treasury sent its Finance List solely to London bankers, who were exhorted to hide it from anyone outside their bank. The first Finance List to include firms in South America was issued on 30 August 1915.[67] Even with this list, the Treasury gave British banks in South America considerable leeway to conduct themselves as they desired. The British government feared that more open attacks would bring complaints that the blacklists violated the neutrality and sovereignty of other nations. The telling feature of these early blacklists was their secrecy, which bred a lack of accountability.

Like shipowners, British bankers in South America opposed restrictions on their activities by the British government, fearing that it would cause them to lose business to their competitors. Some banks acted on their own to clear out unsavory customers. At the start of October 1914, the London and River Plate Bank manager in Rio de Janeiro told the huge German import/export firm of Hasenclever & Co. to liquidate its accounts.[68] Such patriotically inspired moves, however, were only scattered and infrequent. Despite the reputation these banks had for stability in times of crisis, by 20 August 1914 two hundred depositors had withdrawn their accounts from the Buenos Aires branch of the London and River Plate Bank. The manager of the bank fretted that the withdrawals were by Germans who had decided to bank with the Banco Alemán.[69] As before the war, British bankers worried about losing their German clientele, and thus rarely acted on their own against the Germans.

British bankers were aided in their equivocation by the leniency of London officials throughout the opening months of war. On 11 August 1914, the London and River Plate Bank headquarters anticipated regulation when it informed its branches that drafts drawn by Germans on London banks would not be accepted. Two weeks later it stepped back, merely advising that the managers be cautious "in all your transactions with Germans."[70] A revision of the 'Trade with the Enemy' laws, dated 7 January 1915, forbade all London-based banks from conducting business with enemy people, firms and banks outside the United Kingdom. However, the managers of the London and River Plate Bank's flagship branch in Buenos Aires soon were informed by their London home office that the government only aimed to prevent goods from entering Germany.[71] The bank's chairman, Robert A. Thurburn, predicted in a circular to anxious branch managers in South America that a loophole in the law would "leave our business generally unaffected."[72] He was proved correct, when the Treasury granted the British banks and their branches in South America a license to conduct transactions with branches of enemy banks and enemy firms in neutral territory, "so far as it is necessary for them to do so in order to continue their banking business for non-enemy clients, or in order to continue their banking business without breach of any laws or regulations in force in any such territory."[73] The loophole left judgment about the legality of any given business transaction up to the bank itself, which would be allowed to interpret local laws and consider whether halting a transaction would affect any of the bank's "non-enemy clients."

Thereafter, British banks in South America often claimed that they refused business with any house that had branches in Germany.[74] Whether the banks did this in practice, however, remained a contentious issue among the local British. These banks spent the opening months of war accusing their compatriot rivals of violating the spirit or the letter of the 'Trade with the Enemy' laws. For example, while noting in March 1915 that his bank carefully abstained from any enemy business, one of the managers of the London and River Plate in Buenos Aires accused another British bank of drawing on New York to the Banco Germánico on the previous day.[75] The manager was two-faced, however; a number of months later he confided to his chairman that the London and River Plate itself continued to conduct business with Bunge & Born, the grain firm that since the beginning of war had been denounced as an enemy by other local Britons.[76]

Not all of these dealings stayed secret. In October 1915, Hope Gibson of the British Chamber of Commerce in Argentina complained that the local branch of the Anglo-South American Bank had supposedly been forced by its head office in London to grant a credit to the local German house of Brauss, Mahn & Co. After being asked, the bank explained to the government that they did not know of any legal objections to trading with that firm, but would not do so any longer.[77] Such practices did not endear these bankers to many other Britons in South America, especially to partners of the merchant houses that comprised much of the Chambers of Commerce, a group of men who had long questioned the patriotism of British banking.

Most local Britons never knew of the existence of the secret finance or coal blacklists, and often believed that their own anti-German actions were being ignored by the home government. Yet they still continued their anti-German crusade. One common and consistent demand from the most vocal Britons was for all companies controlled by London capital to prove themselves British by ridding themselves of German employees. A typical letter written to the *Buenos Aires Herald* opined that German construction workers at a British-run power station building site should be replaced.[78] By early 1915, Tower had approached a large number of British firms, asking them to get rid of German employees.[79] Despite this clamor, the British government continued to equivocate rather than create a unified, hard-hitting policy regarding such German employees.

One business that came under scrutiny for its German identity was the Argentine Navigation Company, registered in London but managed and largely owned by a man named Nicolás Mihanovich. From the beginning of the war, Consul-General Mackie had asked the Foreign Office to do something to drive Mihanovich out of the management of the firm. The shipowner was well known for his ties to the Austro-Hungarian Empire, having been named a Baron by the Habsburgs as a reward for building a house in Buenos

Aires for the Austrian legation.[80] After meeting in February 1915 with Miguel
Mihanovich, a son of the Baron, Sir Reginald Tower was noncommittal about
the company; but over the next three months he began to suspect that the
company acted as an enemy. According to Tower, Miguel Mihanovich was
the Austrian Vice-Consul and the Baron Nicolás was the honorary Austrian
Consul-General. Tower had also learned that the company's ships had sent
wireless messages to German cruisers since the beginning of the war.[81] But
the WTD was reluctant to place the Argentine Navigation Company on the
coal blacklist, because the Mihanovich line was one of only two carriers
conducting service between Buenos Aires and Montevideo, and its competition was owned by the definitely German Hamburg-Amerika Line.[82] The
British government decided that it was best to do nothing against Mihanovich,
as any such actions would help his German competitors.

Greater outcry erupted over the Liebig's Extract of Meat Company, registered in London. The issue of Liebig's deeply irritated the British in Argentina. One letter to the editor of a British newspaper in Buenos Aires claimed
that Liebig's was obviously controlled by Germans, given the names of its
managers: "Meyer, Dutting, Kroger, Albrecht."[83] Another letter claimed that
Liebig's was founded by a Berlin-born doctor in the 1840s, and was thus
(despite its registration in London) truly a German company.[84] Both writers
demanded that the company prove itself British before it would be treated as
such by British people locally. There was little doubt that Liebig's did have
German employees. The Foreign Office sent a private letter to the head of
Liebig's in January 1915. "No doubt you will agree," the Foreign Office told
Mr Glyn, that British companies abroad should rid themselves of their German
employees.[85] He replied that there were about twenty Germans and Austrians
in the company, but the company and employees were in a neutral country
and the Germans would be hard to replace. Glyn blamed the indignant furor
on the company's competitors. On reading this explanation, a Foreign Office
clerk shrugged with frustration and resignation: "We can, of course, do no
more in the matter."[86]

In Rosario, the Northern Insurance Company retained a supposed German
as their local agent. British residents in Rosario gathered in a fairly raucous
meeting on 22 June 1915. Consul Filleter described how "at the meeting one
of our bankers, under the combined influence of alcohol and patriotism,
vehemently demanded 'publicity', i.e. giving particulars to 'John Bull' or
some such journal, to make a case of" the insurance company. Filliter
explained that he was trying to keep this dispute out of the newspapers, but
he did agree to the formation of a 'British Trade Protection Association',
which would draw up a list of British firms with German employees, while
also taking other suggestions for ways that British business could supplant
German commerce in Rosario.[87]

Probably the largest British company with significant numbers of German employees was the Forestal Company. Forestal, listed in London since 1905 but run by a multinational board and managerial staff, dominated the quebracho industry in the Entre Rios region of north-eastern Argentina, holding a near monopoly in producing extract of quebracho wood, which was important in the tanning of leather, and quebracho logs, for use as railroad sleepers. Many of its employees looked to Europe in 1914, with forty-one volunteering to fight for the Allies.[88] Forestal had taken other steps to appear proper, by moving its selling agency from Hamburg to London; suspending the Germans serving on its London and Buenos Aires boards; and suspending its managers in Argentina, despite the fact that both men, although born in Germany, had lived in Argentina for decades. A member of the London board of the company, Campbell Ogilvie, hoped that such suspensions with pay until their contracts naturally expired would exempt the company from having to permanently dismiss loyal employees "solely on the ground of their nationality." Ogilvie warned that if all such employees were fired, the highly-skilled German technicians and scientists could form a new company that would not just compete with Forestal, but would also be willing to supply Germany with these strategically important products.[89] The Foreign Office initially agreed with Ogilvie's arguments.[90] But denunciations of the company continued to mount, with the Argentine press reporting (and Tower confirming) that on the fall of Antwerp, German employees pulled down and spat upon the British flag, drinking toasts "to the damnation of England."[91] Forestal decided to fire some German employees after the sinking of the *Lusitania*, but still refused to get rid of its most irreplaceable German scientists and technicians.[92]

The Forestal issue flared again in August 1915, when it emerged that A.H. Simon, a member of Forestal's maritime department, had become president of a committee at the German Club of Buenos Aires. H.H. Slater, a British businessman in Argentina, denounced Forestal in a series of strident letters to the Foreign Office. Slater claimed that men like Simon were not technicians and could easily be replaced by British subjects. "For the sake of our British name and character," he pleaded, "these enemies of our country and of civilization should be thrown out, even if this results for a time in a diminished dividend" for Forestal shareholders.[93] Other Britons similarly doubted that these Germans were irreplaceable.[94] Yet as a result of the strategic importance of quebracho products and the fear of retarding its production, until the end of 1915, the British government continued to listen to men like F.C. Stanley, a director of Forestal who explained that any ejected German employees would form their own company. As one Foreign Office commercial department clerk wrote, "The Forestal Company defend their action in retaining Germans in their employment cogently and I think satisfactorily."[95]

At the end of 1915, Tower was instructed merely to reiterate to Forestal's local head, Victor Negri, that he should eject his German employees as soon as possible.[96]

The British government generally lagged behind British officials and civilians in South America in their willingness to tighten the noose around the neck of German commerce in the republics. The reticence of British shipowners, bankers, and government to dive into a war against the German exporters of South America angered many of the British who lived and conducted business in the republics. Commercially-oriented, nationalist community-building efforts flourished as never before in the South American cities. British newspapers, consular and diplomatic officials, and commercial organizations worked in concert to halt trade conducted by local Germans.

The local English-language press played a crucial role in fashioning the new British nationalist spirit among people in South America. Since the start of the war, the *Buenos Aires Herald* had called for the dissolution of the Anglo-German Hospital, which cared for merchant sailors.[97] When the war began, the *Herald*, *Standard*, and *Times* became public forums for Britons griping about their less than patriotic brethren. The issue of transporting volunteers to the armies and navies of the United Kingdom caused a number of awkward situations for the British lines. Letters to the editor called on "leading" British residents and firms to pay the fares of young British men in the republics who, for no reason other than patriotism, were volunteering for the British army. A letter signed with the wordy nom de plume 'One of the Thousands That Think the Same' demanded that the Royal Mail ship British volunteers home without charge.[98] The *Herald* noted the irony when the Royal Mail's slowness to supply a ship for British reservists and volunteers forced local British boys to meet a boat in Uruguay, to which they were ferried aboard the SS *Berlin*, a ship owned by the Austrian Baron Mihanovich.[99]

As time passed, the English-language press grew increasingly vociferous in their campaign against German agents for British firms. In an article published in December 1915, the *Times of Argentina* stated that the British varnish firm Noble & Hoare still used the German, Moller & Co., as its agent in Buenos Aires. The *Times* lamented that a British firm could continue to close their eyes to Moller's nationality merely "for the sake of filthy lucre. What sort of patriotism is this, may we ask?" "[I]n time of war," nationality must be considered "the most important factor of all" in how people conducted business. The newspaper pledged to publicize such cases "in our manifest duty as honest British journalists."[100]

While encouraging and reacting to this local drumbeat for intensifying the Great War, the British diplomats and consuls in the three republics likewise maintained continual pressure on London to augment the effort against German business. The first year of war led most of these British diplomats and consuls to become ardent proponents of a sea-change in British policy. Their interactions with the neutral governments of the republics led such diplomats to believe that a change in tactics could work. Rather than worrying that a British campaign against German businesses would hurt their standing locally, diplomats concluded that the continued use of British ships and fuel by German business damaged the reputation of the United Kingdom. Foreign ministers and other functionaries of the republics appeared bemused that Britain allowed such business between Germans and Britons to continue. Malcolm Robertson claimed that when he was chargé d'affaires in Brazil during the opening months of the war, the Minister of Foreign Affairs dared him to act against firms owned or operated by Germans, even suggesting to Robertson that a firm acting as a German partisan would not be protected by the good offices of the Brazilian state even if registered in Brazil.[101]

These British representatives were, of course, not alone in suggesting that more stringent restrictions could easily be placed on local Germans. For the British Chamber of Commerce in Buenos Aires, pointing out the deficiencies in the economic war quickly became a favorite pastime. Through membership in such commercial organizations, British businessmen participated in the British war effort. Chambers of Commerce provided both a forum to unify the British communities in a manner benefiting the British nation worldwide as well as the primary link between the British businessmen overseas to the British government. In the opening days of war, H.E. Powell-Jones, the Secretary of the Chamber, informed the press that the British Legation would pass relevant general and commercial information about the situation in Europe to the Chamber, which would then post such information in its offices for use by its members.[102] Soon thereafter, the Chairman of the Chamber, Hope Gibson, gave the first annual report to his membership. Gibson noted that British economic interests in the republic "were rather diverse and even at times somewhat opposed to each other." But Gibson struck an ecumenical tone. The Chamber of Commerce must ignore such differences and work for "the advancement of local British commercial interests taken as a whole." The Chamber must have "real practical utility," and must not be "added to the already numerous tribe of (British) institutions here and there whose organisation embraced little more than a brass plate and an annual banquet." To help the group fulfill its duties, Gibson exhorted all British businessmen to join the Chamber. At its meetings, differences among these businessmen could be resolved. Tantalizingly, Gibson suggested that the Chamber had real power to make recommendations on specific improvements to the economic war to Sir Reginald Tower, who would relay suggestions to the British government.[103]

For Tower, Gibson, and many others, the Chambers of Commerce provided British people of South America with a way to attack the Germans with
the aim of permanently taking their trade. These Britons began to operate in
this fashion very quickly after August 1914. In part, the Chambers undertook
propaganda work. When considering the possibility of the Chamber setting
up a boycott of German products and employees, the executive committee of
the Chamber decided that this went beyond their scope to officially undertake
on behalf of the Chamber, but they did decide to "publish in Spanish for wide
circulation some official statements tending to counteract the German propaganda at present being carried on."[104] The Chamber subsequently issued a
press release in Spanish, categorically denying rumors that British manufacturers could no longer supply products to the Argentine market.[105]
They also began a propaganda campaign in the United Kingdom with a pam-
phlet on "German trade in the Argentine Republic," which consisted of a
series of alarmist articles from *The Standard* and was distributed through the
Chamber's London agent to United Kingdom businessmen.[106]

The Chamber in Buenos Aires argued from the start of war that a prohibition on business between British firms and Germans would open "exceptional
possibilities for the British manufacturer to regain lost ground and also seek
new fields in South America." Germany was handicapped by the blockade
and was unable to respond to demands of the South American markets.[107] In
a characteristic move, in October, the Chamber sent to the London Chamber
of Commerce and the Association of Chambers of Commerce an adver-
tisement for Mannesmann, along with a letter "pointing out the opportunity
afforded to British manufacturers of putting on to this market similar goods
to compete" with those made by that German company.[108] In December 1914,
the Chamber in Argentina reiterated to Tower that they perceived tremendous
potential for Britain to gain export share during the war, but first British banks
must "give tangible support to the aspirations of home traders to enter the
enemies' trade preserves."[109] British people everywhere must follow the successful German model of a nationalist foreign trade policy encompassing
manufacturers, traders and government. The British government should
induce British industry to change the way that businesses in Britain conducted
trade in South America, with manufacturers adapting their output to appeal
to the tastes of local consumers, while conducting their business exclusively
through local British importers.

Tower agreed with the Chamber that "if then a real effort is to be made to
take advantage of the present unique opportunity common sense seems to
demand that Great Britain should take a leaf out of the German book."[110]
Tower backed the Chamber's call for manufacturers to appoint British firms
as their agents. In return, manufacturers would be provided with enhanced
commercial intelligence. For instance, the Chamber would obtain samples of

German-produced goods that had proved popular with local consumers, sending the samples to the United Kingdom. Tower explained to the Foreign Office that the Chamber had already in its short existence helped him better to understand the nature of German commerce. Its members "are fully prepared to play their part in the assault on German trade," he announced on Christmas Eve 1914.[111]

Yet the attack from London was slow to come, and the Chamber of Commerce increasingly recognized the Board of Trade as the prime culprit. The Chamber's leaders reacted in fury when the Board of Trade, keeping a bureaucratic distance from the nation's trade, continued to send "requisitions from firms seeking representation in this Republic, without any indication of the names of such firms further than merely quoting a reference number." In a letter to the Board of Trade, the Chamber argued that such practices were outmoded and Byzantine, making it impossible for local firms to judge the likelihood of gaining any business. The ministry would have to become more involved and less secretive if it was going to help increase British trade in Argentina.[112]

It would also have to face reality. By May 1915 the Chamber began to deride the oft-reiterated phrase "business as usual," which "had already been used too extensively without comprehension of the real significance of the (British) position." Clearly, business had changed tremendously due to the war, bringing changed markets and government regulations. British trade would be better served by "facing the facts," concentrating resources on what would most help the British people.[113] In particular, the Chamber hoped that whatever goods could still be exported and imported into the United Kingdom might now travel exclusively through British hands. In June 1915, Tower called together a special meeting of the Chamber's leadership, asking them to discuss and recommend actions to suppress all consignments in British ships to and from German firms in Argentina. They drafted a proposal to bar importers in Britain from purchasing goods shipped by Germans in Buenos Aires, and reiterated the call for British consulates around the world to inspect and stamp the documents of British-owned ships.[114] In general, the Chamber of Commerce clamored for more government involvement in the regulation of international commerce, asking in particular for the servants of the British government overseas to take up a fundamentally new role.

The British Chamber of Commerce in Buenos Aires was the first to make such demands, but it was soon followed by similar organizations in Brazil and Uruguay. At the end of October 1914, Mitchell-Innes sent a letter to the main British firms of Montevideo, calling them to a meeting to discuss how they could help to increase the market share held by British manufacturers.[115] The British Chamber of Commerce in Argentina gained a branch in Rosario in the autumn of 1915, when the 'Rosario British Commercial Protection

Association' decided to affiliate itself with the Buenos Aires organization. Even before then, the Rosario organization had compiled and sent to Sir Reginald Tower lists of German firms and evidence that British ships carried goods for enemy companies.[116]

The frustration of the British traders is apparent throughout the minutes of the meetings of the Executive Committee of the British Chamber of Commerce in Argentina. In effect, the Executive Committee was the Chamber's War Cabinet. Led by Hope Gibson, the committee dealt with the issue of trade with the enemy so often that in August 1915 they began to meet weekly, and in October they made enemy trade a standing item on the agenda, with the results of all relevant deliberations to be communicated immediately to Tower's staff at the Legation. There was an air of intrigue in many sessions, for example, in November 1915 when they discussed "the activities of German secret servicemen and possible attempts upon British property." Perhaps, suggested one member, such German agents could be countered by enhancing joint action with the Chambers of Commerce of the other Allies.[117] With the local French they could create another western front.

In a particularly extraordinary episode, the committee chastised their London representative Donald Begg for answers he gave on behalf of the Chamber to an Admiralty questionnaire about possibly enhancing restrictions of German trade. Begg had suggested that British businessmen in Argentina were far from united behind enhancing such a war versus German traders and that "a boycott of German traders would without doubt damage British interests." The committee bluntly retracted Begg's answers and pledged the loyal cooperation of all British houses during any future commercial war. They claimed that the British public in Argentina fully backed war, but were bewildered about the indecisiveness of the authorities and businessmen in the United Kingdom. It would be easy to attack Germans, who in Argentina were "not consumers, but essentially distributors." All that would be needed were some restriction on British suppliers in the United Kingdom, and London banks, and merchant shipping. But so far these Germans continued to get British supplies, even as these enemies proclaimed to the Argentine public "that the blockade of German ports by the British Navy has entirely failed in its purpose. The prestige of Great Britain," the Chamber drily reported, "is not enhanced by this state of affairs."[118]

Although conditions under which they worked differed due to the attitude of each of the republics' governments, the British in South America generally believed that the war effort must be strengthened. The neutral populace, particularly in Brazil, favored the Entente and feared German expansionism.[119] Few of the British in South America doubted that local Germans contributed directly to Germany's war effort. The pre-war belief that insidious bonds linked German firms, German banks, and the German government led these British people to conceive of a Germany unbound by geographical borders. In the minds of those in South America who already hated the Germans, official regulations against their outposts in South America must be intensified. It was time for Westminster and Whitehall to destroy the livelihoods of Germans in places like Brazil, Uruguay and Argentina.

Conclusion

The opening months of the First World War astonished and angered the British in South America. German cruisers roaming the seas led South Americans to doubt the power of the supposedly invincible British navy. The activities of German businessmen in South America, in supplying their warships and in maintaining their trade with Europe, particularly agonized the British. British expatriate traders and diplomats in South America demanded a fundamental change in the way that their home government conducted economic war against Germany, shifting the focus from the blockade of German territory. Britons in Brazil, Uruguay and Argentina worked to sever their own ties with Germans while laboring tirelessly against profound resistance from banks, shipping lines, and government agencies at home. Only at the end of 1915 did the naysayers in the United Kingdom finally relent under the unremitting pressure from their compatriots across the Atlantic.

3

The British government redefines
Germanness

Of all the ministries of the British government, the Foreign Office certainly heard the most from South America. The Foreign Office had also shown the most concern about Germans in South America. From the opening days of war, its staff on Whitehall grew to see the war as a window of opportunity to attack and permanently cripple the long-lamented German economic presence in South America. At the same time, the proposals from South America might give the Foreign Office an opportunity to gain control of foreign trade policy from the Board of Trade. Foreign Office initiatives, driven by the demands of South America, proved crucial in the formation of the War Trade Advisory Committee (WTAC) in September 1915, which brought together people from a variety of government departments to discuss questions of commercial war. Although some feared changing Britain's overt respect for international law, the committee soon followed the Foreign Office lead by fundamentally redefining the British government's conception of what it meant to be an enemy.

The battle to change the official mind

As 1915 progressed, many in the Foreign Office recognized that reports about the situation in South America languished on reaching the Board of Trade. For example, the Board of Trade failed to demand the dismissal of Germans from British-owned companies. When the Foreign Office learned in November 1914 that a number of British insurers used agents of German nationality to represent them in South American cities, the firms promised to consider a change.[1] Yet nothing happened, and only after repeated prodding from the Foreign Office did the Board, in the autumn of 1915, again ask these insurers to appoint different agents. The furor over British coal reaching the German Coal Depot in Montevideo, and over British shipping lines hauling coffee for German exporters in Santos and Rio de Janeiro, exemplified how the Board of Trade ignored the possibility of extending economic war. Such frustrating episodes taught the Foreign Office to try to enact changes on its own, without reference to the Board of Trade.

Certain recommendations from British officials abroad and, in particular, from the British Chamber of Commerce in the Argentine Republic, guided the Foreign Office. The Chamber's Executive Committee passed four resolutions on 23 June 1915, which demanded that firms in the United Kingdom should stop dealing with German firms in Argentina. With the report, the Chamber appended a list of German firms: 16 exporters, 51 importers, 3 import/export firms, 3 contractors and 5 shipping companies. These firms should be attacked by all possible means at the British government's disposal. The Chamber further proclaimed that, if given the opportunity, loyal British firms would take up the business.[2]

On receiving this enemies list, debate erupted within the Foreign Office about whether present attempts at "moral suasion" would ever influence the actions of businesses in Britain. If not, would a prohibition on such British trade violate the neutrality of the South American countries? H.W. Malkin, an international law specialist, argued that present methods had failed. Despite potentially hurting British foreign trade, Malkin argued that the government must "go the whole hog and prohibit trade with them (German firms in South America)."[3] Malkin recognized that it would be difficult to convert the Board of Trade to this position, but urged that the Foreign Office try. A letter went out to the Board explaining that German residents in Argentina were doing anything they could to carry on their trade. "The time is fast approaching," it declared, "when a serious effort should be made to diminish both now and in the future German trade with neutral countries." The best way to do this would be to extend 'Trade with the Enemy' laws to prohibit trade with Germans in neutral countries.[4] In effect, Britain would change how it defined its enemies. Place of residence, the so-called 'domicile' criteria, was hitherto the sole consideration in Britain's official definition of who was considered an enemy. The FO wanted a system whereby a person's nationality or suspected activities could label one as a German.

In the middle of September, G.H. Villiers, the assistant head of the Commercial Department, decided that rather than continuing to send letters to the Board of Trade calling for action, the Foreign Office should appeal to the committee chaired by Sir Francis Hopwood that aimed to restrict enemy supplies.[5] Upset by the continued flow of products from Argentina to Scandinavia, Villiers despised what he called the "intolerable attitude of the B of T who seem to wish to promote trade with German firms in neutral countries."[6] As a result, on 20 September, Commercial Department clerk Basil Newton wrote a memorandum outlining the Foreign Office position on trading with Germans in neutral countries. "There is abundant evidence," Newton explained, "that enemy subjects in neutral territory are as much our enemies as persons who actually reside in hostile territory." British ships should not be allowed to carry goods sent or received by enemy firms in neutral countries. Newton predicted that neutral governments would not complain about new British regulations, thinking it natural that Britain should eventually pursue this course of action. It must be done, he argued, because British diplomats and consuls "in certain of the lesser developed countries, e.g., in South America," believed that restrictions on trade with Germans there would "be of considerable benefit to the permanent interests of British trade."[7]

The Foreign Office presented Newton's proposal to the WTAC in the autumn of 1915, a new interdepartmental body led by Hopwood that replaced his Restriction of Enemy Supplies Committee. The Foreign Office treated the creation of this committee as an entirely new opportunity to break the logjam. At the first meeting of the WTAC on 29 September 1915, the Foreign Office called for an extension of the definition of 'enemy' so that British enemy trade laws targeted people of German nationality "in certain countries such as the Central and South American Republics."[8]

To gain traction among the various ministries involved in the WTAC, the Foreign Office couched its argument in the language of war, as opening up a new front against the global Reich. The Foreign Office proposal claimed that German firms in South America were stockpiling vital commodities such as wool for shipment to Germany after the war, which would enable Germany's industry and foreign trade to rebound immediately at the end of war. The change would stymie German propaganda efforts in neutral countries, where they were claiming inevitable victory in the war. It would also punish German businesses. If done well, the resulting pain inflicted on German business could lead the government in Berlin to decide that the war should end. But this would only happen, the Foreign Office suggested, if the committee were to approve a complete restructuring of the administration of the economic war to minimize conflicts between the instructions given by various ministries to British traders, shippers and bankers.

When the WTAC immediately decided to form a subcommittee "to consider the definition of 'enemy'," its membership was stacked in favor of the Foreign Office. It was headed by Lord Robert Cecil, the Parliamentary Undersecretary in the Foreign Office since the formation of the coalition government in May 1915. His acceptance of a position in that ministry has been dubbed a "chance decision" by one of his biographers, but Cecil certainly desired the post, and he was most likely aided in gaining it because of his acquaintance with the Foreign Secretary, Sir Edward Grey, with whom he had been at Oxford.[9] Although he sat in the Unionist opposition, Cecil had long supported Grey's conduct of foreign affairs.[10] Cecil's abiding interest in foreign policy was perhaps inevitable considering his family's history – Lord

Salisbury, his father, had repeatedly served as Prime Minister and Foreign Minister over a two-decade span before his death in 1903.

Over the course of 1915, Lord Robert Cecil grasped control of the blockade, which he defined in broad terms as "the organisation of economic pressure of all kinds on the enemy."[11] Sir Edward Grey entrusted Cecil with the blockade owing to his personal disdain for such work.[12] The blockade was not an obvious focus for Cecil who, in the House of Commons, was a noted free trader in a party pledged to tariff reform. He conceived of the superiority of free trade in moral terms, as the fairest system. A man long mistrustful of businessmen interested in personal gain, he believed that tariff reformers immorally looked to enrich British people at the expense of foreigners.[13] However, before the war he had made some concessions to the possibility of retaliatory tariffs and imperial preference.[14] And he had given some thought to the vulnerability of the United Kingdom to foreign trusts, chairing a 1909 Board of Trade committee looking into global cartels in the meat trade. In particular, his committee examined the possibility that US companies could gain control of Argentine meat, which might allow Chicago companies to control the price of beef in Britain.

As the war progressed, Cecil quickly recognized the possible uses of a blockade, outlining his early philosophy of blockade to Edward Grey in a memo in mid-July 1915. He believed it must weaken Germany's "economic position" while depriving her of raw materials and food. Hurting the economy of the Reich might mean, paradoxically, that Britain should continue to allow luxuries to enter German soil. For instance, if goods such as coffee went to Germany, Cecil reasoned, gold would flow from enemy territory with no resulting nutritional benefit for the German populace. Yet, despite such nuanced arguments, he recognized in the end that the flow of goods to Germany should be completely stopped, and that it would not be good for morale if British troops knew that their government allowed their foe in the muddy, treacherous trenches across no man's land such comfort as coffee could provide. The question was how to do so without irritating the most important neutral, the United States, where the government was acutely attuned to the possibility that they might be treated differently from European neutrals when it came to British restrictions on trade with Germany.[15] Cecil, like Grey, understood the importance of the British relationship with the giant neutral power across the North Atlantic, and it led him to attempt to respect the rights of neutrals and to stay within the boundaries of arguable international law even as he turned the screws on the German economy.[16]

By the autumn of 1915, Cecil had become the prime advocate in the House of Commons of the way that the Foreign Office prosecuted the blockade. He labored to teach his fellow politicians the boundaries within which any blockade must be fashioned, arguing that the Foreign Office was walking a tightrope between a desire to weaken Germany by depriving it of war materials and by placing pressure on all German external commerce, while still maintaining for Britain the friendship of the many neutral governments around the world.[17] In his first months in office, Cecil worked with the Contraband Department of the Foreign Office. Headed by Eyre Crowe, this department developed contraband and rationing agreements with the neutral countries adjacent to German-controlled territory. Respect for Cecil's experiences meant that when the WTAC was created, most members deferred initially to him, allowing Cecil to guide the committee's agenda and decisions as he desired. Leo Chiozza Money, a confidante of David Lloyd George and a member of the committee, complained that he and other committee members were completely uninformed of the specifics of a policy created by Cecil with regard to Danish trade, even after it had been implemented in the committee's name.[18] Fully in charge, Cecil undoubtedly was the one who made certain that the subcommittee on defining 'enemy' was created in the first WTAC meeting, and that he would be in charge of this subcommittee.

In his interactions with the governments and traders of the neutrals adjacent to Germany, and with the United States, whose merchants opposed extensions of the British blockade, Cecil constantly dealt with the question of whether it was worthwhile to ruffle the feathers of neutral countries. He learned much about what could be made to appear permissible under prevailing international law. Whether international law weighed at all upon the actions of the British government during the war has been a subject of some debate. It has been argued that the British armed services and even the Foreign Office assumed before the war that issues like neutrality and contraband would mean nothing during wartime.[19] And looking at the first years of war, historians have suggested that the German declaration of the North Sea as a war zone in February 1915, and the British Reprisal Orders soon after, left in tatters all international standards for neutrality.[20] The economic war effort in South America belies these assessments. People such as Cecil recognized the importance of following international law and respecting neutrality, or at least being able to argue effectively that Britain was not breaking it.

The legalistic mentality of Cecil and the Foreign Office built upon the reports from their men in South America. Sir Reginald Tower explained in a memo that British regulations against firms in Argentina, particularly the grain exporting giants, might lead those firms and their partners to register as Argentine citizens, which could entitle them to the "good offices" of the Argentine government. As a result, Tower argued, any 'Trade with the Enemy' law affecting such firms must be carefully crafted to avoid diplomatic hurdles while still hurting such fair-weather Germans.[21] From Uruguay,

Alfred Mitchell Innes claimed that across the continent, there would be much ill will towards Britain if any enhancement of economic warfare in South America were not mirrored by an identical enhancement of regulations towards the United States. Uruguayans wanted to appear both as neutral and as inalienably sovereign as any other state. Innes predicted that if under new British laws the United States could not prove that its sovereignty was being breached, then the Uruguayan government would accept their conclusion.[22]

If this occurred, such a war could work. Innes suggested that "if the policy of boycotting German firms were followed out at both ends, there is a reasonable prospect of some harm being done" to German firms and to *Deutschtum* in general.[23] It would also be a positive signal to the British communities in South America, having "a good moral effect on our citizens" as at least a "platonic expression of the desire of our Government" to pay attention to commerce in South America. Innes believed that a connection existed between the expansion of German trade before the war and the strength and tenacity of the German war effort. He explained that with the elaborate global financial network linking the modern world together: "To-day an operation undertaken in Montevideo may as materially help Germany as if it had been done in Berlin. Money in any country can be utilised the world over. Hence the important thing to-day is no longer domicile, still less nationality, which is often a purely technical thing, but the power and will to help the enemy."[24] This verdict was echoed by M.A. Robertson, British Chargé d'Affaires in Uruguay and then Brazil from November 1912 to April 1915, who explained that his experiences had taught him that trade "is a wheel, and a most important one, in the German war machine."[25] Waging total war against global *Deutschtum* meant waging war in South America.

The subcommittee of the WTAC deliberated in weekly meetings until the end of November 1915, all the time focusing on the situation in South America. R.T. Nugent presented the Foreign Office plan in a memorandum and testimony in the middle of October. He argued that any extension of warfare must "destroy as far as possible the whole German financial and commercial organisation in neutral countries ... [while] assisting British recuperation by the substitution of British commercial organisations and channels of distribution for German." To avoid diplomatic rows, Nugent explained that any measure should legally apply to all neutral countries. However, in application, the measure must vary from country to country. It should be weak in Europe and the United States to mitigate friction with those important governments. But in less strategically vital countries "such as many South American States and the Portuguese and Spanish colonies in Africa, more drastic measures would seem both possible and desirable ... It is fortunately in these very countries," continued Nugent, "that the destruction of German trade promises the most hopeful results, where the political and commercial sentiments of the inhabitants are least likely to be offended, and where the German organisation is at once most vulnerable, and most dangerous in its political, military, and commercial potentialities."[26]

Support for the Foreign Office position came from a variety of other ministries. The Admiralty contributed a memo demanding increased restrictions on the trade of Germans and ridiculed the Board of Trade for its reluctance to take action.[27] H.B. Butler, the head of the 'Trade with the Enemy' department of the Home Office, saw some potential difficulties in administering a policy, but concluded that a publicly announced list of enemy firms could succeed with the support of consuls, diplomats and British businessmen everywhere, and with a new ministry to oversee the campaign. C.J.B. Hurst of the Foreign Office called for the new department to be formed under his ministry.[28]

Resistance to changing the official definition of 'enemy' came, predictably, from the Board of Trade and the bankers. In testimony to the committee, Mr W.H. Hollis, the managing director of the British Bank of South America, claimed that cutting off his business with German exporters in South America would be a futile gesture. After the war, German purchasers of primary goods would still have cash and expertise, allowing them to regain pre-eminence easily. Hollis argued that any British regulations would "choke" the Argentine and Brazilian governments, which relied heavily on customs revenues to fund domestic programs and to service their foreign debts. Such a war, he predicted, would fertilize deep resentment among neutral governments and neutral citizens, possibly leading to retaliatory attacks on highly visible British enterprises by South American radicals who opposed the power of foreign capital. Or even by hitmen hired by the Germans: "You can get a man assassinated in Brazil quite cheaply," Hollis stated alarmingly.[29]

The Board of Trade complained both about the likely efficacy of the measures and the way they would be administered. E.G. Pretyman of the Board of Trade noted that manipulating Britain's merchant tonnage might rouse neutrals against Britain.[30] Thomas Worthington, the Director of the CIB, did not think the main German firms in Brazil could be destroyed.[31] The Board of Trade was undoubtedly concerned about the economic heresy of the Foreign Office proposals, with their overt rejection of the laissez-faire principles that had for so long guided British economic policy. But the Board also balked for reasons of interministerial competition. The Foreign Office proposal would lead the Board and the CIB to lose many of their responsibilities. The Foreign Office planned to create a commercial diplomatic service like that advocated by Victor Wellesley since 1910, linking the Foreign Office directly to manufacturers and exporters in the United Kingdom. Board of Trade officials obstinately declared that the Board would not hand over any functions it presently exercised as the primary intermediary between the government and British traders, manufacturers, and shippers. One ridiculed the idea of creating a new department to administer the war against the Germans in South America, maintaining that it would not reduce interdepartmental correspondence on the subject of enemy trade, which according to him should be the main reason for any change.[32] The qualms of the Board, however, had little impact on the outcome of the subcommittee's debates. Conservative in nature, the arguments utilized by the Board of Trade reflected its philosophical difficulties in coming to terms with total war. The Board of Trade and the bankers who feared change failed to develop a counter-proposal in a climate that demanded attacking Germans wherever possible. Meanwhile, the Foreign Office presented a potentially workable scheme.

"The South American countries are by far the most important in relation to our enquiry," read the subcommittee's final report. "It is mainly with reference to them that the desirability of the new policy must be judged."[33] If passed by Parliament, the new policy would give the government, in Cecil's words, the "power to put a list of prohibited persons in the same position as enemies . . . without calling them enemies."[34] As explained by C.J.B. Hurst, one of the legal advisers of the Foreign Office, under the new law "what is known to everybody as being an enemy firm is a firm which you forbid your subjects to trade with."[35] Such a company might not even be led by a person of enemy nationality, but might instead be owned by a neutral. The government would do so by drawing up a blacklist "with great care and in close consultation with traders at home and abroad."[36] By placing someone on the list, the British government could openly attack any business or individual anywhere in the world.

Was there a need for a new blacklist, when so many already existed? In fact, existing blacklists of a number of ministries were under consolidation at the same time. The General Blacklist Committee (GBLC), a new interdepartmental group headed by T.H. Penson, the head of the TCH, worked after October 1915 to combine the Finance and Customs lists into what they called the general blacklists 'A' and 'B'. Those on the more stringent list, blacklist 'A', could not receive cables or letters transmitted on British-owned wires and ships, could not gain licenses from the WTD for exports from Britain, and had their credit facilities in London cut off. Furthermore, listed firms in the Americas could not import goods into Britain without permission. These new general blacklists, however, did not legally bar British shipping companies from carrying the goods of listed firms to neutral ports.[37] Through the closing months of 1915, the GBLC also maintained that British firms should continue to be allowed to send supplies to German firms in Latin America, because these goods would never reach German territory.[38] By focusing on places beyond German-controlled Europe, the new Statutory List would be unlike any other blacklist.

Also unique and new was its openness. It was the secrecy of earlier lists, including the general blacklists, which made it difficult to enforce the strictures they were intended to impose upon enemy trade. Most of these were only circulated to government departments, particularly the Board of Customs and Excise, which could attempt to stop companies in the United Kingdom from trading with Germans. In stark contrast, the Statutory List would not only be openly acknowledged, but would be routinely circulated and published in the United Kingdom and in participating FTD newspapers abroad. By announcing who the enemies of Britain were, and suggesting that anyone who helped these enemies could be next on the list, it was anticipated that the Statutory List would cause British businesses to regulate their own trade before goods reached customs officials. The Statutory List would be supported by a new law. Unlike the meek strictures of other blacklists, under which British traders were told on an individual basis, as circumstance demanded, of the undesirability of trading with a given firm, British subjects (i.e. anyone living in the United Kingdom) were legally forbidden to engage in business with firms on the Statutory List. The definition of 'enemy' enshrined in the new 'Trade with the Enemy law' required constant scrupulous attention to determine listable enemies at any given time.

Creating the FTD

In order to do this a new department had to be created. Opposing the pessimism shown by the Board of Trade, the subcommittee report stressed that a new department could remedy the confusion between the Foreign Office, Home Office, Board of Trade, Treasury, WTD and TCH. The trade with the enemy departments of the Foreign Office, Home Office and Treasury should be consolidated, the report declared; and hopefully, "it might also be found possible to obtain some assistance from the Board of Trade." The new department should be "an out-lying branch of the Foreign Office" modeled on the Contraband Department, a successful wartime department run by the Foreign Office, with Admiralty assistance, since the start of 1915. Led by "some officers" who would be assisted by "one or two good men of business," the new department should utilize its Foreign Office ties to communicate with British traders around the world.[39]

Yet it was not just a department for the wartime. In the final meeting of the subcommittee, Cecil stated that the new department should "eventually blossom into an important branch dealing with our overseas trade and have the supervision of officials appointed as trade experts." He summarized that it was "most essential that we should make every preparation to expand British trade" both during and after the war.[40] Under the wing of the Foreign Office, the new Foreign Trade Department (FTD) had as its mission not merely the destruction of German-owned and operated businesses in South America but, most importantly, their replacement by British companies. The dreams of Wellesley and others for a new department to boost British foreign commerce had finally come true.

The Trade with the Enemy Extension Act was passed by Parliament on 23 December 1915, and the FTD was soon introduced to the public in Great Britain.[41] Few noticed the change. Newspapers around the country followed much the same line as the *East Anglian Daily Times*, which ran a tiny announcement stating that a department had been set up to carry out the Trade With the Enemy (Extension of Powers) Act of 1915 and that, through Chambers of Commerce and trade organizations, the department would enlist the help of businessmen throughout the United Kingdom. The announcement concluded by imploring the business community to cooperate with this new department "in order to secure full benefit for British interests."[42] Some British journalists who had long clamored for an intensification of measures against Germans and Germany noticed the FTD and gave it a favorable reception. However, journalists displayed no consistent idea as to what the new 'Trade with the Enemy' legislation meant. On the opening of the FTD offices in January 1916, the *Evening Standard* proclaimed hope that the new department would recommend to Parliament further restrictions on enemy trade.[43] The *North Star* explained that the FTD would prevent anyone in "this kingdom" from conducting business with people established in neutral countries who attempted to supply Germany.[44] The *Glasgow News* informed its readers cryptically that the FTD "is charged with the treatment of the operations in this country of German-controlled firms the world over."[45] None of these assessments showed any understanding of the real purpose of the department.

Politicians likewise held differing and largely false understandings about the ramifications of the new law. Cecil explained to the House of Commons that a public blacklist would work to stop trade by Germans abroad. In response to questioning, he denied that the Board of Trade disapproved of the new measure. Yet Cecil presented the bill in a vague, surreptitious manner. In particular, his claim that it was a relatively meager, wartime measure, glossed over the fact that a new, permanent department would be created under the Foreign Office. He also never stated that the law would be aimed primarily at the Germans in South America.[46] The debate was dominated by a hawkish group of Liberal MPs who wanted to tighten regulations on businesses in the United Kingdom. Handel Booth and Sir Arthur Markham demanded that the law be applied to Germans in Britain as well as those Germans abroad.[47] Markham's unhappiness over the foreign focus of this bill led him to join the anti-Asquith Liberal War Committee the next month – a group of MPs who successfully pushed through in late January another Trade

with the Enemy Amendment Act allowing the British government to seques-
ter, sell, or otherwise wind up German-owned businesses in the United
Kingdom.[48]

Undoubtedly, MPs were right to complain that the government had not
fully explained how they meant to apply the law of 23 December.[49] Yet few
would openly oppose a bill that aimed to hurt Germans. The only real objec-
tion came from Sir Archibald Williamson, who complained that stopping
trade with Germans in neutral countries would only hurt British merchants
who could not possibly figure out whether the people they traded with *were*
Germans.[50] As a man involved in a variety of enterprises on the western coast
of South America, including the Balfour Williamson conglomerate, Archibald
Williamson was perhaps the MP most likely to conduct business with such
Germans. Yet he lacked political clout, and his position was ignored by the
consensus calling for tighter regulations.

Few people in the highest reaches of the government understood the
purpose of the new law. Neither the Dardanelles Committee, which between
7 June and 30 October 1915 was the de facto center of British war planning,
nor its successor, the War Committee, paid any attention to the new 'Trade
with the Enemy laws'.[51] Like the House of Commons, and indeed most of
the rest of the world, Britain's leaders were far more interested in the western
front than the south-western Atlantic. The resulting lack of oversight allowed
the Foreign Office and the British overseas to determine the mission and
duties of the department. As it looked likely to curtail trade between British
and German people, the press and politicians approved of it, then moved their
attention on to more obviously pressing matters like the failed Gallipoli
campaign and the likely spring offensive in Flanders.

The Foreign Office grabs the reins

The Trade with the Enemy (Extension of Powers) Act of 23 December 1915,
empowered the FTD to create the Statutory List. As planned, the list was
subsequently published on a bi-weekly basis in the *London Gazette* and
Board of Trade Journal, with copies of the list mailed directly to trade
associations and Chambers of Commerce in the United Kingdom and to
diplomats and consuls overseas. Although they did not ordinarily print the
names of each addition to the Statutory Lists, United Kingdom newspapers
such as *The Times* often ran announcements alerting readers to the publication
of new lists. Attention to such changes was important to the well-being of
British businessmen, as the statute forbade British subjects from trading with
listed firms.

In some ways, the war on German commerce in South America looked
like only a minor innovation. The threat to prosecute offenders followed

earlier laws restricting trade with German-controlled territory in Europe, which had led to a number of fines and other punishments for traders in the United Kingdom during 1915.[52] But aside from controlling merchants in the United Kingdom, the new law envisioned using other British strengths to transform the circuit of commerce in foreign countries. They would create new restrictions on British coal, shipping, and financial facilities, new censorship of postal and cable transmissions, and increase the confiscation of goods and ships intercepted by the Admiralty on the high seas. Customs officers in British ports were to ensure that no British exports were consigned to firms on the Statutory List. The Royal Navy and its blockading forces could stop any ships entering or leaving the North Sea to scrutinize if they held goods or letters for companies on the Statutory List. As the government already largely controlled British-flagged ships, it should be relatively easy to stop blacklisted firms from getting space on ships. British mail censors, who already sifted through thousands of letters and packages traveling between Europe and lands overseas each day, could contribute in helping to discover which firms merited targeting as German. Similarly, British control over the transatlantic cables gave it the ability to monitor all such instantaneous communications between South America and Germany. In short, Britain proposed to cash in on the massive strategic advantages they held over Germany in the South Atlantic by restricting all communications and commerce between South America and Europe.

Despite the reliance on many already established parts of the British blockade, the campaign in South America had an entirely new ethos to it. Blockade, or the act of halting trade to and from enemy lands, had long held a territorial definition. One surrounded an enemy territory, and made life uncomfortable for the people within it. Such sieges aimed to cripple opposing armed forces by causing social unrest. This was not the primary goal of the FTD. H.B. Butler, who in January 1916 became a high-ranking FTD official, openly admitted that the Statutory List "was not primarily intended to assist the blockade."[53] The FTD would attack German economic interests far from Europe, including those that did not attempt to supply Germany.[54] It would utilize tools provided by the blockade such as censorship, yet it would be using them in new ways. Censored communications could unveil neutral businessmen who helped German firms, and who could be placed on the Statutory List themselves.

As a solicitor who focused on company law and had served since January 1910 as a Conservative Member of Parliament, Laming Worthington-Evans was tapped as the first Controller of the FTD. Worthington-Evans was known for his interest in financial issues. Upon his appointment, the press expressed the hope that his "business capacity, alertness of mind, and determination to stop a public scandal," in addition to his reputation as a rising star in the

House of Commons and his wartime work advising the financial secretary of the War Office, made Worthington-Evans a perfect man for the job.[55] The FTD drew its staff from a variety of ministries, but its first members came exclusively from the Foreign Office and its diplomatic and consular services, and from the Home Office. The latter included H.B. Butler, an important Home Office official who had represented his ministry on a number of inter-departmental wartime committees. Beyond reassigning Butler and a few others, the Home Office never showed any inclination to interfere in the activities of the department. Sir John Simon, the Home Secretary, declared in the House of Commons debate that he knew nothing about the Extension Bill, considering it a Foreign Office matter.[56] The main enemy trade duties of the Home Office had been to investigate exporters in Britain who were suspected of trading with the enemy.[57] In sending H.B. Butler and others to the new department, the Home Office gladly divested itself of responsibilities for dealing with German trade in foreign countries.

For its part, the Foreign Office unsurprisingly assigned to the FTD men who had been working for a long time on the issue of South American trade. These Foreign Office clerks included Roland Nugent, the man who presented the Foreign Office case in front of the WTAC; Basil Newton, whose mid-1915 memoranda in support of an economic campaign in South America had initiated the campaign for the new war in the Foreign Office; and M.D. Peterson, a young clerk who had, in the spring of 1915, just passed his foreign service examination in international law. Within the FTD, Newton commanded the American Department, which controlled the Statutory Lists in the western hemisphere and considered all of "the political, contraband [and] commercial questions raised by the application of the powers" of the new enemy trade law.[58] These men who had long encouraged the extension of war were now given tremendous leeway to implement the law that they had fashioned. Other members of the Foreign Office regularly attended to the fledgling department, including Eyre Crowe, Victor Wellesley, and former diplomats Maurice de Bunsen and Walter Townley, who from 1906 to 1910 had served as minister to Argentina.

As the structure of British economic warfare operations solidified in the opening months of 1916, the geographical parameters of FTD activities were soon established. In meetings of the interdepartmental GBLC the FTD immediately drew a geographical line between the general blacklists and the Statutory List. At the end of January 1916, its representative to the committee, C.G. Markbreiter, a one-time Home Office clerk, urged the GBLC to cancel the general blacklist 'A' for all firms outside Europe.[59] In Europe, where contraband agreements made any more tensions with neutral countries undesirable, the general blacklists should continue as the primary blacklists and British traders would continue to be informed individually and privately whenever they tried to trade with firms on the secret general blacklists.[60] Firms in European neutral countries would be placed on the Statutory List only when it was deemed necessary to publicize the fact that they had German owners or managers, and when it was known that blacklisting them would not cause diplomatic troubles or hinder the rationing systems that had been negotiated with the neutral countries. But for countries outside Europe, where there were no rationing agreements, the brazenly open Statutory List made the secret lists redundant.

By the end of March 1916, a similar geographical boundary also divided the intelligence gathering systems of the FTD and the War Trade Intelligence Department (WTID), which succeeded the TCH as the central body for gathering intelligence on German trade from mail and cable censors and other sources. Although they would cooperate by feeding each other information and reports relating to their fields of interest, in practice, the WTID would focus on Europe and the FTD on the rest of the world.[61] As a result of these agreements, by the summer of 1916, the FTD, solidly controlled by the Foreign Office, effectively possessed all of the responsibility for the economic campaign outside the European theater of war.

Conclusion

By the end of 1915, the British government declared as its war aim the eradication of the German economic presence in South America. The case of the Germans in South America led the British government to reorient itself into a new war against Germans around the globe. The FTD inaugurated a new type of global economic warfare using neutral lands as a battlefield. The British weapons were their control of the sinews of economic globalization, the communication, shipping, and finance necessary for South American trade.

The British government expected to draw support from many people in the South American republics, including sympathizers of the Allies and, more interestingly, those who wished to avoid the ire of the British during the war. For one could be placed on the Statutory List simply for having done business with a firm on the Statutory List. Association could suffice for guilt. With the Statutory List, the FTD determined who was an enemy of the British state. The new enemy trade laws could be applied around the world only where it was expedient, allowing Britain to avoid tensions with the United States while focusing tremendous effort on crushing the Germans of South America. The initiation and expansion of the British economic war in South America shows that for many British businessmen and officials, including the once-avid free trader Lord Robert Cecil, free trade was no longer either a strategically viable or economically beneficial option for Britain in its relationship with the republics. In time, ideas broadened about who merited attacks as an enemy. The Foreign Office took the opportunity to leap to the forefront of the British economic war effort, forcing the government to adopt the recommendations of British diplomats and businessmen of the cities of South America. With the new policy, the Foreign Office gained what promised to be a permanent role in actively promoting foreign trade.

Attempting to stop the Germans of South America from conducting their business was not an intuitive act for politicians in Britain, none of whom had, before the war, expected to extend overseas an economic war against Germany. Constant interaction between authorities in London and the British communities of South America shaped commercial warfare in South America, but initially the flow of ideas was from south to north, as British policy makers reacted to the initiatives of the Britons in South America. This placed the fate of the war largely in the hands of this group of proclaimed commercial patriots, businessmen and officials with unquestionable hopes for British commercial advancement but with a proven quirky understanding of the ways of the global economy and plenty of potential for self-serving motives. Yet in the optimistic days of December 1915, any problems of miscommunication and motive were no more than possibilities. British economic warriors on both sides of the Atlantic lauded the new British enemy trade laws for refining the British idea of what it meant to be German. They hoped the Statutory List would destroy the ability of Germans in South America to conduct overseas trade, and believed that this blacklisting might influence trade within the South American marketplaces, or even lead the governments of South America to join the war against Germany. This change in British policy at the end of 1915 brought a type of combat unprecedented in the history of economic war.

4

The "ceaseless vigil":
compiling the Statutory Blacklist

Although it was overlooked and misunderstood in the United Kingdom, the publication of the first Statutory List shook the British and German communities of South America to the core. Citing its immediate effects on local German commerce, the *Buenos Aires Herald* gushed that "in the black list the British Government has forged an instrument of incalculable potency."[1] The Germans openly acknowledged that the Statutory List posed a tremendous threat to their local standing. The German newspaper *Deutsche La Plata Zeitung* lamented that with the British commercial attachés, consuls, and Chambers of Commerce working together to form the Statutory List, the British seemed intent on prosecuting their trade war "with what we may call German thoroughness."[2] "We Britons have played too long at war," declared the *Times of Argentina* in martial tones. "Merchants have to be harsh as well as generals of the army."[3]

Of course, the local British had already begun a war of their own before the Statutory List arrived, and at the start of 1916 they were still intensifying their own anti-German efforts. In a new campaign against shopping at stores that stocked any German-made wares, British newspapers called on all pro-Allied Argentines to wage a "*guerre de boutique* in a neutral country."[4] Businesses refusing to adhere to a strong anti-German line attracted scorn. The *Herald* published a letter to the editor denouncing Slopers, a British-owned clothing retailer, for selling German-made goods.[5] The ultimate goal of these measures was to sway the conduct of Argentines and other neutrals. In the offhandedly racist fashion of the early twentieth century, the *Herald* suggested that, eventually, "the purchase of German or Austrian articles" might become unfashionable, "something in the nature of a reproach and an offence against the common laws of decency and good taste, on a par with the wearing of a paper collar at a West Indian darkies' dignity ball."[6] The long-held British disdain of the local populace enhanced their swagger. Anticipating an intensification of the war by their government in London, these British traders believed that they could mould the local economies and revive their own locally established businesses.

There was no doubt as to the self-conscious patriotism of the British people of South America. From the start of war in 1914, British civic leaders formed committees and organizations to assist the British cause. A British Patriotic Committee was formed in Buenos Aires on 8 August 1914, and a Red Cross Society and various other war charities sprang up as well, drawing millions of pounds of donations over the course of the war. British businessmen led such community building efforts; nine of the nineteen members of the executive committee of the Patriotic Committee also held posts on the Council of the Chamber of Commerce.[7]

Perhaps more than any other nationality living in Argentina, the British community felt the pains of the brutal war at first hand. Early on, the English language press called for men to volunteer. As residents of a neutral country, no man in Argentina, not even one born in Britain, could have been forced to join the ranks even after the United Kingdom mandated conscription in May 1916. But an estimated two thousand Anglo-Argentines enlisted by the start of 1915, and over the course of the war a total of 4,852 men left Argentina to serve in British forces – a massive portion of a British community that, according to some accounts, numbered fewer than 30,000 before the war.[8] Of those men shipped to Europe, 528 died. There is no reason to doubt that Britons in other South American cities volunteered and died in similarly significant proportions.

By early 1916 this literal hemorrhaging of Anglo-South American men appeared as a significant obstacle to the successful prosecution of the commercial war. How could British businesses take the place of their German competitors without their prized British employees? As a result, what it meant for local British men to do their patriotic duty began to change. The British press backed off their earlier call to arms, and the local committee charged with enlisting recruits for British armies began to issue exemptions from the "duty" to serve in the British army. Their efforts declared that men who decided to stay and work in Buenos Aires rather than marching off to Flanders should be considered true patriots and should remain free from pressure from their fellow Britons in Argentina. By the time the British government had created the FTD, Anglo-Argentines generally accepted that their prime war duty was to derive commercial advantage from the abnormal wartime situation.

The FTD immediately buoyed such hopes. Quickly showing its dedication to South American trade, the Foreign Office extended the commercial attaché system to the continent before the end of January. Harry Chalkley, a long-time consular official, became the Commercial Attaché at Buenos Aires and immediately became Sir Reginald Tower's liaison with the local British Chamber of Commerce. Ernest Hambloch, another member of the Consular Service, was assigned to Brazil.[9] The avowed aim of these appointments was to foster links between the government and British traders overseas and to help unite the local British commercial communities, highlighting the readiness of Foreign Office personnel to overturn basic tenets of *laissez-faire* by ending the separation of business from government and of businesses from one another.

To the British of Buenos Aires, Montevideo and Rio de Janeiro, the appointment of commercial attachés promised a whole new war. "THE COMING TRADE WAR: Britain Begins to Move" heralded one headline.[10] They envisioned the FTD as leading a sort of pre-emptive counteroffensive, because after the war, in the words of one British businessman, the Germans were certain to "devote their energies towards trading in the markets of neutral countries."[11] If Britain did not win the commercial conflict in Brazil and dislodge German merchants during the war, the Germans would later dump German-made goods at below-cost prices to regain their pre-war position.[12]

Anticipation of the first Statutory List ratcheted up between the creation of the FTD in January and the issue of the first Statutory List in March. The Council of the British Chamber of Commerce in Argentina gleefully decided to send a copy of the new 'Trade with the Enemy' law to all of its members asking them for suggestions on how to enforce it in the republic.[13] The Statutory List could not arrive soon enough for Britons in Brazil, who fumed that British shipping lines continued to sell space on their vessels to enemy firms. As Admiral de Chair wrote to Lord Robert Cecil at the end of the month, British merchants "on the spot" complained that the Booth line was shipping rubber to New York for German and pro-German firms. Worthington-Evans replied that the FTD was pursuing a "definite policy" to wreck all such German firms.[14] The Minister to Brazil, Sir Arthur Peel, predicted success for the new policy: "German firms are very apprehensive and that is the best sign."[15]

The first Statutory List for South America was issued on 16 March 1916. It targeted, not surprisingly, the wheat exporters of the River Plate. Printed in a variety of publications, including the *London Gazette* of 23 March 1916, this list included the grain firms Bunge & Born, Weil Hermanos, and E. Hardy & Co.[16] A flood of South American firms reached the Statutory List the following week, including the German Coal Depots (Deutsches Kohlen Depôts), German-owned shipping lines such as the Hansa, and Brazilian coffee conglomerates including Theodore Wille & Co. The length of the lists for the South American republics increased throughout the war. People in the republics were notified of changes to the Statutory List by the British legations and consulates, who received word via telegraph from the FTD. Local British Chambers of Commerce were always supplied with up-to-date information and disseminated it among their members. British legations funded the printing of copies of the list to distribute to British businesses, which were encouraged to post it in their offices and stores. British ministers also passed changes to the list to English-language newspapers, which ordinarily printed the lists promptly, even highlighting the names by running them in bold or headline-size type.[17] The British of South America paid close attention to the new measure and celebrated what they hoped would fundamentally change the German position locally, and their own.

From the beginning, the FTD decisions on who to blacklist depended on information and recommendations sent by British diplomats and consuls. In January 1916, the FTD mused over how to rate the quality of their incoming intelligence. After concluding that reports from War Office agents and French operatives were suspect, an FTD report stated that the only foolproof sources of information were letters intercepted by censors and reports from British consuls and diplomats. Mail censorship between Latin America and Europe was coming into full effect in early 1916, as any vessels that wished to gain bunker coal at British ports or to pass the North Sea blockade must submit their post to mail censors.[18] Censors ended up detaining an array of documents that curtailed perhaps as much as £79 million in international transfers of funds that would have aided Germany. They also found much information of interest to those compiling the Statutory List, both in business documents and personal letters. But combing the incredible array of mail for hidden gems was an increasingly difficult task, as correspondents inevitably began to utilize code names and terms in their correspondence. Censorship might yield information on firms that were already suspected to be working for the enemy, but Britons in South America supplied most new names for the Statutory List. As a rule, the FTD applied the standard that any firms "unfavourably reported on" by British officials overseas must be considered highly eligible for the Statutory List.[19] To gather sufficient intelligence data, local ministers should parcel out Statutory List duties to the various consular officers. They would also work to persuade the local British people to support the economic war policy. If a British business legally established in Rio de Janeiro or Patagonia did not want to respect the boycott of Statutory Listed firms, they faced no legal repercussions from any British court. Yet all expected that such British firms would enter the war in high spirits. Diplomats and local British expatriates all gave indications that they would strictly follow the blacklist and endeavor to collect information for the distant London government.[20]

Forming the Statutory List: the case of Argentina

The initiative of Britons in South America in forming the Statutory List is well illustrated by the situation in Argentina. Despite the decision to destroy the vast bulk of FTD files at the conclusion of the war, the construction of the Statutory List can be observed in the written correspondence between the FTD and the British legation in Argentina, a group of records that exists in full, together with the records of the British Chamber of Commerce in Argentina.

As 1916 began, Sir Reginald Tower contemplated how he might help the FTD to build the Statutory List in Argentina. He recognized the need for assistance from the British Chamber of Commerce. Without waiting for the approval of the FTD, he called a meeting of the Chamber's council and asked for help.[21] The list of German businesses that the Chamber had drawn up in 1915 was insufficient, he explained, as the firms on it had been included without any definite proof of improper trade. Tower needed the Chamber to supply an explanation as to why each company or individual should be placed on the blacklist. He also wanted specifics on each company, including their name, address, partners, chief type of business, subsidiaries, and any other companies affiliated with the principles of the Statutory Listed firm.[22] The Council agreed to make "searching enquiries" and to furnish Tower with "the fullest details." Soon after, Tower sent a list of thirty-eight potential names to the Chamber, asking the members to go through it. They agreed that all but one on Tower's list should be blacklisted immediately.[23]

But no one was exactly sure how broad a Statutory Blacklist should be. Tower initially asked the Chamber to divide its recommendations into two lists, one with "the most serious competitors to British Trade in the Argentine Republic" whose actions were motivated by anti-British sentiment, and another "grey" list of firms implicated in trade with Germany or with Germans but which were motivated more by greed than by any concern with whether they might be helping Britain or Germany.[24] Members of the British Chambers of Commerce quarreled over how the Statutory List should be constructed. J.W. Barclay and J.K. Cassels explained that, as representatives of the Manchester textile trade, they feared that halting sales of cotton goods to German importers would lead them to shift their purchases to textiles woven in the United States.[25] These two men, however, were in a minority, and Tower brushed off their complaints.[26] Prominent members of the Chamber, such as A.G. Thornton of the machinery importing firm Evans, Thornton & Co., firmly backed a more stringent attack on German trade interests in Argentina.[27] The President of the Chamber, Hope Gibson, assured the British community in a widely publicized speech in February 1916 that the Chamber was concentrating its full energies on the trade war.[28] The British Chamber of Commerce made certain that it projected a unified face to the public, even when privately some members voiced skepticism about strengthening the trade war.

The newly appointed Commercial Attaché, H.O. Chalkley, took up the theme of unity when he arrived in Buenos Aires. He argued that everyone in the British community must work together for the Statutory List to succeed.[29] Pressure particularly came to bear on the British bankers, almost all of whom inevitably opposed the Statutory List when it was issued in early 1916. Harry Scott of the London and River Plate Bank in Buenos Aires worried that with the Statutory List, "we are only irritating the Argentines for practically nothing."[30] After the blacklisting in July 1916 of the two large German banks, the Banco Alemán Transatlántico and the Banco Germánico de la América del Sud, one British banker complained that such listings angered the Argentine government, and Argentines in general, against Britain.[31]

Yet as 1916 progressed, even these bankers generally felt compelled by patriotic peer pressure to do what was asked of them in regard to the Statutory List. And these reluctant warriors comprised a small minority of the local British community. The Chamber of Commerce ardently and consistently advocated expansion of the Statutory List. Its efforts were assiduous; Tower wrote proudly to Mitchell Innes on 1 February 1916, that "my Chamber of Commerce are always deliberating" on the composition of the list.[32] The Council of the Chamber met far more often than ever before in its short history. Tower attended many of the Chamber's Council meetings and communicated with the Chamber almost daily through February and March, always receiving quick responses to his enquiries. He focused their attentions on the most important goals of wrecking the primary German merchant houses and replacing them with British firms.

Tower did not blindly follow the suggestions of local British businessmen, using discretion in making his recommendations to the FTD.[33] But relations between Tower and the Chamber of Commerce were generally friendly and collaborative. Tower respected the Chamber's suggestions. For instance, he initially disagreed with the inclusion of the import house Eppenstein & Warren on the list that the Chamber had sent to him at the start of February 1916. Tower interviewed Warren, who professed strong pro-British feelings and disavowed rumors of his partner's pro-German proclivities. Yet in an addendum to a telegraphed list mailed to the FTD two weeks later, Tower included Eppenstein & Warren.[34] As the Chamber hoped, this firm was eventually blacklisted in May 1917 and as a result of its listing, Warren renounced his partnership with Eppenstein within a month.

Just as the British minister edited the recommendations of the Chamber of Commerce, the Chamber did not indiscriminately approve all names that Tower suggested. It quickly rejected his suggestion that the Compañia Argentina de Electricidad be placed on the Statutory List. The Chamber recognized that this power company was a public utility necessary for the well-being of the city of Buenos Aires in general and for the British-owned tramway company in particular. Tower soon recognized the validity of the Chamber of Commerce viewpoint, explaining to the FTD that cutting off the flow of coal from the United States to the company might trigger anti-British riots.[35] As this give-and-take relationship developed between the Chamber and Tower, the Statutory List developed in a fashion desired by the British community as a whole. It included Germans and non-Germans, targeting anyone deemed to help the enemy cause.

Information arrived from a wide variety of sources. Often, Tower directed enquiries to the manager of the London and River Plate Bank, from whom he could easily obtain a credit report that briefly described the type and size of the business conducted by a given firm or individual. Individual British businessmen also volunteered information on the activities of suspected firms.[36] At times, gathering information entailed legwork by Tower, legation personnel, or other paid or volunteer detectives. When fifteen cases of electric irons were delivered to the Custom House consigned to a well-known attorney named Arturo Crespo, Tower enlisted a man to watch the customs warehouse around the clock. When a cart picked up the irons and took them to Heinlein & Co., an importer on the Statutory List, Tower had proof that Crespo was acting as an intermediary.[37] He was placed on the Statutory List two months later.

Tower sometimes received incriminating information from the blacklisted or suspected firms themselves. In a series of meetings with Tower aimed at getting the Hansa Mining Company off the list, the president of the company inadvertently presented documents to Tower proving that they used intermediaries to sell to a Statutory Listed United States firm a large quantity of wolfram, a valuable ore.[38] Anonymous tipsters also provided information. Tower, Mackie and Chalkley all received a regular stream of correspondence from unknown sources. Often written in Spanish or choppy English, these letters alerted the British officers to otherwise unknown cases of German business. A writer identifying himself simply as "Un buen amigo de Inglaterra" mailed Tower information about smuggled German-made pharmaceuticals aboard Dutch ships, while another identifying himself as an employee of the British-owned Argentine Central Railroad (Ferro Carril Central Argentino) told about German purchases of wolfram.[39] Sometimes, of course, the anonymous correspondents were apparently wrong, perhaps through overzealousness, or perhaps out of a desire to hurt a commercial competitor or personal enemy. Tower carefully examined any allegations that he considered credible, often delegating the investigation to the British Chamber of Commerce. Leaders of the Chamber of Commerce began to undertake a staggering amount of investigative work. The FTD certainly agreed with Tower that British businessmen abroad were the most crucial sources of information, making the Chamber of Commerce a primary creator of the Statutory List for Argentina.[40] Of the first list of thirty-seven names that Tower cabled to the FTD, thirty-five eventually reached the Statutory List, most of them on the first few lists.[41] Their power to compose the Statutory List, to list and delist, would remain strong through the remainder of the war.

It remains difficult to get into the minds of the individual British business-men who decided to wage the war. Unfortunately, this group of men has left few personal records in South America; they appear to the world as all busi-ness.[42] Yet the decision to fight this war was not an impersonal one, not a fight against a faceless enemy. Looking at a map of Buenos Aires can help us to pin down the early trade warriors, and their early foes. By the end of the war there had been, at one time or another since March 1916, at least 403 different names in Argentina placed on the Statutory Lists. Their full addresses often did not make it to the published Statutory Lists. However, one of the early bundles of names recommended by the Chamber of Commerce to Tower on 23 February 1916 includes the addresses, and also the reasons the firms were recommended. All of the twenty-six "enemies" were headquar-tered in that small section of the city that *porteños* call the Centro (see map 2). Many Council members must have seen their enemies face to face on a daily basis. Those leading the war knew the men they were trying to run out of business. Certain streets where British and German businesses were neigh-bors must have been truly tense. For example, where Calle Cangallo (now Juan Perón) intersected San Martin, two of the leaders of the Chamber, Hope Gibson and Darsie Anderson, operated their businesses directly across the street from both Steffens und Nolle, A.G., a branch of a German steel and cast iron pipe firm, and more painfully, D. Meyer and Co. Tower's report to the FTD on Meyer is worth quoting at length.

> Diego Meyer has been for some years German Consul at Bahia Blanca. He was formerly on the Board of two English Companies at Bahia Blanca, and acted as Agent for the British Bank of S. America at that place. I understand that he has been superseded in all those positions now. His firm has been active in propaganda and in pro-German business generally. Herr Meyer himself has been specially prominent in connection with German shipping. His connection with the importation of arms and ammunition into Port Madryn, and various other questions of a like nature are engaging my close attention, but it is difficult to obtain exact proof of what seems to be going on. Be this as it may, Herr Meyer's name deserves a place in the Black List on many counts.[43]

This account of Meyer's activities seethes. Meyer was the worst type of German, one who had infiltrated British business, then turned wholeheartedly to the Kaiser. It is a personal report, written in conjunction with someone who was keeping a close eye on Meyer; in other words, by Meyer's neighbor Hope Gibson, the adviser on whom Minister Tower relied most heavily. To these leaders of the British war effort, and probably to most of their colleagues who lived and worked among their enemies, the German threat appeared clear and present on an everyday basis.

After the recommendations reached London, the FTD collected evidence.[44] Names were sent off to shippers, bankers, and the major Chambers of Commerce throughout Britain to see what they thought. Suspicions were also circulated to a variety of departments in the government, including the Admiralty, War Office, and Board of Trade. If there was a question about the insufficiency of evidence for immediate inclusion in the Statutory List, then the name would be placed on a Reserve List as evidence accumulated. Most delays in placing German firms on the Statutory List resulted from this vetting process, and from the distance, as the passage of documents across the Atlantic could take over a month. The only names placed on the Statutory List immediately were those working as cloaks, or intermediaries, for firms already on the Statutory List. The FTD pledged that if such cloaks did not immediately halt their pro-German conduct, British diplomats could place the belligerent firm on the Statutory List simply by sending a telegram to the FTD. They also gave Tower access to the Reserve List, asking for his opinions, and by extension, for those of the Chamber of Commerce.

Although extensive Chamber of Commerce and diplomatic records only exist for Argentina, the Statutory List for other South American republics seems to have been fashioned in virtually the same manner. The British ministers in the republics maintained an active correspondence among themselves, feeding each other information about German activities and garnering new opinions on the trade war policy.[45] According to British envoy Alfred Mitchell Innes, the British Chamber of Commerce in Montevideo had labored since January 1916 to draw up lists of German firms. Innes then edited them, sending the amended lists to the FTD by telegraph, and the Chamber's original list through the transatlantic mail. This British minister took more liberties than Tower in editing the recommendations. Of the 41 names on the first list drawn up by the Chamber at the start of February 1916, Innes rejected 21 as minor enterprises too unimportant to bother listing. Administrators in the FTD agreed with many of Innes's ideas, listing 16 of the 20 recommended names by mid-April, and 19 of them before the end of the war. As in Argentina, rejection by the minister to Uruguay did not necessarily mean that a given firm would never be listed. The FTD eventually placed on the Statutory List 10 of the 21 firms initially rejected by Mitchell Innes as unworthy of attack.[46] In all, at least 100 names in Uruguay entered the Statutory List before the end of the war.

It was not commercial importance or lack thereof that mattered. Nor, despite marking a change from the British tradition of using domicile as the criteria for classification as an enemy, did the Statutory List in fact mark a full switch to nationality as the criteria. Not all Germans or German firms were deemed suitable candidates for the list. Some were engaged only in domestic business, or had tight bonds with the local government that could make the situation uncomfortable for Britain. The British of South America were given vast leeway to determine which firms merited being cut off from British shipping and banking. As they were in effect attacking their fellow local citizens, in countries that had declared their neutrality in the world war, all recognized the inevitable need for circumspection in manner, and serious diplomacy in practice.

The South American governments react

In reply to questioning from the Admiralty in late 1915 about how locals would regard a prohibition of trade with Germans, the British Chamber of Commerce in Argentina opined overly optimistically that "general opinion would . . . view such a movement with indifference."[47] Instead, when it was published, the first Statutory List provoked immediate derision from much of the Buenos Aires press and propelled Argentine authorities to action. Calling Sir Reginald Tower into his office, Argentine Minister of Foreign Affairs José Luis Murature acknowledged the right of the British government to control the commerce of its citizens, but protested that since all feared being placed on the Statutory List themselves, the list would force even companies owned by native Argentines to stop trading with Germans. Referring to rumors he heard about the "inquisitorial acts" of the British Chamber of Commerce, Murature complained that the Statutory List policy led Anglo-Argentines to "an excess of patriotic zeal."[48] Finally, Murature grandly declared that the Statutory List circumvented the sovereign right of Argentina to regulate the activity of people within its borders, impeding "commercial transactions of a purely internal character, which neither favour or prejudice the interests of the belligerents, and which . . . are carried on under the jurisdiction and guarantee of Argentine Laws." As firms founded, owned and operated by native-born Argentines could be listed merely at the whim of the British government, Murature complained that "there is arising in the Republic a state of commercial war (*beligerancia*), the perturbations of which fall without distinction on natural-born citizens and residents of all nationalities, and consequently affect the freedom of commerce and industry assured to all inhabitants of the country by the Constitution."[49]

Tower responded with a portrait of the Statutory List operations that he adhered to for the remainder of the war. He argued that the Statutory List did not affect Argentine sovereignty since being listed only affected the listee's international trade, and explained that the FTD placed neutral firms on the

Statutory List "with great reluctance," only after gathering clear evidence that such firms acted "in a matter inimical to British interests."[50] Finally, Tower argued that technically it was not the British people in Argentina who were waging a war against the Germans there, but rather the British government, which, in manipulating the trade and ships of its subjects, was simply exercising its sovereign rights. Tower defended the British Chamber of Commerce, claiming that it acted solely in an information gathering capacity. He knew that this was a lie, that in fact the local Britons had actually instigated and largely continued to run the local British war, but Tower and other Britons consistently denied that there was any local involvement in this war being waged from London.

No one ever explained to the public how the Statutory List was created. The *Buenos Aires Herald* speculated that the list was most likely drawn up by Minister Tower and Consul-General Mackie, with advice contributed by the Chamber of Commerce, individual commercial men, Foreign Office staffers, British censors, and even possibly some British Secret Service officers spying locally.[51] But the degree to which each of these wielded influence remained uncertain. The British Chamber of Commerce attempted to keep its deliberations secret in order to avoid Argentine ire. Tower assured the Chamber that he would always accept full public responsibility for the lists so the Chamber would not be "saddled with the odium of having inserted or withheld any name or names."[52] Innes in Uruguay and Peel in Brazil similarly covered for their local British allies, worrying about the potential negative impact on British business in the republics if British civilians, supposedly under the laws of the neutral states, openly took an active role in attacking local German business.

It was not just the Argentine government that protested. Some South Americans claimed that, in conjunction with the recent centralization of their grain purchasing, the Allies utilized the Statutory List to lower market prices. At the end of June, in reaction to a published warning from the British Consul-General Mackie that doing business with a listed firm could cause a neutral company to be placed on the list, the governing committee of the Buenos Aires Corn Exchange lashed back with a resolution condemning those of its members who refused to purchase grain from Statutory Listed firms. *La Nación* complained that even if the British government only intended the blacklist to exert a "moral pressure over its subjects in order thus to complete the blockade of Germany," the patriotism of the Allied business community and the fear among outsiders of being hit by the Statutory List threatened the ability of Argentina to export its goods. *La Prensa* argued that in denying German interests the ability to use the seas, the Statutory List was "a legitimate measure of hostility in the economic sphere," but in "disqualify[ing] producers and holders of Argentine produce because of their nationality," the Statutory List "attacks the very essence of Argentine sovereignty."[53] A group called the "Argentine Patriotic Committee against the Blacklists" (*El comité patriótico argentino contra las "listas negras"*) produced leaflets explaining how the communiqué issued by Consul-General Mackie subverted the Argentine national constitution.[54] And in the middle of July, Marco A. Avellaneda, a member of the Argentine Chamber of Deputies, introduced a bill making it illegal to insert clauses into contracts excluding deals with firms of certain nationalities and forbidding the press to publish anything that might facilitate the operation of Statutory List policy in Argentina.[55] He was supported by Estanislao S. Zeballos, the former Foreign Minister, who as president of the Argentine Rural Society represented the republic's powerful ranchers. Zeballos, who according to former minister Walter Townley "has always been a strong German supporter" and was in general "a most mischievous windbag," gave a series of well-publicized public lectures on the ways in which the Statutory List infringed on the republic's sovereignty.[56]

Tower pleaded with the FTD to counter such criticism by issuing an official statement emphasizing the extra consideration that had been shown to Argentine interests, such as allowing scarce British ships to carry coal to Argentina from the United States.[57] Yet before such a statement could be released, the complaints dissipated. Although the Argentine government more than any other in South America looked to establish its independence from the United States in hemispheric politics, the announcement in July that a list had been issued for the United States halted charges that Argentina was being subjected to discriminatory treatment. South American governments soon grew to accept the legality of the Statutory List, mainly because Britain applied the list to all neutrals, even the mighty United States.

Issuing a blacklist for the United States certainly ranked as a tremendously bold move, proving indisputably that the British government believed in the importance of the new commercial war in South America. Although President Woodrow Wilson may have held real hopes to supplant British economic connections to Latin America, he was also generally pro-British, making the United States a benevolent neutral after April 1915.[58] Britain increasingly leaned upon the United States for funds and supplies.[59] From the start of the First World War, British economic warfare measures rubbed a sore spot in its relationship with the US government. In March 1915, the German declaration of submarine warfare led the Admiralty, as a "reprisal," to halt all cargo ships carrying goods "of presumed enemy destination, ownership or origin." US authorities responded that the Admiralty action was illegal, and that although Britain had declared a blockade of Germany, they had not made the blockade truly "effective" (and therefore legal) by stopping every ship plying to or from German ports. In the eyes of the neutral US government, and businesses there hoping to maintain as much lucrative trade as possible with both sides in the European conflict, only a complete, "close" blockade that included Baltic Sea traffic could be considered legitimate.[60]

Worried reports from the British Ambassador, Cecil Spring-Rice, poured from Washington to London throughout 1915. United States Ambassador to Britain Walter Hines Page issued a massive treatise on 5 November 1915, which summarized the multitude of US complaints about the blockade.[61] All relevant British ministries paid attention to US objections. Attentiveness to the United States started at the top. Throughout his wartime tenure as Foreign Secretary, Sir Edward Grey fixated on maintaining the attitude that the United States had shown Britain since the war erupted in Europe. To assuage US protests, just a year earlier Grey had even contemplated entirely ending Britain's economic war.[62]

From this perspective of overall British dependence on the United States, the blacklisting of businesses there was shocking. When the Statutory List published on 18 July 1916 included 85 names in the United States the Hearst press denounced the policy, and Irish and German partisans in the United States demonstrated against the British. Although he was generally supportive of the British side throughout the war, the Statutory List greatly frustrated President Woodrow Wilson.[63] On returning from a trip to the United States, Walter Page alerted Grey to the resentment brewing over the Statutory List. Even those Americans who favored the British did not feel that the blacklisting of people in the United States would deprive Germany of food or supplies. While admitting the right of Britain to prevent its subjects from conducting certain business and even to prevent British coal from being given to ships carrying German-owned goods between North and South America, Page wondered if the extension of enemy trade measures to businesses in the United States, aside from possibly violating US neutrality and sovereignty, might also signal that Britain held ill-will toward the North American power.[64]

Yet despite the real possibility that the Statutory List might hurt relations with the United States, the Foreign Office deemed the importance of legitimizing the List in South America worth the cost. Either it was legal for all neutrals, or it was legal nowhere. As Grey explained to Page, "If we gave it up for the United States, we must give it up everywhere." Britain refused to relinquish the Statutory List policy, "for we (have) evidence that in restricting German trade, particularly in South America, it (has) a real effect, and bringing pressure to bear on commercial circles in Germany."[65]

The FTD utilized loopholes built into the 'Trade with the Enemy' law to try to mitigate protests from the United States. The first list for the United States was issued in July, months later than lists for any other country, and the rate at which names were added to the US list was slower. At the end of 1916, there was a continued trend of growth in the lists for South America, with 158 names for Argentina and Uruguay and 225 for Brazil. Only 78 remained on the United States list, seven fewer than on the initial one.[66]

But more important to its acceptance was the process. The United States and Britain acted as if they were arguing a legal case. With perhaps an Anglo-Saxon common law mentality revering legal precedents, or perhaps merely reflecting their own self-images as great powers whose decisions carried global weight, both countries assumed that the decisions made between them would become accepted by all neutrals as de facto international law on this issue, at least during the war. Ambassador Walter Page told Grey that their correspondence should be publicized "to keep the record about international law straight."[67] Much of it would thereafter be printed in newspapers such as *The Times*, and in a British Government White Paper.[68] As with other aspects of the British economic war, such as the blockade in Europe, it was soon accepted by the United States because it was orderly, relatively humane, and seemed likely to be truly effective "not as a mere proclamation of warning, but a procedure comprehensively enforced," and thus seemed broadly to comply with accepted international laws.[69]

By reading the public correspondence, South American governments were led to conclude that Secretary of State Robert Lansing and Ambassador to the United Kingdom Walter Page had adequately addressed issues of international law. In his annual address to the Brazilian Congress in May 1917, President Braz quoted the correspondence between the United States and the Foreign Office when explaining why he had halted efforts to dispute the legitimacy under international law of a Statutory List for Brazil.[70] Foreign Office successes in parrying the United States jabs helped legitimize the British economic war efforts in the eyes of the neutral governments of South America. As M.D. Peterson of the FTD would later note in satisfaction, "the great vindication of the US Statutory List" was the way that, in Tower's words, the Argentines talked up patriotism but were "disposed to hurry to the skirts of the United States in any event needing action or decision."[71]

Rather than continuing to chafe at the list, Argentine opinion makers began to try to understand its ramifications. *La Nación* published an extensive interview with FTD Controller Worthington-Evans, who explained that the Statutory List merely brought British economic war policy into line with that of other belligerents, and stressed that the Statutory List could actually help the truly neutral firms of Argentina to pick up the slack by expanding their operations.[72] After Britain promised that internal transactions between an Argentine firm and those on the Statutory List would be insufficient to warrant placing the Argentine firm on the list, Murature agreed to release correspondence between the British and Argentine governments to the press.[73] In these published letters, Tower and the Foreign Office ardently defended the right of Britain to regulate the commerce of its own subjects. For the British, the release of this correspondence proved the value of sometimes drawing back the curtain obscuring the dark art of diplomacy, as the letters helped to diminish the charge that the Statutory List directly infringed the rights of Argentines. In commenting on the correspondence, *La Nación*, generally a pro-allied newspaper, was led to express its sympathy for the goals of the policy.[74] Murature reassured Tower that the Argentine government would not support Avellaneda's anti-Statutory List legislation in the Argentine Congress.[75] The public nature of this debate over the Statutory List was critical in making the war appear legitimate under international law.

To some extent, Argentina's fear of alienating British investors undoubtedly helped to mitigate official attacks on the Statutory List policy in 1916. Although Germans controlled much of the import and export trade, the City of London provided most of the capital for the development of Argentine railways and other enterprises, and also for financing the Argentine government's debt. In mid-1916, when Murature hinted that the Argentine government might be forced to close any British bank that refused to undertake transactions for listed firms, Tower replied hotly that "if the Argentine Government were so ill-advised as to try conclusions of such a character with His Majesty's Government, there could be only one result, and that spelled financial and industrial ruin for the Republic."[76] Murature quickly dropped the matter. Capital from the United States had barely begun trickling into South America at this time, and until the end of the war it remained fairly inconceivable to Argentine authorities that there could ever be a more ready source of money than London.

But it was the impact of legalistic arguments and the US list, not the power of British capital, that persuaded Argentines to accept the existence of the Statutory List. By the middle of September 1916, even radical newspapers recognized the right of Britain to have the blacklist, and Tower reported a general indifference to agitators clamoring for more significant protests against the Statutory List. The "Argentine Patriotic Committee against the Blacklists" received press only in the *Deutsche La Plata Zeitung*.[77] By June 1917, Tower reported that the Argentine government, and indeed Argentine opinion in general, fully accepted the "international legality" of the list.[78] The technical plausibility of British arguments about the legality of the Statutory List policy, and the acceptance of such arguments by the United States government, led Argentina and the other South American republics to resign themselves to the list's existence.

British goals for the Statutory List

Even as they defended the existence of the list throughout 1916, British trade warriors labored constantly to expand it. In placing a firm on the Statutory List, the British looked for any one of a number of outcomes. For some firms placed on the list, the goal was public supplication to the British Statutory List and a rejection of ties to Germans. In June 1916, Tower announced that any truly Argentine firm would be removed from the Statutory List if the firm provided satisfactory evidence that it no longer acted on behalf of Britain's enemies and signed a written guarantee to not act as an intermediary of imports, exports, or correspondence for listed firms in the future.[79] Some people were delisted after showing Tower legal documents proving that they had severed connections with a listed firm or from German partners.[80]

Two weeks after being listed, the photography supply firm Casa Widmayer closed. Its business was succeeded by the Emporio Fotografico Guillermo Koellner, but Tower felt the new firm too unimportant to merit inclusion on the Statutory List.[81] However, a year later Tower learned that Koellner was buying up certain chemicals at high prices in far larger quantities than his shop needed. Apparently, the firm had expanded by making suspect transactions. Tower called for its inclusion in the Statutory List.[82] Immediately, Guillermo Koellner himself appeared at the Legation with proof that he had been an Argentine citizen since 1893, that his company employed no enemy capital, and that he cherished his long-established relationships with British firms. Tower persuaded him to sign a document pledging that he would never again deal with firms on the Statutory List and would thereafter allow the Legation to scrutinize his books on demand.[83] As a result, Tower recommended leniency and Koellner was removed from the Statutory List. Tower was "subjected to constant visits" from such penitent listees.[84] Tower later compared such grovelling supplicants to the famous medieval episode of the Holy Roman Emperor Henry IV walking barefoot to the castle of Canossa to beg forgiveness from Pope Gregory VIII. In both cases, coercion played a large role in motivating their pleas for forgiveness and professions of undying loyalties to the cause.[85] With British command of the seas imperiling any shipments that they considered suspect, firms that imported or exported had little choice but to sign such pledges. In doing so they in effect signed away their neutrality by guaranteeing that they would not conduct business with anyone that the British and Allies believed to be an enemy.

A number of companies hired lawyers to try to get them off the Statutory List. Some lawyers soon specialized in such efforts, such as Dr Ricardo C. Aldao, who represented Weil Hermanos, the Compañia Hidraulico Agricola, Moller & Co., and Warburg & Goldschmidt. Desperate to be delisted, the Compañia General de Obras Publicas retained Dr Vincente Lopez, the

Solicitor to the Argentine Treasury, promising to give him a place on the company's board of directors if his efforts were successful. What such lawyers were expected to do was uncertain. The Statutory List was not a question of law, at least not Argentine law, and the only court to which an attorney could appeal was Sir Reginald Tower himself. Attorneys who went to Tower's office commonly argued that the listed company was registered and domiciled in Argentina. Such a rationale was never enough on its own to persuade Tower to back a firm's claim for leniency, as he knew that the nationality of the firm would not determine whether or not it was included on the Statutory List.[86]

In fact, the blacklist included a number of companies and individuals that were decidedly not German, yet who were proved to have aided German companies or helped to breach the blockade. For example, Tower fielded many complaints from listed businesses owned and operated from non-South American neutral countries. The Swedish hide and quebracho-exporting firm, Svensson, Ohlsson & Co., was placed on the Statutory List for shipping Argentine products through Sweden to Germany. The company enlisted both the Swedish minister and the pre-eminent shipping agent in Buenos Aires, Pedro Christophersen, to lobby Tower for removal from the list. Although Ernesto Ohlsson was unable to fully explain one suspect shipment, Tower suggested to the FTD that "a lesson has been taught" and, as it would ease tensions with the Swedes, the firm could safely be taken off the list.[87] By exercising such leniency, Tower did his best to keep complaints to a minimum. The British hoped that such confessions and promises meant that applicants, humbled and even humiliated, now recognized the immorality of their pro-German ways. Although it meant a tremendous increase and transformation of the type of work done by British diplomats, such sycophancy could at times be enjoyable.

By removing contrite firms from the Statutory List, the British government made a public statement about its own power. The long reach of the United Kingdom could inflict enough pain to make a neutral person, in a neutral country, far across the ocean, prostrate himself in front of British officialdom. The Statutory List process made the power of the British armed forces, economy and Empire apparent to South Americans. And yet, the British lion hoped to appear to have a heart. Both Tower and the Foreign Office wanted to make mercy rather than stringency the rule of thumb in applying the Statutory List regulations, because they hoped to teach South Americans to avoid Germans, not infuriate local people against Britain.

But the willingness to grant mercy did not apply to all on the Statutory List. The main German and pro-German firms, virtually all of which were blacklisted by the end of 1916, remained on the list until the end of the war. The primary British goal was to drive them into bankruptcy, or at least to prevent them from conducting business during the war while British competitors could be built up. According to Tower, such firms were "genuinely and wholly enemy, and are therefore incapable of reconstruction. They can only be weakened and possibly eventually broken."[88] For example, Germans owned Rathje & Co., a purveyor of tobacco and sheep dip in Buenos Aires. Tower explained in January 1917 that the firm had not done well since the start of war, and that the German bank in Argentina had basically stopped their credit because their payments due to Germany were in arrears. However, the firm had a good reputation, and Tower felt it likely that "if they survive till the end of the war, they will again obtain means to place themselves on a satisfactory basis." Hoping to force Rathje & Co. into bankruptcy, Tower wanted to tighten the noose by placing them on the Statutory List, which was done that May.[89]

Tower was undoubtedly correct that such firms were recalcitrant and unapologetic Germans. Many of those listed refused to beg for mercy, and some even publicly scorned the British trade war. A.M. Delfino & Hijos was a shipping agency that, by the end of 1914, had assumed control of all arrangements for German ships in Argentina, including perhaps the supply of German cruisers offshore. Delfino was placed on the Statutory List of 24 March 1916.[90] Soon thereafter the British grain agent Nicholson & Rathbone refused to load a cargo for the Italian government onto an Italian ship that Delfino represented. Delfino immediately resigned as agent of three Italian shipping lines that had been long-term clients. As the sole agent of the Linea Nacional del Sud, which commanded a virtual monopoly over trade with many smaller Argentine ports, and with the company chairman also holding a number of locally prominent directorships, including one at the Banco de la Nación of Argentina, Antonio Delfino felt tied into the local power structure and did not fear losses enough to kowtow to Minister Tower.[91] His political connections were obviously behind Foreign Minister Murature's approach to Tower protesting against the blacklisting. It was rumored that Señor Delfino even offered his resignation from the Banco de la Nación, but that the resignation was rejected by Argentine President Victorino de la Plaza himself.[92] With such actions, Delfino tried to counteract the legitimacy of the British campaign in South America, by making Britain appear spiteful in attacking a principled and proud man. Tower saw Antonio Delfino as a snake, as a true arch-enemy. He was certain that it was Delfino who informed the German minister, Count von Luxburg, of the discussions in meetings of the Banco de la Nación about Argentine financing for a possible sale of excess grain to Britain in 1916.[93] Yet the Statutory List did seem to hit this enemy hard, as Delfino lost some agencies that definitely hurt his company's bottom line.[94]

Obstinacy had a price, but Delfino was not alone in refusing to give in. Other true believers among the German community openly derided their inclusion on the Statutory List. Fernando Ellerhorst, a public accountant and Argentine citizen, was blacklisted owing to his connections with the new La Germano Argentino insurance company that sprang up at the start of the war. On his listing, Ellerhorst wrote to Tower: "I hasten to express my thanks to you for this distinction. Although I am Argentine and as a neutral have the right to work with whom I please without asking anyone's permission, you have advertised me very well, better than ten advertisements in the newspapers." As Ellerhorst had always done business exclusively with Germans, Tower rued that Ellerhorst might be right.[95] In the same vein, the Deutsches Kohlen Depot in Buenos Aires celebrated its tenth anniversary at the end of 1916 by sending greeting cards to its customers: "In spite of all the intrigues, acts of coercion and reprisals with which our rivals have opposed us in their economic war, we pass this date with full prosperity and with the firmest confidence in the future development of our business." Tower noted, however, that intercepted telegrams between the company and its Hamburg headquarters indicated that the depot was actually just putting a brave face on a difficult climate for its business.[96]

Indeed, the early months of the war brought a number of indications that the British Statutory List was a success. From the start of 1916, reports poured in explaining how firms were pushing their German partners out of the business. Consul Dickson recommended the Rosario firm W. Lohmann & Co. for the list in May, but Tower asked the FTD to hold off, as the partnership was due to dissolve in July and the managing partner, an Argentine named Martinez, should be given a chance to make the business work on his own afterwards.[97] The firm was never placed on the Statutory List. Other firms, such as Luis Aischmann y Cia, an importer of brewery and winery supplies, scrambled to buy out their German partners.[98] It would be difficult to prove that the Statutory List significantly raised the rate at which partnerships splintered in the always tumultuous commercial environment of South America, but the economic war effort determined when a number of partnerships dissolved.

Initial reports from Sir Reginald Tower suggested that the Statutory List was working well, as evidenced by "the keen desire of merchants in B[uenos] A[ires] to hide any enemy connection or association," dropping from their letterhead any mention of their ties to German manufacturers, and calling themselves Argentine, Swedish, and "every nationality save German."[99] In Uruguay, Innes agreed "that the war and the Statutory List combined have seriously crippled German firms in this country." Several importers faced severe financial difficulties owing to an inability to obtain either credit or the

German goods they formerly sold, while exporters had great difficulties conducting business "owing to the operation of the Statutory List, and the influence we exert on American shipping companies."[100] On 30 September 1916, Tower sent to the FTD an extraordinary report entitled "Effects of the Statutory List Policy in the Argentine Republic." His verdict was overwhelmingly positive. The grain giants Bunge & Born and Weil Brothers found their trade tremendously curtailed, the German wool firms found themselves with huge stockpiles of wool that they could not sell because they were on the Statutory List, and the importing firms on the list "have been reduced to 'unconditional surrender'." As companies throughout Argentina began to shed their German partners and managers at an exemplary rate, German businessmen were becoming marginalized in what had until recently been fertile ground for their toil.

The Statutory List was the high point of the British war against enemy traders in South America but it was not the only part of the campaign. Controls on the availability of certain goods, including British coal, were legitimized by appealing to wartime economizing, but they had the further goal of keeping resources from enemy firms. The British made concerted attempts to hurt German grain exporters by exploiting the near-monopoly that the British empire held over the supply of jute. Jute bags were vital to the shipment of the grain crops at least from the farms to train depots, and the lack of grain elevators in Argentina meant that shipment in jute bags was the norm even on most trains and aboard seafaring merchant ships. As control of bags could "inflict injury – perhaps irreparable injury – on the Argentine cereal crop," possibly leaving it rotting in the fields, Tower opposed restrictions on jute imports, fearing that the Argentine government would protest mightily if bags were withheld from Argentine farmers.[101] Under instruction from the British government (and following a model adopted by Ambassador Spring-Rice in the United States), a reluctant Sir Reginald formed a Jute Committee in Buenos Aires in March 1916 to advise the Legation as to which firms should be allowed to import jute. This committee formed a list of approved jute importers that Tower sent to the FTD, and through the war continued to look into cases of suspected bag traders. Other less official boycotts of certain firms developed among local British traders. The firm Tobino & Arvigo was implicated in selling, to British firms, grains that had at one time been owned by Bunge & Born. Thus grain that would eventually reach the Allied forces and civilians financially benefited an enemy company.[102] Outraged, British dealers refused further dealings with Tobino & Arvigo.

A final example of the flexibility and diversity of British warfare is shown by the case of Ernesto Tornquist & Cia. In February 1916, Tower explained that Tornquist should not be placed on the Statutory List, despite the fact that the financial house held the agency of the German bank, Disconto

Gesellschaft, and had been mentioned often in the correspondence of German bankers intercepted by British censors. "It would never do to make an enemy" of a firm run by a third-generation Argentine family deeply intertwined in the structure of the Argentine elite.[103] Tower believed that Carlos Alfredo Tornquist, the present head of the company, personally favored the Allies, "but he is unwilling to sacrifice his German business connections, even if he could, at a moment when the prosecution of his inherited business is more than ever lucrative. In my view," continued Tower, "any blacklisting of the house of Tornquist for their real or supposed delinquencies would have far-reaching consequences, and would be opposed to our best interests."[104] Tower believed that Tornquist & Cia could be utilized in other ways. Tower persuaded Tornquist to force a German named Teodoro de Bary from the boards of two Tornquist-owned companies, after which de Bary was also forced to resign as director of a ranching company that had no connection with Britain. "Surely the long arm of English justice could hardly reach further than this," wrote Tower optimistically.[105] In October, Tornquist opened its books to Tower. Despite the fact that these proved that the company had done some business with Germany, by helping the Argentine government to make debt payments and assisting some firms in remitting funds to their Hamburg home offices, Tornquist pledged to refuse to remit any more funds to Germany, even for Argentine authorities. Tower believed that Tornquist, like many other companies and individuals in Argentina, was jumping aboard the British bandwagon.[106]

Perhaps the most obvious sign of the early successes of the Statutory List was the desire of non-Britons to identify themselves with it. From a local public relations standpoint, probably the most important adherent to the Statutory List was the Italian Legation. The Italians had already been behind-the-scenes contributors to British enemy trade efforts, but the announcement of their First Secretary in Argentina, Vittorio Cerruti, to the local Italian press in October 1916 that he was aiding the Statutory List effort certainly augmented the boycott of listed firms among the large number of people in Argentina with Italian roots.[107] A Belgian paper, the *Cri de Belgique*, published a Belgian blacklist on 10 February 1917 identical to the Statutory List, except that it excluded the grain exporter Bunge & Born, a company claiming to be wholly Belgian.[108]

France, Britain's most important ally, was particularly pleased. In a widely-published correspondence about the Trade with the Enemy Extension Act, Worthington-Evans defended the Statutory List by stating that the new law merely brought Britain into harmony with French practices.[109] France followed a standard that banned trade with all people of enemy nationality, wherever they lived. This nationality-based standard meant that since the start of the war, French businessmen and ships had been forbidden from conducting business with Germans in South America, even while British traders were allowed to do so. The French had long complained that the British unfairly gained from trade that French businessmen shunned.

French authorities always advocated enhancements to the economic campaign, and argued that threatening the ability of Germany to conduct trade *après guerre* could prove decisive in forcing Germany out of the war. France wanted Britain to disavow all of their most favored nation treaties to send a message that after the war, there might be a world trading environment hostile to the Central Powers.[110] At the Economic Conference of the Allies, which ran in Paris from 14 to 17 June 1916, France and Britain pledged to coordinate their post-war commercial policy, enhancing the threat to Germany's post-war trade. The French delegation also pushed through a resolution recommending that the Allies prohibit their subjects and all people in their territories from trading with Germans everywhere.[111] The Board of Trade feared this resolution to such a degree that to prevent it from becoming British law, the Board proposed increasing the size and scope of the Statutory List that the ministry so despised.[112] The labors of the FTD definitely mitigated criticism of Britain from their prime wartime allies, and thus Britain's war in South America helped to keep the Entente together.

As the first year of the Statutory List came to an end, Tower noted that France had created its own blacklist, but as the British controlled the seas and were far more engaged in local business than the French, the British list led the way; the French Confidential Blacklist for Argentina coincided exactly with the British Statutory List.[113] After being instructed by an FTD circular despatch in June 1917 to increase cooperation with the French legation, Tower began to regularly give lists to French Minister Henry Jullemier of names he recommended for the Statutory List, along with the evidence on which he based his conclusions. Jullemier regularly concurred with each of Tower's recommendations.[114] Like the British, their allies were loath to place their own citizens on prohibited lists, but they utilized other threats to stop their countrymen from helping listed firms. For example, the Italian minister decided to punish one Italian textile importer in Buenos Aires who passed British goods to a Statutory List firm by revoking the Italian businessman's exemption from his military service requirement in Italy.[115] The commercial war appeared in such ways to be spreading its tentacles across South America. Surely, the Anglo-South Americans thought, their war could succeed in pushing the Germans back across the Atlantic.

Conclusion

The first year of the Statutory List was considered a tremendous victory for the British trade warriors. Its impact on South American Germans, while incomplete, seemed likely to become tremendous. And they anticipated that future war efforts by the government in London would pour new life into their own businesses. The Statutory List marginalized German capitalists within the South American economies. It also limited the options of many neutral businessmen by leading them to curtail trade with Germans. There were some holes in the British trade war campaign, some indications that the Statutory List policy and the economic campaign as a whole might not be implemented as fully as British war-makers wished. But to people in South America so distant from the front lines of Europe, the list was the sign of British strength, "more than any other measure . . . (bringing) home the effects of sea power to neutrals."[116] Although neutral countries complained about the Statutory List, the FTD believed that the list enhanced the image of Great Britain abroad, highlighting the many aspects of British power and the likelihood of their eventual victory over Germany.

By the end of the year, neutral governments accepted the existence of the Statutory List, and allied governments such as France applauded it. The FTD and British diplomats stationed abroad successfully fended off challenges to the economic warfare policy. Latin American countries grew to feel that they were being treated in the same manner as their neighbor to the north, the United States. The ability of the FTD to parry criticism that the Statutory List violated the sovereignty or neutrality of the South American republics lent luster to the initial successes of the war.

At the end of 1916, the FTD confirmed that it had made huge strides to seal relations between British traders and officials abroad and businessmen in the United Kingdom. According to Sir Reginald Tower, the FTD drew together the local British Chambers of Commerce, the consulates and legations, and the general British and even neutral populace, all working hand in hand in the war on German commerce.[117] The FTD claimed to have weakened the German hold over the Argentine grain and the Brazilian rubber and coffee trades, while systematizing the creation of lists of enemy and British firms.[118] Over the first year of the war, the Statutory List wrecked some once-grand German businesses and inspired fear among neutral businessmen that they would be placed on the list, which led them to halt their business with listed firms. The FTD seemed to be fulfilling its promise to crush German traders abroad, but would it succeed in replacing them with British businessmen?

5

Fighting a "constructive" war

Much of the diplomacy of the British economic war was open for the world to see. As Parliamentary Under-Secretary in the Foreign Office, and later as the Minister of Blockade, Lord Robert Cecil attended frequent interviews with journalists in the United Kingdom, Europe and the United States, and responded to complaints from other governments in newspapers and pamphlets.[1] From its creation, the FTD likewise openly asserted its purpose and the legitimacy of its mission. The FTD propagandized among the traders of Britain and the broader public, both in Britain and abroad, as to the need for the Statutory List against Germans in the Americas.[2] Departmental staffers translated articles written by journalists and economic nationalist organizations in Germany, and issued releases to the British press indicating that Germany's main war aim was to crush British dominance in global trade.[3] Over the next two years, the FTD constantly produced and broadly circulated reports as to the effectiveness of the Statutory List.[4]

This propaganda championed a number of reasons why the Statutory List was an important aspect of the overall British war effort against Germany. In a report entitled the "Effect of the Statutory List on the Conduct of the War," H.B. Butler claimed that the Statutory List "has a very direct bearing on naval operations" because it crippled German merchants in South America who had given aid to German cruisers early in the war. If allowed to continue operations, Butler insinuated, these same men would provision any German submarines that might slink to the distant continent during the remainder of the war. Butler also believed that the Statutory List restricted the possibility that the German economy could recover after the war. The longer the war continued, the more onerous the Statutory List would feel to German businessmen in South America who were the agents of German economic expansion overseas.[5] Hopefully, German traders, shippers and bankers, all fearing difficulties in restarting international business after the war, would pressure the Kaiser to sign a peace treaty as quickly as possible even if it meant capitulating to the Entente's territorial and financial terms.[6]

Yet prosecuting the European war was not the only purpose of the South American war. Rather than just destroying the German businesses, the FTD looked to help nurture their British competitors.[7] British commercial warriors aimed to manipulate wartime conditions to build postwar economic dominance across South America. Destruction of *Deutschtum* would be a failure without the construction of Greater Britain.

The "constructive" aspects of war

During the three years of the overt trade war in South America, from March 1916 to April 1919, the British undertook a variety of new efforts to enhance the role of British companies and individuals in the republics' commerce. The assumption that underlay the "constructive" war was that the importance of the United Kingdom as a trading partner to South America would enable Britain to erect a system that benefited British businessmen both at home and overseas. Even during this "total war," often portrayed as a time when the United Kingdom hoarded all of its resources for the war effort, Britain remained a vital supplier of many goods to South America. Over 28 percent of the total Argentine imports in 1916 still came from Britain.[8] By funneling these to specific British merchant houses, exporters in the United Kingdom could trade in a patriotic way. And by purchasing South American goods only from reputable British exporters, importers in the United Kingdom would help to overcome the enemy giants such as Bunge & Born and Theodore Wille & Co.

As with the Statutory List, Sir Reginald Tower leaned on the British Chamber of Commerce when deciding how to help British trade take the place of Germans handicapped by the economic war. Even before the first Statutory List for South America appeared, the FTD telegraphed its representatives abroad to ask for recommendations for a 'white list' of British firms that could pick up the German trade.[9] Tower immediately told the Chamber of Commerce to shift its focus from attacking Germans. As he and the Chamber had already agreed on the names of the primary enemy firms in Buenos Aires to be included in the first Statutory Lists, Tower now wanted the Chamber to concentrate on the creation of "the alternative or constructive list."[10] In a special meeting of the Chamber's Council on 24 February 1916, Tower made a point of noting that "this constructive task . . . was intended directly to further British trade in the Argentine Republic."[11]

In a telling embodiment of the new mantra of partnership between government and business, Tower sat as chairman of the Chamber's council throughout March 1916. Together they drew up special white lists largely of Chamber members who could take the place of Germans on the Statutory List. Tower had already telegraphed to the FTD the names of British firms in hardware, machinery, and pottery, and the Chamber worked quickly to expand this list, compiling the information it had already been collecting.[12] A week later Tower sent to the FTD the Chamber's thirty-one page report including a list of 137 "white" firms, each one placed within one or more categories such as general merchants, commission agents, and importers or exporters of specific goods and commodities.[13] The Chamber assumed that the list would be used by all manufacturers and exporters in the United Kingdom looking to boost their business with the River Plate. As factories in the United Kingdom focused on war production, and as the amount of shipping available to South America dropped, the Chamber did not believe that their list would necessarily mean that a flood of British-made goods would pour into whitelisted importers, but its members assumed that the British government would force United Kingdom firms to utilize the white list when searching for local agents or representatives. Tower likewise hoped for the best in thanking the Chamber: "I can only add that I sincerely trust that the care expended by the Council in this compilation may be seen repaid by a sensible increase in British Trade in the Argentine Republic."[14] The Buenos Aires correspondent of *The Times* of London supported such hopes:

> Our local firms will require assistance – a more generous measure of support from our Government, and a less conservative attitude on the part of our banks. There are British houses – and if, in some instances, they do not yet exist, they can be established and will be warmly welcomed – capable of taking the place of the German firms who for too long have held too great a proportion of our trade. From local sources here such houses can be indicated and recommended, and the Chamber of Commerce is at present engaged upon this most useful constructive work. The Government should see to it that they are encouraged and supported.[15]

The Chamber, looking to train the government how best to promote the trade of Greater Britain, began molding Chalkley, the newly appointed commercial attaché. As the idea of a commercial attaché to a South American country remained controversial in the British government, Chalkley's position was ill-defined. When he began to receive enquiries from companies in the United Kingdom asking about the prospects for specific trades in Argentina, he went to the Chamber and worked out a special agreement with Powell-Jones. The Chamber would subsequently receive all such enquiries, working out a response that would be reported to Chalkley, with an extra copy for him to send "to his Department for their information and guidance in subsequent enquiries of the same nature."[16] The Chamber and Chalkley also collaborated on his proposal to push United Kingdom manufacturers to work together to send out "technical trade representatives" to study certain Latin American markets. Council members saw this as an opportunity to teach British manufacturers about the specific needs of the Argentine marketplace and the ways that German competitors had gained dominance in certain trades.[17] They quickly compiled trade statistics to bolster Chalkley's claim that British manufacturers needed either to organize themselves or be swamped by the well-organized Germans.[18] Soon the Chamber created an "electrical trade committee," which compiled lists, samples, and prices of certain goods previously supplied by German manufacturers through local German merchants.[19] They hoped that by using this information, and by banding together as the Germans did, British manufacturers could figure out how to enter the local market. By the middle of December 1916, British officials in the eastern South American republics had already recommended more substitutes than there were names on the Statutory List. Whereas 158 names were on the Statutory List for Argentina and Uruguay, the FTD had 345 names in its 'Substitute Index' for the two countries. In Brazil, the 225 companies on the Statutory List were also outnumbered by the 324 substitutes.

Tower lauded the enthusiasm of the Chamber of Commerce. He worried somewhat that many firms whitelisted by the Chamber claimed an ability to undertake business in branches of trade beyond their expertise, but Tower believed that for Buenos Aires, this should not matter.[20] Most British manufacturers already had agents in Buenos Aires, he explained, and these were already securing orders from acceptable firms and refused orders from Statutory Listed firms. He suggested that British manufacturers without agents, and those who previously made use of the Germans, should contact the commercial attaché or the British Chamber of Commerce in Argentina, who could suggest a variety of legitimate substitutes.[21]

By the end of 1916, a number of indicators suggested that British businesses were gaining ground in South America at the expense of the Germans. The Chamber pitched itself to possible members as a pipeline for trade with the United Kingdom. Those Anglo-Argentines initially wary of the Chamber soon recognized the benefits of being associated with it, and from a membership of 94 in August 1914 the Chamber ballooned to 163 members by May 1916.[22] It seemed an excellent moment to ask again for the ultimate prize – an annual subsidy from the government "to further British commercial interests in the Argentine."[23] The idea of a subsidy suggests that Chamber leaders envisioned a new, permanent, corporatist model, the penetration of commercial and government interests with one another. At the same time, Anglo-South American businessmen had fully come to accept the FTD line that this new department, rather than the Board of Trade, would be their critical connection to British businesses at home.[24]

The expansion of the Foreign Office and
the Ministry of Blockade

Men working in the FTD already knew that to build British overseas trade, they would have to undertake tasks that the Foreign Office had never done before. In a memo to trade associations and Chambers of Commerce in the United Kingdom, Nugent explained that "the constructive side of the Department's work follows as a natural corollary to (the) destructive activities." British channels for trade must be built up in order to ensure that the destruction of German firms was not a "purely temporary and evanescent" wartime phenomenon, but rather permanent. British replacement businesses rooted in place by the end of the war could block Germans attempting to regain their pre-war position. Nugent appealed to businessmen in the United Kingdom for suggestions.[25] In making such an appeal, the "constructive" war in South America led the FTD to encroach on the Board of Trade, which had long been the point of contact between the British state and British business. As Nugent's memorandum suggested, this was a change that would last beyond the conclusion of the world war.

Most histories of the British war stress, in Nugent's words, the "temporary and evanescent" aspects of Britain's war. Too often the post-bellum reassertion of free trade and laissez-faire policy, of unobtrusive British government, seems inevitable and even well planned. Much has been written about the phenomenon of British government departments and ministries popping into existence over the course of the First World War, only to turn to dust at the conclusion of the conflict.[26] As the traditional story goes, bureaucracies such as the Ministry of Munitions embodied the temporary nature of the wartime suspension of laissez-faire. Officials accepted that businessmen would come in to help run new departments that would impose unprecedented restrictions upon British business, but all expected the situation to revert to normal after the conclusion of peace.

The British economic war was one of these new contingencies necessitating the creation of new departments and ministries. Yet this war seemed potentially longer-lasting in its effects on British government. In supporting the FTD, the Foreign Office looked to remake the entire system of British foreign trade by bringing together the government and British traders at home and overseas. Unsurprisingly, the war in South America led directly to a fierce confrontation between rival bureaucracies, the Foreign Office and the Board of Trade, over the future of government promotion of British commerce. In short, the British decision to engage in commercial warfare stoked an already smoldering bitter bureaucratic turf war.

After spending much of 1915 as Foreign Office undersecretary in charge of blockade issues, Cecil believed he understood the difficulties of coordinating the economic war. In the months since entering the Foreign Office in May 1915, Cecil had labored in a high-profile role defending the prosecution of the economic war and repudiating those who thought British measures against German trade were too lenient or too harsh. Although it might have appeared at odds with his avid and well-known support of free trade, the war left Cecil with a strong distrust of the Germans, and he favored "an uncompromising economic policy" against them.[27] As illustrated by his decisive intervention in the WTAC, Cecil undoubtedly believed by late 1915 that "a harsher line" must be taken against the Germans, that a total war must be waged.[28]

Yet despite the creation of the FTD and other efforts to support the economic war, Cecil remained exacerbated by the confusing maze of departments and committees that ran the British blockade effort. Despite its importance as an "operation of war," the blockade was being run by various departments that decided on policy "in half a dozen different ways successively." Although the recently created War Trade Advisory Committee had consistently supported the policies he favored, Cecil believed that the committee would never become the clearing-house for blockade-related departments that he dreamed of. Only a minister of blockade could bring the "unity of direction and responsibility" necessary to the success of an economic campaign against Germany.[29]

In early 1916, Cecil's call for better coordination of blockade efforts resonated. Lord Emmott, who as the head of the WTD controlled the granting of licenses to United Kingdom exporters, believed that a unified blockade department should be placed under the aegis of the diplomatically-oriented Foreign Office, the ministry equipped to deal with the "delicate matters" of maintaining friendly relations with neutrals that came part and parcel with the blockade.[30] Cecil was the obvious choice to run the new ministry. He was liked and respected both by Liberals and Conservatives in the Asquith-led coalition, and Grey, who had long considered blockade work "nauseous," pledged that having two cabinet ministers from the Foreign Office would cause no friction.[31] Grey happily relinquished to the new Minister of Blockade responsibility for duties he would rather ignore.

In the eyes of some historians, failure to avert the war in July 1914 and further failures over the following years destroyed the confidence and the clout of the Foreign Office during the war.[32] However, in creating the Ministry of Blockade, Cecil amassed new powers for the Foreign Office. The ministry appeared on the Foreign Office List throughout the war years. The naming of Cecil as Minister of Blockade in February 1916, even as he pointedly retained his position as Under-Secretary at the Foreign Office, enhanced the importance of the latter ministry to the conduct of the war. Throughout the remainder of the war, most believed that Cecil performed his duties as much an official of the Foreign Office as the head of the Ministry of Blockade.[33] Cecil himself would later claim that the new ministry did not mean a change in his workload but merely an obvious increase in status and visibility.[34] It enhanced his profile among ministerial circles, in Parliament, and with the public at large, allowing him to function as a counterweight to Sir Edward Grey, who lost much prestige after failing to avert the war in the confusing days of July 1914, and whose subsequent expressions of pessimism and unhappiness made him increasingly irrelevant within the Cabinet.[35]

The Ministry of Blockade gave Foreign Office personnel a new wartime role, something they had been craving since the start of this devastating war much blamed on the failure of diplomacy. The personnel and duties of departments in the Foreign and Blockade Ministries overlapped. The de facto secretariat of the Ministry of Blockade was in fact the Contraband Department of the Foreign Office, headed by the able and independent-minded Eyre Crowe.[36] This department had done formidable work in negotiations with European neutrals to seal holes in the economic wall that Britain hoped to build around German territory. The creation of contraband agreements recognized "as a workable contract between businessmen" the halting of neutral ships and cargoes that were bound for Germany through a neutral state.[37] These complex and contentious agreements proved that, despite their failure to avert Europe's descent into war in the summer of 1914, men in the Foreign Office had not lost their diplomatic skills.

The creation of the Ministry of Blockade made the Foreign Office much larger by enveloping an 'alphabet soup' of departments and committees from other ministries and also by creating entirely new units such as the War Trade Statistical Department and the War Trade Intelligence Department (WTID), which accumulated and distributed information on enemy firms and individuals.[38] By far the largest new department was the FTD, which owing to the ballooning of the staff at the Foreign Office was forced to take up quarters away from Whitehall, in Lancaster House across St James's Park.

Members of the FTD inherited the wariness towards the Board of Trade that had long prevailed among the Foreign Office staff. In December 1915, Roland Nugent advised Worthington-Evans that if he should happen to run into people from the Board of Trade, he should ask for their assistance. The new department needed manpower, and Nugent hoped for a single "good man" from the Board's CIB, but no more than that. "We would also of course take anyone them offered from the Commercial Branch, but would on the whole rather be without them!"[39] In a pointed memorandum received by the FTD on 30 December 1915, the Board of Trade outlined what it saw as the duties of each department that dealt with aspects of trading with the enemy, claiming for the Board of Trade authority over all questions "not specifically assigned to other Departments."[40] "This requires a counterblast," demanded Nugent, who directed each section of the FTD to draw up "a fairly exhaustive list of its activities" in order to stake its claims immediately. Nugent felt that if the Board were left to determine foreign trade policy, a lenient attitude towards British firms that traded with Germans would prevail.[41]

In May 1916, Henry Fountain of the Board of Trade complained that the FTD was advising British firms about alternative outlets for business that they had formerly done with firms now on the Statutory List. Nugent pledged that the FTD would send officers to brief the CIB on a regular basis about reports it received from abroad, but Fountain noted three weeks later that no FTD representatives had yet arrived.[42]

Particularly annoying to the FTD were lectures from the Board on the need to pay attention to the concerns of the four British banks that operated in South America.[43] The FTD had been founded in large part to give commercial interests other than bankers a voice in trade policy, and its members considered it counterproductive to spend much effort on the wishes of bankers. The Board of Trade also rejected FTD and Admiralty calls for a system of certificates that would ensure that British ships did not carry goods in which enemy firms owned an interest.[44] The Board claimed that such a system would breed congestion in ports and cause costly delays in shipping, but officials at the FTD saw the Board's recalcitrance as symptomatic of that ministry's principled opposition to a stringent enemy trade policy.

The FTD was not alone in its hostility toward the Board of Trade. Although relations between the Admiralty and Foreign Office have been described as less than wonderful in the opening months of war, the Admiralty had itself engaged in a number of disputes with the Board.[45] Early in 1915, the Board blamed the Admiralty for a shortage of shipping, claiming that the navy had requisitioned a wasteful amount of British-flag tonnage for war purposes. The Admiralty countered that the Board was at fault for failing to gain control of the world's neutral shipping by chartering it at the outbreak of war.[46] The Admiralty also scoffed at fears that restricting British manufacturers from trading with enemy firms in neutral countries would devastate British interests at home and abroad while causing no pain to Germany.[47] At the start of January 1916 the Trade Division of the Admiralty pledged to help the FTD in any way it could. The Trade Division soon began to send along to the FTD reports that it received from overseas, particularly from shipping agents, informants and naval attachés, about suspected cases of trading between British subjects and Germans in South America.[48]

The Admiralty was happy to relinquish some of the burden of attacking German commerce overseas. Their administration of the Coal and Ships Blacklists had been less than completely successful. The Trade Division fielded numerous complaints in 1915 from British steam lines claiming that other British ships had willingly sold to German firms a significant amount of scarce cargo space on ships leaving Brazil during 1915. By 1916, Frederick

Leverton-Harris of the Trade Division (soon to become a member of the Ministry of Blockade) expressed relief that the Statutory List would prevent British ships from undertaking such business.[49] The Admiralty recognized the limited capabilities of warships to hurt German traders overseas, and believed that the FTD could accomplish more.

As the economic war in South America initially succeeded in curtailing German business, the ineptitude of Board of Trade practices had never been more apparent to the Foreign Office. Information from the CIB – mostly general trade statistics – proved useless in forming the Statutory List. The Board had no non-statistical information about the commercial situation existing in many foreign countries, knew nothing of the nationality of individual businessmen and companies, and seemed incapable of understanding that nationality mattered.[50] Walter Runciman, the President of the Board of Trade, complained that the FTD was encroaching on Board duties, but the FTD countered that it was the failures of the CIB to supply useful information that helped nurture the FTD's direct ties with traders in the United Kingdom and abroad.[51]

Initially, there were indications of resistance to the war from British businessmen who wanted to complete the terms of contracts they already had with companies on the Statutory List. Nugent and Townley demanded stringent restrictions against the completion of pre-existing contracts, stressing "that the bulk of the people who apply to us (for a licence to conduct such trade) will be desperately anxious to keep up their Hun connections and nothing but unbending severity will ever make them believe that we mean what we say and that they have got to break it if they possibly can."[52] Some merchants in Britain seemed unlikely to accept the white lists as accurate lists of substitutes, as they were compiled by obviously self-interested groups of British businessmen in South America.[53]

Yet as 1916 progressed, much of the business community in the United Kingdom was coming over to the side of the FTD. The Federation of British Industries (FBI), a new trade group of British manufacturers founded in the summer of 1916, immediately attached itself to the FTD, eventually hiring two men from the department: Roland Nugent and Guy Locock. The founding president of the FBI, the Birmingham railway carriage and armament manufacturer Dudley Docker, made it abundantly clear that the Foreign Office rather than the Board of Trade should run the government's foreign trade policy. A proselytizer for what has been termed "British corporatism," Docker believed it likely that the FTD would help him to erect the export monopolies and combined sales forces overseas that he believed necessary if Britain were to win in their industrial rivalry with Germany.[54] Docker was only the most prominent of many industrialists who supported the FTD. On receiving a letter from Oswald Nettlefold of the Wholesale Hardware Club attesting to the fact that the FTD has made it easier than ever before "for traders to get information with regard to foreign markets," one FTD clerk gloated that "I don't think any Govt. Dept. [*sic*] has received a better testimonial."[55]

In December 1916, the FTD claimed that Chambers of Commerce and trade associations in the United Kingdom regularly applied to the department for information on whom they should contact abroad to boost their trade.[56] The department exhorted trade associations in Britain to trade only through FTD-approved firms, and also looked to entice merchants in the United Kingdom to increase their trade with neutral countries by sending UK trade associations a number of reports from diplomats and consuls about commercial conditions and possible openings for trade in their districts.[57] In October 1916, the FTD bragged to the Board of Trade that its new contacts with British trade associations led to the creation of a British consortium to replace the German firms that formerly controlled Brazil's rubber exports.[58]

In response, the Board looked to rejuvenate itself by calling in personal favors. Hilda Runciman, the wife of President of the Board of Trade Walter Runciman, wrote directly to Grey, expressing her worries about her husband, who, she claimed, had sunk into a depression due to the animosity between the Board of Trade and Foreign Office. She forwarded a memo outlining a scheme that her husband believed vital to Britain's post-war commercial recovery. Runciman's plan envisioned the discontinuation of the Foreign Office-led Commercial Attaché program and the extension, instead, of the Board of Trade-controlled Trade Commissioners, who presently labored only in the British Dominions, to countries beyond the Empire.[59] To rebuff this, a committee of Foreign Office personnel was formed to draw up recommendations "in regard to the proper organisation of the government service of commercial intelligence in foreign countries."[60] It was led by a proven warrior in the economic fight against Germany, Eyre Crowe, the Under-Secretary of State and head of the Contraband Department, whose father had been Britain's first commercial attaché covering all of Europe in 1880. The Crowe Committee, as it became known, included Victor Wellesley, Algernon Law and C.H. Tufton of the Foreign Office Commercial Department, Nugent and Worthington-Evans of the FTD, and Walter Townley, the retired ex-minister to Argentina.

Their final report explained that because "there cannot be a British foreign policy as regards commercial matters abroad separate from general foreign policy," the Foreign Office should be given control of all aspects of foreign trade policy. The Foreign Office was "now committed to a national trade policy which will enter largely into the conduct of our foreign relations and may dominate them."[61] The report called for a permanent, professionalized overseas commercial attaché service, run by the Foreign Office as a direct link between "the business community at home and the intelligence service abroad in all matters of current commercial intelligence."[62] Commercial attachés should be paid remunerative, alluring salaries, be presented with a clear career path with periodic and regular promotions, and have their own staffs and offices, separate from consulates and legations. In other words, they were to form a new service, positioned (in the mentality of the Foreign Office) between the lowly, ship-counting duties of the consuls and the high politics of the diplomats.[63] Yet having this new corps of officers overseas would hopefully make all diplomats and consuls more cognizant of the needs of Great Britain's foreign traders. The Crowe Committee envisioned all members of the diplomatic corps passing a period in the FTD before being sent abroad, as "it should be clearly understood that every diplomat is expected to occupy himself with commercial matters."[64] Meanwhile, the Consular Service would become a preparatory service for the post of commercial attaché, and consuls would be reallocated around the world according to the needs of British commerce.

The Crowe report is striking in how little it overtly focused on the war. Yet of course the war was always on the minds of committee members, as it had allowed the Foreign Office to create the FTD and begin operating a commercial intelligence service abroad in the manner it desired. The FTD had gained experience in dealing with the Chambers of Commerce and other British business interests at home and abroad, and had exposed some signal failures in the Board of Trade. The Crowe report skewered the Board for failing to compile even basic commercial information on tariffs and taxes that could help British businessmen build their trade in markets they did not personally know. The report recommended a systematization of annual forms filled out by embassies and consulates to increase the quality of information. Current information should be kept in a card index, with consuls and commercial attachés furnishing all information for given industries or firms on prescribed cards. This centralization of information would allow for informed reassessment of policy toward a given firm or industry at a moment's notice, and would enable British companies to contact their counterparts overseas more easily than ever before. In short, the Crowe committee advocated making the FTD a permanent part of the British government.

Runciman immediately announced his displeasure. "The report of Crowe's Committee frankly shocks me," he wrote to Grey, claiming that the committee members failed to take into account the wishes of British businessmen to retain their traditional relationship with the Board of Trade. He predicted that it would be met by vociferous opposition from commercial men in the United Kingdom.[65] Exhibiting an abject lack of interest in questions of British commerce, Grey replied that he had not yet read the report, and appeared bewildered at the venom displayed by Runciman. He explained to his private secretary Eric Drummond that he had no knowledge of any divide between the Board of Trade and the Foreign Office, and supported Runciman's call for a meeting where he and Cecil could settle the issue.[66]

Drummond, however, was more attuned than his boss to the mentality of Foreign Office officials. He told Runciman "quite unofficially and frankly" that the Foreign Office backed the Crowe recommendations and feared that if the Board got its way it would abolish the commercial attaché system and establish trade commissioners instead, thus dividing foreign policy between two departments and making it impossible for British commerce to reap benefits from the activities of diplomats and consuls overseas. Denying that Crowe committee members were motivated by anything but "the best national interests," Drummond backed vehemently the committee's recommendations as the ones most likely to benefit British commerce.[67]

But Grey was less intransigent than his advisers. By August 1916 he had grown depressed and exhausted, preoccupied with Europe and the United States. He was willing to give ground and hatched a compromise with Runciman. But Runciman soon complained to Foreign Under-Secretary Lord Hardinge that nothing had changed, that FTD letters to Chambers of Commerce and other trade associations in Britain asking for and distributing information about enemy firms had led to an overlap between the Foreign Office and the Board of Trade. Hardinge, like Grey, had no interest in commercial work and had kept aloof of the entire debate.[68] Those in the Foreign Office who favored the FTD worked to educate Hardinge as to the benefits of the department. Townley wrote a memo for Hardinge claiming that the Board had spurned all FTD requests for cooperation, leaving the FTD "to do all its own trade organisation." To fulfill its duty to hinder enemy trade and improve British trade abroad, the FTD had no choice but to directly contact Chambers of Commerce and manufacturers associations in the United Kingdom.[69]

As the overall leader of the Foreign Office's economic war, Lord Robert Cecil then became involved. Cecil explained to Prime Minister Asquith at the end of October 1916 that he had decided, with Runciman, to appoint a joint committee to heal the rift between the two ministries.[70] Yet the committee Cecil envisioned would probably have been less than even-handed. He had already written to Lord Milner, a noted imperialist and tariff reformer who sympathized with the general need to expand British trade, asking Milner to chair this committee looking at what machinery Britain "ought to possess in order to push our trade in foreign countries. The Germans, as you know, have had a very complete and elaborate organisation for that purpose which has, without doubt, been of great service to them." With Milner's "unique knowledge of both the official and the commercial sides of the question," he could render a decisive verdict, one Cecil believed would be in favor of significant changes in government assistance to foreign trade.[71] But before such a committee could form, Lloyd George took over as Prime Minister in December 1916, and Milner became occupied by new duties in the War Cabinet.

The accession of Lloyd George into the premiership in December 1916 meant a more open rejection of *laissez-faire*, and enabled Cecil to cater to those in Britain who favored, in his words, a thorough "anti-German economics." The Welshman brought a definitive change in ideology and manner, and surrounded himself with businessmen, populists, and nationalists who were increasingly wary of the political, financial, and commercial power of the United States.[72] These tendencies seemed likely to benefit the cause of Britain's economic war within the corridors of Whitehall and Westminster. Importantly for those fighting in South America, the new Prime Minister immediately created a Ministry of Shipping, which took over from the Admiralty in controlling the requisitioning and apportioning of British merchant shipping. The new ministry soon decided to requisition all British tonnage, including all tramps and liners.[73] Such changes appear, if anything, to have strengthened the ability of British officials to wage their trade war. Lloyd George replaced Grey with Cecil's cousin, Arthur Balfour. At the same time, Cecil nudged Lord Hardinge out of his role as the number two man in the Foreign Office even while maintaining his position as Minister of Blockade.[74]

For part of 1918, Cecil found himself as acting Foreign Secretary, and in July 1918 was granted the unique title 'Assistant Secretary of State for Foreign Affairs'. He had many allies among the Foreign Office staff. Eyre Crowe wrote to him: "I look forward with complete assurance to the day when you will be our Secretary of State and/or (as our business men say) Prime Minister."[75] Rather than being a career dead-end, Cecil's control of the Ministry of Blockade appeared as a step upwards within the Foreign Office, only enhancing the possibility that he might eventually fill the chair as Foreign Secretary as his father had done decades before. He soon replaced Worthington-Evans as Controller of the FTD with Ernest Pollock, a known Chamberlainite tariff reform MP and leader of the staunchly anti-German Unionist Business Committee.[76] Pollock had tremendous economic war experience as chairman of the earlier Contraband Committee and member of the WTAC. The intensity of the linkage between the Ministry of Blockade and the Foreign Office was particularly apparent in the operations of the FTD, and Foreign Office personnel, both in London and overseas, proved continually vital to its functioning. Conversely, the impact of the FTD on the Foreign Office also proved striking, as the operations and successes of the FTD supported the long-running attempts of the Foreign Office to take British trade promotion away from the lackadaisical control of the Board of Trade.

By creating the FTD and the Ministry of Blockade, the Foreign Office staked out a truly belligerent stance against the Board of Trade. Walter Townley summed up the sentiment in a private letter to Innes at the end of November 1916:

> Ever since this department came into existence we have taken advantage of our special position, which necessitated our endeavouring to build up British trade interests to replace the German interests put out of action by the Statutory List, to collect as much information of a commercial nature from abroad as possible. The results of our efforts have enabled us to make the Board of Trade look very small when they endeavoured to substantiate their claim that the Commercial Intelligence Branch was well up to date in this respect, but we want to go one better, and establish under Foreign Office auspices such a system of collection of commercial intelligence that it will be proved beyond question that the Foreign Office has shown itself capable of devising a system of trade information which will satisfy all national trade requirements.[77]

Confident that the operations of the FTD would prove its commercial usefulness, at the end of 1916, the Foreign Office felt in the lead in its competition with the Board of Trade.

The Form K system

The war in Europe posed a tremendous problem for the economic warriors of South America by changing the way international trade occurred. In many ways this complaining was a case of sour grapes – the nineteenth-century system of international trade had, after all, largely benefited Britain, and the resulting maintenance of British dominance on the seas enabled them to create an unprecedented barrier between Germany and South America during the first few years of war. The British Admiralty's blockade in the North Sea, and the contraband and rationing agreements forced upon the neutral countries of Europe, cut off virtually all South American trade with Germany by the early months of 1916. According to perhaps the best, although undoubtedly flawed statistics, compiled by the prominent Argentine company Ernesto Tornquist & Cia, the value of German goods entering Argentine ports decreased from $83,933,786 (Argentine gold dollars) in 1913 to $221,628 in 1918.[78] The sizeable bilateral trade that connected the republics with Germany before the war had completely disintegrated.

But while trade from Germany plummeted, exports from the United Kingdom to the republics also decreased in both quantity and value, even as British imports from South America increased dramatically. Once the workshop of the world, even before the war British industry had shown its limitations. To conserve for war needs, within months of the start of the war, officials in the WTD restricted many exports, while production adjusted to supplying military needs. As industry focused on supplying the war in Europe, the flow of British goods to South America diminished. The paucity of available goods was such that in October 1916 Sir Reginald Tower urged the government to instruct any British firms capable of exporting any merchandise to tell their clients and agents in Argentina exactly what was available.[79] Virtually anything would find welcome customers across the republic.

At the same time as British machinery, hardware, and other manufactured goods became largely unavailable in South America, imports began to pour in from the United States. The role of South America's chief supplier abruptly shifted from Britain to the United States. British importers recognized both the fickleness and the brand consciousness of consumers, and worried that Latin consumers would became accustomed to US products and would never again buy British. They pleaded for at least some of every United Kingdom product to be shipped to Argentina during the war, if only to keep consumers aware of their continued existence.

One example of such a product was antibacterial dip used to disinfect wool. Although perhaps unglamorous, sheep dip was big business. In 1913, Great Britain supplied 6.5 million of the 7 million kilograms of sheep dip imported into the River Plate. After the war began, manufacturers in the United States began to produce dip, while it became more difficult to procure from Britain. In June 1917, one sheep dip importer in Buenos Aires complained to Commercial Attaché Chalkley that stockmen and land companies were growing accustomed to bathing their flocks with dip from the United States. British suppliers also found themselves battling against sheep dip manufactured locally by the Statutory Listed firm H. Fuhrmann & Co. With the English moniker 'Triumph', this product, manufactured by Germans in Argentina, could be easily mistaken by consumers as a product of the United Kingdom.[80] Worrying that, after the war, they might be excluded from one of the most important sheep-rearing regions of the globe, officials and businessmen in the wool-producing River Plate asked the government in London to ensure that British manufacturers could continue to supply at least some dip during the war.[81] Mitchell Innes supported the calls of Wilson & Co. for 300 drums of sheep dip per month for Uruguay – a mere trickle compared to the pre-war average of 6000 drums, but enough to keep it on the market. Wilson worried that otherwise, "we shall lose all our customers who are already using inferior and cheaper dips manufactured in other countries, and later on it will be very difficult to get them back again."[82] The same was requested for a number of other products, but with little success. As the Board of Trade explained to the Chamber, most of the articles desired by the Chamber were restricted to military requirements, or were no longer being produced as their factories had been turned into munitions plants.[83]

In some cases, the issue was less the inability of the home company to manufacture the product than the lack of available shipping space to send it on the long southwesterly journey across the Atlantic. But whether it was due to lack of freight or inability to produce or export, the paucity of available British goods undoubtedly punished British importers and commission agents in the ports of South America. Many of these merchants had relied for the past decades on their connections with the United Kingdom as a last bastion of strength in their competition against traders of other nationalities. They reached out to the British business community in the United Kingdom, hoping to persuade their distant brethren of the merits of a new nationalist form of trade. They began to sponsor propaganda to be disseminated through the Association of British Chambers of Commerce, compiling a memorandum for the Association describing in detail and with ample statistics the types of imports that Germany had dominated before the war. The Chamber concluded that British manufacturers in certain trades should combine together to produce and market cheaper goods made specifically for the tastes and budgets of the South American consumers.[84] Other South American Britons chimed in with their opinions. Gordon Ross, the former financial editor of the *Standard*, an important English-language newspaper in Buenos Aires, published in London a lengthy book describing the tantalizingly wide open commercial conditions of Argentina and Uruguay. With the Germans smashed by the Statutory List, Britain faced "the golden opportunity." If British manufacturers became attentive to local standards, such as the metric system and the Spanish language, the war was certainly the moment "not only for the recovery of lost ground, but for grasping a very large share of new opening. Will they?"[85]

Tantalized by their prospects for the future, by the end of 1916, these Britons in South America certainly saw themselves as fully engaged in the "constructive" aspect of the war. Yet they also recognized that the "constructive" war policy remained far from a success. The Chamber of Commerce in Buenos Aires spent much of the Argentine summer of 1916 and 1917 demanding an answer to why Eugenio C. Noé & Co., a questionable company with German ties, was able to obtain wire from Britain while at least four members of the Chamber were unable to do so. According to the Chamber's sources, Noé had previously sold German-made wire under the name San Martin; he was now selling the British wire under the same mark, and was thus using a British-made product to support the maintenance in the market of a German brand.[86] Despite the question bouncing through Whitehall, Tower found that he could give the Chamber no good answer. According to the Admiralty, the export of such goods had been banned since May 1916, and according to the WTD no license for exporting such goods would be granted unless it was required for war manufacturers. Yet Noé had recently received the wire, Tower acknowledged to the Chamber.[87] The Council was indignant. "British firms in the Argentine Republic are (not) one whit behind their colleagues elsewhere in loyalty and in willingness to accept the restrictions upon their trade which are rendered necessary by the war," yet under the present system followed by the government in Britain, "neutral firms are able to obtain goods from Great Britain which are refused to British firms."[88]

The Chamber followed with an extensive memorandum on the "opportunity of ousting Germany from one of her special trades," a list that included products as varied as dynamos, emery cloth, screws, and hams. The Council claimed that it was not presenting the list in a "critical (or) complaining spirit," but both the hopes and anxieties of its members were palpable. The government should let exporters in the United Kingdom know about the Chamber's needs, and those exporters should contact the Chamber to let their members know of the goods they had available.[89] Innes similarly reported that a British store in Montevideo, La Muebleria Inglesa, found itself unable to import bedsteads that had already been manufactured for them by a company in England, while another non-British local company faced no difficulties receiving a license for bedsteads of their own.[90] The British in South America concluded that officials and businessmen in the United Kingdom were failing in their duty to coordinate efforts to help their countrymen overseas.

In particular they worried about the failure of the FTD to utilize the information that the British Chambers of Commerce and legations in South America had collected. When firms in Britain asked the FTD for the names of suitable agents in Argentina, the FTD repeatedly pestered Tower for recommendations, leading Tower to suggest in April 1917 that the FTD examine the huge list of reputable British businesses that the Chamber of Commerce had compiled a year previously.[91] At times, the FTD seemed to lose track of the Chambers' work.

But this early list had not been misplaced. Rather it had been disregarded by the FTD, a department that increasingly pandered to the business community of the United Kingdom rather than that of British Buenos Aires. In part, the department had grown disillusioned about the commercial capabilities of their countrymen in South America. At the end of 1916, Sir Reginald Tower, who certainly placed great value on most of the efforts of the Britons of Argentina, complained to the FTD that his local compatriots had failed to take up the slack in the grain trade. In the months since the Big Four grain firms were blacklisted, the British firms had succeeded only in squabbling among themselves and continuing to trade in the murky local grain options market, even though it inevitably helped the Big Four. Similarly, no British company had stepped into the breach left by the Statutory Listing of the wool exporting giants Staudt, Engelbert Hardt, and Lahusen. A number of British firms had earlier claimed that they could undertake such work, but the list of substitutes they had compiled was ridiculous, "the answers being in many cases so vague to be practically useless, and the light-heartedness in expressing willingness to undertake the most extravagant and impossible branches of trade making one doubt how far the matter has been taken seriously." This undoubtedly referred to the extensive, and confusingly indexed, 'white list' put together by the Chamber, and sent along to London in May 1916.

This white list included two lists of importing firms in each sector of trade; tellingly, one of the lists showed those who were already importing such goods, while the second included those who nebulously claimed they were "prepared to import" them.[92] At the FTD, clerks like Eady and Townley wondered what to do with such a list. They wanted to help British business-men at home connect to new overseas markets. But, as Townley recognized, to recommend to United Kingdom businessmen those British importers and exporters was "likely to bring ridicule on the FTD" from the United Kingdom businesses that might waste their time looking into false opportunities.[93] In October 1916, Chalkley found himself chastising his Chamber for using misleading statistics in a memorandum to the Board of Trade and Association of Chambers of Commerce. The Chamber quickly retracted its claim that Germany dominated before the war in imports of cotton and woolen textiles, noting that Germany dominated only in the relatively small trade for "made up clothing."[94]

In the eyes of the FTD officials at Lancaster House, leaving the construc-tive war in the hands of the locals had led to enthusiastic but haphazard results. They needed guidance, a system. At the end of 1916 the FTD were determined to start again. In doing so, they repeated the mantra that their duty would be to lay the foundations of a system of commercial intelligence that would permanently assist British trade.[95] But it took a while for the Britons in South America to hear about it. The British Chamber of Commerce in Buenos Aires only learned of the scheme via a letter from the Chamber in Rio de Janeiro, which had been asked by the FTD to compile a report on how the department might compile information for home firms that would enable them to determine if they should try to open up trade in foreign markets.[96]

The Chamber in Buenos Aires immediately pushed itself into the debate. As the plan unfolded, it became apparent that the FTD hoped to compile a tremendous database of information about all business in foreign countries, answering questions that home traders were asking, while also serving as a commercial library at British missions and legations across the world for the use of any British firms. The FTD proposed gaining much information by sending out a questionnaire to "non-enemy importers who already had business relations with the United Kingdom."[97] Eventually known as the "Key Form" or "Form K," the issue of this questionnaire bred a huge rift between the FTD and the Britons of Buenos Aires. In the eyes of the Chamber of Commerce, such a circular "would very probably do more harm than good," irritating and confusing neutral firms. Gibson and Pearson argued that Argentine businessmen would find the circular offensive.[98] Tower was perplexed at this, and called together a special meeting of the Council, whose members claimed again that it would cause resentment and suspicion among neutral importers who, as a result, would most likely "divert their trade into the hands of our competitors." Even with Tower present, a formidable man whom they certainly respected and even admired, a minister who had done more for them than any British official previously, the Council reiterated its unanimous vote against the proposed circular.

Tower fumed. Although the Council minutes provide a synopsis rather than an exact transcript of the meeting, the minister was clearly sharp in his criticism. He undoubtedly expected the Chamber to support and work avidly toward any policy determined by the British government. Gibson evidently felt offended by some of Tower's remarks chastising the Chamber, and the two exchanged some letters over the next week, but Tower refused to apologize. "If the soreness of the Chamber is because they were not consulted early enough or because I did not at once agree to their sweeping rejection of the procedure which appeared to me the only one to adopt with any chance of success, I am afraid we must differ on this point . . . Let us leave the personal offence etc. to less wise people than ourselves and go on with our good work in the interests of our country."[99]

Amazingly, Tower's stubbornness did not shake the Chamber, which remained set against the FTD plan. Gibson and the rest of the Council claimed to be most concerned with the supposedly impolitic wording of Form K itself. But their greater problem, their greatest fear, was what such information might do to their members. According to the Chamber, the preferred way for United Kingdom businesses who wanted to enter the market to learn about it would be for them to enquire "through the regular sources," such as British banks, and through other British businessmen, including the willing members of the Chamber's Council, who would give advice not as officials of the Chamber but as individuals.[100] In other words, the Council rejected Form K because it bypassed the Chamber, ruining the hopes that its members would, by government order, become the conveyors of all British trade with Argentina.

Yet the FTD went through with it, and had consuls send out questionnaires to thousands of supposedly neutral businesses in neutral markets across the world. Indeed, the Form K scheme shows that what most impressed the

FTD was the perception that traders in Britain needed global uniformity and ubiquitous information, not just information about distant British merchant houses. Because the overall information gathering effort would be done by British consuls, the form should be as clear as possible to limit the growth of their workload. It should also be straightforward so that traders in the United Kingdom could immediately judge whether it was worth while to attempt to trade with a given firm, or in a given locale.

By mid-1917, the FTD bureaucracy in London was set to operate its constructive efforts. They wrote to all British Chambers of Commerce sending a copy of an actual Form K, along with a memorandum explaining the development of the Form K program and describing the way that traders should utilize them. Not surprisingly, the example came from a South American consulate, the one in Asuncion, Paraguay, which, despite being in another country, rested on a tributary of the Rio de la Plata and thus was dependent on the Buenos Aires market. Every three months, consuls would update "cover forms" that would briefly describe the local market conditions, including weights and measures, languages, size of population, and also statistics on the total annual value of local imports and exports, the value of trade with the United Kingdom, and the amount of competition from foreign traders. The Form K itself attempted to make the relevant information immediately comprehensible to any British businessman, once they became accustomed to the FTD shorthand. For example, the top of the sample form had "R.4 direct," which indicated that the firm was the fourth on the Consulate's master list of recommended firms, and that it was capable of buying direct from the United Kingdom.

The forms included information about the nationality of the partners of the firm, their commercial reputation and financial standing, their references, the nature of their business, the language they preferred to use, their local competitors, and a judgment as to whether the firm could take the place of companies on the Statutory List as recipients of the products of the United Kingdom. On receipt from abroad, the FTD sent a copy of each report on each firm to the Association of Chambers of Commerce and the FBI. The Chambers of Commerce in the United Kingdom compiled lists of their own members interested in a particular class of trade. If they received a report on a company dealing with lumber or cement, all of their members interested in "building materials" would receive a copy.[101] Within the FTD offices in Lancaster House, the geographically divided sub-departments of the FTD took responsibility "for all local constructive work," and for distributing any specific commercial intelligence to firms in Britain. The "general" department of the FTD digested the information that arrived from merchants and trade associations in the United Kingdom, and distributed the results of Form K queries to these businessmen.[102]

Form K were compiled for all traders, not just the enemy or the British ones, but according to Controller Ernest Pollock, this was not inconsistent with the nationalist trading mission of his department. The Form K system was at least partially built upon the belief that the real ailments of British trade were in the inability of their products to penetrate neutral marketplaces beyond the larger metropolises. Rear-Admiral Henry Campbell, the former head of the Admiralty Trade Division now seconded to the FTD and, according to FTD Deputy Controller Ronald Macleay, the mastermind behind Form K, envisioned that the new information would be useful not only for exporting firms in the United Kingdom, but also for local British trading houses in neutral countries. According to Campbell, such pioneering British merchant houses had lost their position due to the way trade developed in the "hinterlands" of their countries. To help Britons in South America, there were two types of Form K. The "direct" series would help British exporters to know the overseas markets. The "indirect" series, examining local firms not ordinarily engaged in importing or exporting, would be available in British consulates for the use of locally-established British firms overseas, giving them a deeper knowledge of the trade within their own country.[103] Form K reports on indirect traders would be quite beneficial to the large British merchant houses in port cities like Buenos Aires that hoped to develop their inland trade with booming provincial towns like Tucuman and Rosario.[104] Both ends of the transatlantic British nationalist trade machine would thus understand the competition they were dealing with, helping the FTD to complete its mission to seal together transnational Britons in bonds of mutually beneficial commerce. Yet in the eyes of Britons in South America in the middle of 1917, the Form K was doing no such thing. Most claimed to understand the local marketplaces sufficiently, and were unlikely to benefit from the Form K system. Instead, it serviced businessmen in Britain in a way that might not benefit the Britons of South America.

Despite his support for Form K in his relations with the Chamber, Sir Reginald Tower repeatedly wrote to the FTD throughout 1917 supporting the Chamber's proposal for export preferences to be given to foreign branches of British firms, particularly for goods competing in sectors that had been dominated by Germans before the war.[105] After the question passed through the government, in January 1918 the FTD explained that the government had deemed impractical any arrangements for favoring British firms overseas when issuing export licenses.[106] The FTD undoubtedly fumbled efforts to coordinate the British bureaucracy behind the constructive war, and had difficulty getting the rest of the government to implement schemes of trade preferences that would help the British in South America. The WTD determined which British products could be exported, the Ministry of Shipping distributed space on British-controlled merchant vessels, and the customs monitored the goods and mail that flowed in and out of the United Kingdom. All appeared skeptical of placing restrictions on which recipients British exporters could send things to, especially when the normal trade of British exporters was already hampered by wartime circumstance.

Planning for a post-bellum constructive war:
The Department of Overseas Trade

Throughout 1917, the Board of Trade worked to repudiate the FTD's efforts to squeeze between the Board and United Kingdom manufacturers and exporters. The Board of Trade may still have doubted whether Britain's economic war could actually work, but they finally jumped on the band-wagon.[107] From the start of the Form K system, the Board demanded that carbon copies of every report be sent to the Board's Department of Commercial Intelligence.[108] Pandering to the Chamber of Commerce in Buenos Aires, in October 1917 the head of the Board's new Latin American section conveyed his opposition to the Form K scheme.[109] The Board further listened to South America when it appointed an advisory committee on commercial intelligence to discuss a proposal, made by the Commercial Attaché Chalkley in Buenos Aires, calling for traveling representatives of associations of manu-facturers to be sent abroad to show British wares and to learn about openings for trade. The advisory committee agreed and attempted to draw together groups of manufacturers in each sector of trade. The Board of Trade agreed to assign officers to help groups in certain sectors such as silversmithing in their efforts to federate their industry "for export purposes."[110] Finally, the Board reached out to the Association of Chambers of Commerce, asking for suggestions on how to raise the status of the Chambers and to help secure "closer co-operation between them and Government Departments."[111] All British companies could be excused for any confusion as to which ministry ran the British government's promised efforts to support trade in South America.

Inevitably, this question of control would have to be resolved in London, perhaps by the committee that Cecil had proposed to Asquith before the government reshuffle. In February 1917 this group finally came together, chaired not by Milner, as Cecil had suggested, but by Lord Faringdon, a wealthy railway director and Liberal Unionist MP. Each of the five members came to the meeting with his own agenda, and none showed signs of flexibil-ity. The preferences of Victor Wellesley, the delegate from the Foreign Office, were well known, and the industrialist Dudley Docker had deep ties to the FTD. Interestingly enough, despite the Board of Trade's constant reiteration that they firmly held the pulse of British commerce, businessmen in the United Kingdom largely fell in line behind the Foreign Office. The

Association of Chambers of Commerce and the Federation of British Industries often held antagonistic stances on trade policy, yet both proclaimed their support for the Foreign Office report.[112]

Thus braced, the Foreign Office showed no signs of backing down. Cecil declared that the Crowe report was the official opinion of the Foreign Office, and Sir Eyre Crowe vociferously defended the report during his testimony.[113] The Board of Trade rejected the idea that any future commercial intelligence effort should utilize or communicate with British Chambers of Commerce because, the Board argued, members of such Chambers often dealt in non-British goods.[114] Faringdon showed a bias against the Foreign Office in his bristling cross-examination of Crowe and in his terse, incredulous rejection of arguments put forward by Crowe and Worthington-Evans that the Foreign Office might be better equipped than the Board of Trade to lead foreign trade promotion and intelligence. The Foreign Office deeply annoyed Lord Faringdon by asking the Treasury for funds to pay for a new commercial attaché position in Italy, thereby pre-empting the committee's decision on whether such attachés should even exist.[115]

The Foreign Office position embodied in the earlier Crowe committee was well represented in the majority report signed by Wellesley, Docker, and D.F. Pennefather, a Member of Parliament and member of the Association of British Chambers of Commerce's Consular Service and Foreign Trade Department Committee.[116] Docker explicitly backed the reasoning of the Foreign Office about the need to keep commercial intelligence under one roof, and he believed that the Foreign Office was much more likely than the Board of Trade to help a manufacturer such as himself looking to sell goods abroad.[117] Refusing to concede defeat, the committee chairman Lord Faringdon and Sir William Clark of the Board of Trade wrote a minority report rejecting the Foreign Office stance.[118]

Undoubtedly, the FTD hoped to establish a presence in commercial intelligence before the Board could regain the lead, and the desire to compete against the Board was a primary reason for the FTD to push the Form K system so hard during early 1917. As FTD Deputy Controller Macleay admitted privately to Tower, he was unsure what would result from the failure of the Faringdon committee to fashion a compromise. But Macleay remained optimistic about the prospects for the FTD, believing that the information in Form K "ought to prove very useful when at the end of the war this department becomes as it appears destined to do a sub-department of the Commercial Dept at the FO."[119] Yet, at the same time, the Board of Trade launched a new effort to bypass the FTD, writing directly to the British Chamber of Commerce in Argentina. In its letter, the Board expressed its "keenest appreciation of the value of the Argentine market and of the necessity of strengthening the national hold upon it," and was setting up a new Latin American branch in its Commercial Intelligence Department. The Board claimed that it merely wanted to ask the Chamber of Commerce for information on what goods previously supplied by United Kingdom manufacturers would be in demand again at the end of the war, but undoubtedly the Board's motivation was that it could weaken the FTD among its core constituency.[120]

The continuation of the squabble forced the heads of the feuding ministries to step in again. The newly appointed President of the Board of Trade, Albert Stanley, met with Cecil in August 1917. Stanley's lack of history with the interdepartmental dispute made it easier for him to address it without the rancor shown by other Board officials, and together the two ministers crafted a memorandum on foreign commercial intelligence. Under the Stanley-Cecil plan, the collection and distribution of commercial intelligence would take place in a single department, as both the Board of Trade and the Foreign Office had wished. Unlike the competing schemes, however, neither department would wield absolute control. Instead, Cecil and Stanley proposed amalgamating the Foreign Trade, War Trade Intelligence, and War Trade Statistical Departments of the Ministry of Blockade with the Department of Commercial Intelligence of the Board of Trade. This new Commercial Intelligence Department would be tied equally to the Foreign Office and the Board of Trade and through those departments to British diplomats and businessmen.[121] Cecil's exact motivation for making the compromise is unknown, but he was certainly not alone in wanting to get it settled once and for all, and it is possible that his dual Foreign Office-Blockade Ministry role led him to believe that more permeable borders between ministries might allow better utilization of government resources. He showed no sign of believing that the compromise was in any way a betrayal of the Foreign Office position, convincingly arguing to the War Cabinet that "the war had proved that it was not possible to separate political from trade matters in the Diplomatic and Consular services." The War Cabinet adopted the plan on 15 August 1917.[122]

Yet even this top-level decision did not end difficulties between the Foreign Office and the Board of Trade. The Foreign Office remained unsatisfied with the Stanley-Cecil compromise. Arthur Steel-Maitland, appointed as the Parliamentary Secretary of the new department, was known as a difficult man who, as Conservative party manager, was unpopular among many of his fellow politicians.[123] Politically, he was a tariff reformer allied with Ernest Pollock, Dudley Docker, and others who demanded change in the way that the government promoted British exports. Dissatisfied with his junior post at the Colonial Office, feeling that it was insufficient recompense for his five years of thankless work for the Unionists, in July Steel-Maitland had asked the Conservative leader Andrew Bonar Law for a higher office.[124] Although Bonar Law voiced his doubts that a joint department could work, recognizing the state of high animosity that existed between the Foreign

Office and Board of Trade, Steel-Maitland took the position, and immediately faced difficulties.[125]

Although the department was to be run jointly and equally by the Foreign Office and Board of Trade, Steel-Maitland found it difficult to promote his relationship with the Foreign Office, despite his own preference for that ministry over the Board of Trade. He was physically distant from Whitehall, the new department taking over the offices of the CIB in the City of London, and the bulk of his employees came from that section of the Board of Trade.[126] Only two Foreign Office officials entered the new department, Guy Locock and Basil Newton.[127] Newton was the only one with any experience at the FTD. In the halls of the Foreign Office, the FTD still held a pre-eminent place over Steel-Maitland's department. In December 1917, FTD Controller Ernest Pollock expressed unhappiness over an interview given to *The Times* by Steel-Maitland, in which Steel-Maitland declared that his department would take over all the constructive work that was part of the economic war. Steel-Maitland, in a telling proof of the primacy of the FTD within the Foreign Office, apologized and explained that he would correct the confusion when he issued a press release about his organization. He recognized that the FTD would continue to do all of the Statutory List work, and that his department had only been given that part of the constructive work dealing with Form K. The only reason he had not yet issued a press release to this effect was because the Board of Trade and Foreign Office could not yet agree as to its name.[128]

Following the wartime premise that breeding relationships between business and government would benefit both, Steel-Maitland spent from November 1917 to February 1918 gathering together an advisory committee, including men from a variety of manufacturing and service industries. Recognizing the importance of publicity to the future of the department, in making itself known and appreciated by British businessmen and in engaging in pro-British propaganda in foreign countries, he urged that a member of the press be included among the committee members.[129] Steel-Maitland looked to establish a few local branches in Leeds or Sheffield, to advise traders who wanted to do business abroad, but did not know how to go about doing it.[130] He also backed commercial missions abroad to investigate the markets for certain British produce, the first one going to South America in early 1918 to look at the market for jewelry.

At the start of 1918, the Board of Trade announced to the business community that the new Department of Overseas Trade (DOT) had been given the reins of the Form K system. FTD partisans like Ernest Pollock would later report much overlapping of work, delays, and missed opportunities.[131] Yet the FTD had also found Form K a thankless task, despised by those consuls and British businessmen abroad who compiled it. But the creation of the DOT confused the question of which department should be in charge of commercial intelligence. The DOT was at least nominally interested in many of the same duties as those undertaken by the FTD, particularly those associated with the "constructive" aspects of the war.

The intransigent Foreign Office support for the FTD showed that they by no means regarded as final a DOT jointly run with the loathed Board of Trade. They hoped to use the remainder of the war to prove the vast superiority of a service run by the Foreign Office. Leaders of the FTD such as Ernest Pollock believed they could ignore the DOT because the FTD had de facto control over the most useful commercial intelligence and had the ear of many influential British businessmen. Until the end of the war, the Foreign Office continued to pour its trade-oriented resources into the FTD, refusing to merge the FTD into the DOT. The commercial attachés in South America did not begin to work fully on behalf of the DOT until 1919, instead concentrating their full energies on the FTD's economic war. From Buenos Aires, all of Commercial Attaché Chalkley's letters to the DOT throughout 1918 were addressed to Balfour, not to Steel-Maitland or Stanley at the Board of Trade.[132] The Commercial Attaché program was still definitively a Foreign Office operation. Members of the FTD jealously guarded their control over both the destructive and constructive aspects of the economic war, even after the flaws in their handling of both had become apparent.

They were certain that the Board remained obstructionist at heart. In a rare moment of togetherness, junior representatives of the FTD, DOT, and Board of Trade met on 6 March 1918, to write a memo explaining the Treasury's need to consider "the development of British interests in South and Central America" when giving permission to invest capital abroad. They cited particularly the possibility that British investors could take over the Compañía Alemana Transatlántica de Electricidad, which owned power stations in Buenos Aires and other cities in Chile and Uruguay. Balfour at the Foreign Office was receptive when Cecil presented the idea, but when Steel-Maitland excitedly took the proposal to the President of the Board of Trade, it was shot down. The FTD could write such a plea to the Treasury, but not jointly with the Board.[133]

Finding he could not deal with the conflicting demands and expectations of the Foreign Office and Board of Trade, Steel-Maitland threatened to resign as its head in April 1918. He recognized the futility of going to his superiors at the Board of Trade, and he was exacerbated by the Foreign Office, which he considered the natural home of his department. He did not understand why the Foreign Office had rebuffed his attempts to draw the DOT closer. In a

letter to Cecil, Steel-Maitland particularly cited the resistance of Eyre Crowe
to the effective working of the DOT with its supposed partners in the Foreign
Office.[134] Crowe and Wellesley worried that Steel-Maitland would confuse
the system whereby British diplomats sent all their correspondence to the
Foreign Office.[135]

None of the departments involved really understood the boundaries
between their duties, and there is little doubt that the British communities of
South America never truly knew what to make of the conflicting signals they
received from the British government. Throughout 1918 they received news
and queries from the FTD, DOT, and the Latin American Section of the
Commercial Intelligence Branch of the Board of Trade. The Chamber of
Commerce in Buenos Aires did not much trust the Board of Trade, whose
representative, Mr Bray, appeared more keen to help Argentines emigrate to
Britain to spur transatlantic commerce rather than focusing on nurturing trade
through the Anglo-Argentines.[136] The DOT looked similarly uninterested in
the fate of local British traders. The first direct letter from the DOT to the
British Legation in Buenos Aires, on 18 June 1918, rejected a request by
Tower that a list of firms on the Statutory List and the articles they traded in
could be circulated in Britain, with any replies from British manufacturers
being sent to Chalkley, who could parcel them out to British firms in Argentina. A superior way to inform British manufacturers of opportunities in
Buenos Aires, stated the DOT, would be to disseminate Form K reports to
companies in Britain, who could then communicate directly with whatever
local houses they wished.[137] As the Board of Trade had long argued, commercial intelligence should aim to bolster trade for United Kingdom companies, rather than building trade with Britons beyond the Empire.

Conclusion

The formation of the economic war in the overseas neutral nations took place
in the context of a broader reconstruction of the bureaucracy of the British
government. This reorganization was shaped in part by pre-war disputes
among ministries but even more by criticism of the disorganized conduct of
the economic campaign against Germans during the first year and a half of
the war. British economic warfare efforts were centralized underneath a
single man, Minister of Blockade Lord Robert Cecil, a change that in effect
brought the blockade under the control of the Foreign Office. The existence
of the FTD enabled the Foreign Office to attempt to amalgamate under itself
powers formerly reserved for the Board of Trade. A vicious but predictable
bureaucratic turf war ensued. Rejecting the traditional, uninvolved ways of
the Board of Trade, the FTD worked to connect British businessmen abroad
to their counterparts in the United Kingdom, with the aim of setting up a

permanent system of trade benefiting the British everywhere. Far from being uninterested in questions of commerce, the members of the Foreign Office looked to take control of official policy towards foreign trade and to install a completely new commercial ethos among government and businessmen. Throughout 1916, the far-reaching schemes of the FTD stood as perhaps the most extreme embodiment of Britain's rejection of *laissez-faire*. Beyond muddling through, beyond temporary measures, the FTD operated under the assumption that government involvement in international trade was not just for wartime, but beyond. Deviating decisively from its traditional support for the globalization of free trade, open markets, and economic integration, the British government hoped now to globalize the nationalist commercial practices of British businessmen.

Yet as the commercial war moved into its second year, the FTD grew increasingly anxious about the possibility of creating this new transatlantic British commercial identity, as rifts between the businessmen of South America and those in the United Kingdom remained apparent, and wartime circumstance exposed the limitations of all Britons for effective nationalist action.

6

Cloaks, Turks, the Octopus, and other Undesirables: Travails of the trade warriors in South America

A year after its creation, Sir Reginald Tower judged that the Statutory List as initially envisioned was fully implemented. British people no longer traded with Germans, and the Statutory List included all of the largest German and pro-German companies. "Enemy firms in Argentina who are included in the Statutory List are deprived of British goods, British markets, British shipping and British finance – a formidable loss to them," wrote Tower in a special report on the trade war. "Every month has increased their difficulties and reduced their opportunities." Nevertheless, across South America, Germans continued to conduct business. With his characteristic bombast, Tower conveyed a stark reality:

> The enemy firms remain, powerful and hostile, antagonized and bitter at the exercise of our temporary supremacy, bound together by what they regard as an outrage on their moral prestige as well as on their material prosperity, ready to make a ruthless onslaught on our trade when the time comes. It is at their destruction while we have the power that we must aim."[1]

Like Tower, other British economic warriors remained hopeful, even optimistic, but they had obviously encountered a number of obstacles in their attempt to destroy German commerce in the South American republics.

Through 1917 it was not just defects in the constructive war that became obvious to British observers in South America, but also problems with the Statutory List. According to FTD propaganda, it had successfully conducted an effective, precise, and harsh war against wily enemies. In an eleven-page memo to the Cabinet and other ministries in November 1916, the FTD bragged of how the Statutory List permanently crippled various German firms "on the Atlantic coast of South America." German correspondence already shown high anxiety on both sides of the Atlantic, and the pain inflicted by the Statutory List would inevitably increase the longer the war went on.[2]

Yet they had a notably difficult time getting the word out about the Statutory List to businessmen in the United Kingdom. In May 1917, the FTD published a consolidated list of the more than 2,000 names of people and companies around the world that they had placed on Statutory Lists. Many British companies complained that it was too difficult to keep up to date with the revisions printed each week in the *London Gazette* and *Board of Trade Journal*. The FTD were still finding cases where United Kingdom firms caught corresponding with people on the Statutory List claimed that "they have never heard of the List."[3] And despite their evident intentions, the FTD did not target all of those people whom the British in South America believed merited attack.

As the war progressed, the once belligerent FTD seemed increasingly to support the skittishness of many United Kingdom businessmen, who had a harder time than their compatriots in South America seeing the possible benefits of a trade regime focused on "Greater Britain." Even Roland Nugent, who in 1915 had proved to be a prime proponent of the Foreign Office's commercial war in South America, tempered his demands for anti-German measures with the caveat that British manufacturing needed whatever encouragement it could get. Nugent, who in 1917 would take a position in the FBI, explained that questionable cases would not be included in the Statutory List when big interests such as Chambers of Commerce in the United Kingdom opposed the inclusion of a name.[4] Interference by British manufacturers fearful of changing their trading partners in South America accounted for some of those names proposed by Tower – and by other British diplomats abroad – that never reached the Statutory List, or were listed only after long delay. The FTD's desire to stretch a hand to businessmen in the United Kingdom, thereby bypassing the Board of Trade, left the department increasingly susceptible to lobbying from these businessmen.

The FTD had the responsibility to issue licenses allowing British firms to trade with individuals and firms on the Statutory List. The department initially declared it would issue such licenses only to allow companies to fulfill contractual obligations which, if neglected, could leave the British companies open to lawsuits under local laws.[5] "The guiding principle in such cases is, in fact, expediency pure and simple," explained an FTD circular to the diplomats in the Americas.[6] In a July 1916 memo to diplomats in the Americas the FTD declared that it would no longer issue licenses for British firms to trade with businesses on the Statutory List "save in very exceptional circumstances." Anyone who contracted to sell goods to firms of enemy nationality or association not yet on the Statutory List "would be well advised to seek other outlets for his sales, and as the eventual placing of a firm on the Statutory List may affect its credit, he would be advised to so arrange his business that he may not suffer future inconvenience."[7] Yet the FTD often relented in the face of British manufacturers who believed that the war had placed enough restrictions on their trade. Many industrialists argued that if they had an opportunity to fabricate goods for export, they should be allowed to ship such goods abroad, and if this meant that they had to conduct their trade through German firms, then sometimes they should be allowed to do so in order to keep the wheels of foreign trade rolling. From Uruguay, Innes complained in August 1916 that the FTD too willingly granted licenses to exporters in the United Kingdom, allowing them to trade with firms on the Statutory List.[8]

The FTD also faced criticism for taking the Statutory List too far. Such problems resulted in large part from the inevitable bureaucratic and logistical delays in FTD reactions to the recommendations of the British in South America. One example of delay leading to controversy was the blacklisting of Cassini & Co., implicated by its connections to the German-run, Argentina-based textile importers and clothing manufacturers Mitau & Grether and H. Sternberg & Co. All three firms held close relationships with the Berlin-based company Sternberg & Co., and documentation proved that they were integrally related, as all conducted trades through the Italian, Cassini. Yet when asked, Emilio Grether pleaded to Tower that he used Cassini's name without authorization. Cassini desperately wanted to get off the list and signed an undertaking in July stating that his firm would never trade with companies on the Statutory List.[9] Tower and Chalkley maintained that the Italian businessman had suffered enough, and opined that if his firm liquidated its debt to Sternberg, Cassini should be removed from the Statutory List.[10] And from Rosario, the British Consul Dickson pleaded for Cassini's removal from the list, saying that most locals (many of whom were Italian) sympathized with Cassini. "Should any disaster overtake him as a result of his being on the Statutory List," warned Dickson, "that sympathy would very likely take active form."[11] When six months later, Cassini remained on the Statutory List, Tower wrote to the FTD that the firm "is popularly regarded even by allied persons here as something of a 'martyr' and as a victim of injustice."[12] Cassini was finally removed, but only after three more uncomfortable months had passed.

At the other extreme, critics lamented the few obviously gaping local holes in the Statutory List. The FTD exempted British-owned railroads, enterprises subject to the laws of the republics, from having to comply with the Statutory List. This enabled listed firms to continue hauling their goods around the country, a particular boon to firms specializing in bulky export commodities like grain, which relied on the rails to get the goods from the pampas to the sea. British insurance companies in the republics also continued to conduct business with German firms throughout the war. These insurers were given an exemption from the 'Trade with the Enemy' law on 23 May 1916, after arguing that to do otherwise would be catastrophic for their business.[13] Such loopholes made the British government's policy appear half-hearted or inconsistent to some increasingly agitated Britons living in the republics. One optimistic observer claimed that the "bitter complaints" within the British community over omissions from the Statutory List "are unsolicited testimony to its efficacy."[14] Yet in the eyes of some Britons, the Statutory List was undoubtedly tainted by such exceptions, bringing into question the intentions of Britain's supposedly strict enemy trade policy.

Cloaks and the United States

But all Britons agreed that the greatest challenge to the Statutory List effort came from listed firms that conducted foreign trade not in their own names, but rather through intermediaries. These soon became known as "cloaks" because they enabled Statutory Listed companies to disguise their activities. Individuals and companies worked on behalf of firms on the Statutory List by allowing their names to be used in shipping manifests and bills of exchange so that goods on British ships could reach them. Others stored the goods of listed firms in their warehouses, or sold to Statutory Listed firms goods that they had imported themselves. British mail censors could be evaded through use of cloak addresses and code words. Many cloaks were true 'straw men', individuals (often of local nationality) who were unlikely to conduct any trade other than as cloaks. Straw men throughout South America who helped to circumvent the Statutory List did so through a mix of fearlessness of the consequences of being listed, desire for potentially easy profits, and either a pro-German or disinterested position toward the war in Europe. Tower suggested in a letter to the FTD that the cloak problem revealed "the facile and complaisant character of the Latin American generally," with their constant friendliness and desire to please easily abused "by the German tempter," a phrase perhaps most revealing of Tower's wartime paranoia about the German threat.[15] Friends, employees, and opportunists shipped goods for importers such as Hasenclever & Co. and exporters like Staudt & Co. When the names of the Statutory Listed firms did not appear in shipping documents, cables and mail, their business conduct was inscrutable, at least from the perspective of London.

The cloak problem was initially underappreciated by the British on both sides of the Atlantic, and seemed solvable. In Montevideo, Innes expressed hope in the last days of August 1916 that the recent placement on the Statutory List of a number of cloaks would be a sufficient threat to stop others in the city from acting in the same way.[16] Yet a variety of people in South America remained willing and able to act as cloaks, helping listed firms send and receive goods, and thus continue their lucrative international trade. As Sir Reginald Tower reckoned, cloaks could be anyone affiliated with a company. He thus forwarded a comprehensive list of the employees of Hasenclever & Co., a listed firm, to the FTD.[17] British consulates, legations and Chambers of Commerce could learn who worked as a cloak only through constant, close inspection of intercepted communications and shipping manifests, and by paying attention to informants in the ports and customs houses. When discovered, some cloaks were placed on the Statutory List, particularly those working for the most despised companies such as Staudt & Co., Hasenclever & Co., and Bunge & Born. But by the middle of July 1917, British officials understood that there was a virtually inexhaustible supply of potential cloaks, and placing them on the Statutory List was, in Tower's words, "like pouring water into the sea." "The 'cloak' system is my despair," he lamented.[18]

The best hope was that the United States could solve the cloak problem. By declaring war on 6 April 1917, Germany's defeat on the European battlefield was secured. It would be easy to assume that US involvement similarly enhanced the effectiveness of the British economic war in Latin America.[19] The difficulty in receiving supplies from Europe had motivated firms on the Statutory List to look north through the first year of the British commercial war. Profiting by the hardships that war imposed on British business, the American Transatlantic Line in November 1916 began a steamship service between the US and South America which was known to supply cloaks.[20] British people concerned with the economic war hoped this problem with inter-American trade might be solved if the United States declared war against Germany. In February 1917, officials at the FTD drooled over the possibilities of what might happen if the United States entered the war and adopted British measures: "In many cases the adherence of the United States to our Statutory List would remove the last prop by which enemy houses are struggling to support their existence until peace is signed."[21] Eyre Crowe was hopeful that a belligerent United States would adopt the British war, noting that even if they decided against prohibiting the trade of the large German immigrant population within its own borders, it would still be "perfectly logical for them to prohibit trade with enemy firms in neutral territories."[22]

The FTD tried to persuade their new allies that the Statutory List actually hurt Germany. They seized on a confidential report from a former *Daily Mail* correspondent in Berlin, whose meeting with a confidant of Chancellor Bethmann-Hollweg suggested that the German leader would sign a peace treaty if he received guarantees that the British trade war would not continue after the conclusion of peace. Members of the FTD were ecstatic, noting that this confirmed that the Statutory List was a "most valuable weapon" that had a significant impact on German decision-making. The pain of Germans in South America was registering in Berlin. If the United States cooperated, the screws could be further tightened. The FTD wrote to Ambassador Spring-Rice in Washington, asking him to reiterate to US authorities that the Statutory List was a crucial campaign of the total war:

It does of course involve attacks on individuals who may regret the action of their national government. So does every shot fired in the present war. The decisive consideration must be whether such measures bring nearer a peace which is acceptable. In present conditions this consideration renders it no longer possible to refrain, as heretofore, from commercial warfare.[23]

Suggesting that the threat of commercial loss in South America could defeat Germany was certainly optimistic. In the hypercharged patriotic atmosphere of 1917 Germany, an Allied economic war would more likely lead German industrialists and merchants to demand highly punitive peace terms from the Allies.[24] If the economic war in South America had any effect on the length of the First World War, the animosities stirred up could only have served to extend it. The fear of a post-bellum trade war in South America was far down the list of things that pressured the German government to capitulate in the war – a war whose end would only be determined by conditions on the battlefield.

Yet this war-shortening argument played to the desire of the Wilson administration for peace as soon as possible. The resulting initial coordination to curb the cloak problem looked promising. In May 1917, Tower told the FTD that the best way to tighten regulations against cloaks would be to forbid US shipping lines from shipping cargo for unreliable consignees. By June, a "cloaks list" was created under the British Consulate General in New York. The British consuls in South America informed their colleague to the north, via telegraph, of the people in South America who acted as cloaks and who should not be allowed to receive goods from the United States.[25] The nominally secret list was distributed to both allied and neutral shipping companies which, under pressure as a result of their reliance on British coal depots in various foreign ports, had signed voluntary agreements to respect the Statutory List.[26] Yet the recently founded American Transatlantic Company, for one, disagreed that their agreement with the FTD not to ship goods to firms on the Statutory List also meant that they should refuse to carry goods "consigned to palpable cloaks."[27]

Soon some Britons claimed, like the British military intelligence officer stationed in Rio de Janeiro in June 1917, that "the entry of the United States into the war against the Central Empires . . . has proved an unmixed blessing to German commercial houses in South America." By studying the manifests of merchant ships, he found that over the previous two months nearly 42,000 different items arrived consigned to known cloaks of three German firms. The US government did not seem eager to implement measures of its own, and the American Chamber of Commerce in Brazil resisted suggestions that it take steps against trading with Germans.[28] Sir Reginald Tower recognized stark differences in the conduct of his US colleagues compared to that of other Allies. "They [the US] are hesitating about accepting a S.L. policy," he wrote to Macleay in July 1917. "The Ambassador here shows little interest in the matter [and] has so far not joined me at all, nor tried to meet halfway my various advances for confidence and cooperation."[29] Tower was apoplectic about the reluctance of the United States to enter the war in South America. "For the last three years I have been about twelve hours a day, often even more, in the Chancery, and the time is coming when this will prove beyond one's strength." He became a self-described grouse during the months after the United States entered the war, increasingly pessimistic about the prospects for the economic war.

From Montevideo, Innes confirmed that US representatives were less than friendly. After the Foreign Office sent a telegram commanding him to secure full cooperation with his US colleagues, Innes replied that the US government should issue similar instructions. Relationships between British and US diplomats were "impaired by local suspicions," which Innes blamed on the US representatives.[30] "The fact is that the German firms now take such precautions to cover up their traces that it would require an organised secret service to get at the bottom of their manoeuvres. For the moment I am feeling rather 'fed-up' with it all," explained the overwhelmed minister. "My only clerk is in hospital, and I cannot replace him; I have important negotiations on hand and cannot attend to the chasing of cloaks."[31] Only with the help of his US colleagues could the trade war possibly succeed.

Officials at home understood these difficulties, and likewise registered their unhappiness about the activities of the United States. The FTD wrote a memo for the War Cabinet advocating an extension of the Statutory List policy "to exploit the alarm already manifested by Germany at the idea of *post bellum* trade war." The War Cabinet sent this memorandum to Washington.[32] Yet there was no action. Two months later, at the end of September 1917, Lord Robert Cecil complained to the War Cabinet that as far as the British economic war in South America was concerned, the United States might as well have remained neutral.[33]

But Britain held little leverage against the United States in Latin America at a time when cooperation in the European theatre was critical. The United States would have to be persuaded, rather than forced, to take up the Statutory List. The FTD lobbied Washington to recognize that the British policy was the correct one. For German firms outside Britain, the department lectured, it had grown obvious "that if a firm or company is German owned or controlled the question of enemy activity is merely one of opportunity." FTD standards for determining enemy status should be adopted by the United States.[34] Yet they refused to simply adopt the Statutory List, as the French and Italians had done. People in the United States had developed an aversion to the concept of the Statutory List when it was applied there in July 1916.

In the days leading up to US entry into the war, the US Ambassador to Britain demanded that Britain withdraw the Statutory List there.[35] The War Cabinet obviously complied; after all, the Statutory List for the United States had only been created to justify the more extensive economic warfare efforts in South America. But for the US government, angry about the British war, schooled in the Monroe Doctrine, and somewhat enamored by the possibility of Pan-Americanism, it would be deeply embarrassing to appear to submit to British authority over policy towards Latin America. To do so might sow doubt among South Americans about the power of the United States.

At root, the reluctance to adopt the British commercial war rested on the wishes of businessmen and politicians in the United States, who looked to supersede both Germany and Britain in South America.[36] When Britain and Germany began fighting in August 1914, myriad delegations from Chambers of Commerce and other trade and industry groups traveled southward from the United States in search of commercial opportunities. Wartime penetration by US banking was particularly striking. Just before the war began, in June 1914, the Federal Reserve Act made it legal for American banks to establish branches in foreign countries. The New York-based National City Bank wasted little time, setting up its Buenos Aires branch in November.[37] All assumed that German businesses in Latin America, disadvantaged by wartime circumstances, would make the easiest targets for US businessmen.[38] But these entrepreneurs were also willing to profit from the problems faced by British businessmen during the war, owing to lack of merchandise and cargo space. Even after entering the war, traders, bankers, and government officials in the United States believed that competition would be the rule for the Allied relationship in South America.

They believed that Britons were likewise competitive, certain that the prime intention of the British government in creating the Statutory List was not to hurt Germany, but rather to foster British trade.[39] As Emily Rosenberg has explained, many North Americans viewed the British blacklist as an unfair method of competition aimed against United States business.[40] US policy makers bore in mind the possibility that US and British trade might be in conflict after the war. In a letter to his superior in Rio de Janeiro, W.H. Lawrence, the United States consul at the coffee port of Santos, demanded that his government do more to aid its citizens who, during the war, were working to claim a larger slice of Brazilian commerce. Lawrence feared a British resurgence after the war and called on the US government to extend loans to commercial ventures, tariff preferences to US shipping lines, and business training in US schools.[41] He even suggested that there might come a time when the United States would combine with the commercially able Germans against the British, particularly if the latter created an economic alliance with France.[42] There had been some consternation in the United States over a possible alliance between France and Britain that arose during the mid-1916 Paris Economic Conference, where the two countries vaguely resolved to implement a post-bellum scheme of commercial favoritism for each other and their worldwide empires.[43] But clearly Lawrence's musings were triggered not by the Paris resolutions, which had led to little action in the intervening months, but rather by the competitive commercial situation he witnessed in Brazil. Even after their government declared war against the German empire, United States officials could see the British, rather than the Germans, as their primary foe.

US authorities and businessmen did not believe that any benefit might result from joining Britain's war. US businessmen who dealt with the South American republics respected the Germans for their successes during the previous decades, were happy to profit from the urgent desire of these German firms to keep their business going, and believed that after the war, connections to these successful German businessmen would bring continued profits. The British recognized this. An agent sent to Argentina by the British Ministry of Information in October 1917 reported to his superiors that "our greatest trade and general antagonist in South America is the United States. Every ship that comes from the United States with passengers is a Mayflower of commerce." New US banks were poaching the staff of British banks by offering to double their pay.[44] Competition remained the rule. Yet of course it would not do for the United States to overtly reject an economic war against Germans, who were, at least while battles raged in Europe, so obviously their enemies. In December 1917, the United States finally stepped into the fray when it published a blacklist of enemy firms in Latin America. The first US 'Enemy Trading List' included some names that were not on the British Statutory List.[45] British officials, excited to strengthen the economic campaign, swiftly placed those names on their own Statutory List.[46] They hoped their misgivings about the United States were finally being allayed.

Creating a new front in the commercial war

In June of 1917, the members of the British Chamber of Commerce in Buenos Aires began to establish committees focusing on individual trades. The first, an ad hoc group of importers in the electrical trade, decided at its first meeting that it would compile a list of goods that previously had been supplied from Germany, with prices and terms of trade. Led by James Asher, the manager of the British importer Agar Cross & Co., the committee also suggested that British manufacturers of such goods should begin to coordinate themselves, standardizing production and distribution while using their leverage as a group to guarantee that shipping lines provide them with competitively priced space from Britain.[47] Asher's voice came not from the ruling Council of the Chamber, but rather from the grassroots British businessmen of Argentina, eager to ratchet up both the constructive and destructive wars. Following this demand for greater and broader participation in the Chamber's wartime activities, the Council soon set up committees in a variety of other trades.[48] These committees provided innovative new services in the commercial war, and their activities re-energized the activists in the Chambers who hoped for greater command over the course of British trade. Even as hurdles arose, the British business communities in all the South American republics refused to stop fighting, continually developing new ways to attack their ever-changing enemies.

Although the development of local manufacturing may have been surprisingly meager in retrospect, many local industries did grow across South America, and where they did, they usually worked to thwart the war effort.[49] In Argentina, the Statutory Listed firms Curt Berger & Co. and Hoffman & Stocker continued their lucrative trade in various types of paper simply by manufacturing the paper locally, in their own factories, or by purchasing it from other local producers.[50] Despite the fact that the South American republics relied on imports to supply many needs, it became apparent that businesses less reliant on foreign supplies remained largely untouched by the British war. The Statutory List did not limit trade within the republics, other than for British merchants and others who voluntarily adhered to it. British trade warriors recognized that more merchants must become involved in the fight, and they must take it beyond the ports, to the retail and wholesale markets across each country. To truly hurt the Germans, the British would have to find a way to directly meddle with local trade.

By the end of 1917, British authorities and their businessmen allies had successfully gained control of the trafficking of certain goods in Buenos Aires, making them impossible for listed firms to obtain. For example, electric lamps came from only two foreign sources, Philips and General Electric. The Chamber of Commerce drew up a list of ten houses (four British, three Italian, two US, and one Argentine) that local agents of these two manufacturers could sell their lamps to. These ten merchants in turn limited their sales to a list of twenty-eight wholesalers and large consumers. Copies of the business logs of all these firms were sent to the Legation each month to ensure they did not sell directly or indirectly to firms such as the Compañía Alemana Transatlántica de Electricidad, the electricity producing company that Tower had recently persuaded the FTD to place on the Statutory List.[51]

But Sir Reginald Tower's meager staff could not replicate these tedious processes for all trades, many of which dealt with a far broader array of suppliers. At Tower's request in July 1917, the Chamber's Sectional Trade committees brainstormed new ways to ferret out and control trade being conducted by Germans. Tower urged the British government to force all shipping lines to adhere to lists of specific approved consignees for certain goods, and the sectional committees began to draw up these "approved lists."[52] By November 1917, the hardware and machinery committees had created an approved list that they anticipated would be accepted both in Britain and the United States.[53] The classifications they created were followed by other committees. Each importer was placed on list 'A' for reliable companies, list 'B' for suspect firms, and list 'C' for companies that definitely assisted firms on the Statutory List. Tower promised that the new lists would be sent to the British Consul-General at New York, much like the cloaks list, with the difference that they included only real importing companies, rather than "men of straw."[54] In New York, customs officials would detain shipments for companies on list 'B.' This should lead afflicted firms to come to the British legation in Buenos Aires, where they would guarantee that in the future they would not deal with enemy firms and open their books to accountants recommended by the Chamber of Commerce.

With their new "approved lists of importers," the Chamber attempted to recreate a white list – one they hoped would finally determine the direction of British trade. Tower appreciated the Chamber's efforts, telling Gibson and Powell-Jones that the Chamber itself was the only body "equipped for the task of destroying German trade and future trade prospects." Recognizing this, in January 1918, the government answered one of the Chamber's calls for subsidies. Tower promised that if the Chamber used "all its energies in open combat with German local trade," it would be reimbursed for the expenses of commercial warfare.[55] It was a moment of mobilization. The Council of the Chamber deliberated about what powers Tower would be willing to give them, and in their quandary they instructed Gibson to ask Tower what to do next. Gibson considered his Council's instructions for a day, and then refused to act. As he explained to his fellow members on the Executive Committee a few days later, the Chamber had been requested by the government to extend its activities, and they should simply go about doing so. They knew what to do, and it was time to do it. Gibson carried the day, as the Council immediately created more sectional trade committees and assigned all Chamber members to at least one of them.

They also recognized the importance of increasing publicity for the economic war, hoping to persuade pro-Allied businessmen in Argentina to join. This was an idea that had been in the air for a while, at least since November 1917, when the Executive Committee explained to Tower their wish to publish the Statutory List more broadly in newspapers across Argentina, and also to obtain the cooperation of "the Italian, French, and Belgian Legations" to get these countries' blacklists published as well (note the omission of the US Legation from this list).[56] Now, in January, on Gibson's urging, the Council created a new Press Committee that would distribute "judicious information to the Press," and the Chamber would undertake the publication of as many as 100,000 copies of the Statutory List in Spanish to be distributed across the Republic.[57] Gibson was proposing that the Chamber work more openly on the British war, while trying to persuade or coerce others in Argentina to join the cause.

Already, in December 1917, the Chamber had begun to compile a list of "purely local cloaks" who bought Allied merchandise locally and delivered the goods to Statutory Listed firms. The Council also unanimously supported the proposal of its Electrical Trade Committee that all Chamber members should pledge to refuse to conduct any business with "any known or self professed German Firms or individuals, whether or not on the British Statutory List."[58] After the Council meeting on 17 January, the new sectional committees broadened this effort to uncover Germans and their fellow travelers. The committees soon created a fundamentally new blacklist – one that listed local cloaks and also "known Germans" who were not eligible for the Statutory List. By the end of January, this 'Undesirable List' was circulated for private distribution to members of the British Chamber of Commerce, and also to the other Allied Chambers of Commerce.[59]

Unsurprisingly, the Chamber wanted to broadcast it further. In March they asked Tower for permission to distribute the Undesirable List (which already included 186 names) to the local French and Italian newspapers. The Chamber hoped it would be published and that this would result in more businesses joining their local boycott, but Tower refused.[60] Although he applauded the "very militant" attitude that the Chamber increasingly exhibited over the preceding months, Tower worried that because the list contained names of non-German neutrals, publication would make it appear that companies on the list were official enemies of the Allies.[61] Any published list should include only true Germans, people of admitted or proven German nationality.

Yet the Chamber would not back down. After meeting with Tower, the Hardware Committee remained aghast that their minister still rejected the publication of the Undesirable List in the press. The new list was "an indispensable complement to the Statutory List and should be an all Allied list, as it deals with innumerable cases of minor importance individually, but which collectively form an important part of local enemy activity."[62]

The work undertaken in devising the Undesirable List was unlike any the Chamber had ever conducted before. When the FTD asked for a list of expenses, the Chamber estimated in March that it would soon be spending

£1,100 per month just on intelligence gathering, a figure that did not include money spent on increasing the size of the Chamber's offices and their paid staff.[63] In May the Electrical Committee assigned one of its members, J.F.W. Argent, the local agent of the North British Rubber Company, to suspend his normal work and spend all his time coordinating investigations.[64] In July, the Chamber was forced to increase its expenses by renting out some new rooms, where Mr Argent would head the Investigation Office.[65] The Chamber needed the extra space.[66]

But they also opened the new office because they wanted their investigations to remain separate from the Chamber itself. Leaders attempted to keep these investigations as clandestine as possible. In late January, the Council voted to refrain from discussing this work during a forthcoming Special General Meeting "on the ground of possible leakage."[67] Although there are only oblique references to it in Chamber of Commerce records, an increasing amount of work was apparently done by private investigators hired and guided by the committees.[68] Tower explained to the FTD that spying was a huge endeavor, as there were over two hundred firms on the Statutory List in Buenos Aires alone, with many of them owning vast warehouses on the outskirts of the city.[69] Such distances necessitated the purchase of an automobile by the electrical trade and hardware and machinery committees in January.[70] The investigators received some information from "inside sources," but much of it came simply by watching the carts that entered and left the warehouses and yards of firms on the Statutory List.[71] In one note bolstering his claims for increased funding for investigations from the FTD, Tower suggested that two men would be required to watch the huge factory owned by the blacklisted firm H. Sternberg Jr & Co. that was being supplied by some unknown local intermediary.[72] Obviously it would have taken hundreds of investigators to watch all the German targets, a number far beyond what their expenses could have paid for. Yet the committees certainly hired enough investigators, and conducted enough stakeouts of German businesses themselves, to become noticed. The Statutory Listed firms knew, or at least assumed, that they were being watched. In July 1918, Tower relayed a report written by an inside source at a recent meeting at the German Club, where a "Señor Hindler" suggested that they could find the British spies if they themselves hired agents to stake out their own businesses. Tower's source (it is unknown who it was, perhaps a servant or waiter) had been called away twice during the middle of the debate, but when present he witnessed the representatives of a number of German companies pledging monthly dues totaling $30,500 to a new effort to combat the Statutory List.[73] This was nearly three times the amount spent monthly by the British Chamber's investigators, and it is doubtful whether the Germans ever actually followed through on creating a system to counter the British investigations, to watch the watchers. But the account does suggest how the war in South America was waged literally on the streets, with German trade becoming more scurrilous and fitful, their wagon drivers and wealthy merchants looking over their shoulders at who might be following them while they went about their business around the city.

And at the same time, the whiff of secret agents, clandestine offices, and stakeouts, must have been intoxicating to many of the British men active in gathering this commercial intelligence. They tried to keep the clandestine effort secret but, at the same time, they could not help bragging about it. Their published annual report for the year ending on 30 June 1918 listed fifteen sectional trade committees with 124 members, and acclaimed the committees who had "been extremely valuable to national interests," the "heavy and continuous" labors of their members proving their devotion and loyalty to the cause.[74] These Britons had become consumed with fighting Germans, and were fully engaged in the battle.

The creation of the Undesirable List illuminated the desire of British businessmen and officials to remedy the troubling problems with the existing Statutory List, in particular its slowness to react to changes in who acted as an enemy. At the start of 1918, Sir Reginald Tower still advocated further expansion of the Statutory List as the way to attack Germans, suggesting to the FTD that it widen its standards for the Statutory List by including firms of enemy nationality "whose business operations have hitherto been regarded as on too small a scale to justify their inclusion in the Statutory List."[75] At least one of the British government's agents in Argentina suggested that to remedy this problem, Tower himself should be given "full discretionary powers" to put names on or take them off the Statutory List.[76]

But by the middle of the year, Tower had come to favor the Chamber's new Undesirables List. When telling the FTD of the myriad companies that he suspected of being owned by Bunge & Born, Tower explained that asking Allied colleagues to place these names on the official blacklists would enable the enemy businesses to continue to operate unimpeded for at least another few months, as the machinery of the Statutory List chugged along slowly in London. He recommended instead the immediate placement of these names on the Undesirables List and printing them, under the heading of Bunge & Born, on copies of the Statutory Lists that were published for use by Allied partisans in Argentina.[77] Tower realized that changes in blacklisting had to happen more quickly, with more publicity, and should be directed against a broader array of German companies.[78] These things could only happen by maximizing unity with the other Allies – not so difficult when it came to the French, Italians, and Belgians, but a problem when it came to the Americans.

Making the war an Allied effort

Although it was certainly a hopeful sign for the British, even after the US published its first Enemy Trading List in Buenos Aires on 9 February 1918, there were indications that the US war might be less than Britain had hoped. Many listed firms expressed confidence that they would continue to receive goods by taking advantage of the decision of the US War Trade Board to allow the fulfillment of pending contracts. Meanwhile, the US Consul-General in Buenos Aires continued to balk at cooperation with the British Consul-General Mackie and Commercial Attaché Chalkley.[79]

Finally, in March, the Foreign Office instructed British envoys across Latin America to meet at least once each week with their US, French and Italian colleagues to decide on recommendations for the Allied lists. With the merging of Allied blacklisting efforts, British diplomats, rather than acting unilaterally and contacting the FTD directly, had to make a case in front of their Allied colleagues before any company would be placed on the Statutory List. Each British minister would relay to the British embassy in Washington the recommendations composed by himself and his colleagues. An Allied committee would then meet in Washington on a weekly basis to determine the additions and reductions of the list in each Latin American country.[80] By centralizing in Washington the blacklisting procedures for all Allied lists in the western hemisphere, the British seemed to give in to US terms.

Yet even after this directive, inter-allied cooperation in Argentina remained slow to appear. Sir Reginald Tower explained in April 1918 that he and the US ambassador decided to build the list by having the US and British legations meet weekly, with their decisions referred by Tower to the French and Italians. But new delays ensued, owing to the bureaucratic transition in US embassies. When the United States assigned a commercial attaché to Buenos Aires, it took some time for him to learn about US enemy trade policy from the Consul-General, who until then had done all the preliminary work on the Enemy Trading List. It took two further months before the US State Department decided that the US ambassador should be the one to attend consultations with the other Allies, and that the US commercial attaché would do the investigative work.[81]

In the meantime, Tower and his Allied colleagues routinely submitted the names of possible listees to each other. Yet in June, the US commercial attaché reported on the:

> lack of co-operation between concerns whose owners are of nationality of the Allies in that those of one nation feel at liberty to ignore the list of another and many times it happens that firms considered as 'enemy' by one are not so considered by the other because the name does not appear on its own black list. This leads to confusion and dissatisfaction between the Allies and in the meanwhile the enemy concerns are keeping themselves alive.[82]

The process of converging the various national blacklists sometimes enabled enemy companies to escape listing. In May 1918, fifteen names were removed from the Statutory List for Argentina, against the vociferous opposition of the British Chamber of Commerce, to help unify the Statutory List and the US Enemy Trading List.[83]

The difficulties in coordination rested in part on differences between the two Allied governments' enemy trade laws. US and British laws used different definitions of 'enemy.' The US refused to regard German nationality or sympathies as sufficient reasons to be listed. Instead, under US regulations, a firm had to be a branch of a firm based in Germany, engage in trade with Germany, work as an agent of German propaganda, or have a partner or a manager who lived in German-controlled territory.[84] In short, the US regulations were less broad, less open to anyone who aided the enemy than the British rules. Through to the end of the war, the British Statutory List included names that were not on the US Enemy Trading List. For instance, Tower asked the FTD to place a handful of companies on the Statutory List for acting as cloaks for the Hansa Mining Company and for L.D. Meyer & Co. He did not bother reporting these cloaks to the United States, however, because neither Hansa nor L.D. Meyer were on the US Enemy Trading List.[85] Britain maintained the right to place names on their own Statutory List even if the United States did not agree.[86]

Despite their disagreements with the United States, British officials in the republics found that they could often shape the other Allied blacklists. The long experience of men such as Chalkley, Mackie, and Tower in Argentina, Atlee and Peel in Brazil, and Innes in Uruguay gave them significant voices in meetings with their Allied counterparts. In Argentina, Tower was considered until at least August 1918 as the primary intermediary between his US colleague, with whom Tower decided on recommendations for the blacklists, and their French and Italian colleagues, who had long followed Tower's lead.

At the same time, in April 1918, the British Chamber of Commerce in Argentina similarly internationalized their war. In Buenos Aires, the British Chamber created an Inter Ally Committee (IAC) to fashion new Allied white and black lists.[87] In June 1918, the FTD called for the resulting Allied list 'A' (which initially followed the ones drawn up by the British Chamber's Sectional committees) to be turned into an official white list, and lists 'B' and 'C' to be considered as an 'unpublished' but broadly circulated black list.[88]

For the British businessmen in South America, the relabeling of these lists magnified their powers. The Council hoped that the existence of the new committee would deflect from the British some of the public opprobrium about the commercial war.[89] They also expected to be able to circulate the various lists on a much broader basis, and thereby persuade more people in Argentina to abide by the war against Germans. The experiences of British Chambers of Commerce in prosecuting the economic war gave them an importance to the Allied war effort beyond that of the other Allied business communities.[90] The relationship of the British Chamber to the other Allies mirrored that that of Tower to his Allied colleagues. The IAC in many ways became a rubber stamp for the decisions made by the sectional trade committees of the British Chamber of Commerce. Respect for the British experience in the war against the local enemy led to the naming of Hope Gibson as IAC president and Powell-Jones as its secretary.[91] Rarely were the recommendations of the British Chamber "seriously challenged" by other members of the IAC.[92] By eliciting the support of the other Allies, the British trade warriors significantly expanded the scope of their war, leading untold numbers of merchants representing a broad variety of nationalities to adhere to it.

But despite the success of the British in broadening their new economic war, the internationalization of the lists had a downside for Britons in Buenos Aires. Their long-time hopes for the creation of a British nationalist trade system in Argentina could not easily coexist with this drive for increased unity between the Allies. Any preferences for British businessmen would leave the British government open to criticism from the Allies that their own traders were being discriminated against. Thus, as the Hardware and Machinery Committee complained despondently in August 1918, there remained no sign that the British government would ever start favoring British firms over others when issuing export licenses or space on ships from United Kingdom ports.[93]

The official character of the eventual white list also necessitated that things were defined in a far more (for lack of a better term) black or white manner than ever before. In reviewing the activities of the Swedish grain exporting firm Brander Bergstrom & Co. in November 1918, the FTD asked Tower to get the Allies to decide whether the company should be placed either on the Enemy Trading List, or on the White List.[94] By the end of 1918, there was no recognition of any middle ground between enemies and allies. Exporters in the United Kingdom had to make no discrimination between truly British companies and those, like Brander Bergstrom, which were highly suspect, yet which pledged that they did not trade with Germans.

British officials both in London and in South America had hoped to continue to dominate the Allied war against German trade.[95] Throughout 1918, British trade warriors in South America remained angry at the United States. Although the United States recognized the validity of the Statutory List policy as an act of war, they only warily implemented similar measures. This official US attitude, nurtured by a mistrust of British intentions and a desire to reap the spoils of war for themselves, diminished the ability of Britain to conduct its commercial war in South America.

Reinforcing the war effort: the de Bunsen mission

The result was a tremendous swell of dissatisfaction among British trade warriors with the FTD's leadership in the war. The ability of firms on the Statutory List to maintain their operations in new ways led some British merchants to begin acting in a manner that could be seen as opposing the spirit of the Statutory List policy.[96] In part, it was a failure of the FTD to sufficiently control the flow of trade from Britain: "There is no knowing what licenses are now being granted by the FTD!" exclaimed one Admiralty official in October 1918.[97] Some charged that the FTD had not sufficiently pressured certain UK-based businesses to repudiate and break all of their contacts with Germans. In particular, trade war hawks continued to mistrust the British banks. As patriotism demanded, the local managers of the London and River Plate Bank and the London & Brazilian Bank aided the British Legations, Consulates, and Chambers of Commerce, supplying information on the creditworthiness (and thus the commercial importance) of suspect companies. The historian of these British banks notes accurately that the staff of these banks was depleted tremendously as men volunteered for the British army, and claims that the remaining staff generally worked to curtail their transactions with German banks and with companies on the Statutory List.[98] Yet the British banks remained highly suspect in the eyes of other British businessmen. When Harry Scott of the London and River Plate Bank resisted a proposal that all British companies refuse to accept any cheques on German banks, he provoked a general outcry from Chamber members, who demanded and received an even more stringent policy.[99] Bankers were left out in the cold when important decisions were made by their local compatriots. In the spring of 1918, the manager of one of the British banks in Rosario complained to the British Consul that a sub-committee of Rosario's British Chamber of Commerce had been meeting in secret, outside of the purview of the British bankers, and had placed firms on local blacklists for reasons "which are difficult to understand."[100] British banks remained out of the inner circle of the economic warriors.

Such divisions within the British communities were not fully smoothed over by the FTD. It would be difficult to charge that the department had lost the will to attack Germans in South America. In May 1918, the FTD sent Sir Maurice de Bunsen, a life-long Foreign Service official and diplomat, to South America in a high profile mission. A number of historians have argued that the main purpose of de Bunsen's journey was to ensure that the United States dollar would not replace the British pound as the dominant medium of trade and investment on the continent.[101] Belying this analysis, de Bunsen's personal diaries and letters illuminate that his primary goal was to increase the effectiveness of the economic war. When Foreign Secretary Balfour asked the Cabinet to allow de Bunsen to offer to the presidents of Brazil, Argentina, and Chile, an augmentation of their diplomatic relations from the envoy to the ambassadorial level, Balfour explained that this would demonstrate the British "determination not to lose our political and economic position in Latin America, but rather to develop it still further, and to protect it against German competition after the war."[102]

In South America, crippling Germans remained the paramount concern. De Bunsen's meetings in the republics centered on issues relating to the Statutory List. De Bunsen spent much of his time "bucking up" the British communities in South America, "who have felt rather neglected and cut off from home, though playing up most splendidly in the war."[103] This meant, in part, appearing at dinners and other functions to commend their efforts in prosecuting the trade war, as he and his entourage looked to cement the wartime linkages of the British government to these British businessmen.[104] De Bunsen hoped to prove that the British government truly wanted to satisfy the needs of these Britons. "I make them really my first object after doing the official things," he wrote to his wife, "and it is touching to hear their acknowledgments and how they seek every opportunity of a few words more."[105] "I think the real good we do is by seeing so much of the British Chambers of Commerce and colonies generally."[106] He delivered a message to each Chamber, approved by the King, commending the way that Englishmen in South America were working to build "the collective organized effort now necessary to preserve our place in the world."[107] And the results of such meetings appeared to be more than just breeding goodwill. De Bunsen's discussions with the Chamber in Buenos Aires led to a requested memorandum from the Chamber's secretary, Powell-Jones, detailing suggestions for reorganizing commercial intelligence efforts in London.[108] De Bunsen believed that these British commercial warriors should be rewarded for their war efforts.

De Bunsen's positive attitude to the British expatriate business communities in general contrasted sharply with the refusal of his mission to spend any of its time with British bankers. "I can't make out what they are here for," wrote James Dey of the London and River Plate Bank in Buenos Aires to his superiors in London. Follett Holt, the mission's representative from the newly formed DOT, did not even take the time to go personally to the bank and present a letter he had brought from London.[109] All the while, Follett Holt, A.C. Kerr of the FTD, and W.S. Barclay (who, de Bunsen declared, was the "real brains of the mission" and who had recently stepped down from a top post in the FBI) focused their energies on hashing out the workings of British 'Trading with the Enemy' laws with the British Chambers of Commerce at each stop on the continent-wide tour.[110]

In this respect, the mission's efforts in Chile were particularly important. There the British community was more divided than elsewhere in South

America over the British economic offensive. In Valparaiso, a group of particularly conservative British merchants doubted that combining themselves into a Chamber of Commerce would be useful, and the eventual creation of a Chamber in July 1917 was due only to the assiduous efforts of British Consul-General Maclean.[111] Many Anglo-Chilean businessmen, following Archibald Williamson (MP) of Williamson Balfour & Co., focused pessimistically on ways that the Statutory List hurt the British position in Chile. Rather than looking for ways to augment their links to their home country, some of these instead followed the practice of Statutory Listed companies by looking during the war to US suppliers.[112] Yet, at the same time, other Britons in Valparaiso engaged in the same blacklist-building procedures as their compatriots in Buenos Aires and Rio de Janeiro, all the while vociferously denouncing their less patriotic British neighbors. De Bunsen was certain that his mission succeeded in calming this internecine feud. Particularly through the efforts of Allen Kerr to mediate between these economic war hawks and doves in Chile, the mission "did something in the way of pouring oil on troubled waters."[113] In Chile as elsewhere on this South American tour, the de Bunsen mission focused steadily on ways to augment the trade war.

Despite the evident appeal of patriotism, it remained obvious that some Britons were far more hawkish than others when it came to the trade war. Perhaps, in the end, this mitigated the success of the British mission, which after all rested on maximizing national pride and unity. On top of the other problems, such internal difficulties gave rise to pessimism among those in South America who identified themselves as British and who once had high hopes for the commercial war against their German competitors.

British textiles and the Turkish connection

The textile trade provides an ideal case study of the wide variety of difficulties faced by Britain in their economic war. The ability of Statutory Listed firms to receive fabric and clothing from overseas constantly perplexed British trade warriors in Argentina throughout 1919. Many blamed it on Turkish traders: "Levantines of every denomination, Mohammedan, Christian, Jewish," whose numbers mushroomed after the war began.[114] In 1913, the Textile Committee of the British Chamber of Commerce in Buenos Aires estimated that Turkish entrepreneurs imported £260,000-worth of cotton goods from Britain, controlling a mere 8 percent of the imports from the United Kingdom. In 1917, they received £1,167,000, or 32 percent of all British imports. In December 1916, the British Chamber of Commerce found at least 152 Turkish firms that had imported textiles from the United Kingdom over the course of the year, and 55 others would have done so had they been able to obtain credit. Most of these firms were one-person shops, existing in name only, and working solely as intermediaries for textile and clothing firms on the Statutory List.

Although the Ottoman empire sided with Germany during the war, and "undoubtedly there are some with pro-German sympathies," explained the Textile Committee of the British Chamber of Commerce, "perhaps the majority care little one way or the other so long as they can make money."[115] The stereotypical Turkish trader, in British eyes, had very little capital and willingly worked for very little profit, using cash to purchase goods and then selling them quickly to firms on the Statutory List.[116] In British eyes, the Turk supported himself solely with the commissions he charged as intermediary between the importer and those on the Statutory List. "The Turkish importer is a man of little education and less morality, and has no particular desire to maintain British goods and will transfer trade to other countries without hesitation," explained the British textile merchants. "He will, by various sharp practices, lower the prestige of British goods."[117]

In the hope of of curtailing imports from Britain by these Turkish firms, the British Chamber of Commerce in March 1917 advocated a system allowing exporters in Britain to send goods only to firms approved by them and by Consul-General Mackie.[118] From the heart of Great Britain's textile manufacturing region, the Manchester and Bradford Chambers of Commerce expressed support for the proposed policy. But it became apparent that the FTD favored granting general guarantees to importers in South America, rather than issuing approvals on a shipment-by-shipment basis. Turkish firms with general guarantees could purchase unlimited amounts of any available textiles directly from the United Kingdom. British merchants in South America demanded, instead, a system favoring themselves. Scarce British-made goods should be sold purely through British merchants, they argued. By the start of 1918, the textile committee of the British Chamber of Commerce in Buenos Aires grew increasingly exasperated at the failure of British authorities to stop shipments to the Turkish firms. There already existed at least one hundred respectable British, Allied and neutral firms that could take up this business. Tower agreed with the textile committee as to "the unhealthiness of the trade" conducted by the Turkish merchants.[119]

Initially, the FTD reacted defensively, saying that the British merchants of Buenos Aires had obviously gained an "erroneous impression" of the efficacy of British government measures to limit the leakage of textiles to firms on the Statutory List.[120] But soon the FTD threw its support behind a more stringent system that would closely regulate the flow of goods from Manchester. The plan, devised in Buenos Aires by Commercial Attaché Chalkley, allowed Turkish firms to receive goods from Britain only through a single British company, Moore & Tudor. Turkish business had to open their books to the British firm, and answer a questionnaire regarding their partners, banking references, types of trade, main customers, and the value of goods they imported from the United Kingdom each year since 1913. The Turkish firms had to then sign guarantees not to trade any goods to firms on the Statutory List, nor to re-export the merchandise to another country without the consent of Moore & Tudor.[121] The Manchester Chamber of Commerce advised that such a system might work.[122] But British traders in Buenos Aires were not pleased. Not only would the system allow Turkish businesses to continue to receive goods from Manchester, but there were also reports that the Manchester exporters had offered credits to some of these Turkish importers to facilitate the trade. The Textile Committee alarmingly reported, at the end of June, that orders amounting to £840,000 had passed through Moore & Tudor in only the previous two months.[123]

What the British textile merchants in Argentina, and their fellow trade warriors, really wanted was a system forcing United Kingdom producers to prefer deals with the British businessmen in Argentina.[124] "Loss of the Turkish trade would certainly be in the best interests of British trade," explained J.K. Cassels of the importer Ashworth & Co., the chairman of the Textile Committee, in August.[125] Yet it was impossible to place Turkish firms en masse on the Undesirables List or on one of the restricted lists 'B' or 'C'.[126] The United States would never go along with it, their textile manufacturers increasingly pleased to find easy access to a new market.[127] Turkish importers increasingly shipped goods from the United States by utilizing credits easily procured from the newly established US banks.[128] In October 1918, in an astonishing testimony to the continuation of much international trade during the First World War, the over-importing of textiles due largely to Turkish trading contributed to a collapse of local prices.[129] Of course, this price drop only made it more likely that desperate Turkish traders might sell more goods to German firms on the Statutory List.

After the guns were silenced in Europe in November, Sir Reginald Tower advised the FTD to rescind all the restrictions that had been placed on Turkish people trading with the United Kingdom.[130] Controlling these merchants was a hopeless cause, and Tower reasonably threw up his hands in recognition of the utter failure of Britain's war against these intermediaries. The Turkish textile merchants provide a telling example of the ways that new business practices, and a new group of businessmen, could help Statutory Listed firms to repel British attacks.

Targeting a slippery "Octopus": The pivotal case of Bunge & Born

Rolling up Bunge & Born and the rest of the Big Four grain exporters ranked as probably the primary goal of the British trade war in South America.

Argentine farmers called Bunge & Born – a massive, transnational trading conglomerate – "the Octopus," its tentacles reaching through all steps in the trade. In Tower's eyes, this Belgian firm was a front for pro-German Jews, led by Alfredo Hirsch, one of the wealthiest Germans in Buenos Aires. The company's massive shipments of wheat to Germany through the northern European neutrals aggravated British blockaders throughout 1915 and were an important reason for the imposition of rationing agreements on the Scandinavian countries.[131]

After the first Statutory List was published in March 1916, the company initially panicked. Newspapers reported rumors that Bunge & Born would fire all of its German employees.[132] The firm's lawyer, R.C. Aldao, came to the legation to ask Tower if the company could be removed from the list if it dismissed Hirsch. But their self-defense soon grew cannier. In April, another lawyer explained that both George Born and Ernest Bunge were Belgians, who, through no fault of their own, found themselves living in German-occupied Antwerp. This lawyer also argued that Hirsch had proven his allegiances when he founded the Belgian Relief Commission in Argentina, that the company did not sell goods to enemies of Britain, and that it had dismissed all of its German employees.[133] But Tower stood unmoved. Still buoyed by his hopes for the new war, and recognizing that Bunge & Born was a fundamentally pro-German company in personnel, activities, and intents, he told their lawyers that even "documentary proof of death-bed repentance" would not lead British authorities to take the firm off the Statutory List.[134] By September 1916, Tower optimistically reported to the FTD that the company was really hurting.[135]

But Tower also recognized that Britain faced some difficulties in finishing off the grain giant. Initially, an argument over whether Bunge & Born was Belgian split the Allies over how to treat the firm, with the Belgian minister in Argentina resisting attempts to destroy the grain trading monolith. The Belgian Minister to Argentina worked to "rehabilitate" the firm by advocating plans to eject the "German element" from the company. Tower refused to back down, even though in February 1917 the Belgians published a blacklist that was identical to the British one, other than in the omission of Bunge & Born. In a country where Belgian trade had never been dominant, Tower could easily ignore his Allied counterpart, Belgian Minister Mélot, whose home country was occupied.

Tower found that a more difficult problem in attacking Bunge & Born was the variety of guises utilized by the company. Like other listed companies, Bunge & Born sent some of its exports through cloaks, at least half a dozen of whom eventually reached the Statutory List themselves. Bunge & Born shifted some operations into new companies, such as the Sociedad Financiera e Industrial SudAmericana, formed in August 1915 by Hirsch and other managers of Bunge & Born. Some real estate holdings were spun off into a firm called La Inmobiliaria, a company that similarly had at least nominally existed earlier, but which did not begin active operations until March 1916. La Inmobiliaria entered the Statutory List three months later. Another company, the Société Anonyme des Minoteries et d'Elevateurs a Grains, was denounced by local Britons as being owned by Bunge & Born. But after Hirsch resigned from his managing position at that company, and Tower failed to exhume conclusive proof that the company's shares were held by any of the directors of Bunge & Born, Tower decided that he could not recommend the firm for the Statutory List.[136] Likewise, the trade of a number of farms and cattle ranches owned by Bunge & Born or Alfredo Hirsch were "purely local in character," and thus untouchable by the Statutory List regulations that focused on foreign trade.[137]

The multiplicity of Bunge & Born's guises made it a difficult target. The lumbering Statutory List always seemed months behind. Tower recommended Pels & Lakatos, a company of ex-employees of Bunge & Born, for the Statutory List on 5 January 1917, but the company was not listed until 11 May.[138] In Argentina, Tower proved that Jorge Engelhard imported specialized milling machinery from Switzerland through an Italian in Argentina, Antonio Battilana, who, on receipt, was instructed to transfer it to Bunge & Born.[139] Engelhard entered the Statutory List, but only three months later, far too late for those conducting the rationing of Swiss exports to stop the shipment.

Tower hoped the constructive war would succeed, with British grain firms taking Bunge & Born's place. But a disappointed Tower found himself scolding British firms for being more interested in sparring among themselves than cooperating for their mutual benefit. Within days of the publication of the first Statutory List in March 1916, the British company Sanday & Co. claimed that purchases of huge quantities of grain by a compatriot, Ross Smyth & Co., had caused a rise in prices, hurting both Argentine wheat on the world market and Sanday's position within Argentina. The British Chamber of Commerce supported this claim that prices were artificially high owing to such purchases, which they assumed, correctly, were financed by the British government. Tower grew annoyed both at the bickering British grain firms, and at the British government for not informing him that they were purchasing grain through Smyth & Co. at prescribed, above-market rates.[140] Obviously, the FTD had not done enough to coordinate the British government to use its strengths, such as its role as the main purchaser of a prime Argentine product, behind a policy that would aid the economic war.

Perhaps most shockingly, instances continually arose of even reliable, allied grain exporters accidentally buying stocks of grain from Bunge & Born. Tower rounded up the Allied grain houses, and with assistance from Chalkley and Mackie, representatives of the six main Allied houses set up a 'disapproved list' of firms thought to be intermediaries locally for Bunge & Born. Most British people blamed their failure to live up to enemy trade laws on the way that local futures markets operated.[141] Yet they were split over whether to stop their own operations there. Ross Smyth & Co., the main purchaser of grain on behalf of the British government, opposed any ban. Tensions among the British grain brokers grew when Sanday & Co. accused Dreyfus & Co., a French firm, of dealing with Bunge & Born.[142]

But soon after, in March 1917, Sanday & Co. itself received 1,800 tons of oats from Bunge & Born. It had arrived in Sanday's hands very indirectly. They made a contract with the Buenos Aires firm Mellado & Bridger for the grain to be delivered in Bahia Blanca. Mellado & Bridger bought the grain from Mauricio Zuckerberg in a contract stamped 'allied'. Zuckerberg bought the grain in the option market, from J.P. Baas Jr, who, as it turned out, was actually just a straw man for Bunge & Born. When Sanday & Co. discovered the chain of exchanges, they refused to take the shipment, but Zuckerberg appealed to the Cereal Exchange. The board of the Exchange, refusing to recognize the significance of any "allied" stamp on a contract, ruled that Sanday must accept the oats. Tower relented and allowed Sanday to do so.[143] The options markets, in both Buenos Aires and Rosario, allowed Bunge & Born a tangled mass of transactions through which they could, in effect, launder their grain. Even attentive Allied grain firms caught themselves purchasing in the options market oats or wheat that had at one time been owned by Statutory Listed firms. Only after options trading was temporarily suspended by the Argentine government in November 1917 did Allied firms announce their withdrawal from the market.[144]

By that time, the British government had already lost its faith in the ability of British firms in Argentina to sort out their differences. The Royal Commission on Wheat Supplies, the buying agency for all wheat coming into Britain, undertook a massive amount of business in Argentina, purchasing more than 9 million tons of cereals from its creation in October 1916 until the end of the war. Since late in 1916, the Wheat Commission initially made purchases in Argentina through two British controlled cereal firms. But after a year, the Commission decided that the British firms were not capable of making the massive purchases necessary during the 1917–18 season and appointed a Wheat Commissioner in Argentina.

Highlighting once again the patriotism of local Britons, Wheat Commission staffers in Argentina were mostly unpaid volunteers, particularly the wives of British businessmen who undertook the clerical work. The Commission purchased the 1917–1918 crop by converting eight Allied cereal firms into buying agencies, allowing them to make some profit from fixed allowances and brokerage fees, while the price offered by the Commission was made known to farmers and thus could not be manipulated for the profit of the middlemen. During that season, the Wheat Commission purchased 45 percent of the total Argentine wheat crop, nearly 12 million quarters (units of 480 lbs) out of the total 26.7 million quarter Argentine crop.[145]

Yet despite the overwhelming presence of the Wheat Commission in local markets, Statutory Listed firms like Bunge & Born still operated. Bunge & Born continued to grant credit to farmers, to sell and buy grain through the options markets of Rosario and Buenos Aires, to ship abroad through cloaks, and to maintain its tremendous importance within domestic markets and marketplaces in the region like Brazil. The Wheat Commission attempted to purchase grain exclusively from non-blacklisted firms, but it was difficult to determine whether a given firm was a cover for one of the blacklisted giants, or even whether one of the Allied firms had intentionally, or inadvertently, bought its grain from a Statutory Listed firm.

With the failure of the Statutory List to shut down the cloaks, intermediaries, and subsidiaries of Bunge & Born, other locally-directed measures against the enemy grain dealer intensified. One way was to attempt to control the trade in jute bags. The Argentine cereal trade was still not done in bulk, with grain elevators, but rather in jute bags. Most raw jute came from India and was thus controlled by Britain. As Britain was the primary purchaser of Argentine grain, they also commanded the thriving market in used bags. British intervention in the £7.5 million Argentine jute market was described as close to philanthropy in a post-war Wheat Commission report, claiming that by 1918 it sold bags directly to farmers at half the previous market rate. The profits were reinvested in wheat purchases for the United Kingdom. The Wheat Commission claimed that only in rare cases could they not get in contact with the wheat producers, who instead bought from middlemen at higher prices.[146] Command over jute had actually begun in early 1916, when Tower appointed a Jute Committee, chaired by J.K. Cassels of the textile importer Ashworth & Co., to compile an approved list of jute importers.[147] Companies who wanted to enter the approved list often came calling at the Legation – one more example of how wartime duties increasingly taxed Tower's staff.[148] But despite their efforts throughout 1917, much jute had leaked to Statutory Listed firms.

In January 1918, in a further measure designed by Tower to prove to the two hundred businesses in Argentina that dealt in raw jute and jute bags the "uncompromising attitude of H[is] M[ajesty's] G[overnment] in regard to trade with the enemy," the Jute Committee made inclusion in the list of approved importers in Buenos Aires contingent on the firm signing a guarantee that they would abstain "from all dealings *whatsoever* with (Statutory) listed firms." Even most bag traders not implicated in trade with Germans would be initially placed on list 'B', with the Consul-General issuing individual certificates for each of their transactions. Only those few placed on list 'A' would be given an unlimited license to receive jute from British sources. The division of the approved list into two classes would not be made public, but firms on list 'B' would be sent letters informing them of the need to apply for such certificates.[149] Wheat Commissioner Herbert Gibson then took over all imports of raw jute (which came from India) and set up controls over the resale of used bags.[150]

Yet jute kept leaking to undesirable firms like Bunge & Born. In January 1918, Bunge & Born rubbed British noses in its achievement by mailing a circular to many firms informing them of the 750,000 new bags that their own factory had produced, and advertising their plans to sell many of these on the open market, thus flaunting British attempts at control. "If I had fifty additional clerks in His Majesty's Legation I could not hope to give sufficient time to investigate each case," lamented the British minister.[151] Tower learned how one of Bunge & Born's employees purchased 500 bales of jute from a bag factory owner named Manuel Fuente, who approached an intermediary named Casteran, who arranged with a broker to purchase jute from an approved British importer, Hardcastle & Co. via a legitimate dealer, Portalis & Co. All steps of the transaction were paid for in cash. Tower wanted all of the men involved in this convoluted chain to be placed on the Statutory List, and he publicized his discovery of the plot in hopes of having "a deterrent effect on others desire to act in a similar fashion." However, only one of the firms was ever placed on the list, and Tower did not truly believe any longer that blacklisting would do much to stop such transactions. One of the companies involved, Portalis & Co., was headed by Victor Negri, a direc- tor of the British quebracho firm Forestal & Co. who Tower knew well. Undoubtedly, Negri would not have made such a transaction if he had known about it, Tower surmised, but the steps in sending the jute between Hardcastle and Bunge involved at least five intermediaries, none of whom necessarily knew the final destination of the goods. For Tower, the case was "illustrative of what is doubtless going on all through the country and which seems unavoidable."[152]

And after further investigation, the story of this jute only became more complicated. Over the course of the next few months, Tower interrogated a number of the participants, and reviewed an array of documents. In August he proved that Juan Casteran had received letters from Bunge & Born that held them responsible for payment to Fuente. Casteran obviously knew he was delivering British goods to enemy firms, and should be placed on the Statutory List. But this man was never blacklisted. In November, Tower related the heated criticism that he was taking from both British businessmen and the Italian press for the way the situation was handled. The British Chamber of Commerce continued to demand that all the companies involved be placed on the Statutory List, for fear that to do otherwise would give the impression locally that any guarantees that companies sign with Britain "may be broken with impunity." The Italian newspaper *L'Italia del Popolo* asked why the British jute controllers had not done anything about Portalis. The paper had discovered that Casteran & Co. had in fact been a virtual subsidiary of Portalis and was forbidden to enter into trades of over $1,000 without Portalis's approval. The amount of jute that had been traded was worth at least £70,000, and thus Portalis, and the supposed ally Victor Negri, had probably known about the trade with Bunge & Born.

On top of this, the Briton involved in the transaction, P.A. Hardcastle, should have known better. Tower called Hardcastle in for a harsh lecture, explaining that as neither Portalis nor Casteran were bag manufacturers, Hardcastle should never have sold them so much raw jute.[153] Did Hardcastle know what he was doing in working against his country's war? Tower doubted he could ever find the truth.[154]

On top of all the other difficulties in uncovering the surreptitious dealings of Bunge & Born, throughout 1918, Tower continued to find himself harassed by efforts to rehabilitate the firm, to gain its removal from the Statutory List. By then, Belgian Minister Mélot had accepted Tower's long-held assertion that a company so dominated by Alfred Hirsch could never be recognized as anything but pro-German. But in 1918 it turned out that Bunge & Born had other influential supporters. In August, the US Commercial Attaché, Robert Barrett, visited the British Legation, where he suggested to Tower that it was in the interest of the Allies to get the company on their side after the war. Barrett suggested that a Belgian man, Casimir de Bruyn, be approved as the new manager of a reconstituted Bunge & Born. Tower saw through the scheme. It had been suggested to Barrett by Hirsch's lawyer, Julio Garcia, and was also being propelled forward by the desires of US Chargé d'Affaires Robbins, who was married to de Bruyn's daughter.

Tower knew that de Bruyn presently ran the "Molinos Harineros y Elevadores de Grano," a supposedly Belgian mill that the British Wheat Commission had purchased grain from in 1917, but which was increasingly suspected of operating in secret accord with Bunge & Born.[155] He also noted that Barrett's proposal to rehabilitate Bunge & Born would still allow Hirsch to own a third of the capital of the new company. Tower could never agree to such terms.[156] Like many other aspects of the war, the issue of Bunge & Born further enhanced the mistrust that Tower and other Britons felt towards their supposed American allies.

Until the end of 1918, Bunge & Born continued to use cloaks and shift resources to evade British scrutiny. In February 1918, one British grain firm listed at least eleven individuals and companies in Argentina that helped Bunge & Born to maintain its highly lucrative general merchant trade with Brazil.[157] The company found new ways to invest its capital, including granting short-term loans to the Argentine government.[158] "It is impossible to exaggerate the serious consequences of that organization [Bunge & Born] remaining intact," fretted Tower in September 1918.[159] Yet intact it stayed. In June 1918, an intercepted letter written by one of Bunge & Born's competitors to a correspondent in Rotterdam reaffirmed the continued inestimable importance of Bunge & Born across the grain-growing pampas. Many farmers, unable to stand on their own financially, remained indebted to Bunge & Born through the end of the war.[160] Britain completely failed to root out and destroy Bunge & Born, their prime target. Britain also failed to nurture British traders as adequate replacements for the German firm. From the start of the trade war through the signing of the armistice, Tower and other trade warriors found it impossible to sink their claws into "the Octopus."

Conclusion

In waging war against German business in South America, the British faced myriad difficulties. Even as they installed ever more stringent restrictions upon their enemies throughout 1918, their targets found new ways around the British restrictions. The agency in control of the economic war, the FTD, proved incapable of keeping up with the ever-changing situation in South America. Many of the failures of the British commercial war might have been alleviated had the United States adopted the measures designed by the British. The US government and businessmen resisted this, reasonably seeing their own position in South America as much in competition against the British as against the Germans. As far as the war in South America was concerned, the Anglo-American alliance was a fiction.

Despite increasing pessimism and some divisiveness about the trade war, through the signing of the armistice on 11 November 1918, most British people in Argentina maintained complete, even fanatical, support for all measures against the Germans. Many of these partisans continued working in their Sectional Trade Committees on new ways to intensify the war. One might argue that by creating the IAC, the British war was just in the last months of 1918 reaching its peak, as enlisting European allies in the creation of blacklists and boycotts created new disruptions to local trade. They claimed some successes in their attacks on German business. The records are scantier for the other South American republics, and it is unlikely that the British communities in countries like Brazil and Uruguay were as hyperactive as those in Buenos Aires. But in early 1918 the idea of the restricted lists 'A', 'B', and 'C' spread to include businesses across the continent. And many Britons beyond those in Buenos Aires were certainly involved in the war. In Brazil, British Minister Peel enlisted the publisher of the weekly English language paper, *Wileman's Brazilian Review*, to regularly print the Statutory List, and by early 1918 that publisher was working for Peel to examine the manifests of the Lloyd Brazileiro Steamship Company to ensure that the line was observing blacklisting regulations.[161]

Among the letters preserved from the files of Innes's legation are a number that he received from a variety of informants in Montevideo, both known and anonymous. A note signed simply "An Englishman" informed the British minister that the Statutory Listed company Staudt & Co. was using the name Giovanni Sassoli as a cloak in Montevideo.[162] Other Anglo-Uruguayan efforts were more organized. In February 1917, the British Chamber of Commerce in Uruguay asked for a grant to cover the $100 it was spending each month to assist the FTD.[163] Through 1918, in an attempt to ferret out cloaks, Innes labored to examine the names on shipping manifests telegraphed from the British Consul-General in New York, assisted by the local branch of the London and River Plate Bank.[164] He also supported a variety of efforts by local British companies to improve the availability of British goods, particularly in trades like grain machinery and scientific instruments, which had hitherto been supplied solely by Germany.[165] Innes's efforts were prodigious. In February 1918, Peek Bros & Winch, Ltd, a London tea exporter, wrote to him saying that they were unable to obtain from the government any names of suitable agents in Uruguay. He replied in a series of letters, successfully setting up the London business with an acceptable local Briton.[166] Diplomats and the local British communities worked hand in hand throughout 1918 to fight both the destructive and constructive wars, not just in Argentina, but across South America.

At their peak, Britain's trade warriors openly interfered with the domestic markets of the South American republics, looking to control and redirect trade to further their agenda of destroying German business and replacing it with British. The textile trade exemplifies the willingness of the British government to completely overturn basic tenets of the free trade regime they had long supported in South America. If interfering in the flow of trade in another country is imperialism, then this was an imperialist moment for Britain, with imperialist intentions.

But by the end of 1918, these were exposed as mere imperialist pretensions. It appeared that there was nothing that Britain could truly do to ensure the dissolution of many German companies in South America. The resources of enemy firms were too large and too diversified between various economic sectors and among various republics. German merchants kept business going by tapping into the vibrant, ever-changing local markets of the bustling, cosmopolitan cities like Rio de Janeiro, Montevideo, and Buenos Aires. And even the many German businesses that had been negatively affected by British measures remained far from liquidation.

Sir Reginald Tower received reports in June 1918 that the two German banks in Buenos Aires conducted virtually no international business, and had lost most of their allied and neutral clients, because Allied banks refused to accept cheques drawn on the German banks. The banks were making no money. But they were not losing money either. Tower reported to the FTD that both the Banco Germánico and Banco Alemán remained quite solvent, holding large cash reserves in the accounts of German clients, and maintaining the ability to restart their international business whenever cable and mail traffic was reopened.[167] These German banks were not alone in placing themselves, during the war, into a stasis from which they could not be pushed by any British or Allied regulations. Only with help from local authorities might such German companies be successfully attacked. As shown in the next chapter, the governments of the South American republics reacted in a variety of ways to British overtures, as the British utilized both the carrot and the stick to try to get their way in a region that had long been regarded as a de facto part of the British world.

7

How the economic war shaped South American engagement in the World War

Perhaps the most important decision that any South American government could make between 1914 and 1918 was in its stance towards the European war. Not only did each republic have to decide between neutrality and a declaration of war, they also worked at defining exactly what neutrality or belligerency meant in practice. Argentina remained neutral throughout, Uruguay broke its relations with Germany without fully signing on to the Allied cause, while Brazil declared war against Germany. Historians have suggested that each government's stance towards the war was motivated by concern for their relationships with other American countries, by respect for the Allies – particularly for France – and by the impact of German U-boat warfare on South American shipping.[1] This chapter suggests instead that the British commercial war was perhaps the most crucial determinant in how each South American administration confronted the "world war." The decision of each country's leaders whether to join or remain neutral in the European war was integrally related to the war they lived through, the one fought in their countries by Britain against local *Deutschtum*.

Argentina

For Britain, the relationship with Argentina had long been its most important in Latin America. Since obtaining independence from Spain in the early nineteenth century, Argentina became a prime venue for British foreign investments and for British exports. As the historians Peter Cain and Antony Hopkins famously argue, the British had so penetrated Argentina's economy by the early twentieth century that Argentina should be described as the ultimate example of British informal imperialism, where de facto dominance proved preferable to the less lucrative direct control they wielded in Africa and Asia. Argentine leaders traditionally held a close relationship with Britain.

British economic warriors hoped that Argentina might join Britain in fighting the Great War against German imperialism. They believed that if

Argentina were to enter the war, Argentine authorities might liquidate the German companies that British economic warriors had targeted. Initially, of course, Argentina was not alone in staying out of the war. The United States notably refused to get involved until the German submarine war in February 1917 made American retaliation inevitable. Yet the United States was not the only country whose ships were indiscriminately sunk by U-boats. German torpedos sank a number of Argentine steamers during the war, one of many mistakes the Reich made in its often hamfisted treatment of the Argentine government. And yet, Argentina remained neutral.

Neutrality had not been a significant issue under President Victorino de la Plaza, as Germany refrained from attacking Argentine ships and the British economic war had not yet intensified. But things changed when Hipólito Yrigoyen and his Radical party came to power in October 1916. A modest-living man in a country accustomed to rule by a virtual aristocracy, his leadership gave the Radical party a moralizing, ethical, anti-corruption flavor. Yet the Radicals were far from being a revolutionary party, and despite the similarly spartan lifestyle, Yrigoyen was no Robespierre. His party was largely made up of middle-class interests rallying together other classes under a banner of patriotism, a "Tory democracy" according to the historian of Argentine radicalism, David Rock.[2] At times this meant he was allied with the old rural elite, but it also meant he could pander to the growing urban working classes increasingly inclined towards trade unionism, social-ism, and anarchism. This caused much fear among Britons in Buenos Aires and Rosario, where large British enterprises such as shipping lines and railroads employed many of the restive workers. In the eyes of the British government, Yrigoyen was reasonably classified as a mysterious man, an unknown factor.

It is impossible to determine whether Yrigoyen and the members of his government were ideologically anti-British. Some Britons believed that he was more anti-American than anything else, that he chafed more at the Monroe Doctrine than at the economic dominance of London.[3] His foreign minister claimed to Maurice de Bunsen that Argentina was "the most pro-British country in South America."[4] But it was always apparent that Yrigoyen recognized the opening in Argentina for an anti-British, anti-globalization politics.[5] Although at heart Yrigoyen may have accepted the existence of Argentine dependence upon Britain markets, at face value Yrigoyen's rheto-ric and actions marked, in the words of Joseph Tulchin, "a significant depar-ture in Argentine foreign policy," striking "an aggressive posture in relations with nations outside Latin America."[6]

This aggression appeared in Yrigoyen's stance toward British capital. The domination of Argentine railroads by British capital and management lent an anti-British aura to labor agitation and strikes that spontaneously erupted in July and August 1917. When lay-offs racked the British-owned Central Argentine Railway in Rosario, British managers faced actual physical confrontation with their unhappy workers, who destroyed train tracks and threatened their lives. British-owned businesses depended upon the goodwill of the police and the Argentine government for their protection, but Yrigoyen was slow to call in troops to quell the violent riots, and he sided with the workers in demanding concessions from the foreign owners.[7] However, he later reversed his stance towards railway strikers, coming down on the side of the owners and even calling out troops in February 1918. And it should be noted that Yrigoyen was hardly the first Argentine ruler to have a tense relationship with British railroads. Even as the oligarchic Argentine governments had supported their expansion since the 1860s, estanciero-led administrations feared railways' monopolization of transport and passed legislation regulating their activities. Most notably, after the Baring Crisis in 1890, an unhappy government dropped the whole system of profit guarantees that had propped up earlier investment.[8]

A far more consistent measure, throughout the First World War, of Yrigoyen's aggressiveness towards the outside world was, perhaps paradoxically, his ardent support for maintaining Argentina's neutrality. Many Britons hoped that the German submarine war in early 1917 would push Argentina to join the Allies, in which case "the advantages to our after-war trade with the Argentine of the present trend of events are obvious and considerable."[9] As the FTD noted, if Argentina or another South American country entered the war, German businesses could be simply sequestrated and sold off.[10] British officials at the highest levels consistently recognized the possible benefits of an Argentine alliance. In December 1917, Sir Edward Carson persuaded the War Cabinet to spend £20,000 on an unknown but undoubtedly spurious scheme, suggested by Admiral Hall of Naval Intelligence, in the hope that it would secure Argentine intervention in the war.[11]

Yet despite British cajoling and corruption, Argentina remained neutral. Yrigoyen accepted German reparations for sunken Argentine merchant ships, rather than using these as pretexts to join the war, like Brazil and the United States.[12] In September 1917, the United States released intercepted telegrams from the German minister in Buenos Aires, Count Luxburg. In his telegrams to Berlin, Luxburg pegged Foreign Minister Pueyrredón as "a notorious ass and an anglophile," and recommended that all Argentine ships leaving European ports should be "sunk without a trace," despite his earlier promise to Yrigoyen that no further Argentine ships would be attacked. Luxburg's telegrams led to the revocation of his diplomatic credentials and his ejection from the republic, but not even the ensuing uproar in the Congress for action against Germany and the smashing up of the Deutscher Klub by a pro-Allied mob could shake Yrigoyen's staunch neutrality.[13]

Many contemporary Britons, like the British Consul in Rosario, were certain "that it is enemy activity which is behind the pro-neutrality cry."[14] Tower particularly worried about the threats from German agents sabotaging food shipments and stirring up strikers. Historians have since downplayed the importance of such enemy agents provocateurs in influencing Yrigoyen's neutrality. Others, following dependency theories, focus on the structure of the economic relationships between Argentina and Britain, explaining that, in effect, Argentina remained neutral because it supposedly suited Great Britain. As the efforts of Carson show, this is patently false.

Argentine historians have followed another track, recognizing the link between the maintenance of Argentine neutrality and the ideologies of Argentine leaders. To Ricardo Weinmann, Argentine neutrality was the result of Yrigoyen's intense and stubborn nationalism and anti-imperialism, his unwillingness to bend to outside pressure.[15] In the eyes of Raimundo Siepe, Yrigoyen's neutrality was rooted in a principled pacifism that he would carry into post-war work at the League of Nations. Yrigoyen believed that only by maintaining neutrality could Argentina speak up for international rights and humanitarianism.[16]

By giving agency to Yrigoyen, these Argentine historians have certainly improved over the economic determinists. Yet in praising Yrigoyen's professed desires for peace or national power, they overlook another primary reason for maintenance of Argentine neutrality, namely the existence of the British economic war, which pushed Argentines away from Britain at the same time as ship sinking and Count Luxburg pushed Argentina away from Germany. The Statutory List was always despised by Argentines, who could little imagine joining a campaign they disliked. Most Argentines had, even before Yrigoyen's presidency, recognized the legality of the British commercial war. In a coherent summary of the generally accepted position, *La Nación* recognized that firms in Argentina had a right to conduct commerce with whomsoever they wished, and thus local British firms could follow the Statutory List.[17] Such "spontaneous collaboration" was not "an infringement of the jurisdiction" of Argentina, as such collaboration could not be overtly mandated by a British law.

Yet the Statutory List obviously did intrude on Argentine life, and the Argentine government always opposed it. De la Plaza's conservative administration at the start of the British trade war was to most appearances pro-British, yet even they clandestinely sponsored attacks on the British economic campaign. In August 1916 Foreign Minister José Luis Murature denied that the Argentine government had any influence over an anti-Statutory List bill that was introduced in the Chamber of Deputies by a pro-German parliamentarian. However, after the opposition Radical party took the reins of government, Murature admitted to Tower that he had personally helped to draft the bill.[18]

Compared with the acquiescence of the Conservative government to the existence of the Statutory List in early 1916, condemnations of the List increased in number and intensity under Yrigoyen.[19] Yrigoyen's unpredictability exacerbated the difficulties that Britons faced in waging their economic war, and appeasing him became a significant British goal that transformed the Statutory List. After he took over as Foreign Minister in early 1917, Honorio Pueyrredón, the 41-year-old lawyer and Radical party politician, proved a particularly pushy opponent in meetings where he sparred with Sir Reginald Tower, a formidable man known as the most serious and respectable member of the diplomatic corps. The issue of the Crespo brothers and the Hansa Mining Company proved particularly contentious after their blacklisting in February. Arturo Crespo, an Argentine lawyer, was placed on the Statutory List for acting as a cloak for Heinlein & Co., which received 2000 flat-irons from a British ship. When Crespo came to Tower to complain, his attitude was exceptionally casual, laughing that he was a free Argentine citizen and could trade with whom he pleased. But Eduardo Crespo, his brother, soon came to apologise, and Tower recommended dropping Arturo from the Statutory List – in his words, it was not worth provoking the resentment of more Argentine lawyers.

But Eduardo, as president of the newly blacklisted Hansa Mining Company, had his own bone to pick with Tower. When Tower showed him proof that Hansa had three German directors, and that they sold wolfram and tungsten to Primos Chemical Co. of Pennsylvania, a known pro-German firm on the Statutory List for the United States, Crespo was indignant. He met with Pueyrredón, who summoned Tower to issue a protest. Pueyrredón worried that the mine, which employed 1,500 people, might be crushed by its inclusion on the Statutory List. Tower retorted that it was obviously German. A flurry of meetings with Crespo over the next few days led Tower back to Pueyrredón, who again asked Tower to remove the mine from the Statutory List, even though it was obviously mostly owned by German capital and directed by Germans. Tower wrote to the FTD with his advice. Hansa was obviously German, but "from my point of view, it would obviously make my position here easier and more agreeable" if Hansa were dropped from the Statutory List. Tower recognized that the question was one of general principle: "Is the representation of the Argentine Government of sufficient weight to induce HM Government to remove the name from the Statutory List, in the particular case of an Argentine national industry being concerned?"[20] When Crespo found that Tower's efforts were not working, he persuaded the Argentine Legation in London to support the company's case to the British government.[21] Although Hansa was not taken off the Statutory List until April 1919, the British government in August 1917 suspended the prohibition on British subjects trading with the company, acknowledging their own desire to gain wolfram ore for the war effort and the need expressed by Pueyrredón to maintain employment for the hundreds of mine workers.[22]

Inevitably, Yrigoyen's reticence to give in to the warring Britons bled into his treatment of other aspects of the Argentine-British relationship. The animosity between Argentine and British officials engendered by the British economic war proved to be a significant undercurrent in the saga of wheat purchasing, which embroiled Anglo-Argentine relations throughout Yrigoyen's administration. Wheat gave Argentina significant strategic importance to Great Britain.[23] Since agricultural protectionism had been jettisoned by the repeal of the Corn Laws in 1846, British consumers relied on foreign produced grains. When Argentina became a large-scale producer around 1900, Britain began to consume an ever-greater amount of wheat and corn from the River Plate. At the same time, the advent of freezing technology and improvements in livestock breeding allowed Argentina and Uruguay to become important exporters of beef and mutton, and Great Britain became their main purchaser. By 1914, the River Plate region had become an irreplaceable source of food for the United Kingdom. During the war, the British government needed to do whatever was necessary to ensure that these foods continued to flow into the United Kingdom.

Early on during Britain's war in Argentina, it appeared that the importance of Britain as a wheat consumer might be a source of leverage for Britain, helping to get Argentina to sell it on favorable terms or even to revoke its neutrality. In June 1916, the Argentine Minister of Agriculture, worried about a surplus of 2 million tons of unsold wheat, proposed that the British government purchase it through bankers and merchant houses in Buenos Aires, with payments to be made after the war.[24] "In view of the fact that there is no other apparent outlet for the crop," the War Office believed it could buy the grain at a low price.[25] The Treasury noted that such a purchase would be "extremely advantageous from the financial standpoint." Obtaining funds in Argentina would help exchange, which had gone against the United Kingdom owing to the tremendous rise in Britain's trade deficit with the republic. It would also conserve cash that otherwise would have been used to buy grain from the United States. But such purchases from Argentina would require longer journeys than comparable purchases from the United States, and therefore a less efficient use of limited freighter space. One remedy, the Treasury noted, would be for Argentina to requisition the German steamships that were being interned in their ports.[26] British officials began an unabashed effort to persuade Argentina to do so.[27]

A bounty of between twelve and nineteen German merchant ships, with a gross tonnage of at least 62,000 tons, had taken refuge in Argentine harbors at the start of the war rather than risk capture by the British navy on the high seas.[28] Various ministries in London drooled over these ships and schemed how to persuade Argentina to put them into use. The Board of Agriculture, which at that point conducted Britain's wheat purchases, agreed that if the Argentine government would use the German vessels, then British authorities would buy everything they could ship.[29] But Argentina believed that by requisitioning the ships, they would breach their neutrality, as Germany would consider the loss of the ships a virtual declaration of economic war by Argentina. Tower recognized that it was unlikely that President de la Plaza's government, so soon before a hotly contested election, would do anything so drastic.[30]

The Radicals under Yrigoyen who took office in October 1916 brought a stark change in the official stance toward Argentine grain. The first Foreign Minister, Carlos A. Becú, signaled at his first meeting with Tower that Argentina would no longer be willing to extend credits to Britain to finance British grain purchases.[31] The change of heart infuriated the British. The Royal Commission on Wheat Supplies proclaimed that any reluctance on the part of Argentina to grant financial facilities to Britain would be met with "a corresponding reluctance to provide the tonnage" necessary for Argentina's foreign trade.[32]

Yet the British lust for food quickly stifled their threats. Rumors had spread for weeks that Argentina might prohibit wheat exports for fear that the new crop was smaller than usual and would be needed for home consumption, but it was still a shock when Tower learned, on 27 March 1917, that such a prohibition would begin the next day. In a panic, the Royal Commission demanded that the 310,000 tons of wheat that they owned in Argentina be loaded as soon as ships en route to Argentina arrived. The commission urged Tower to threaten that Britain might curtail its coal exports to Argentina.[33] The historian Bill Albert has argued that coal was the British import "most widely and sorely missed" in Argentina, which had no pits of its own, as shortages led to a rise in fuel prices.[34] But coal shortages did not cripple the Argentine economy, as the railways and power plants increasingly operated on native wood, US coal, and newly developing domestic sources of oil.

Over the six months ending 28 February 1917, more than twice as much US than British coal was consumed in Argentina.[35] And most of the coal imported into Argentina was needed by British companies, in particular, by British-owned railroads. The British government was unlikely to hold over the heads of Argentine officials the possibility of discontinuing coal supplies if such an embargo would merely hurt enterprises owned by London investors.[36] Foreign Office officials regretted the lack of other obvious reprisals. They could not threaten to stop buying other Argentine products, because the

Allies clearly needed food. By 1916, the Allied governments took a majority of their meat imports, 570,783 tons out of a total of 969,275 tons, from the River Plate and Patagonia.[37] Although Britain would have preferred to ship beef and mutton from Australia or New Zealand (both of which were over-producing during the war), the far shorter route between the River Plate and Europe made Argentine and Uruguayan suppliers preferable, as it allowed more efficient use of the 51 available British refrigerated steamers. Argentina held the upper hand.[38]

The resulting British response was meekly to dispute that a shortage of wheat existed, to speculate on the basis of flimsy evidence that German commercial houses had forced the Argentine government to place an embargo on wheat by purchasing and storing large supplies of grain on the account of the German government, and to note that Argentina continued to allow grain exports to Brazil and thus was not treating all countries equally.[39] Argentine authorities probably truly feared a wheat shortage, and the overspeculation and rising prices that such a shortage might bring in their wake, especially at a time when war-related inflation had already hurt many Argentine workers.[40] But it was also reasonable to see the Argentine moratorium as a shot across Britain's bow. It is notable that this heightened tension between Britain and Argentina occurred at virtually the same time as the United States revoked its neutrality and joined Britain.

An agreement was eventually reached the following month, allowing the British-owned grain to be shipped, but only after the British promised to ship wheat from Australia to Argentina if it were needed.[41] To be forced to fulfill this obligation would tie up valuable shipping in southern oceans far from the war zone, but Britain had to gamble, as the immediate need for wheat in Europe made the much closer Argentine supplies a great deal more valuable than those from Australia.

Yrigoyen initially accepted the British proposal. Then, in May, as the British ships were plying the seas toward Argentina to pick up the wheat, he reinstituted the ban on exports. It was a startling move. Tower warned that if the ships arrived and could not load their cargoes, it would bring a permanent rerouting of shipping away from Argentina. In London, Foreign Under-Secretary Eyre Crowe contemplated the abandonment of all wheat purchases in Argentina.[42] But Britain needed the food. Only in October was Britain finally allowed to ship the remainder of the wheat that they had purchased the previous season.[43] Not only had the British failed to persuade Argentina to augment the grain fleet by taking over German ships in its harbors, but Britain was forced to tie up a number of its own ships. Argentine authorities never needed to call on the supplies from Australia, but their ability to wring advantages out of Britain was well noted, even as their neutrality remained intact.

Finally, in late 1917, Britain gained what many have considered a huge concession from Yrigoyen. To finance that season's grain shipments, Yrigoyen extended a loan from the Argentine government to the British of 200 million gold pesos, worth about £40 million.[44] Historians have seen this unprecedented loan convention as a de facto breach of Argentine neutrality – a moment when Argentina came down squarely on the side of Britain. Roger Gravil argues that Argentine officials were forced to offer the loan. With buyers in Central Europe cut off by blockade, the Argentines had nowhere else to sell their grain, and thus had to accept woefully low prices from the Allies. To Gravil, "the Argentine grain trade in wartime was subjected to the most draconian foreign manipulation in the republic's history up to that time."[45] Carl Solberg agrees that the British had their way in negotiations for grain purchases, with the threat to curtail coal supplies to Argentina and the lack of alternative markets for Argentine produce allowing the Allies to buy grain at rates below those deserved by the farmers in the pampas.[46] Hew Strachan suggests that the United States pushed the Argentines to accept the deal.[47] A few others note, more even-handedly, that the deal had some benefits for Argentina including the stabilization of exchange and the promise of obtaining coal from Britain.[48] H.S. Ferns suggests that, in general, Argentine supplies of food and raw materials during the war occurred "on commercial terms generally of advantage to themselves."[49]

In fact, all these historians undervalue the ways the grain finance scheme favored the republic. Sir Reginald Tower, for one, recognized that the scheme was "of great benefit to Argentina." After the war, he wrote that "Argentina [which] was then making money hand over fist out of exports to the Allies could well afford it, and the arrangement was certainly a sound proposition from her point of view."[50] The set prices and quantities of grain shipped under that agreement gave the Argentine government an unprecedented sense of security in the future of the grain industry, allowing it to levy a tax on agricultural exports in January 1918.[51] Despite the scarcity of British shipping, and the earlier sense that Britain might only conduct a wheat purchase if the Argentine government requisitioned the German ships in its ports, the loan agreement was concluded without mention of these ships; Britain could not use wheat to force Argentina to break its relations with Germany. Perhaps most importantly, the British need for loans must have been psychologically delightful for Argentine leaders. The need for Britain to obtain the wheat called into question the financial hegemony of London, suggesting to the Argentines that their financial strength was relatively improving. In the relationship between Argentina and Britain, the traditional roles of borrower and lender had been reversed, and Argentina had reason to hope that this change would be permanent.[52]

What the loan agreement also did was to change completely the dynamics of the Argentine grain trade, to the detriment of Britain's economic war. In 1917–18, the Wheat Commission bought 45 percent of the total Argentine wheat crop. Its purchases guaranteed that Argentine exports would remain at high levels, thus undermining the ability of the Argentine government to argue that the Statutory List restrictions wrecked the republic's foreign trade. Yet the convention also indicated that the British government would no longer attempt to foster the growth of British-run wheat companies. After the loan convention with Argentina was signed at the end of 1917, a commissioner was appointed in Buenos Aires to oversee the details of wheat purchase, including inspection of shipments, storage at the ports, and control of the jute bags in which Plate grain was shipped. Herbert Gibson, a partner in the sheep-rearing concern Gibson Brothers, and the brother of the president of the British Chamber of Commerce, was named the Wheat Commissioner, eventually receiving a knighthood for his services.[53]

Many local British subjects (including a number of women) joined his staff as clerks, and Gibson even requisitioned the services of Powell-Jones, the secretary of his brother's Chamber of Commerce. But this system was far from what was intended by the concept of a "constructive" commercial war, as British grain firms found their permanent growth stunted by the centralization of grain purchase. Under the Wheat Commissioner, Allied cereal firms were transformed into mere buying agencies, given fixed allowances and brokerage fees on purchasing goods from producers at prices whose lowest level was fixed by the loan convention.[54] And the Wheat Commissioner took a heavy hand in all of the business of these Allied firms; when one English exporter was offered a contract to purchase wheat to send to Spain, the Wheat Commission requested that the English exporter refuse the business, as it would breed competition with the Commission. Of course, there was a Statutory Listed wheat trader available to pick up the Spanish contract instead.[55] The wheat sale, in effect, brought an end to the attempts of Britain's constructive warriors to gird Anglo-Argentine grain exporters for continued success post-bellum, when it was assumed that free trade in wheat would resume.

The wheat sale also created new troubles for Britain's destructive war. Rather than enhancing the status of Britain in Argentina, the wheat sale made it apparent that Argentina held the upper hand in its relationship with Britain. By the middle of 1918, Yrigoyen's officials began to use this new-found strength to intensify their attacks on the British economic war. During the visit of Maurice de Bunsen's mission to Buenos Aires, Foreign Minister Pueyrredón described to de Bunsen the many ways that Argentina had acted in an ostensibly pro-British manner, with the creation of the wheat deal and the expulsion of Luxburg. But according to de Bunsen, "Sr. Pueyrredón, in conversation, was chiefly preoccupied with the effect of our Statutory List policy, which he thinks in some cases is calculated to do our cause more harm than good."[56]

Pueyrredón's growing obsession with the British trade war was also apparent to Reginald Tower. Starting in late June 1918, Reginald Tower began to look into reports of the enemy proclivities of the Werner Mills, a large flour producer in Rosario. Tower actually went twice to Rosario to speak with the British Chamber of Commerce there, and also to meet with Emil Werner. The mill owner admitted that he was German, and that the former German minister, the notorious Count Luxburg, had attended his son's wedding. Werner also admitted that he had purchased German war bonds, that a few of his managers were German, and that his partner, Jorge Boehming, was not just a German but was also the president of the local German Club. On top of this, Werner was also known by the FTD as someone who had assisted the strikers during a contentious walkout against a handful of British-owned railways. Undoubtedly, the Werner Mills were an ideal candidate for the Statutory List. According to Tower, there was no way that anyone could claim that the mills were a vital source of flour in local markets.

Yet that is just what the local national deputy claimed, raising a minor agitation that led Foreign Minister Pueyrredón to request to Tower that the mills remain off the Statutory List. In deference to Pueyrredón, Tower recommended that the Werner Mills should not be added to the Statutory List, and the FTD complied.[57] Likewise, in July 1918 the Argentine government succeeded in pressuring Tower and the Foreign Office to remove Florencio Martinez de Hoz from the Statutory List. From early 1916, Foreign Minister Murature and his Radical successors Carlos Becú and Honorio Pueyrredón had repeatedly complained about de Hoz's blacklisting. As a propagandist for the German cause and an intermediary for German companies receiving European goods, de Hoz was placed on the Statutory List in May 1916. De Hoz was an obstinate German partisan. Despite the fact that his business undoubtedly suffered on account to his listing, unlike many other Argentine firms, "he did not . . . knock at the door of the British Legation offering his books for examination, financial guarantees, etc."[58] But after a series of complaints from Pueyrredón, de Hoz escaped the list in July 1918 without signing a written commitment not to trade with Statutory List firms. Tower told Pueyrredón that he was letting de Hoz off solely out of "deference to the verbal representations made by His Excellency," the Foreign Minister.[59]

Yrigoyen's government found other new ways to actively oppose the Statutory List, such as by extending laws that were intended to thwart the British war. As companies whose operations faced specific local regulations, British-owned railroads had never fallen under the restrictions of the Statutory List and had to carry goods for firms on the blacklist just as they would for anyone else. In March 1918, Yrigoyen extended this doctrine to the seas by decreeing that Argentine Navigation Company (a British-registered coastal steamship line operated by the Mihanovich family) must carry goods to other Argentine ports for firms on the Statutory List. According to reports in *La Nación*, the ruling had been championed by the German Chamber of Commerce, which made known to Pueyrredón their unhappiness at their inability to use the steamship line even for trade within Argentina. Tower explained to the FTD that Britain should back off from pressuring the steamship line; to demand compliance with the Statutory List "in their coasting trade must bring them into conflict with the local law, and I fear their action could not be success-fully defended."[60] In effect, this new law reopened a route for trade among Germans in Argentina, in growing cities like Bahia Blanca and Rosario, significantly weakening the strictures of the Statutory List which relied so heavily on British command of shipping and coal in the South Atlantic.

Clearly the British war against Germans in Argentina would have had a much greater chance of success if the Argentine government could have been persuaded to join the Allied cause. Instead, the Argentines fortified their neutrality as the war progressed. Britain's commercial war faced significant opposition from many Argentines, the resulting spite and mistrust penetrating all aspects of the official relationship between the two countries. The republic did not hold all the cards in their bilateral relationship during the war, and had not even truly broken from its long-term state of economic dependence on the United Kingdom. However, Britain's tremendous wartime needs for Argentine food forced British authorities to listen to Argentine concerns and even to act before the Argentines could complain. Not only did the British increasingly respect Argentina's inherent power, the complaints further weakened British resolve in their war against German commerce.

As the diplomatic advantage tilted towards the Argentine government, increased moderation marked the British economic war in Argentina. British trade warriors grew wary of provoking controversy, while the Argentine government tested out the increased power it held in its relationship with the British government. British grain purchases continued, but only after the Argentines felt assured that they were not giving in to British demands or otherwise compromising their sovereignty or their neutrality. Until the end of the war, Argentines undoubtedly felt, as one Anglo-Argentine financial journalist wrote, that the republic would continue to profit "from the troubles of European nations."[61] Argentina could maintain its neutrality if it wanted to. This may have been founded on Yrigoyen's ideals, or his pandering to local anti-foreign sentiments, but the British trade war also proved an insuperable barrier between an alliance of Argentina and Britain. By the end of the war, their need to trade with Argentina meant the British government could do little but prostrate itself at Yrigoyen's feet.

Brazil

As in Argentina, the economic war in Brazil molded all other aspects of that country's relationship with the United Kingdom. Related issues included the possibility of requisitioning interned German ships, financial claims by British firms against municipal and state governments, the availability of supplies of coal and jute, and the desire of both Britain and Brazil to maintain each others' solvency. Brazil needed British shipping to keep its international trade flowing and British coal for its railroads and electrical plants, but like Argentina, Brazil found some alternative sources of fuel and manipulated Britain's deep desire for the German ships in its harbors. Two primary issues, however, set Brazil apart from Argentina. First, Britain was not a customer of the main Brazilian export, coffee, much of which was moved by German middlemen in Santos and Rio de Janeiro who were the primary targets of British economic warfare in the republic. The United Kingdom had few consumers of Brazilian coffee, a situation contrasting sharply with the demand for Argentine wheat. Second, Brazilian foreign policy had for decades tended to follow the United States. Far more than in Argentina, the British competed for primacy not just with Germans, but also with the Americans and even, to a lesser extent, the French. During the war, traders and officials from all four countries clawed for favors and concessions from the Brazilian government.

As the historian Emily Rosenberg has shown, US attempts to enhance its presence in Latin America, both before and during the war, were couched in the rhetoric of pan-Americanism, idealizing the supposedly inherent unity of the New World. The United States especially courted Brazil, and the republic responded. Some Brazilians believed that enhancing ties to the United States might bolster their country in its long-running competition against Argentina for dominance in South America. But Brazilians were also attracted by the way that pan-Americanism appeared synonymous with economic anti-Europeanism. US officials nurtured this latter idea. In November 1916, the US Secretary of State declared to the Brazilian ambassador in Washington that "the time for monopolies has ceased and it is now opportune to allow the Americas that is South and North to compete with European organisations in the enormous field which Europeans have been allowed to exploit for many years in South America."[62] The Brazilians wished for an alternative to European capital and products, and although they were unsure whether the United States could supply enough of either, they welcomed the chance to break their dependence on Europe. Dislocation of the start of war further linked together Brazil and the United States. The North American power had long been the primary consumer of Brazilian goods; during the war, the United States also became the primary supplier of manufactured products. As British envoy Sir Arthur Peel recognized, Brazil desperately needed US imports during the war and would never risk antagonizing its powerful neighbor to the north.[63]

As in Argentina, the Statutory List for Brazil attacked some of the most important businesses in the republic, in particular, those companies that controlled the main export crops. Early in the economic war, the British trumpeted their successes against German rubber firms that dominated the Amazon. Rubber was always a strength for the British, and in 1913 ranked as the only South American export in which British ports worked as an êntrepot for the European market.[64] By October 1916 the FTD had helped to set up a consortium of British rubber firms, allowing them to place German rubber traders on the Statutory List with devastating effects.[65] This negated the power of the Pralow-Scholz group of German rubber firms that had reigned in the states of Manaos and Pará. Yet before the start of the war, the Brazilian rubber trade was already noticeably declining. Rubber prices had collapsed in 1910, and it was found that the wild varieties harvested in Brazil were less accessible and more expensive than the rubber grown on recently planted plantations in Asia.[66]

Coffee was obviously of far greater importance than rubber both to Brazil as a whole, and particularly to the Germans in Brazil. By far Brazil's primary export, coffee passed almost exclusively through the hands of German merchant houses that were the prime targets of the British economic war. In some ways it must have appeared that Brazilian authorities would welcome measures against these Germans. Germany deeply annoyed Brazil early in the war by requisitioning the coffee stocks in Hamburg and Bremen, owned and warehoused there by the government of the state of São Paulo. In Brazil, many believed that the two largest coffee exporters, Theodore Wille & Co. and Eugen Urban & Co., held too much power over the country's coffee business. As Peel explained, German firms such as Theodore Wille "are not mere businesses but enterprises with great capital employed and ramified into a very complex network of controlled enterprises which comprise Brazilian firms indebted to German merchants, Brazilian registered companies, branches in interior, local manufacturers and industries."[67]

Brazilian coffee was different from Argentine wheat in two important ways. Although some might beg to differ, coffee was not a necessity but rather a luxury, bringing no nutritional value to a populace or to an army. For this reason, it remained less than certain through early 1916 that coffee shipments to Germany would be stopped by the British blockading forces, as some British officials suggested that the expenditure of German gold on a commodity with minimal dietary benefits should be encouraged.[68] Furthermore, coffee was something that tea-sipping British customers did not want. Indeed, the willingness of some Britons to consider allowing the coffee trade to continue to Germany indicates their incomprehension of the psychological benefits of a warm cup of the bitter brew. With little demand in the United Kingdom, any coffee imports into Great Britain were ordinarily sent along to customers in continental Europe. During the war, the British shied from committing tonnage to a commodity that they had no taste for. British ships, therefore, stopped carrying coffee, and subsequently Brazilian coffee exports plummeted. In this way, British control of shipping was a much greater problem for Brazil than for Argentina or even, as we shall see, Uruguay.

Yet British officials and businessmen ideally did not want to crush the lucrative Brazilian coffee industry, but rather to redirect it, loosening the hold of German firms while replacing Hamburg with London as the primary European coffee entrepôt. From the start of the commercial war, British authorities hatched plans for a large-scale purchase of Brazilian coffee, with the aim of increasing the solvency of Brazil, wrecking Theodore Wille and other German exporters, and installing British exporters in their place. During the first months of 1916, rumors circulated in the Brazilian port of Santos that German firms were stockpiling coffee for shipment on the declaration of peace. The British General Staff commissioned a paper on a systematic campaign of Germans overseas to build up stocks that could be rushed to Germany "on the termination of hostilities."[69] In Brazil, the commercial attaché, Ernest Hambloch, suggested ways to make Britain the center of the coffee trade. Still only a few months into the campaign, Hambloch believed that the Statutory List was hampering the business of the German firms, and that Brazilian firms had not moved in to pick up the slack. British firms could take over, he argued, if the state of São Paulo would only eject Theodore Wille & Co. as representative of the European financiers of the state's coffee valorization scheme. To get the government to do this, Britain would have to finance purchases of the coffee beans that were piling up in Brazilian ports, loaning São Paulo and the Brazilian federal government the hefty sum of between £6–7 million. Perhaps stocks of coffee in the United Kingdom could be built up from their present 500,000 bags to 3,000,000. At the conclusion of war, these could be sold to Scandinavia, Russia, and Hamburg, remaking Britain as the coffee entrepôt for the lucrative markets of northern Europe.[70] Edward Wysard, who held a number of directorships in Brazil and was an informant for the FTD about São Paulo, hoped to set up a British company, which would have a concession from the Tsar for a monopoly on coffee sales in Russia.[71]

A primary difficulty was the opposition of the Treasury to spend on a commodity that had no wartime use. The Admiralty wanted to help the Marconi Company to gain a concession from the Brazilian government to set up wireless telegraph stations, in order to have South American wireless operations, and thus communication with shipping, in British hands. This concession was bitterly fought over by Telefunken, which supposedly received assistance from the German government.[72] The issue of whether to support Marconi came back to coffee. Eyre Crowe was reluctant to intervene diplomatically in favor of Marconi as the British government would then be "morally bound" to finance the purchase of Brazilian coffee, even before they had gathered together the money to do so.[73] Lord Rothschild promised Edward Grey that he would finance a British takeover of the Brazilian coffee industry if the Allied governments agreed to buy the coffee for their armies.[74]

In November 1916, the Foreign Office, which favored a coffee purchase, looked to bypass the Treasury. In a memo to Asquith's core War Committee, the Foreign Office explained that without measures to purchase Brazilian coffee, German companies would regain full control over the coffee trade after the war.[75] Lord Robert Cecil argued that it would be worth while for Britain to spend £2.5 million to buy and store Brazilian coffee if, in return, Brazil would seize the forty-four German ships interned in Brazilian ports, putting them into use on behalf of the Allies. Both Grey and Lloyd George spoke in support of the idea, noting that the requisitioning of ships would in effect be an act of war by Brazil against Germany. In November, the War Committee overrode Treasury objections and gave Cecil the authority to negotiate a coffee-for-ships exchange with the Brazilian government.[76] At the end of 1916, the prospects for a British bail-out of the Brazilian coffee industry appeared fairly rosy.

British coffee exporters also appeared to be gaining market share at the expense of their German counterparts. On 15 August 1916, *Wileman's Brazilian Review* reported that exports by British firms rose from 2,547,081 bags in 1914–15 to 3,329,814 bags in 1915–16, while exports by French firms rose from 659,943 to 1,023,223, and those from Italian firms grew from 252,025 to 527,738. Meanwhile, exports by blacklisted enemy firms declined from 2,864,274 bags to 1,734,998. An FTD report noted optimistically that these statistics had been compiled in June and July 1916, when the Statutory List had only been in force for three months.[77] Surely such trends could only get better as the list clamped down on the Germans.

Yet despite growing British interest over the course of 1916, as with all other aspects of the British war, 1917 went poorly. Rather than following through with a coffee purchase plan, the government came up with a new way to put pressure on Brazil to revoke its neutrality and take the German ships. Pleading the need to conserve shipping for necessities, Britain prohibited imports of coffee.[78] Brazil reacted furiously. Although Britain was not an important coffee consuming country and the prohibition openly aimed at saving scarce tonnage space, the halt in British coffee shipments was denounced, rightly, as a measure to force Brazil to declare war and to requisition the German tonnage in Brazilian ports. In a meeting with the Brazilian minister in London, de Bunsen admitted that Britain would allow coffee imports again if Brazil took the German ships.[79] Peel, for one, did not think the British ploy could work; if they really wanted to conserve tonnage, British import prohibitions should be on *all* Brazilian exports, rather than just coffee.[80] Brazilians generally believed that the British import ban was intended to force Brazil to join the Allies.[81] President Wenceslau Braz threatened to retaliate by canceling repayments on government debts held in London.

The Brazilians had other options available for financial assistance. According to Foreign Office clerk Gerald Villiers, Brazil "is throwing herself financially into the arms of the US with results which are bound to be most prejudicial to British interests after the war."[82] And the Brazilian Minister of Finance in February 1917 even claimed that the German government had offered to place at the disposal of the Brazilian government some £6 million in gold belonging to German banks, which had recently been transferred from New York to Buenos Aires.[83] But German lures proved insufficient for Brazil compared to the magnetism of the United States. After the latter declared war against Germany in April 1917, Brazil also broke off official relations with Germany. Over the following months, the republic slowly and legalistically lurched towards war, finally declaring war against the Central Powers on 26 October 1917.[84]

Throughout this interim period, the British government considered how Brazil might help the war effort. British military officers belittled the possibility of Brazil contributing anything militarily to the fight versus Germany. The Admiralty, adhering to the low opinion of the abilities of the Brazilian people that prevailed throughout British officialdom, agreed that Brazil could not aid the Allies militarily other than by allowing British warships to use its harbors.[85] "Heaven forbid that we should have a Brazilian Division on the Western front or too many Brazilian men of war adrift on the ocean or Brazilian air craft darkening the sun," scoffed Admiral Lloyd Hirst.[86] To British officials, the most important ways for Brazil to contribute to the war would be for the republic to liquidate enemy merchant houses and banks and to requisition the German and Austrian ships in Brazilian ports. In other words, Brazil must engage in the British commercial war.[87]

Yet Brazil's entry into the war did not result in a new adherent to the British assault on German trade, nor did it improve relations with Britain. On the same day Brazil declared war, foreign minister Dr Nilo Peçanha argued that the British Statutory List was no longer justifiable and must be withdrawn immediately. Brazil could deal with its Germans on its own. They began to do so with the War Law of 16 November 1917, which gave the government the right to declare a state of siege in any part of the country. This was aimed to head off any possible civil disruptions in the southern states, where Germans made up a large portion of the population. The War Law also allowed the government to cancel contracts with enemy subjects, to seques-trate their property, and to establish control over or liquidate their businesses. The War Law was a potentially lethal weapon against the German businesses long targeted by Britain.

However, during the first months of its war, the Brazilian government shied from attacking the German companies. Brazil established control over the three German banks in November 1917, but thereafter authorized them to continue to conduct business.[88] British minister Sir Robert Peel complained that "the present unsatisfactory position of enemy subjects being allowed to deal with Brazilians but forbidden to trade with the Allies is to continue. German commercial interests in Brazil will be kept alive, and general trade with Germany will naturally follow the return of peace conditions."[89] The Brazilian economic war had very different goals from the British war. When Brazil drew up its own blacklist, the British firm Cory Brothers was listed, apparently because President Braz was annoyed about Cory's efforts to get the state-owned railways to repay an overdue debt. The Brazilian Foreign Minister suggested that Cory would be removed only when Fonseca & Co. of Para was taken off the British Statutory List. After the Foreign Office and FTD lectured that such blackmail was "a most improper use to make of a Black List," the Brazilians rescinded Cory's listing, yet they remained mis-trustful and resentful of the British commercial war.[90]

As a result of the half-hearted Brazilian attitude toward the economic war, Peel recommended that Britain maintain the Statutory List for Brazil.[91] The British government agreed, making Brazil the only ally in which Britain maintained its economic war. This deeply annoyed Brazilians, scarring every aspect of Brazil's relationship with Britain over the next year. In reviewing the March 1918 Brazilian 'Green Book', a published collection of official foreign correspondence from the years 1914 to 1917, the Brazilian press focused their entire attention on what the book said about the Statutory List policy and about the United Kingdom's prohibition of coffee imports.[92] Bra-zilian Minister of Foreign Affairs Nilo Peçanha broke the secrecy of earlier agreements he had made, where the FTD had pledged to notify Peçanha of the names of firms and people recommended for the Statutory List, and in return for maintaining their coal supplies, Brazilian-flagged ships would refuse cargo space for Statutory List firms.[93] Peçanha believed that since

Brazil had implemented its own economic measures against Germans, there was, "no further justification for the exercise of an authority which was thought to be inconsistent with the sovereignty of Brazil."[94] Brazilian courts ruled against Brazilian registered businesses that cited British Statutory List regulations when breaking contracts with German firms, affirming that only Brazilian enemy trade measures were the law of the land.[95]

British economic warriors had no doubt that Brazil was failing to battle German trade as a good ally should. When the United Press of America asked the British government in May 1918 to write a statement for circulation in South America about Brazil's contribution to the war, laudatory yet false banalities spewed from the Admiralty (Hirst declared that his piece was "written with my tongue in my cheek"), and from the Foreign Office (Eustace Percy declared that his contribution was a "piece of turgidity"). Others, however, expressed frankly their disgust with Brazil. M.D. Peterson of the FTD wanted the communiqué to state that Brazil still allowed "its vital industries to rest under the control of a foreign enemy," and that Brazil must "set its own house in order" by following British regulations against German firms.[96]

This obvious animosity between British and Brazilians over how to fight against Germany crippled British chances to gain control of the German ships interned in Brazilian ports. Brazil sequestered German ships in June 1917.[97] After negotiating with each of the Allies for the substantial privilege of using the ships, at the end of November 1917, Brazil awarded France the right to charter most of the interned German vessels in return for purchasing two million bags of coffee.[98] It was a telling blow to the British position in Brazil. In the eyes of Florence O'Driscoll, the agent in Brazil for the Marconi Company, giving the ships to France was "a way of spitting at the English."[99]

Yet despite no longer having the bounty of ships available for the taking, the British interest in coffee remained strong. This was a testament to the importance that the destruction of German trade and its replacement by the British held for many in the British government. The paired questions of coffee and economic war dominated the efforts building towards the de Bunsen mission's visit to Brazil. The mission's staff acknowledged that coffee financing and attacking German firms were interlinked and inseparable issues.[100]

Allen Kerr, the former minister to Chile and the mission's delegate from the FTD, speculated that if Britain purchased the coffee piling up in Brazilian ports, Brazil would take action against Theodore Wille & Co. Kerr believed that any coffee purchase must be led by British merchants, rather than bankers. Rothschild's cash would be important, but Rothschild's "knowledge is confined to finance, not the handling of coffee," and he could thus not successfully attack German trade. The FTD should help to create a pro-British group capable of replacing Theodore Wille & Co. as the operators of the coffee valorizations on behalf of Brazilian governments.[101] Yet others in the FTD recognized that the Brazilians had seen no indication yet "that we retain the power to put forward a constructive effort" to create an organization capable of taking Wille's place.[102] In Brazil, Peel worried that the main issue was the present instability of Brazil's coffee economy, and proposed that a British coffee purchase scheme could be done in conjunction with France and the United States.[103] The manager of the London and River Plate Bank in São Paulo likewise fretted that the Brazilian coffee trade needed an Allied bail-out.[104]

Some in the FTD speculated that if France, Italy and Belgium participated, Britain could dangle before Brazil the prospect of Brazilian cooperation in an inter-Allied combine that would market all existing and future coffee stocks.[105] If the United States had to become involved in it, wrote one FTD clerk, the US stake must be smaller than that of Britain, as otherwise Britain would merely be helping the United States to "attain a predominant place in the coffee market at our own as well as at the Germans' expense." Once British coffee houses were set up, they could "make the market their own without heavier initial expenditure."[106]

But unsurprisingly, the FTD came down on the side of inter-allied conflict rather than cooperation. In a memo for the War Cabinet-appointed Economic Offensive Committee, the FTD explained that a British coffee purchase would ensure quick action against Germans in Brazil, while counteracting the growing Brazilian assumption that the United States would dominate the republic after the war. Around £13 million would have to be spent to buy the coffee stocks, and another £2–3 million to buy the assets of Wille and to replace their loans to planters.[107] Interested in the possibilities of maintaining economic war even after an armistice, the Economic Offensive Committee called for the creation of an interdepartmental committee to examine the idea of a coffee purchase.

At the same time, in early May 1918, the de Bunsen mission entered Brazil. De Bunsen quickly learned the depths of Brazilians' need for purchasers of their coffee stocks. In a telegram to Balfour he explained that the Brazilians would never destroy Wille & Co. unless Britain found a market for their coffee. He supported Peel's suggestion that Britain and the United States should buy equal proportions of it, and suggested that the Brazilian government might allow part of the British money to stay in London in return for liquidation of some of Brazil's debts.[108] However, building any agreement with US participation was stymied by the pointed absence of US Ambassador Edwin V. Morgan from Rio de Janeiro when the mission arrived. The United States was unwilling to sign on to British efforts to gain trade for Britons, and de Bunsen soon recognized that negotiations would have, in any case, been impossible "under the limelight conditions" of the mission.[109]

Yet attempts to build an agreement with Brazil continued behind the scenes. Before leaving Sao Paulo, A.C. Kerr spoke frankly with members of the Brazilian Ministry of Foreign Affairs. He sympathized with their worries about how liquidating German banks and firms might bring havoc to the Brazilian economy, noting that it could cause huge losses to planters and to industries financed by Germans and might spur on the increasingly active labor movement in the republic. Kerr proposed that the Allies take over the two German banks operating in the republic, hiring new managers and changing the entire ownership of the banks, with the means of payment determined in post-war negotiations with Germany. Kerr believed this would bring Brazil completely into the Allied camp, while dealing an "unexpected material and moral blow at Germany (the) importance of which it is difficult to over-estimate." German trade in Brazil would be "controlled and discriminated against at its fountain head," and a precedent would be set for the liquidation of other companies, such as Theodore Wille & Co.[110] Peel fully supported this plan, saying that the change in the ownership of the German banks would lead to a rapid series of bankruptcies among German interests.[111]

Yet this scheme floundered when the de Bunsen mission left, and the United States re-entered the picture. Apparently satisfied with their ships, the French supported the United States to lead all further Allied negotiations with Brazil. Already despising France for having gained control of the German ships, British observers also suspected that the French had already used their position as the local Allied wheat purchasers to continue to shore up their position in this small but promising trade. With an astonishing lack of self-reflection, the Foreign Office complained that "the action of the French Government in Brazil has been devoted rather to the extension of French influence in that country than to the promotion of the interests of the Allies as a whole."[112] To top it off, the British-led commercial war effort against German firms meant that, as Peel rued, "all the odium of the Black List falls on us."[113] Brazilian Foreign Minister Peçanha exposed the terrible position that the Statutory List placed Britain in when he told Peel at the end of June that Brazil would no longer even consider raising funds from Britain unless they ended the Statutory List.[114] The British war against Germans in Brazil made it impossible for a true Allied coffee plan to ever develop; all parties were too jealous, too mistrustful.

And entering July 1918, a takeover of German exporting contracts by British interests was looking increasingly far fetched. British bureaucrats who hoped that the United Kingdom could reap all of the benefits of a coffee purchase scheme assumed that the Brazilian Warrants Company, a British firm tied to E. Johnston & Co., would be the one replacing Theodore Wille as the agent in charge of the valorization. However, Brazilian Warrants was shown to be associated with a financing company of questionable reputation, one that would probably warn Wille about any measures that Brazilian Warrants might take against it.[115] As with the wheat trade in Argentina, it was difficult for British trade warriors to fully trust the British companies who stood to benefit from a destruction of German export houses, as the structures of local trade conspired against their ability to curtail their own interactions with German firms.

In the end, the complicated machinations in Rio de Janeiro, London, Washington and Paris were rendered moot by the weather. A frost later in July killed millions of coffee trees and drove up the price of coffee. This made Brazil's previously unsellable piles of beans valuable again, which mitigated the need for the Brazilian government to accept any of the financing schemes proposed by the Allies.[116] It became apparent by August 1918 that the Brazilians would not liquidate Wille or the German banks, even if Britain offered to abolish the Statutory List in return.[117] Theodore Wille, an enemy firm within the territory of a British ally, survived the war intact and strong.[118]

Coffee was not the only commodity controlled by Germans and coveted by British traders. For other goods, such as Brazilian tobacco, the British had better luck in removing Germans from the export trade. Yet tobacco illustrates the complexity of the German position in Brazil and the likelihood that they would regain their position after the war ended. Despite the fact that German tobacco exporters had stopped operating, in February 1918 the Germans still owned the cigar factories of Bahia, still had the knowledge and skills to operate a system of cash advances for farmers against their growing crops, and still had Hamburg, where expert tobacco merchants lived and made it possible for the city to regain its place as the great tobacco clearing center for all of Europe. If the Germans were later able to obtain reasonable shipping and credit facilities, the "hard hit" they took from the British during the war would soon be shrugged off.[119] It would be surprising if they could not. The German cigar factories and other tobacco firms, employing hundreds of Brazilians, had no difficulty receiving financial facilities from the Banco do Brasil in 1918. The Admiralty called on the FTD to somehow persuade the Brazilians to liquidate, or at least sequestrate and administrate, the German cigar factories, "in order that as much lasting damage as possible should be inflicted upon enemy trade."[120] Yet the FTD could do very little to persuade a government unwilling to kowtow to Britain.

As shown, British people proffered a variety of schemes to take control of Brazilian export trades. They were hampered in part by failures of the British state, as ideas for a scheme to control Brazilian coffee bounced around without consolidating into a concrete plan.[121] Although it might help the Allies, the Brazilian government refused to implement any economic warfare measures that might hurt it, and Britain found that any attempts to compel Brazil to do so merely augmented anti-British feelings in the republic. In Brazil, Britain confronted not just a solidly rooted German commercial structure, but also machinations by its allies, France and the United States. The economic war nurtured a mistrust of Britain among Brazilians, hurting rather than helping British attempts to extend its power and influence in the republic. Writing of the travails of his company in dealing with officials in Brazil, the head of British Marconi fretted that his company was "in a hopeless position as a result of the relationship between the Foreign Office and the Brazilian Government."[122] He could have been writing about the problems faced by the British in general. In 1918, Commercial Attaché Hambloch was not the only British official to lament that "nearly five years of war and blockade have not uprooted" the Germans from the Brazilian economy.[123]

Uruguay

The First World War affected Uruguay in a way that was different from its larger neighbors. Throughout the war, Uruguay's rulers displayed a desire to do things their own way, in their own time, without taking orders from any of its neighbors or from any of the great powers. Uruguayans took tremendous pride in maintaining the independence of their foreign policy. Many in Uruguay loathed their southern neighbor, Argentina, fearing its expansionist tendencies. According to the ever-voluble British Minister, Alfred Mitchell Innes, in local circles, "Argentina one not infrequently hears called the Germany of South America."[124] For similar reasons, Uruguay would never follow Brazil. In June 1917 the Uruguayan government declared its friendship with all American nations that had joined the war, and in October the Chamber of Deputies voted to rupture relations with Germany. Yet unlike Brazil, Uruguay never declared war against Germany, despite the fact that most Uruguayans preferred the Allies and even feared German expansion from Southern Brazil.[125]

In 1918 Innes himself argued that Uruguay was in a de facto state of war against Germany, proven by their use of government wireless stations for messages to British cruisers, their declaration of solidarity with the United States, and their seizure of German ships in their ports. In Innes's words, "Germany has, in fact, swallowed insult after insult from a contemptible little country."[126] The Uruguayan republic definitely came down against Germany by the end of the war.[127] And its generally pro-Allied stance reflected the country's support for the United States. Men like Baltasar Brum, the Foreign Minister, were especially enamored with the pan-Americanist ideas coming from some quarters in the United States, unsurprisingly seeing the distant power as a reasonable counterweight to its less powerful, but more menacing neighbors, Argentina and Brazil.

The rupture of relations with Germany was, however, not purely built on sympathy for the United States. Speculation about German intentions in southern Brazil produced an astonishing degree of paranoia among the leaders of the republic including Foreign Minister (and in 1919, President) Baltasar Brum. In a bizarre episode that began in late March 1918, a German submarine stopped a Spanish ship on the high seas that carried a mission from the Uruguayan armed forces to France. The Uruguayans were affronted; as far as they were concerned, they were neutrals riding on a neutral-flagged ship, yet the German submarine captain showed them documentation that Germany considered Uruguay an enemy. The German captain kindly allowed them to return home, but the Uruguayans were indignant, demanding verification of whether Germany considered the two countries at war.[128]

A month later, Germany finally responded negatively.[129] Brum speculated to Innes that it took the German government so long to respond because they were at that moment engaged in their final, last-ditch offensive on the western front, which looked initially to be going well. Germany's government, confident in its success, was looking to create a peace treaty with the great powers with a clause that would give the Reich a free hand to deal with its other lesser enemies, that is, Uruguay. In Brum's view, "Germany's programme was then to take possession of, at least, the southern provinces of Brazil and of the whole of Uruguay." However, once Ludendorff's offensive collapsed, so did German hopes for conquering this slice of South America.[130] The timing of the German response was a reasonable cause for speculation, although one might imagine that the issue of Uruguay's status was far from being the most important thing on the minds of Berlin during the bloody month of April 1918. Undoubtedly, Uruguayan leaders held a much greater fear of Germany than either Argentina or even Brazil, where a sizeable population of Germans lived.

Yet despite Uruguay's true fear of Germany, and its supposedly significant rupture of relations with Germany, Uruguay's position during the war would be better termed as flexible neutrality rather than belligerency. "Associated" is too strong a term for the relationship between Uruguay and the Allies. There were a number of reasons why Uruguay refused to break its neutrality and become fully allied. Uruguayans were stereotyped as being more inflexibly principled, and less opportunist, than their Argentine neighbors, wanting to join the war on the Allied side, but unwilling to revoke the guarantees of neutrality towards Germany that they had pledged in 1914.[131] Yet ideals aside, Uruguayan desire to maintain neutrality was certainly based almost entirely on their dislike of Britain, an enmity of long standing only enhanced by witnessing Britain's commercial war. Far from bolstering Uruguayan respect for British strength, the British commercial war ran directly against mentalities rooted in the Uruguayan psyche. The war irritated a government whose policies were in many ways predicated on the belief that they were besieged by foreign powers, both within and beyond the South American continent.

The Uruguayan government, led by José Batlle y Ordóñez as either president or behind-the-scenes power broker since 1906, enshrined nationalist, economically progressive programs before and during the war, including the eight-hour day for workers and protectionist measures to bolster local industry. In effect, Batlle looked to break Uruguay from its underdeveloped, dependent place in the world economy. Such policies were anathema to the British capitalists who owned most Uruguayan utilities and all the railroads. Britons held a tremendous stake in Uruguay, and it is worth while to remember that in 1900, British investments in Uruguay of over £40 million equaled their investments in China. Batlle had never made a secret of his wish to reverse the penetration of the economy by British interests since Uruguayan independence in 1826.[132]

British officials notably lacked respect for the Uruguayan government or for the issues important to them. The British infantilized Uruguayans even more than they did Brazilians and Argentines, seeing Uruguay as a small and vulnerable country, with only a short experience in self-government, and leaders lacking in experience, more prone to follow their impulses than to engage in rational behavior. British minister Alfred Mitchell Innes wrote caustically in 1914 that President José Batlle y Ordóñez was "an intellectual hermit, who personally conducts the whole machinery [of government], assisted by a body of young men, active, intelligent, progressive, but without any of the experience necessary . . . and with many temptations thrown in their way."[133] Corruption would overtake them, he assumed. Seeing Batlle himself as a power-hungry rabble rouser, the British could little comprehend *battlista* efforts to put in place a quasi-socialist order in Uruguay.

In part, the British commercial war augmented and highlighted the preexisting propensity of the British government to ignore the republic. Uruguay had always been an inconsequential pawn in South America. Britain had supported Uruguayan independence in the nineteenth century merely to limit the power of both Argentina and Brazil.[134] UK businessmen and officials considered Montevideo as an adjunct of Buenos Aires, rather than as the center of its own national economy. During the war, Britain continued to treat Uruguay as economically and politically unimportant – an attitude which made it difficult to wage a commercial war against the Germans there. Many British manufacturers and exporters skipped the markets of the republic out of ignorance, assuming that by appointing an agent in Buenos Aires, they had sufficiently covered the entire River Plate market.[135] The British government similarly failed to assign a commercial attaché to Uruguay during the war. The attaché assigned to Buenos Aires had Uruguay on his official agenda, yet Chalkley was overburdened by his duties in Argentina and paid no attention to Uruguay.[136] To Britain, Uruguay was small and unimportant, and therefore even the campaign against the substantial German commercial presence there was neglected.

Two issues in particular illustrate the way that Britain overlooked the economic possibilities of Uruguay in refusing to treat Uruguay and Argentina as separate entities, to the ultimate detriment of the British position in Uruguay. One was the effort to gain the use of German merchant ships at anchor in Montevideo. Britain hoped that Uruguay would requisition the eight German ships of an estimated 42,000 tons interned in the harbor.[137] Innes said that the Uruguayan government might requisition the ships if Britain issued a guarantee that the republic would be adequately supplied with coal and steel throughout the rest of the war.[138] The Foreign Office rejected the idea by saying that they were planning to use coal instead in their negotiations for South American cereals. However, the cereal export trade was not one in which Uruguay participated on any large scale. Only 3 percent of the value of Uruguay's exports between 1911 and 1915 were from grains, and only 2 percent over the following five years.[139] Grain purchases in Uruguay by the Royal Wheat Commission during 1918 were a mere 39,813 tons, an infinitesimal amount compared to the 4,358,340 tons bought in Argentina.[140]

Obviously, substantive wheat purchase negotiations only took place with Argentina. The Foreign Office failed to recognize that the unimportance of wheat and other grains to Uruguayan exports meant that Britain could have utilized coal when bargaining for the German ships in Uruguayan harbors. After brisk and lengthy argument between Uruguayan authorities and the British, French, and Americans, finally in the middle of 1918 the Uruguayans leased the boats to the Allies through the Emergency Fleet Corporation of the United States. Although Britain supposedly received guarantees that at least a few of the ships would be used for trade between Uruguay and Britain, they were quickly shunted to US routes.[141]

The allocation of the British-flagged refrigerated shipping fleet likewise highlighted British ignorance of the tiny republic. The growth in the value of Uruguayan exports during the war was in large part due to shipments of meat products to Britain and to the Allied armies. The republic exported a record 95,200 tons of frozen and chilled beef in 1915 and the *frigorífico* slaughter between 1917 and 1919 was at twice the level of 1914. The historian Martin

Finch believes that Uruguay was satisfied with their surging wartime meat exports.[142] But British records show that the Uruguayan government certainly desired more, and believed that the British government unfairly discriminated against their country in favor of Argentina.

In both Argentina and Uruguay, foreign-owned *frigoríficos* dominated the business of slaughtering, preparing and shipping frozen and chilled beef and sheep. In relations between Britain and Argentina, the beef business became an issue after 1910 primarily owing to the threat that a group of Chicago-headquartered firms might eventually monopolize Argentina's international meat sales.[143] But in relations between the Uruguayan and British governments, the primary focus was not on US capitalists grasping control over the meat trade, but rather on competition between Uruguayan establishments and the *frigoríficos* of Argentina. During the war, the primary meat-related goal of the British government was to fill refrigerated tonnage and return it to Britain as soon as possible. The system for allocating shipping space built on pre-war price-stabilization arrangements developed by the *frigoríficos* themselves. These granted each company a set proportion of meat exports from Argentina. In early 1915, the Board of Trade had gained control of purchases both for the War Office and for the French government, and with the requisitioning of Plate tonnage, the Board of Trade controlled all Allied meat supplies by early 1916.[144] The Board remained satisfied with the pre-existing centralization of the Plate beef trade because it provided an easy platform for negotiating agreements.

In the eyes of Uruguayan officials during the war, the problem was that their two main *frigoríficos* were owned by Sansinena and Swift, which operated large establishments across the Rio de la Plata in Argentina from which they filled most of their allocated tonnage. At the start of 1916, the Frigorífico Uruguaya, owned by Sansinena, quickly slaughtered and stored enough meat for months of future shipments, and then stopped their production, laying off employees and limiting the options of those Uruguayan ranchers who wanted to sell cattle.[145] The Uruguayan government preferred a system giving each country, rather than each company, a set percentage of the refrigerated tonnage, but the Board of Trade rejected these pleas, arguing that it was up to Sansinena and Swift to decide how to focus their resources. The hands-off attitude of the Board was possibly influenced by the fact that neither of the *frigoríficos* of Uruguay was owned by London investors. But most of all, the Board of Trade rejected the Uruguayan claims for fear of rocking the boat. To give Sansinena a special contract focusing on maintaining continued output from their Uruguayan works might cause the other companies to pull out of the agreement, thus imperiling the steady supply of meat bound largely for troops in the field.[146]

The Uruguayan government complained that the committee that allocated space on the insulated cargo ships traveling from the River Plate ignored the needs of Uruguayan exporters.[147] The committee met in Buenos Aires, and Innes pointed out that the Uruguayan government "always resent business of this country being dealt with in Buenos Aires."[148] Yet the Ministry of Shipping explained that it was impossible to give Uruguay a set proportion of tonnage as it might interfere with imports of higher priority goods and that, as a result, any committee formed in Montevideo to deal with shipping would have to work "under the instructions of the Committee at Buenos Ayres."[149] After weathering years of complaints from the Uruguayan government, Innes was certain by the start of 1918 that the unyielding attitude of the British government ensured that Uruguay would continue to believe that Britain treated the country unfairly in comparison to Argentina.[150]

As with every other aspect of British policy, the way that Britain waged its economic war in Uruguay connected integrally with the war in Argentina. When most Uruguayan additions to the Statutory List were published in the *London Gazette*, they were done so under the heading ' "Argentina and Uruguay." This was perhaps inevitable and advisable, considering that the main German companies in Uruguay had establishments in Argentina as well, and because the main trades in which German exporters in Uruguay operated, namely hides and wool, were also important in the pastoral country of Argentina. Companies such as Staudt & Co. (which Innes indicated was the most important German company in Uruguay), Lahusen & Co., and Engelbert Hardt & Co., all conducted extensive business across the pampas in both of the republics.[151]

Given their subordinate position in the world of British diplomacy, the British economic warriors in Uruguay unsurprisingly grew quite cynical. In particular, the British minister, Alfred Mitchell Innes, became known at the FTD and in the Foreign Office as a caustic and erratic adviser. Innes had been a strong economic warrior from the start, keeping a particularly close eye on the wool and hide trades over the first years of the war. He noted the increasing propensity of these companies to ship their goods to the United States, and worried about the apparent stockpiling of goods in Montevideo for shipment to Germany after the war.[152] Innes advocated stopping all British trade with these Germans, and he got his wish when the Statutory List was created. But even more, he hoped that British firms could be persuaded to take the place of the Germans. "No temporary boycott of German firms will destroy their commercial ability. They will spring up again like mushrooms after the war" unless British business learned how to compete.[153] Only with a fundamental change in the way that Britain conducted itself in Uruguay could British business overtake that of Germans locally. British-owned utilities needed at least some local ownership, and business decisions should be made locally rather than by slow to react London boards of directors. Innes used as an example the London-owned Montevideo Telephone Company, which in failing to run an efficient service working for the good of the community was really failing to live up to the duties implied in concessions granted them by the Uruguayan government.[154] He believed that by swindling the locals, such companies sullied the reputation of British enterprise as a whole and might lead the rulers of Uruguay to adopt measures less than favorable to British interests.

In early 1917, Innes stated that over the previous decades, the British had failed to utilize their "formidable advantages" of ownership of the railways, the water company, the gas company, and the import houses.[155] The economic war was futile because German houses refused to fold and British replacements did not open.[156] British merchants must be stimulated to compete against German wool and hide exporters by getting "into touch with the importers in the United States" who bought heavily in Uruguay. Only "two old English firms" conducted such business as of March 1918, and whether one of those would continue to do so was uncertain. Its owner, "a very old man," had just died. "The head of the other (British house) is also old, and not very pushing, I fancy." It was felt that British capitalists should combine their efforts in Uruguay, perhaps managing the railroads, water and telephone companies through a single corporation, which would then take on the German controlled wool and hide export trades. Perhaps the Uruguayan government might get involved. "If we could get hold of the German bank . . . we should have a good foundation to work on" speculated the British minister. Innes stressed the need for new blood and a new attitude among all of the British who decided to undertake any form business in the republic. "If we are to succeed, we must make a religion of our work. This, I feel, is the real basis of German success, far more than the combinations and cartels."[157]

Despite his constant cajoling, there are no records of any attempts by the British government to foster a British presence in the lucrative, German-dominated wool and hide markets. Unlike efforts made for Argentine grain and Brazilian coffee, there seems to have been no concerted attempts to seize control of these main Uruguayan export trades in which German companies predominated. Innes's plans remained more a pipe-dream than a reality. Unable to see Uruguay as important, the British government would not spend resources on the economic war in the tiny republic. The economic war in Uruguay suffered as a result of the attitudes of officials in London.

Innes constantly clamored for more leeway to be able to alter the Statutory List himself.[158] As in Argentina and Brazil, certain blacklistings fed tension between Uruguayan authorities and Britain. Just a week after a contentious vote in the Chamber of Deputies led to Uruguay breaking its relations with Germany, in October 1917, Innes related the unfortunate tale of the recent Statutory Listing of Juan and Alfredo Schroeder, a father-and-son agency that, since the beginning of the war, had channeled the significant south Brazilian salted meat trade through Montevideo. One of the eminent members of the Blanco opposition party, Rodriguez Larreta, a man who had crossed his party lines to vote with the government on the rupture, appealed to Foreign Minister Brum to get his friend Schroeder's name removed from the Statutory List. Brum met with Innes and explained the political embarrassment, and the subsequent tremendous resentment of the British government, that was due to Schroeder's blacklisting. Innes lamented to the FTD that the blacklisting had been wholly unnecessary in any case, as he was personally working on building up a small firm of young Englishmen who he believed would have succeeded in usurping Schroeder's connections to these meat processing factories, known as *saladeros*, over the next two or three months.[159]

But Schroeder was not removed from the Statutory List, and Innes soon grew to fear that the British trade war offended Uruguayans so deeply that it might permanently limit British influence in the republic. "We must not, in the prosecution of our Enemy Trading policy, do what may be *contraproducente*; we must not do more harm to ourselves in the prosecution of our policy than any good that we are likely to derive from it." By focusing on the destructive side of the commercial war, Innes worried that Britain was generating "a current of sentiment adverse to us, which would do more to help the Germans after the war than could be offset by the positive harm that our policy would do to them."[160] Attempting to deprive Uruguay of its "liberty of action brings us into conflict with their determination to defend their independence. One must have lived here to realise how powerful this sentiment is."[161] But people in the Foreign Office did not trust Innes as they did ministers such as Tower and Peel. Their envoy in Montevideo was seen as unpredictable and overly critical of the activities of British capital and London-based companies in the republic. Scoffing at Innes augmented the propensity of the FTD and the British government in general to overlook the possibilities that existed for Britain in Uruguay.

The Uruguayan government was thus left to make up its own mind about the world war, and their leaders proved this independence when determining the republic's stance toward the European war. The pre-existing disregard that Batlle and the other leaders of Argentina held towards British economic domination of their country tempered their willingness to truly become an Ally. As elsewhere in South America, Britain's commercial war in Uruguay was not augmented by the local government. In Uruguay, the British conducted its war both inefficiently and without regard to local susceptibilities, making failure inevitable.

Conclusion

As shown, the British commercial war dominated their relations with Argentina, Brazil, and Uruguay during the First World War. The Statutory List and other overt British incursions into the sovereignty of each of these republics provoked outrage, annoyance, and opportunism from officials, politicians, and the public across South America. Although this chapter details only the cases of Argentina, Brazil, and Uruguay, similar anger towards the Statutory List prevailed in other republics. For example, Maurice de Bunsen explained that the Chilean President and Foreign Minister, and the Bolivian President, complained to him about the Statutory List, and its application by British "super-patriots," while threatening that the British war could transform the position of British business in these countries.[162] The British campaign against German business decreased the likelihood that the South American republics would actively support the broader worldwide Allied war effort. The commercial war fertilized the segment of public opinion that opposed the Allies or supported the Germans. In waging their war, the British knowingly sacrificed reserves of South American goodwill. British authorities obviously believed the goals of the economic war were worth some substantial cost. It also indicates the lack of an escape strategy: once having entered into a war against bona fide Germans, they could not declare a retreat if the campaign did not work out, even if it backfired and drove the local republics away from Britain.

The persistence of British warfare also indicates British condescension towards local authorities. The unwillingness of Britain to revoke the Statutory List for Brazil, even after the republic declared war on Germany, showed that the British did not believe that Brazilians could implement any successful campaign against the Germans in their own territory, and also that Brazil was no more than a second-class ally, not entitled to the same considerations given by Britain toward other allies such as the United States. In every republic, the British economic war embarrassed local governments in the eyes of their people and heightened their resentment of British informal imperialism.

The differences between the attitudes of governments of each of the republics toward the war were significantly based on practical, tangible aspects of their relationships with Britain. Argentina had far more leverage over Britain than did its neighbors to the north. The British need for Argentine-produced food tempered the British war effort there, making it less likely that the British could succeed in obtaining their war goals. Even though Brazil eventually formally allied itself with Britain and France, Britain found it difficult to persuade the Brazilians to sign on to a warfare campaign that targeted some of the largest companies in the republic. The commercial war in Uruguay highlighted the British tendency to ignore the tiny republic, and augmented

Uruguayan rejection of its ties to Europe. In each of these republics, the British commercial war dealt a painful blow to the prestige and resulting power of the United Kingdom; and the commercial war paved the way for successes of nationalist politicians campaigning against all foreign influences and skeptical of continued membership in the global economy.

A deep distrust of the Statutory List existed in South America, where many complained that it infringed their sovereignty and their right to maintain neutrality in the war between the European powers. Argentina, Brazil, and Uruguay took a variety of stances toward the British war on Germans in South America, which changed as the war progressed. These three republics demonstrate a variety of definitions of neutrality and belligerency, and a surprising level of agency in determining what their definition would be. Many South Americans believed that the commercial war against Germans in the republics was really a British war against the republics themselves. Their resistance against Britain contributed powerfully to each country's belligerent status in the war. It also, ultimately, crippled Britain's trade war against the Germans of South America. Rather than highlighting British power in its relations with the South American republics, the counterproductive commercial war underscored fatal British weaknesses.

8

Attempting to bring Greater Britain into the post-war

The sudden end to the shooting in November 1918 caught people around the world by surprise. Only over the previous month or so had it appeared that the Allies were bound to beat the Germans in Europe, and the shape of the peace remained uncertain. The possibility of maintaining the economic war perplexed the British government. Some, bent on revenge and lustful for reparations, urged the maintenance of the blockade until the Germans capitulated fully to Allied terms. Others feared a humanitarian catastrophe and demanded the end of the blockade to alleviate the suffering of the conquered and starving German populace.[1] The vengeful won, and the British government baldly retained the blockade against Germany as a hefty bargaining chip to be utilized during the peace talks in early 1919.

The issue of whether to maintain economic war against South American Germans agitated the Britons on both sides of the Atlantic. The Argentine press applauded indications that the war was finished, but some anticipated future great power conflict over the republic. *La Argentina* suggested that the British announcement "may be considered as a certain intimation that the commercial war for the capture of the markets is commencing."[2] There were some indications that the British government was gearing up for such a commercial battle; for instance, the War Cabinet authorized the swift demobilization of soldiers previously involved in business overseas.[3] The British Chamber of Commerce of São Paulo and Southern Brazil published a book-length report on Brazilian trade, subtitled "Hints and Information for Manufacturers and Merchants." It adhered closely to the wartime line that coffee merchants and bankers in Britain now had the opportunity of a lifetime to "become the European distributors of the bean," and that British manufacturers could best gain a foothold in local markets for machinery and other goods if they hired and used the local expert British merchant houses, rather than sending non-Spanish speaking salesmen ignorant of the products they were hired to sell.[4] At the armistice, British businessmen in South America were girding up for the continuation of commercial struggle.

"No more will they harass the outlying Hun":
dismantling the Foreign Trade Department

In a frenzy of self-congratulation, the emotions of victory led to lofty claims with regard to the British war in South America. The FTD trumpeted its successes, as Controller Ernest Pollock bragged that the trade of German exporters from the River Plate had been completely crushed by the war, and that German firms of all sorts across South America had lost much business.[5] Pollock had long claimed that the Statutory List in South America chipped at the efficacy of the German war machine and nudged the Kaiser toward capitulation. Yet after the battlefields quietened, Pollock no longer argued that maintaining the list could help to ensure the creation of a successful peace. He wrote on Armistice Day that although the British blockade of Germany should only be withdrawn slowly, step by step, the bulk of the names on the Statutory List, other than those necessary "for the efficiency of the blockade," should be immediately removed from the list. In a reversal of his hitherto vociferous defense of the List, Pollock conceded that many firms had been included for trivial offenses. He also suggested that its continuation would feed grudges against the Allies that would hurt British trade.[6]

Many in South America were appalled at this decision. The British Chamber of Commerce in Argentina had long portrayed its wartime work as aiming for its permanent integration into a commercially unified Greater Britain. Their entire efforts since their founding had been, in their own words, "very largely concerned in affairs affecting what can only be termed Imperial Trade and Commerce, with special concern to preparations for the commercial war which will be waged on this continent so soon as hostilities cease."[7] What was needed, wrote one British machinery and tool importer in Argentina, was for the Chamber of Commerce to use its influence to maintain an Allied boycott against German firms in the republics, even after the end of the war.[8] The conflict in South America must go on, even if an armistice ended hostilities against Germans in Europe. They anticipated support from the Controller of the FTD, Ernest Pollock who, in the House of Commons since the start of the war, had led a block of MPs lobbying for extreme anti-German measures, and had earlier argued that the Statutory List could last even after an armistice.[9] Many of the Chamber's sectional committees, including the crucial one on export trade, were only just completing their classified lists during the month following the armistice.[10] If perhaps these blacklists and whitelists were put into place, local Germans might finally lose their grasp of the wool, hides, and grain trades.

These Anglo-South Americans who wanted to continue prosecuting their war hoped in vain. Some had probably recognized over the previous year that the post-bellum continuation of measures against the trade of Germans was growing less likely. Many non-British locals still despised the Statutory

List as too arbitrary and mean spirited, and the United States remained unwilling to fight. It came as no surprise, in mid-December 1918, when the US government commanded its legations to discontinue all local, unofficial, "prohibitive" blacklists.[11] The other Allied Chambers of Commerce, led inevitably by the British, urged their governments to overturn this edict, immediately telegraphing to the FTD reasons to maintain these lists.[12] Only when commanded by all home governments two weeks later did the Inter-Ally Commercial Committee publish a notice in Buenos Aires withdrawing all non-official blacklists.[13] The IAC immediately disbanded itself on 20 January yet, even then, the leaders of the British Chamber of Commerce remained recalcitrant.

President Hope Gibson pressed the case in person at the FTD. He had left Argentina in October 1918 for a short trip to Britain. It was obviously undertaken for more than business or personal reasons, although the latter were certainly important – at the end of January he was awarded the CBE in recognition of his wartime work. But before he left Buenos Aires, the Chamber's Council appointed him as their "special delegate," and he acted as such during his visit. A few days before Christmas, Maurice de Bunsen of the FTD held a luncheon in Gibson's honor. Gibson spoke to the assembled guests about the work of his Chamber of Commerce, and of their hope that the government might enact a permanent 'reliable list' of importers in Argentina through which British trade could flow.[14]

In going to Lancaster House a few days later to meet with members of the FTD, Gibson undoubtedly hoped that his physical presence at the department he had long aided might persuade them to maintain the prohibitive lists. He considered these blacklists crucial to continuing the commercial war, and the FTD pledged to him, their most loyal warrior in the South American campaign, that they would reconsider their stance. No one in the FTD meant it, however, soon writing to Tower that "firms included in the unofficial lists are notoriously neutral rather than enemy," and thus should no longer be attacked.[15]

After this, the administrative structures erected to prosecute the war in South America disintegrated both in South America and London. At the end of January 1919, Tower discontinued the grant of £100 per month to the trade committees of the British Chamber of Commerce, and these committees subsequently stopped investigations for the Statutory List.[16] When the IAC disbanded – the group that had for a few months published the Statutory List under the title the Unified Black List – the Chamber decided that it would not pick up the slack by printing and distributing the list on its own.[17] The Chamber soon dropped its leases on two extra offices, laid off a number of female staff workers, and auctioned off the furniture that the Legation had once paid for.[18] The British government's decision to renounce financial ties to the Chamber undoubtedly hurt. The organization had done considerable quasi-official work during the war, much of it never reimbursed. Chamber leaders hoped, on principle – even before the creation of the Statutory List – that they might begin to receive regularly at least a small sum from the British Treasury. The first months of peace dashed such hopes.

In 1915, FTD founders all anticipated that the department would evolve into an agency with a long-term, post-war mandate. However, the failures of the commercial war had caused a decline in its fortunes during 1918. Even before the Statutory List was withdrawn in April 1919, many members of the FTD had abandoned ship. In a memo to Maurice Hankey, always planning for the future at the CID, Pollock suggested that it was unnecessary for any nucleus of the department to be kept going in case of a future war.[19] In May, the remains of the FTD were amalgamated into the Commercial Department of the Foreign Office, not into the DOT as anticipated.[20]

The end of the Statutory List was the occasion for final tributes. Ernest Pollock sent individual telegrams to each British minister abroad praising their efforts. In his telegram to Argentina, he justly lauded "the wholehearted and effective co-operation of the British community," and the "unceasing and strenuous labour" of the legation and consulate staffs.[21] The celebration in London was downright jovial. Deputy Controller Sir F.E.H. Elliot's 'Ode to the FTD' offers one man's insight into the accomplishments of his department:

> The fiat has issued from gay Paree
> That there is an end of the FTD.
> Their task is finished, their work is done,
> No more will they harass the outlying Hun,
> No more will they brandish the grim S/L,
> As a terror to those who would serve him well,
> No more will they be 'prepared to condone',
> The offences of those who have none to own,
> No more will they 'note with satisfaction'
> The 'attitude taken' 'in this connection',
> Their minutes and drafts are no more to be,
> But saddest of all, there'll be no more Tea!
> For the FTD were a cheery band,
> And their work and enjoyment went hand in hand,
> And while memory lingers, I'm sure there will be,
> A soft spot in our heart for the old FTD.[22]

Elliot aptly captures the bureaucratic jargon of FTD letters to companies it wanted to comply with the Statutory List. Trench poetry this was not, in quality or in seriousness. The "cheery band" of armchair economic warriors in Lancaster House were unlikely to suffer from shellshock. The members of the FTD did enjoy camaraderie, and a sense of shared purpose. But Elliot's poem is also rather dismissive of the war that he helped to lead, expecting the memory of what they had done to fade into a rosy nostalgia, ignoring the overall failure of the war. By the start of 1919, Elliot, and the other FTD leaders, did not believe that their war should continue, nor that such a war would ever be recreated in the future.

Similarly the end of war brought a complete turnover in British officialdom overseas. In both Uruguay and Brazil, the Foreign Office appointed new ministers in the middle of 1919. And after nine years at his post in Buenos Aires, Sir Reginald Tower was replaced by Ronald Macleay. Out of the door with Tower went his diplomatic secretary, Millington-Drake, some other staffers hired for the wartime, and all of their accumulated knowledge, their hard-earned war experiences, and their close contacts with local British business leaders. With Tower's sense of urgency gone, the legation in Buenos Aires remained woefully understaffed and was led once again by old-school diplomats, at least one of whom regarded the advent of commercial attachés as "a regrettable innovation."[23]

The Foreign Office clerks, diplomats, and businessmen who developed expertise in the operation of trade war in neutral lands scattered, and the lessons of the South American war with them. When the Admiralty later set up a committee to compile a summary of the conduct of the economic war for use in any future war, it included representatives from the Foreign Office, Board of Trade, DOT, Admiralty and Treasury, but, inexplicably, no one who had served in the FTD.[24] At about the same time, the vast bulk of FTD records were destroyed. The Department had clearly accumulated an incredible array of records; as one of the last remaining clerks at the department wrote in May 1919, undoubtedly looking across the largely unmanned offices in Lancaster House, desks and cabinets bursting with files, with further correspondence still pouring in from wartime contacts overseas, "the very amplitude of the material is what affrights me."[25]

Destruction probably also helped to protect the confidentiality of informants and the decision making process by which the department created the Statutory List. Unfortunately, the incinerators destroyed much information that might have been of use to British business. In July 1919, the DOT hoped to give the White List for Argentina, which was finalized only in December 1918, to traders who wished to send commercial propaganda and business feelers to the republic. The Foreign Office shrugged that it was impossible, because it no longer had any copies of the list.[26]

The stillborn Department of Overseas Trade

At the end of the war, it appeared that at least a few UK-based firms would attempt to run their operations in South America in a nationalistic fashion.

After his stint on the de Bunsen mission, Allen Kerr entered the private sector when the London investor Emile d'Erlanger appointed him to return to South America to "further strengthen the British spirit" of the South American Stores Ltd, the Argentine Iron & Steel Co. Ltd, and the Argentine Tobacco Co. Ltd.[27] From Brazil, Ernest Hambloch urged the British government to be "courageously partial" by helping individual British companies in their quest to receive concessions. "If I may say so," ventured the Commercial Secretary, "I believe these are the lines on which the German Government would have worked in the old days."[28]

Hope Gibson, for one, savored the possibilities. Immediately upon his return to Buenos Aires in February 1919, he put before the Chamber a proposal to convene a special meeting of all members, asking them to establish a permanent office in London, so that "a direct and rapid means of communication would be established between business centers in London and Buenos Aires." The Chamber would have to hire two full-time secretaries, who would spend time alternately in both countries so that they were both knowledgeable about commercial matters on both sides of the Atlantic, along with a permanent head who would likewise split his time between Argentina and the United Kingdom. Gibson claimed to be upbeat, buoyed by those he spoke to in government and business circles back home who did not plan "to abandon, in the remotest degree, British interests in this country." But the Chamber needed to act immediately if its members were to take advantage of a situation in flux. According to Gibson, British manufacturers and exporters, and the British government, had not yet defined the country's post-war commercial policy, and would most likely end up trading with anyone who could offer them facilities. The Chamber's new transatlantic secretaries would help enable members to do this.[29]

At the start of March, the Executive Committee decided that the Chamber would be represented by a salaried official in London, but that no offices "except on a modest scale" should be opened. With the end of government subsidies, and the unlikelihood that they would ever be offered again, the pressure in the council to economize struck hard against Gibson's hopes that the Chamber might invest significant funds in projecting itself into the United Kingdom. Yet, over the next few months, the Chamber continued other efforts to reach out to businessmen in the homeland. The members of the Executive Committee agreed to a 400 percent increase in its subscription rate to the Association of Chambers of Commerce, with the assurance that the Association would pay "special attention to the interests of British Chambers abroad." Along with other British Chambers in Rio de Janeiro and Montevideo, they weighed in favor of the proposal of the FBI to appoint trade commissioners in foreign markets.[30] They decided to print a thousand copies of a memo written by A.G. Thornton in 1915, showing statistics for pre-war

German trade with the republic, and planned to send these copies to the Association of Chambers of Commerce in London to distribute to any of its members interested in entering the Argentine market. Studying the numbers, hopefully, would lead them to "devote their attention to the lines of business formerly in German hands."[31]

But in the United Kingdom, this outreach was largely ignored. At the end of the war, a desire permeated many in the United Kingdom business community and in the government to have things return to the way they were before 1914.[32] Most wartime ministries were, in the words of A.J.P. Taylor, "slaughtered" as quickly as possible at the end of the war, as economic freedom "burst out overnight" in the United Kingdom.[33] Some manufacturers who had profited handsomely during the war spent their gains on amalgamations, rather than on new technologies and better management. The initial post-war days were highly profitable, and most industrialists scorned the neo-corporatism and protectionism favored by men like Dudley Docker.[34] Overt support for commercial controls was astonishingly low in post-bellum Britain, with organizations like Association of Chambers of Commerce and the FBI unwilling to take a pro-tariff reform stance for fear of alienating some of their members.[35] The crafters of British economic policy, trying to turn back the clock to the free-trade past, a *belle époque* that perhaps never truly existed, ignored the ways that the war changed the place of Britain in the world economy.

In the last days of 1918, the DOT told British diplomats abroad to publicize the lifting of most restrictions on British manufacturers and on British imports and exports. The United Kingdom was again open for business, but not in a fashion that particularly benefited Britons in South America, and complaints flowed in to London. For instance, Innes observed that British shipping lines consistently failed to appoint British representatives in Montevideo, and in the months after the war, these lines looked as if they might appoint Germans. In the Foreign Office, Victor Wellesley agreed that this posed a tremendous threat.[36] But shipowners' associations rejected making the hiring of British agents a general policy, and the Ministry of Shipping agreed.[37]

Officials at the DOT debated the possibility of enhancing post-bellum commercial nationalism. The jargon of blacklisting and economic war was not forgotten by Steel-Maitland, who argued that keeping an eye on the Germans was a priority, "especially in those countries which she may wish to use as camouflage after the war to conceal her activities under a neutral cloak."[38] He continued to agitate for an increased link with the Foreign Office, suggesting to the Prime Minister in January 1919 that he be appointed Assistant Foreign Secretary so that he could control the commercial side of foreign affairs. According to Steel-Maitland, Balfour took no interest in commercial affairs and Hardinge was incompetent about them, making it impossible for Steel-Maitland to get the DOT business accomplished.[39] Being placed thus in the Foreign Office would allow him to guide the development of the consular and commercial diplomatic services to help British business exploit trade possibilities. The British needed to augment their official presence both in the markets of competing industrial powers, such as Germany, and in markets with potential for development, such as South America. Consular posts abroad should be expanded from the pre-war level of 299 to 404. Steel-Maitland assured that the cost of his scheme "will not amount to a farthing in the £ of our foreign trade" and "will give the nation value for its money."

But Auckland Geddes, the minister in charge of reconstruction soon to be appointed President of the Board of Trade, had little faith in the DOT or its leader. "Steel Maitland is a trial and his whole department is in an impossible position," he explained to Conservative leader Andrew Bonar Law in May 1919.[40] Steel-Maitland seems to have truly believed in the cause of creating a commerce ministry within the Foreign Office. But his scheme was cursed by the inattention of the Foreign Office, the blatancy of his grasping careerism, and the impolitic tone of his requests. Steel-Maitland believed heartily in his DOT, but his leadership of the department made it suspect in the eyes of his peers in London. Exacerbated with obstruction from the Board of Trade, he resigned on 23 June, while calling on the government to place the DOT solidly under the auspices of the Foreign Office.[41]

British businessmen in South America gasped at the news that Steel-Maitland had abandoned ship. The British Chamber of Commerce in São Paulo wired the DOT expressing "grave concern" over Steel-Maitland's resignation, while reiterating a long-standing demand for the formation of a wholly independent ministry of commerce.[42] The Argentine Chamber's recently-elected new chairman, the furniture importer and retailer H.C. Thompson, wrote to the Foreign Office supporting the genuine efforts of the DOT to increase British trade in Argentina, but he feared that the present turmoil had made it impossible for the department to operate.[43]

It is notable that it took the DOT a few months to reply to the Chambers of Commerce. Undoubtedly, worries about disorganization in London were well founded, with terrible understaffing plaguing the ability of the DOT to keep abreast of its responsibilities.[44] It must have been exasperating for the Chambers to finally receive a reply in November from the secretary to the new head of the DOT, Sir Hamar Greenwood, who bombastically claimed that "never before in British history were governments at home and in the outer Empire more alive to the paramount need of stimulating and developing trade and commerce."[45] Greenwood turned out to be a short-term replacement and was followed quickly by Frank Kellaway, and in April 1921, Sir Philip Lloyd-Graeme, a true Board of Trade man. British commercial interests in South America grew appalled as the DOT drew closer to the Board of Trade, a ministry that had never supported the creation of the DOT in the first place.

The DOT would not be assisted by the Foreign Office, chastened by their wartime experience. The Foreign Office showed no signs of retaining the mantle of trade champion that it had held during the war. The ministry's power within the British government suffered dearly for other reasons in the immediate post-war years, as Lloyd George took a direct role in much British foreign policy. Under Lord Curzon until 1924, the Foreign Office apparently lost all interest in issues of trade, focusing more on the maintenance of peace in Europe and (following Curzon's predilections) on policy towards the Far East.[46] By the early 1930s, at least one clerk in the Foreign Office's American department complained that the ministry again blithely passed along to the Board of Trade and Treasury, without comment, most commercial and financial questions dealing with South America.[47] This reinstitution of the Foreign Office's traditional willful ignorance of commerce augured poorly for the ability of Britain to compete internationally when nationalism reasserted itself in the global economy during the 1930s. Outside the Foreign Office, a variety of businessmen and politicians in the United Kingdom were interested in implementing some form of British-centered commercial policy, but most of these focused on the idea of imperial preference, an inherently territorial concept of commercial nationalism that could not easily include the British of non-Empire South America.

Favoring trade within the Empire, the DOT initially refused to give importers in Britain information about alternate sources of goods if the department considered imperial sources sufficiently plentiful. In August 1919 the DOT backtracked, noting that this policy did not "take full account of the useful services rendered to British trade by British exporting houses in foreign countries," and declared that from then on, the names of such British houses would be given to companies in the United Kingdom that requested information on the country in question.[48] Yet such potential gains were erased just months later when the DOT explained to its commercial diplomats and consuls abroad that the names of firms on the now defunct Statutory List should also be given as suitable connections abroad to any querying United Kingdom exporting firms.[49] With this, the DOT proved itself to be acting purely on behalf of exporters in Britain, not British importers in South America. To the British overseas, their government was acting as if the war had never happened. In response, the British Chamber of Commerce in Buenos Aires declared that its own mission had changed, that the Chamber "should revert to its original objects, which are firstly to promote the trade of local British firms, members of the Chamber, and secondly that of the Empire."[50] With the turning away of the Chamber of Commerce in Argentina, the DOT lost what might have been its greatest ally and its best source of information about local markets – businessmen who had declared their deep loyalty to Britain and who had been repaid poorly for it.

What ensued over the next few years was the disintegration of innovation and risk-taking by the DOT. Rather than fostering the dreams of overseas businessmen who yearned for fundamental change in their relationship with the government, the DOT resisted such advice. The British government and the DOT announced in a circular in April 1920 that they had no power to enforce commercial nationalist practices.[51] When a position on its advisory committee opened up in April 1921, the idea of appointing Follett Holt, formerly of the British Chamber of Commerce in Argentina, was vetoed on the grounds that he held "strong – and in present circumstances quite impracticable – views on how commercial intelligence should be organized."[52] In September 1921 the DOT told the Association of British Chambers of Commerce that owing to a lack of funds, they would not sponsor any official British participation in the Rio de Janeiro Centenary Exhibition. The Association's Foreign and Colonial Affairs Committee was aghast, responding that this would hurt British trade in Brazil and that Britain should "strongly support the Exhibition."[53]

But the DOT was not a department of visionaries, and the few potentially fruitful schemes hatched by its members were easily crushed by tight-fisted Treasury officials, who viewed the DOT as an optional, and therefore expendable, department. By the time Lloyd George's coalition government fell in 1922, the department had become an appendage of the Board of Trade.[54] As the department had failed to lobby support for its mission, at the onset of economic slump, the Treasury reduced DOT funds by 30 percent for the years 1922–23.[55] Despite wartime pretensions to permanence, the British effort to regain commercial hegemony in South America became merely one more example of a policy being overturned when the British government reinstituted laissez-faire policies.[56]

In a true testament to the inertia of bureaucracies, the DOT limped along for a further two decades, but there is no indication that the department ever utilized even its reduced funds to much gainful purpose. A decade after the war ended, complaints about the failures of British trade remained identical to those before the war. British manufacturers lacked the necessary drive to meet competition from the United States, explained one British railwayman in Argentina. British industries failed to send out British men trained in local languages, refused to make the products desired by local consumers, and did not extend credit on terms comparable with American firms.[57] The London Chamber of Commerce lamented in 1928 that despite repeated reports and suggestions from Commercial Secretary Chalkley in Buenos Aires, no one had yet created a real collective effort among businessmen in the United Kingdom to address the continuing decline in the competitiveness of British exports to South America.[58] "Our methods of production, representation, marketing and sale require thorough revision," concluded the report of the high profile mission led by Lord D'Abernon, who visited the South American republics in 1929, exactly replicating criticism that had been made thirty years earlier. The DOT obviously failed to improve the ability of British manufacturers and exporters to service the South American marketplace.

Perhaps most unforgivable was the department's failure to maintain the links with the British communities in South America that the FTD had fostered during the war. Even after the trade committees of the British Chamber in Buenos Aires stopped their investigations in connection with the Statutory List in January 1919, some of them continued to work to supply monthly reports to Commercial Attaché Chalkley, but they were never sure whether these reports went to the Board of Trade or the Foreign Office. As a result of this uncertainty over their efficacy, and the halting of subsidies from the government to conduct such enquiries, most of these trade committees eventually stopped compiling up-to-date information, a gap that would be deeply felt and never filled by the British commercial intelligence establishment. When asked by the DOT in early 1920 to send home information on rubber importers in Argentina, Commercial Attaché Chalkley could do nothing but mail a list he had on file of approved rubber importers, written by the Rubber Committee of the Chamber of Commerce on 14 August 1918.[59]

By the 1930s the Chambers of Commerce in the republics had virtually no ties to the British government. When Sir Herbert Gibson visited Britain in 1932, he did so as the head of the most prominent British family in Argentina, as the former British Wheat Commissioner in Argentina, and as the present President of the British Chamber of Commerce in Argentina. Gibson gave a well-publicized speech to a Federation of British Industries audience, yet the DOT expressed surprise on learning that he was in the country. Gibson was hurt that the department had ignored him.[60] Created to foster ties between British businessmen at home and British businessmen overseas, by 1932 the DOT had no idea whether any relationship even existed between the two.

The German threat re-emerges

Given the British paranoia about their own relative decline, and anticipation of fierce post-war competition in South America, it is unsurprising that even after the war ended, the debate continued over which country most threatened Britain there. Despite the tremendous across-the-board gains by the United States during the war, many British traders and businessmen in South America continued to downplay the threat from US financial and commercial competition. Herbert Gibson was one of many in 1919 who repeated the mantra that US commercial propaganda backfired owing to the tactlessness of US businessmen.[61] With much hope for the future, Chalkley reported that Argentina preferred British merchants and goods, that wartime growth of the share supplied by the United States rested solely on their ability to supply goods, and that this US trade was precarious as it was based on merchanting, rather than investments.[62] Innes wrote of the troubles of American companies such as General Electric, which because of failures to deliver and the shoddiness of its products "seems to have incurred the ill-will of at least some of the local dealers."[63] In Brazil, Commercial Attaché Ernest Hambloch reported that US businessmen had missed their window of opportunity during the war and would now face problems caused by inexperience and a tendency to make themselves unpopular.[64] Such reports aimed to reinforce the optimism of British businessmen contemplating whether to enter the South American marketplace. However, such rosy reports might have backfired by giving those in the British government wary of trade promotion a reason to refuse to appropriate scarce funds for it.[65]

Rather than making a substantive critique of the actual situation, those who downplayed the capabilities of the North Americans repeated notions long held by the British about the national character of US commerce. Even local non-British businessmen repeated the mantra. In April 1919, the *Journal of the Argentine Industrial Union* stated bluntly that "American commerce is not British commerce, that is to say, the commerce to which the whole world has rendered and still renders the most complete homage."[66] But more honest assessments noted that US businessmen showed no signs of reducing their efforts to enter the market. In December 1918, the American Commercial Club in Buenos Aires decided to expand itself into a Chamber of Commerce that would associate with other chambers in the United States.[67] Some British officials who mocked the personalities of US businessmen still recognized the inherent potential strength of the American economy. Chalkley believed that the wartime diversion of some Argentine trade to the United States would likely prove permanent.[68] "Englishmen generally pooh-pooh the competition of the United States," wrote Innes, but "when the Americans have corrected their initial mistakes due to ignorance of the export business, they may become serious competitors." US businessmen undoubtedly hoped to dominate South American trade, and Innes, for one, found few reasons to believe that they could not.[69]

Of course the primary reason why many Britons underestimated the Americans had nothing to do with the actual threat posed by US business. In the years immediately following such an all-consuming war, paranoia about Germany was bound to far outweigh any other considerations among the apprehensive British. In his 1918 assessment of the war in South America, the British historian F.A. Kirkpatrick worried that the vast numbers of German businessmen in the River Plate outnumbered their English competitors, many of whom had returned to Britain to fight in the war. German merchants cut off from international trade had begun investing locally, bringing in huge profits during the war. "From this far western front Germany has mobilized a business army," claimed Kirkpatrick, prepared to continue the commercial conflict after an armistice.[70]

And in the months after the armistice, this prediction appeared wise. Activity by German businesses in the republics surged, as the German Chamber of Commerce claimed boastfully that no German business had been driven into bankruptcy by Entente economic warfare.[71] US postal censors intercepted a flurry of letters to and from blacklisted German firms in South America. German companies were looking to place orders and start up business with companies in the Unites States, with firms that appeared keen to reciprocate.[72] In November 1919, the formerly Statutory Listed firm Staudt & Co. cheekily sent two buying agents, both of them German, to the United Kingdom to make purchases.[73] By the end of 1920, Chalkley had no doubt about the regeneration of German business. "German agents are active in their endeavours to secure orders," and merchandise from Germany was already being offered in large quantities in Argentina.[74] German manufacturers, aided by the declining exchange value of the mark, slashed their prices and, as a result, quickly regained prominence in such trades as agricultural machinery.[75] Imports from Germany seeped into the republics, despite the confiscation of the German merchant fleet by the Allies under terms of the peace treaty. From Bahia, Brazil, Consul White reported that German-made goods arrived on Dutch ships as early as August 1919.[76] Across the continent, German banks worked ardently, and generally successfully, to recoup their positions.[77]

The South American British continued to express their fears of Germany to home authorities and businessmen. Their representatives persuaded the London Chamber of Commerce to create committees for Brazil in 1921, and for Argentina and Uruguay in 1922, bringing together businessmen in London who were interested in Latin America. Donald Begg was elected chairman, with Follett Holt as his deputy; both were agents for British Chambers of Commerce in these countries, and they understood the concerns of their distant Chambers. As Begg explained in an April 1923 report, the regrowth of foreign competition continued to crush British business in the republics. He particularly lamented the fact that British manufacturers hired non-Britons as their agents in South America, warning that this was bound to hurt British industry in the long run. British traders were caught between two competitors, the United States and Germany, but one in particular stood out: "Strange as it may seem, I believe Germany is the more dangerous of the two owing to her greater experience and adaptability in foreign trade and the great wealth of her Nationals who are willing – in fact anxious – to facilitate business by ample credits. Under these circumstances British commerce must carefully and minutely study every detail in order to hold its own."[78]

And so the Germans easily brushed off the war. In many British eyes, the war had been utterly worthless, the German threat unmitigated by the years of struggle. Even in 1923, when perhaps the worst economic crisis ever to hit an industrialized nation sank the *Deutschmark* into worthlessness, British observers in South America perceived little but German strengths. In Buenos Aires, H.O. Chalkley, now with the title Commercial Secretary, fully agreed with an assessment by the British Chamber of Commerce in Rio de Janeiro that German goods could dominate South American marketplaces. Property and capital in Argentina controlled by Germans had grown rapidly since the end of the war, explained Chalkley, and German-owned shipping had regained a lucrative place in both the commodity and passenger trades. Some people lost money with the fall of the mark, but local Germans continued to take orders, at low prices, for goods that had to be sent from Germany, knowing that with their thorough knowledge of the requirements of the Argentine market and of the going prices, they could continue to conduct profitable business.

Chalkley had no doubt that no matter how bad things became in Germany, the Germans would still prosper in Argentina.[79] The British Chamber of Commerce in Argentina described how many German firms in Buenos Aires were enlarging or rebuilding their offices and warehouses and did not suffer from any lack of capital. "Generally speaking they leave no stone unturned to push sales" and they "seem to be able to quote lower prices whenever competition renders this necessary." German companies dominated the purchase of raw wool, and their buyers appeared "to be flush with money." Importers of German-made electrical goods declared huge profits, even as those merchants who imported British goods faced an extremely low volume of trade and tight profit margins. And the Germans continued to deliver goods swiftly out of their large, locally-warehoused stocks, while British firms could only quote for delivery in six to eight weeks.[80]

For the British, the most disappointing aspect of the resurgence of German businessmen was in the export trades. The Brazilian coffee trade remained entrenched in German hands in 1919.[81] By the middle of the year, British coffee firms such as Naumann Gepp & Co. clamored for permission to rehire the Germans they had once fired at the insistence of the FTD. The Foreign Office felt powerless to stop such rehirings.[82] The DOT said that it would tell any firm asking for advice that it was best for British trade interests overseas to be represented by British people or by subjects of the country in question.[83]

However, Foreign Office clerk Duff Cooper ridiculed such attempts to warn British firms against hiring Germans or using them as their agents. "It is absurd for H[is] M[ajesty's] G[overnment] to say 'Don't Employ Germans' when they have no power to stop anyone doing so."[84] In the 1920s, Germans remained integrally important to the Brazilian coffee trade, even trade conducted by supposedly British firms.[85]

Enemy firms also quickly retook the River Plate grain trade. At the end of war, the Allied grain traders of Buenos Aires desperately hoped to maintain sanctions on their German competitors. They telegraphed Prime Minister Lloyd George, pleading for him to bar Bunge & Born, Weil Hermanos, and General Mercantile Co. from competing in Allied markets and from chartering Allied tonnage. With virtually all of the world's shipping under Allied control, this would have meant virtually maintaining the Statutory List restrictions.[86] Yet restrictions were lifted from these companies. It soon became apparent that the blacklisting of German-tainted grain firms during the war had done little to limit their business, nor did the war help British shippers to gain predominance. Acknowledging the continued strength of the German firms in January 1919, the US Food Administrator Herbert Hoover suggested at the Paris Peace Conference that the credit resources of the German merchant firms in South America could finance purchases of as much as 200,000 tons of cereals a month for their famished homeland.[87] It would certainly be wrong to conclude that the Statutory List "drastically reduced" German involvement in the Argentine grain trade.[88]

Bunge & Born, for one, emerged unscathed. They remained an attractive trading partner even for London-based firms such as Taylor Buckell & Co., which in June 1919 asked the Foreign Office if it could legally resume dealings with Britain's one-time arch enemy.[89] Bunge & Born flourished in the years after the war, profiting much from the speculation in wheat futures that proliferated after the declaration of peace, and further diversifying within Argentina by building paint factories and textile mills. Bunge & Born extended its financial domination of the countryside, continuing to advance to farmers and agents the funds to buy their seeds – a practice that allowed the firm to establish the prices of the crop.

The ubiquity of the firm overwhelmed Argentine farmers after the war, among whom it was said, "Bunge gives the farmer his credit, sells him his seed, and buys his grain. And when the crops are in, Bunge sells the farmer the rope to hang himself."[90] In his report after leading a mission to South America in 1929, Lord d'Abernon futilely called for British firms to enter the grain trade between Argentina and Britain, as the entire trade remained in the hands of "continental" European shippers.[91] In 1931, Bunge & Born handled 43 percent of the wheat exported from Argentina, doubling its pre-war percentage.[92] Perhaps the most painful blow to the British in

Buenos Aires was that their wartime arch enemy, Alfredo Hirsch, became the company's global president in 1927. He guided the giant grain firm, which remains one of the largest in the world, until 1957, long after the Second World War had come and gone, and long after the evaporation of the possibility that British goods and traders could ever again rule in South America.

Hirsch's successes were merely an extreme example of the general post-bellum German recovery in South America. British coffee houses gained no ground against their German competitors during the 1920s or 1930s.[93] By 1922, Germany regained its pre-war share of Argentina's foreign trade, and in 1927 their bilateral trade reached an all-time high, with Germany consuming 16.5 percent of Argentine exports. Along with this expansion of trade came unprecedented levels of investment capital from Germany and the creation by Weimar businessmen of local subsidiaries in the South American republics.[94] The British campaign during the Great War had fundamentally failed to make these republics less attractive to the businessmen of the German world.

Even as they experienced this economic boom during the 1920s and 1930s, the Germans of South America grew increasingly nationalistic and built stronger bonds with their homeland than ever before. Although some Germans retained only a cultural separateness from the local populace and were, in fact, loyal and assimilated citizens of the states in which they lived, historians have shown that many of these Germans who ended the war prosperous and arrogant considered themselves as potential "imperial outliers", proud of their intimate connections to Germany.[95] These ties were enhanced by a relative flood of new immigrants escaping the challenges faced by Weimar Germany, particularly after the hyperinflation of 1923. According to Ronald Newton, members of all classes within the German community of Buenos Aires united in support of Hitler in the 1930s, setting up Nazi party organizations and Nazifying many existing clubs and German-language schools.[96] Richard Staudt, the head of the enormous Staudt & Co. import-export empire, led a rousing mass meeting of 10,000 Germans celebrating the Anschluss in 1938.

Even those German-Argentines like Alfredo Hirsch who opposed the Nazis did so in a culturally German context; in 1934, Hirsch helped to found an anti-Nazi German language school employing a number of German intellectuals fleeing the Third Reich.[97] In Brazil during the late 1930s and early 1940s, German behemoths like Theodor Wille and Hermann Stoltz employed many of the Nazi secret agents who supplied their government, and its submarines, with vital information regarding merchant and naval targets.[98] The failure to destroy these Statutory Listed firms during the First World War thus exacerbated Allied difficulties during the second one. Jonathan Barton writes that in the case of Chile, this political and imperial dimension of the German commercial expansion exacerbated the frustration of British businessmen in South America who were unhappy about the resurgence of German trade, "even more so than with US business."[99] South American governments during the interwar period focused their fears not on the British role in their countries, but rather on the powerful, colony-seeking Nazis, enabling US authorities to persuade local governments to deport many Germans to internment camps in the United States in the early 1940s.[100] Britain, searching for pre-eminence but largely out of the picture by the 1930s, certainly lost the Great War in South America.

The decline of "Greater Britain" in South America

At the end of the war, expressions of global British unity remained constant and unwavering across South America. In September 1919 the Chamber in Buenos Aires sent a circular to its members recommending that, whenever possible, they should employ Britons, thus preserving "for the future the continuity in British houses of a British 'atmosphere'."[101] The Chamber's hardware and machinery subcommittee asked members to inform the Chamber of instances of foreign competition in freight rates, quality of goods, methods of delivery, salesmanship, availability of credits, and other aspects of trade in Argentina, with the information sent along to the commercial attaché.[102] They looked to maintain the "us versus them" wartime mentality, fostering the transatlantic bonds of Britishness, even after the war ended.

A proposal by the Chamber in Rio de Janeiro, dated May 1920, urging changes in how British passports were obtained, provides insight into how the war reshaped British identity in South America. According to the Chamber, the British government would not allow Britons to obtain British passports from consulates in Brazil, and the Chamber wanted this policy to be changed. In a particularly jarring example of the new British identity, attached to the Chamber's report was a petition from twenty-six workers at a British mining company, some of whom were former British servicemen, including one man disabled by war wounds. "We, the undersigned British subjects, who were born in Brazil . . . refuse to apply for Brazilian passports, since such action implies our recognition of Brazilian nationality, whereas we are British born subjects and consider ourselves fully entitled to possess British passports."[103]

Born in the sovereign state of Brazil, yet defiantly 'British-born subjects', such Britons in South America proclaimed a unique nationalism. "British subjects," the Chamber agreed, "place a high value on their British nationality and regard it as important that they should not have to identify themselves against their will with the subjects of the country in which the accident of birth has given them second nationality." It was felt that the British government must do everything it could "to promote loyal British sentiment in every part of the world." Thousands had responded "in the hour of England's need," volunteering to fight in the armies, but they also fought in South America, where British businessmen "were assured during the progress of the war that their devotion to trade interests there was of more importance to the Empire than their personal service with HM Forces in Europe." If British merchants and returning volunteers from the ranks were unable to obtain British passports, "it comes as a blow to national prestige amounting to an affont," and it might cause these men to switch their loyalties to their "second nationalities," in other words, to the country of their birth. Both the British ambassador to Brazil, Ralph Paget, and the British Chamber of Commerce in Buenos Aires signed in support of this proposal.

These Britons got their passports. Brazilian and Argentine authorities might well wish good riddance to a group of locals who, during the war, could hardly have done more to claim their British allegiances. Yet the Foreign Office told local governments that these were special passports, and did not entitle the "British subjects born in the Argentine" and in Brazil who held these passports to claim protection from British diplomatic representatives when in Brazil or Argentina. Foreigners in the lands of their birth, these Britons were not entirely welcome at home either, holding different rights from real subjects of the British Crown. For this group of people, at home neither in South America nor in the United Kingdom, a truly greater Britain remained an impossible goal.

The surge of patriotism and belligerency left the British of South America with some organizations, such as Chambers of Commerce, that have lasted until the present day. In August 2004 the Chamber in Buenos Aires celebrated its ninetieth anniversary with an impressive reception at the British Embassy. But insular Britishness has largely faded away. British unity, which seemed so necessary and even inevitable during a period of international conflict, made less and less sense to many Britons in South America after the war. They felt abandoned by their supposed compatriots back home. Some judged their own Britain-centered policies to be a failure and assimilated with the locals – a decision that also probably helped them to maintain business in the increasingly anti-foreign atmosphere of the republics during the 1920s and 1930s. British clubs and organizations fell into the hands of Argentines or fell apart altogether; the lawn tennis club lost most of its British members by the early 1920s, as did the Hurlingham Club, where Britons had at one time introduced polo to Argentina. Efforts by British businessmen to maintain their elite status were hampered by their continued decline in the economies of the South American republics. As others became wealthy and prosperous, local British businessmen "lost all contact with the governing class" of Argentina. By the early 1940s, the British ambassador there lamented the fact that there was no one in the British community through whom he could informally communicate with the Argentine government, as no local Briton any longer had those kinds of high level contacts in local political circles.[104]

British merchant houses still attempted to maintain unity within the local British communities, but the interests of merchant traders increasingly diverged from the interests of the less nationally-oriented British business-men who helped to build South American manufacturing. The British Chambers of Commerce lost their place as the embodiment of British commercial nationalism.[105] The Chamber in Buenos Aires remains, in the early twenty-first century, an organization that avowedly aims to breed con-nections with the United Kingdom for the prosperity of British people locally. They still hold their council meetings at the grand, oblong, boardroom table that the Chamber bought for itself during its frenzied expansion in the heated days of the First World War. But its members have certainly assimilated; tellingly, the Chamber's official name now is the Cámara de Comercio Argentino-Británica.

Conclusion

Jonathan Barton, among other historians, has argued that the failure of post-war Britain to regain its pre-war share of trade resulted in part from the "lack of coordination within British government, between government and finance, and between finance, government and business."[106] But it is worth-while to remember that this lack of coordination was not inevitable. Rather than becoming a solid department that looked likely to support British trade for years to come, the DOT sank only very shallow roots. At the end of the war, a chastened Foreign Office allowed the Board of Trade to largely reassert its authority over commercial issues. The shift in power back to the Board of Trade made the definitive reassertion of free trade, and the rejection of preferences for Britons in South America, almost inevitable. Even before the severe budget cuts known as the Geddes Axe fell upon British ministries, and even before British businessmen reasserted their own practices of business as usual during the 1920s, it was obvious that the constructive war – the attempt to permanently reorganize Britain's foreign trade by nationalizing the mentalities and actions of British businessmen and officialdom – would never succeed.

The British government, and particularly the Board of Trade, consciously dismantled structures that had been built during the war with an eye to helping

British trade succeed in peacetime. In what was a certain admission of its failure to live up to the dreams of the economic warriors, the career Board of Trade official Sir Hubert Llewellyn-Smith smugly wrote in 1928 that the DOT had, since its founding, worked smoothly and successfully.[107] Few businessmen, and few in the British government, would remember how close the Foreign Office had come to snatching away control of foreign trade policy from the Board of Trade, or how far they had once progressed along the path of institutionalizing and bureaucratizing the rejection of laissez-faire.

Conclusion: remembering
the Great War in South America

In 1919, many in South America mistakenly assumed that the British war against German trade would be long remembered, if ignominiously for the British. In April 1919, only weeks before the dissolution of the British Statutory List and the Allied Enemy Trading List, the pro-German Buenos Aires newspaper *Handels-Zeitung* ran an article condemning the British economic war as a failure. "The final balance of the Black List will show a great moral deficit against England, which will never be compensated by the ephemeral benefits resulting from her arbitrary action against her commercial rivals."[1] *La Union* predicted that the Statutory List policy "will remain one of the greatest blots on the conduct of the war by the Allies," an outrageous breach of the sovereignty of neutral nations and an encroachment on the rights of businessmen.[2]

British authorities wanted to forget the whole episode quickly. Despite his public bluster that the war had succeeded, Ernest Pollock's renunciation of the Statutory List on the day of the armistice indicated that the British government recognized its failure. The paucity of remaining records on the FTD – a department with dozens of full time staff members and a wide range of responsibilities – suggests that the purging of all Blockade Ministry records around 1926 struck this department with particular severity. Initial efforts culled all the FTD papers into two, rather slim, bound volumes.[3] A third was compiled in March 1939 by someone who came across a musty box of FTD papers when looking at the basement of the Foreign Office as a possible air raid shelter. These were quickly examined and weeded, keeping the information that was "of general interest and likely to be of guidance in the future."[4] An ominous phrase, but the need for guidance probably seemed realistic on the eve of the Second World War.

The repudiation of the economic war, and particularly the campaign in South America, appears throughout the subsequent official blockade histories. Popular histories of the naval war were commissioned from Julian Corbett and C. Ernest Fayle by the CID, but these published works largely ignored the ways that blockade went beyond the halting of ships on the high seas. The first and only historian of the Ministry of Blockade, H.W. Carless Davis, wrote a triumphalist history of the British blockade. Davis particularly lauded the bureaucracy that developed in London to control it, perhaps not surprising coming from the deputy chairman of the WTID. But the chapter on the Statutory List was by far his weakest. Concluding the manuscript, it reads as a throwaway chapter, written by an Oxford don rushing to finish and return to his normal life. He accepted blithely the assertion of Pollock and the FTD that the war in South America had been instigated by London officials, and that they had succeeded in crushing German businesses in South America. Despite its limitations, Davis's history remained classified as secret until 1957 and has never been published.[5]

Among other long classified works, W. Arnold-Forster's book for the Admiralty, and A.C. Bell's *History of the Blockade*, written in the 1930s, using Admiralty and Foreign Office records, both focused their attentions on the curtailment of trade with enemy lands in Europe. Even among Whitehall's historians, the South American campaign remained ignored and unknown as the Second World War began. At the beginning of the Second World War, a Statutory List policy for the non-European neutrals was again put in place, but a more globally marginal Britain held no more illusions about the possibility of waging such a significant economic war as they had attempted in 1916. Even before the attack on Pearl Harbor in December 1941, Britain's blacklists for Latin America followed the so-called Proclaimed List of the United States, which was an effort by the United States at "hemispheric defense," protecting itself and the "other American Republics" from the Axis powers.[6] There would be no second British attempt to wage a constructive war.

Like officials at home, the British communities in South America swept the commercial war under the rug. With the blessing of the British Legation and Consulate-General, various British organizations in Argentina banded together after the armistice to publish a record of their war efforts. They produced a large book that included thorough biographies of each of the more than five thousand men who voluntarily left Argentina to join British armies, and a complete account of the sums contributed in Buenos Aires to the various British charities and war loans. However, the writers considered it impolitic to detail how British people in the neutral republic attacked their neighbors. Their efforts had been kept as secret as possible during the war, and the book's editor concluded that "the inner history of the ceaseless vigil over British interests, and devoted attention to British trade and commerce, will probably never be written."[7]

Few reminisced about the war. Six years after it ended, Sir Reginald Tower, retired at home in England, revised his wartime verdict on the campaign against the Germans. He now suggested that the impact of the Statutory

List grew over time, and that attempts by US businessmen to grab the Argentine market failed.[8] Tower, however, wrote this in a report for the Prince of Wales, who traveled to South America in 1925, and may have been patriotically overstating the power of the United Kingdom. On the eve of the Second World War, another old South America hand who worked under Tower recalled that "in the intense war time diplomatic activities one got to know the country and the people in a way one would never have dreamt of in the old easy-going days, and even now. One had to delve into everything and Black Lists often savoured of patriotic blackmail!"[9]

Looking back, the commercial war quickly became anomalous and abnormal. Few Britons wanted to memorialize a failed economic war, one that diametrically opposed the resurgent orthodoxy of free trade, especially during a period when Britain's endemic economic problems were growing obvious to increasing numbers of people in the United Kingdom. From the perspective of the 1920s, the Statutory List seemed pathetic and ill-tempered, embarrassing and forgettable. It is hard to escape the conclusion that the Great War in South America has been ignored by historians for so long because it was intentionally forgotten and erased by the many Britons who waged it.

The results of waging commercial war

Did the South American campaign matter to the overall war, helping the Allies to win or reducing the time it took for them to do so? Probably not. The collapse of Germany undoubtedly occurred in Europe, within a population and army concerned not with foreign trade somewhere else, but rather with their own survival in the present. Yet the intensity and complexity of the fight in South America illuminates very well the global, total scale on which this First World War was waged. Traditional definitions of total war focus on bringing in new forms of combat and weaponry, on mobilizing civilians on the home front and on attacking civilians in enemy territory, on waging "unlimited warfare" both as a strategy and as a war aim. The war in South America adds geographic breadth and personalized depth to this vision of total war by exposing how war transformed civilian life in South America, where a group of self-identified Britons helped the British government to fight against a much-despised enemy, not just in Europe but in South America itself, utilizing forms of economic warfare previously unimagined. It exposes yet again the way that decisions during war can be determined by misperceptions, overexcitement, and even paranoia, as rationality often takes a back seat to emotion.

It has often been said that in Africa, the failure of the Germans and British to understand each others' actions led to a 'scramble for empire' that both fostered and exemplified the tension between the two countries.[10] As in

Africa, so in South America, where throughout the years before 1914 Britain and Germany failed to comprehend or accept each other. To many wary British people, the Germans seemed intent on destroying British trade with the republics. Among Britons in South America during the decade before the war, long-held arrogance coexisted uneasily with a growing sense of insecurity. Many held an unrealistic sense of Britain's power, their belief that Britain could successfully step in and force the ejection from sovereign countries of an opposing national group of businessmen exemplifying their imperialist mentality. Permeated by ideas of the racial inferiority of the people and governments of South America, many British believed that this war could succeed in damaging German companies and that without the German presence, British businessmen would be left to take over. The British assumed that the local governments could do little about this. They also believed that if they did not wage war in South America, then Britain would lose its place in the republics to the wily Germans who had built such a strong position in a shockingly short period of time. Their unity, their nationalism, was based on the shared enemy, Germany.

During the First World War, South America with its resources and its economic potential came to be seen as strategically vital to the United Kingdom. The presence of British people within the South American countries and in their economies subsequently came to be thought of by the British government as a strategic necessity. This new understanding of South America led the British people of South America to see themselves as part of a Greater Britain whose *raison d'être* was commercial dominance over belligerent and untrustworthy transnational Germany. To many of the British in South America, the idea of a nationalist trade policy, with British people everywhere favoring business with one another, seemed potentially beneficial for everyone involved.

Their pre-war loathing of Germans ensured that if the Britons of South America were to have a say in it, the British government would strive to force German business in South America to close its doors. Rather surprisingly, they had their way. In waging war against the Germans of South America, the British government followed not the dictates of City of London financiers, but rather (in part) the desires of British industrialists and (even more) the demands of British traders in the distant republics. The wishes of British merchant bankers were often pointedly ignored by those who continually refashioned and implemented the economic warfare policy and who blamed British finance for many of Britain's pre-war failures to maintain dominance in regional trade. The commercial war against the Germans was a prominent example of British imperialism that definitely did not grow from the wishes of the City of London. As the First World War passed, British bankers in South America completely lost the ear of economic war policy makers, and it briefly appeared possible that, after the war, in an era when conflict between the Great Powers was expected to continue, finance might permanently lose its place as the anchor of British imperial policy toward the continent.

The unveiling of the Statutory List indicates the tremendous respect paid to international law even during the midst of a brutal war. The British were passionate about legalistically upholding the international commitments regarding the freedom of trade during war that Britain had made since the 1850s. By quietening protests from the governments of South America in 1916, Britain's legalisms allowed the economic war there to gain a foothold. Britain, the South American republics, and the United States all appeared susceptible to the idea that international law guaranteed broad neutral rights. What is ultimately surprising about the British effort is not its ultimate de facto repudiation of the rights of neutrals to freely engage in trade, but rather the consistent and vociferous adherence to the idea of neutral rights by British diplomats and officials throughout the First World War. The belief that international law actually mattered contributed to the growth (if only temporary) of support for international organizations after the war, such as the League of Nations, created to codify and stretch international cooperation.

The wartime system proved temporary, in part because of the resurgence of the post-war ideological consensus behind reinstating liberal orthodoxy. Gentlemanly capitalist sentiment again permeated London. Yet government cutbacks and the decision to ignore trade, seen in the defanging of the DOT, was also the by-product of the failure of the interventionist state model during the commercial war. Historians have long disagreed as to the extent to which Britain was able to "muddle through" the war, following no plan but relying on the British talent for inventiveness, tempered by a strong work ethic.[11] This commercial war shows that the ability to even muddle was often stunted by inter-ministerial turf wars, squabbles over war strategy, and ideological divisions over state intervention in the economy. Rifts within the British government, particularly between the permanent officials of the Foreign Office and Board of Trade, diminished the effectiveness of the commercial war in South America and made it less likely that potentially useful wartime structures linking government to business would be maintained post-bellum. Those who hoped that the war would permanently augment transatlantic British nationalism had their hopes dashed by the war they waged.

The failure of the South American idea of commercial Britishness to take root in the United Kingdom had lasting consequences. It may be true, as Correlli Barnett has argued, that the absolute acceptance of liberal economic doctrine by virtually everyone in post-war Britain was "catastrophically inappropriate" and contributed heavily to the collapse of British power during the interwar years.[12] The British could have taken up the nationalist policy of trading preferences for British people, which would have been more in tune with the ragged international trading system of the interwar years. Yet the problems with waging the war in South America made it less likely that the British government would install such protectionism after the war. The British government had tried something significantly different from doctrinaire free trade, *laissez-faire* practices, and had judged this experiment as a failure. It was not just the overwhelming intellectual appeal of free trade, or the British desire to return to an idealized pre-war world, that led to the revocation of wartime trade policies, but also the fact that many of Britain's wartime trade policies had not worked.

The war in South America runs against the ordinary chronology of the war. Most historians perceive that the likelihood of Allied victory over the Germans increased during the course of the war between August 1914 and November 1918. Yet from the examples of Uruguay, Argentina, and Brazil, the likelihood that the British could meet their goals for the war against German business in South America actually declined as the war progressed. The increasing difficulties reflect how South America was a venue for mistrust not just between Britain and Germany, but between the Allies. Competition between Britain and the United States over which would guide the war against Germans in South America, and who would take the anticipated spoils, consistently interfered with the effort to implement effective sanctions against German trade. The situation in South America highlights how the various Allies fought together not merely in support of abstract ideals of democracy, sovereignty, and neutrality, nor as a result of historical ties to each other, nor out of a mutual hatred of Germans, but also in the hope that their own nation could benefit. In South America, each foreign power held strangely mercantilist assumptions, acting as if they were playing in an economic zero-sum game where a gain for one entailed a loss for another. All were aware that the world war made the role of commercial hegemony in South America open for the taking by whichever power could manage to do so. In South America, the only Ally whose war goals were met was the United States, which gained predominance in South American trade. Although squabbling over the war in South America was not the only reason for the post-war disintegration of the alliance between Britain and the United States, it certainly fed the growing mistrust between officials of these two great powers, contributing to the general isolationism and international instability of the 1920s.[13]

Without a doubt, the war negatively affected Britain's relationships with the South American republics. It has often been stated that early twentieth-century South American states languished in a state of dependency, subject to the world economy in which they marketed their goods, with the primary benefits accruing to countries in the center of the world economy, especially Britain. In bidding for the destruction of the Germans in South America, the British consciously sought to deprive the economies of the South American republics of their German component, and, in pursuing the war, Britain trampled on the sovereignty of each South American country. Yet British records suggest that, during the war, Britain felt an unprecedented dependence on South America. The neediness of Britain for staple primary goods enabled Argentina, at least, to gain concessions that helped to shield it from the full pressures of the global economy and of the Allies' wartime economic restrictions.

The openness with which Britain invoked war measures that impinged on local economic freedoms deeply annoyed many people in the republics, and the resultant public pressure helped bolster those South American governments that wanted to prove that they were "masters in their own homes."[14] By maintaining their neutrality, or, in the case of Brazil, by not blindly following British economic war policies after entering the war, the governments of Brazil, Argentina, and Uruguay refused to be victimized by the British restrictions. The British war in South America crucially limited the willingness of South American governments to take a pro-Allied stance, and helped to map for each republic the parameters of their neutrality or, in the case of Brazil, their belligerency. British officials grew to see the commercial war as a public relations nightmare, eroding much of the goodwill felt by South Americans for the British people and making it difficult for Britain to get its way on other important issues. The commercial war on Germans stimulated South American governments to act independently of Britain and to scorn British desires. Even in the 1920s, after the commercial war ended, its recent memory contributed to political and social movements in Argentina, Brazil, and Uruguay, This clamor for a reduction of foreign involvement in their economies after the war fertilized the subsequent wave of populist nationalist governments in each republic.

In short, the First World War was not just a European conflict, but one with global implications. Instead of exemplifying the power of the major industrialized countries, the core of the world economy, the war in South America forces us to understand the strengths of the periphery. It shows how transnational British identities developed and interacted with the shifting national identities of South Americans. It remains true to state that with such actions as blockades the First World War exemplified the rejection of global integration, yet the transnational complexity of this war in South America also shows that the First World War may be seen as the ultimate expression of the complexity of globalization in the early twentieth century. The interactivity and paradoxes of globalization mark this war far more than do the asymmetries of imperialism or dependency.

In the British economic war in South America, one sees the creation of a new type of war: the advent of economic sanctions. These have since become a widely accepted aspect of international conflict resolution. With such sanctions, a great power (and its allies) makes use of its apparently dominant position in the chain of transactions that exemplify modern global capitalism to influence the activities of countries and companies not directly under their control. After the First World War, the bloodless campaigns of this kind of war appealed greatly to Lord Robert Cecil and many others, who hoped that judicious use of economic weapons might empower the League of Nations to assure world peace. But despite such idealistic uses, since that time, economic weapons have more often been used by a single power for its own benefit, and to wage its own war.

As the British came to realize, the temptation to utilize dominance in world trade as a weapon can be overwhelming, yet it holds a tremendous risk. Waging such trade wars often simply exposes how truly independent and free many world markets have been and continue to be. Even dominant, imperial, powers have only limited abilities to influence the activities of distant governments or businesses.[15] Capitalism had by 1914 become quite sophisticated and multidirectional even on the periphery of world trade. The episode of the British war illustrates the difficulty, if not the impossibility, of attacking vertically integrated multinational companies like Bunge & Born and Theodore Wille & Co., whose primary defense was the scale and scope of their business and the multidirectional nature of the globalized marketplaces in which they operated. The war tested long-held British assumptions of their power in South America, and found them lacking. It would not be the last time that a war launched by a great power in a flood of righteous nationalistic optimism would backfire, exposing the inherent weaknesses of that power while nurturing new resentments among an unnecessarily broad array of once friendly foreigners.

Eventually, in the 1930s, wallowing in the depths of the global economic slump, the United Kingdom renounced free trade. Rather than creating preferences for overseas businessmen with British blood, as the British business community in South America had yearned for during the war, British authorities followed the more obvious option of favoring imperial markets and erecting tariff barriers. By that time, the relative and apparently irreversible decline of the British presence in South America appeared obvious to Britain's commercial competitors and to British businessmen themselves.[16] After the First World War, the economic and cultural role played by the British communities in the vibrant metropolises of South America withered under the pressure of foreign competitors and the lure of assimilation into local cultures. During the 1930s, the connections of British merchants in South America with their counterparts in the United Kingdom remained no more exclusive than in 1914, even as the trend continued, so apparent since the turn of the century, of British commercial decline in South America.

Notes

Introduction

1 Roger Chickering and Stig Förster (eds), *Great War, Total War: Combat and Mobilization on the Western Front, 1914–1918* (Cambridge: Cambridge University Press, 2000).

2 John Keegan, *The First World War* (New York: Knopf, 1998); Niall Ferguson, *The Pity of War* (New York: Basic Books, 1999); David Stevenson, *Cataclysm: The First World War as Political Tragedy* (New York: Basic Books, 2004); Hew Strachan, *The First World War, Vol. 1: To Arms* (Oxford: Oxford University Press, 2001).

3 The lack of histories of the First World War in South America compares unfavorably with the strong work on how the Second World War was waged there. For example, see Stanley E. Hilton, *Hitler's Secret War in South America, 1939–1945: German Military Espionage and Allied Counterespionage in Brazil* (Baton Rouge: Louisiana State University Press, 1999); and Ronald C. Newton, *The 'Nazi Menace' in Argentina, 1931–1947* (Stanford: Stanford University Press, 1992).

4 For the irreconcilable differences between blockade planners and British businessmen before the war, and the fundamental inconsistencies in the resulting blockade plans, see Paul Kennedy, "Strategy *versus* Finance in Twentieth-century Britain," in his *Strategy and Diplomacy* (London: Fontana Press, 1984). For the continuing debates between blockaders and businessmen after August 1914, see John McDermott, "Total War and the Merchant State: Aspects of British Economic Warfare against Germany, 1914–16," *Canadian Journal of History*, xxi (April 1986): 61–76. Eric Osborne writes about squabbles between a belligerent Admiralty and a weak Foreign Office, in *Britain's Economic Blockade of Germany, 1914–1919* (London and New York: Frank Cass, 2004).

5 For a laudatory take on the effectiveness of the blockade, see the official history by A.C. Bell, *A History of the Blockade of Germany and of the Countries Associated with her in the Great War, Austria-Hungary, Bulgaria, and Turkey, 1914–1918* (London: HMSO, 1961 [1937]). Paul Vincent agrees that the blockade was "the most potent weapon in the Allied arsenal." Vincent, *The Politics*

of Hunger: The Allied Blockade of Germany, 1915–1919 (Athens, OH and London: Ohio University Press, 1985) 50–60. Arthur Marsden called the blockade "the most devastating use of sea power devised in the war." Marsden, "The Blockade," *British Foreign Policy Under Sir Edward Grey*, ed. F.H. Hinsley (Cambridge: Cambridge University Press, 1977), 514–515. For an account of the failure of British blockade diplomacy, see M.W.W.P. Consett, *The Triumph of Unarmed Forces* (New York: Brentano's, 1923). Niall Ferguson, always the persuasive contrarian, argues that virtually all British measures against the German economy were ineffective; *The Pity of War* ch. 9.

6   Maurice Parmelee, among others, believed the blockade definitely shortened the war, in *Blockade and Sea Power: The Blockade, 1914–1919, and its Significance for a World State* (New York: Thomas Y. Crowell Co., 1924). More recently, the idea that blockade made a difference in the timing of the end of the war has been generally rejected; e.g. Gerd Hardach, *The First World War, 1914–1918* (Berkeley and Los Angeles: University of California Press, 1977), ch. 2.

7   Avner Offer thinks the blockade led Germany to give in to harsh terms, in *The First World War: An Agrarian Interpretation* (Oxford: Clarendon Press, 1989), ch. 5. Also, see Ferguson, *The Pity of War*, 276–281.

8   Marion Siney argues that the blockade primarily effected German civilians at the end of 1916, not German armies; *The Allied Blockade of Germany, 1914–1916* (Westport, CT: Greenwood Press, 1973 [1957]). But on the other hand, A.C. Bell and most since him have argued virulently that the blockade was a legitimate tool of war. The debate becomes more heated when the specific question of the continuance of blockade after the armistice is considered. Paul Vincent argues that the continuation of the blockade through 1919 led to unnecessary and cruel starvation in Germany. Offer doubts that the Germans truly starved; *The First World War*, 45–53.

9   Førland, Tor Egil, "The History of Economic Warfare: International Law, Effectiveness, Strategies," *Journal of Peace Research* 30: 2 (1993). In an acknowledgment of the overly restrictive definition of the term "blockade," British war planners during the 1930s adopted the broader term "economic warfare." W.N. Medlicott, *The Economic Blockade* (London: HMSO and Longmans, Green & Co., 1952), 1:16.

10   John Gallagher and Ronald Robinson, "The Imperialism of Free Trade," *Economic History Review*, 2nd series, 6:1 (1953); Rory Miller, "Informal Empire in Latin America," *Oxford History of the British Empire. Vol. V: Historiography*, ed. Robin Winks and Wm. Roger Louis (Oxford and New York: Oxford University Press, 1999).

11   D.C.M. Platt, *Finance, Trade, and Politics in British Foreign Policy, 1815–1914* (Oxford: Clarendon Press, 1968) 312, 258.

12   Seen in their *British Imperialism: Innovation and Expansion, 1688–1914* (London: Longman, 1993), cited as *Vol. I*; and *British Imperialism: Crisis and Deconstruction 1914–1990* (London: Longman, 1993), cited as *Vol. II*.

13 Cain and Hopkins, *Vol. I*, ch. 9; and *Vol. II*, ch. 7.

14 A.G. Hopkins, "Informal Empire in Argentina: an Alternative View," *Journal of Latin American Studies* 26 (1994): 479.

15 Cain and Hopkins, *Vol. I*, 314.

16 Roger Gravil, *The Anglo-Argentine Connection, 1900–1939* (Boulder, CO and London: Westview Press, 1985), 139–140.

17 Bill Albert, *South America and the First World War: The Impact of the War on Brazil, Argentina, Peru and Chile* (Cambridge: Cambridge University Press, 1988), 58.

18 Miller, *Britain and Latin America*, 180–186; Cain and Hopkins, *Vol. II*, 154–155.

19 Some dependentistas ignore the war altogether; for example, see the brief paragraph on the war in Frederick S. Weaver, *Latin America in the World Economy: Mercantile Colonialism to Global Capitalism* (Boulder, CO: Westview Press, 2000), 77.

20 VCJurgen Osterhammel and Niels P. Petersson, *Globalization: A Short History* (Princeton: Princeton University Press, 2005).

21 P.J. Cain and A.G. Hopkins, *British Imperialism, 1688–2000*, 2nd edn (Harlow, England: Longman, 2002), 664.

22 On the many ways that the pre-1914 economy existed as far more integrated and globalized than that of the early twenty-first century, see "The Rise and Fall (and Rise) of Market Integration," in Michael D. Bordo et al. (eds) *Globalization in Historical Perspective* (Chicago and London: University of Chicago Press, National Bureau of Economic Research, 2003).

23 See especially Parts Two and Three of Offer, *The First World War*.

24 Jeffry Frieden, *Global Capitalism: Its Fall and Rise in the Twentieth Century* (New York and London: W.W. Norton & Co., 2006), ch. 5.

25 C.A. Bayly, *The Birth of the Modern World 1780–1914: Global Connections and Comparisons* (Oxford: Blackwell, 2004), 228–234.

26 C.A. Bayly, "On Transnational History," *American Historical Review*, 111 (2006): 1449.

27 Mark Proudman has an excellent discussion of the development of the idea of "Greater Britain" in "The Most Important History: The *American Historical Review* and Our English Past," *The Journal of the Historical Society*, VI (June 2006): 177–212.

28 Ronald C. Newton, *German Buenos Aires, 1900–1933: Social Change and Cultural Crisis* (Austin and London: University of Texas Press, 1977); for Brazil in Frederick C. Luebke, *Germans in Brazil: A Comparative History of Cultural Conflict During World War I* (Baton Rouge and London: Louisiana State University Press, 1987); for Chile in George F.W. Young, *The Germans in Chile: Immigration and Colonization, 1849–1914* (New York: Center for Migration Studies, 1974).

29 Juan Ricardo Couyoumdjian, *Chile y Gran Bretaña Durante la Primera Guerra Mundial y la Postguerra, 1914–1921* (Santiago, Chile: Editorial Andres Bello, 1986), 42.

30 Jonathan R. Barton, "Struggling against Decline: British Business in Chile, 1919–33," *Journal of Latin American Studies* 32 (2000): 235–264.

1 The rise of the Anglo-German antagonism in South America, 1900–14

1 Report for 1899 and 1900 on the Trade and Commerce of the Consular District of Rio Grande do Sul. No. 2702, P.P. 1902, cv, Cd. 786–6.

2 Report for the years 1902–04 on the Trade of Santos. No. 3521, P.P. 1906, cxxiii, Cd. 2682.

3 Britain held 34.1 percent of Argentina's imports in 1900, a decline from their 37.3 percent share the year before. Both figures are far larger than Germany's 11.1 percent share in 1899 and 14.7 percent share in 1900. Report for the year 1900 on the Trade and Commerce of the Consular District of Buenos Aires. No. 2615, P.P. 1901, lxxxi, Cd. 429–73.

4 D.C.M. Platt, *Latin America and British Trade, 1806–1914* (NY: Harper & Row, 1972), 286, 289, 294–295.

5 Albert, *South America*, 147.

6 Colin Lewis, *British Railways in Argentina 1857–1914* (London: Athlone, 1983), 196–204.

7 These statistics do not include the tonnage under Argentine flag, as this was used exclusively in coastal trade with other South American nations. Shipping statistics are found in Ernesto Tornquist & Cia, *El Desarrollo Económico de la República Argentina en los ultimos cinquenta años* (Buenos Aires, 1920), 189–190.

8 See Alan K. Manchester, *British Preëminence in Brazil. Its Rise and Decline. A Study in European Expansion* (Chapel Hill: University of North Carolina Press, 1933); Eugene Ridings, *Business Interest Groups in Nineteenth-Century Brazil* (Cambridge: Cambridge University Press, 1994); and Richard Graham, *Britain and the Onset of Moderrnization in Brazil, 1850–1914* (Cambridge: Cambridge University Press, 1968).

9 Vera Blinn Reber, *British Mercantile Houses in Buenos Aires, 1810–1880* (Cambridge, MA: Harvard University Press, 1979).

10 Robert Greenhill, "Merchants and the Latin American Trades: an Introduction." *Business Imperialism, 1840–1930: An Inquiry Based on British Experience in Latin America*, ed. D.C.M. Platt (Oxford: Clarendon Press, 1977) 159–197; Geoffrey Jones, *Merchants to Multinationals: British Trading Companies in the Nineteenth and Twentieth Centuries* (Oxford: Oxford University Press, 2000), 62–64.

11 Bayly, *The Birth of the Modern World*, 472; Ferguson, *The Pity of War*, and Kennedy's review, supporting his position on the German antagonism, "In the Shadow of the Great War," *New York Review of Books*, 12 August 1999.

12 Platt, *Latin America*, 173–250.

13 Report for the year 1912 on the Trade of the State of São Paulo. No. 5160, P.P. 1913, lxix, Cd. 6665–118.

14 Sir Reginald Tower's Annual Report for 1912 on Argentina. CP 5066, in Kenneth Bourne and D. Cameron Watt (eds), *British Documents on Foreign Affairs – reports and papers from the Foreign Office Confidential Print* (Frederick, MD: University Publications of America, various dates), Part I, D, Vol. 9, paragraph 128 (hereafter Bourne and Watt).

15 Report for the year 1902 (January to September) on the Trade and Commerce of Brazil. No. 3050, P.P. 1903, lxxvi, Cd. 1386–127.

16 Charles Jones, "Commercial Banks and Mortgage Companies," in Platt, *Business Imperialism*, 36–40.

17 Report for the year 1902 (January to September) on the Trade and Commerce of Brazil. No. 3050, P.P. 1903, lxxvi, Cd. 1386–127.

18 Report for the year 1906 on the Trade and Finances of the Republic of Uruguay. No. 3855, P.P. 1907, xciii, Cd. 3283–116.

19 Innes to FO No. 47 Com'l, 6 July 1914. FO No. 35731 of 4 Aug. 1914. FO368/1164.

20 From the map entitled "Volume and distribution of British Trade on January 1st 1912," in Archibald Hurd, *The Merchant Navy*, Vol. I (New York: Longman, Green & Co., 1921).

21 Report for the year 1912 on the Trade of the State of São Paulo. No. 5160, P.P. 1913, lxix, Cd. 6665–118.

22 Philipps to the *Daily Mail* on 4 June 1914, quoted in Hoffman, *Great Britain and the German Trade Rivalry*, 268.

23 *Hansard*, 20 Mar. 1906, 4th series, vol. 154, 199–200.

24 Report for the year 1910 and part of the year 1911 on the Trade of the Consular District of Rio de Janeiro. No. 4686, P.P. 1911, xc, Cd. 5465–79.

25 Sir Reginald Tower's Annual Report for 1912 on Argentina. CP 5066. Bourne and Watt, part I, D, Vol. 9, paragraph 13.

26 Report for the year 1905 on the Trade, Commerce, &c. of Santa Catharina. No. 3737, P.P. 1906, cxxiii, Cd. 2682.

27 Report for the years 1902–04 on the Trade of Santos. No. 3521, P.P. 1906, cxxiii, Cd. 2682.

28 Report for the years 1899 and 1900 on the Trade and Commerce of the Consular District of Rio Grande do Sul. No. 2702, P.P. 1902, cv, Cd. 786–6.

29 Platt, *Latin America*, ch. 10.

30 Tower's annual report for 1912 on Argentina. CP 5066. Bourne and Watt, Part I, D, Vol. 9, paragraph 128.

31 Report on the Trade of the Consular District of Pernambuco. No. 4685, P.P. 1911, xc, Cd. 5465–78.

32 N.L. Watson, *The Argentine as a Market: A report to the Electors to the Gartside Scholarships on the Results of a Tour in the Argentine in 1906–7* (Manchester: Manchester University Press, 1908), 25–40.

33 G. Shaw-Lefevre, "A visit to the Argentine Republic," *The Nineteenth Century*, Vol. L (July–Dec. 1901): 830–843.

34 In this, I agree with Gravil, *The Anglo-Argentine Connection*, 103–104.
35 Remark by W. C. Kenny in the bank's annual report of 1912, p. 2. Box A47, BOLSA.
36 Memo by Edward Greene at Brazil House in London on 28 Feb. 1916, entitled 'Report on the Santos Coffee Trade'. No. 59356 of 15 Mar. 1916. FO 368/1495.
37 James Bryce, *South America: Observations and Impressions*, revised edn (New York: Macmillan, 1917), 510.
38 Report for the years 1904–06 on the Trade of Bahia. No. 3901, P.P. 1907, lxxxviii, Cd. 3901.
39 Victor Bulmer-Thomas, *The Economic History of Latin America since Independence* (Cambridge: Cambridge University Press, 1994), 169; William Glade, "Latin America and the international economy, 1870–1914," *The Cambridge History of Latin America, Volume IV, c.1870 to 1930*, ed. Leslie Bethell (Cambridge: Cambridge University Press, 1986), 14.
40 Memo by Edward Greene at Brazil House in London on 28 Feb. 1916, entitled "Report on the Santos Coffee Trade" FO No. 59356 of 15 Mar. 1916. FO368/1495. Also, Greenhill, "The Brazilian Coffee Trade," in Platt, *Business Imperialism*, 213–218.
41 'Memorandum respecting German Trade with Brazil' from Consul-General O'Sullivan-Beare to the Board of Trade, enclosed in his FO No. 28 of 30 Mar. 1914. CP No. 17271. FO368/941.
42 Greenhill, "The Brazilian Coffee Trade," 211–212.
43 David Joslin, *A Century of Banking in Latin America: To Commemorate the Centenary in 1962 of The Bank of London & South America Limited* (London: Oxford University Press, 1963), 159–167.
44 Report for the year 1908 on the Trade of Brazil. No. 4358, P.P. 1909, xcii, Cd. 4446–182.
45 Report for the years 1902–04 on the Trade of Santos. No. 3521, P.P. 1906, cxxiii, Cd. 2682.
46 On the tendency of transatlantic European companies to adopt very flexible management models, with "evidence of both centralizing and decentralizing approaches," see Robert Greenhill, "Investment group, free-standing company or multinational? Brazilian Warrant, 1909–52," *Business History*, 37 (1995): 86–111.
47 James R. Scobie, *Revolution on the Pampas: A Social History of Argentine Wheat, 1860–1910* (Austin: University of Texas Press, 1964), 92–93.
48 Roger Gravil explains that "the grain trade was primarily in German hands," relying for this assessment of nationality on characterizations by Britons during the war. Gravil, *The Anglo-Argentine Connection*, 40. Eager to demonstrate the overall weakness of British economic penetration in Argentina and the ability of the Argentines to rule their own house, D.C.M. Platt claims that the 'Big Four' were Argentine. Platt, "Economic imperialism and the businessman: Britain and Latin America before 1914." Roger Owen and Bob Sutcliffe (eds) *Studies in the Theory of Imperialism* (London: Longman, 1972), 300. But no

one in Argentina seemed to believe that Bunge & Born or others were "Argentine." For example, Consul Hugh Mallet in Rosario in 1904 explained that "there are several British firms engaged in shipping grain, but the bulk of this trade is in the hands of foreigners, principally Germans." In the Report for the year 1903 on the Trade and Commerce, &c., of the Consular District of Rosario, No. 3157, P.P. 1904, xcvii, Cd. 1766–91.

49 Tower's annual report for 1913. CP 10379. Bourne and Watt, part I, D, vol. 9, paragraph 177.

50 Gravil, *The Anglo-Argentine Connection*, 44–54.

51 Letters of 24 Apr. and 28 May 1914, from Harry Scott to Thurburn, private. Box D76/2, BOLSA.

52 "The Wool Trade and Germany," Board of Trade memo of 7 Feb. 1912. Appendix XVI of the Report and Proceedings of the Standing Sub-Committee of the Committee of Imperial Defence on Trading with the Enemy, 1912. CAB16/18A.

53 Report for the year 1907 on the Trade and Commerce of the Consular District of Buenos Ayres, No. 4064, P.P. 1908, cix, Cd. 3727–147.

54 "The Wool Trade and Germany," Board of Trade memo of 7 Feb. 1912. CAB16/18A.

55 Platt, *Latin America*, 306–310.

56 Graham, *Britain and the Onset of Modernization in Brazil*, ch. 3.

57 On the importance of "national print-languages" in enabling modern nationalism, see Benedict Anderson, *Imagined Communities: Reflections on the Origin and Spread of Nationalism* (London: Verso, 1991), 44–46.

58 Alistair Hennessy, "Argentines, Anglo-Argentines and Others," *The Land that England Lost: Argentina and Britain, a Special Relationship*, ed. Hennessy and John King (London: British Academic Press, 1992), 23.

59 Sir David Kelly, *The Ruling Few, or the Human Background to Diplomacy* (London: Hollis & Carter, 1952), 111.

60 Manuscript by Sir R. Tower, "Argentina: Notes for H.R.H. The Prince of Wales' Visit 1925," written in June 1925. University of London Library, Senate House. Also, Kelly, *The Ruling Few*, 109.

61 Report by Sir R. Tower for 1912. CP 5066. Bourne and Watt, Part I, D, Vol. 9. In relation to the sports-madness of local Britons, it is worthwhile to remember that the English brought football to South America.

62 On the belle époque vogue for building monuments, see Eric Hobsbawm, "Mass Producing Traditions: Europe, 1870–1914," *The Invention of Tradition*, ed. Hobsbawm and Terence Ranger (Cambridge: Cambridge University Press, 1992), 271–276.

63 Proudman, "The Most Important History." Also, see Offer, *The First World War*; Andrew Thompson, *Imperial Britain: The Empire in British Politics c.1880–1932* (London: Longman, 2000); David Armitage, "Greater Britain: A Useful Category of Historical Analysis?" *American Historical Review*, 104:2 (April 1999): 427–445.

64 Hennessy, "Argentines, Anglo-Argentines and Others," 23.

65   G.R. Searle, *The Quest for National Efficiency: A Study in British Politics and Political Thought, 1899–1914* (Berkeley and Los Angeles: University of California Press, 1971).

66   Haggard annual report on Brazil for 1912. CP 10286. Bourne and Watt, Part I, D, Vol. 9.

67   "Report on a Journey in the South of Brazil," Sir William Haggard, October 1912. No. 684 Misc, P.P. 1913, lxix, Cd. 6666.

68   Newton, *German Buenos Aires*, xv.

69   Richard Graham, "Introduction," *The Idea of Race in Latin America, 1870–1940,* ed. Graham (Austin: University of Texas Press, 1990), 1.

70   Hennessy, "Argentines, Anglo-Argentines and Others," 24–25.

71   On Brazil, see Thomas Skidmore, "Racial Ideas and Social Policy in Brazil, 1870–1940," and Aline Helg, "Race in Argentina and Cuba, 1880–1930," in Skidmore (ed.) *The Idea of Race in Latin America.*

72   Ronald Newton shows that this British tendency to compare themselves to the Germans was mirrored by the Germans, who "ceaselessly measured themselves" against the British. Newton, *German Buenos Aires*, 29.

73   R.J. Kennedy's annual report for 1911 on Uruguay. CP 5009. Bourne and Watt, part I, D, vol. 9.

74   Newton, *German Buenos Aires*, 11, 26.

75   Report for the year 1905 on the Trade, Commerce, &c. of Santa Catharina, No. 3737, P.P. 1906, cxxiii, Cd. 2682.

76   Robert Freeman Smith, "Latin America, the United States and the European powers, 1830–1930," in Bethell, *The Cambridge History of Latin America, Vol. IV, c.1870 to 1930*, 98.

77   Luebke, *Germans in Brazil*, 70–82.

78   Germans made up only a small minority of those emigrating to South America, and even to Brazil. Of the nearly four million immigrants to Brazil between 1881 and 1930, a mere 5 percent came from Germany. Nicolás Sánchez-Albornoz, "The population of Latin America, 1850–1930," in Bethell, *The Cambridge History of Latin America, Vol. IV*, 131. Germans were a small minority of the populations in the immigrant-laden cities; for instance, in 1914 there were around 30,000 members of the German community in Buenos Aires, of whom only 11,000 were *Reichsdeutsche*, or German nationals. Newton, *German Buenos Aires*, 28. Germany and Britain had similar numbers of subjects in Argentina. Throughout Argentina in 1914, out of a population of nearly eight million, only 26,995 men and women indicated to the Argentine census authorities that they were German, a number comparable to the 27,692 British. Tornquist, *El Desarrollo Económico de la República Argentina en los últimos cincuenta años*, 4–5.

79   Percy Alvin Martin, *Latin America and the War* (Baltimore: Johns Hopkins, 1925), 12–13.

80   R.J. Kennedy's annual report for 1911 on Uruguay. CP 5009. Bourne and Watt, part I, D, vol. 9.

81   "England and the Americas," *The Saturday Review*, 4 Jan. 1902, 5–6.

82　F.W. Wile, "German Colonisation in Brazil," *The Fortnightly Review*, January–June 1906, 129–138.

83　Haggard's annual report for 1912 on Brazil. CP 10286. Bourne and Watt, part I, D, vol. 9.

84　Robertson's annual report on Brazil for 1913. CP 5814. Bourne and Watt, part I, D, vol. 9.

85　Report for the year 1909 on the Trade and Finances of the Republic of Uruguay. No. 4605, P.P. 1910, ciii, Cd. 4962–217.

86　R.J. Kennedy's annual report for 1911 on Uruguay. C.P. 5009. Bourne and Watt, part I, D, vol. 9.

87　Fritz T. Epstein, "European military influences in Latin America" (unpublished, Library of Congress manuscript, 1941), 214–220.

88　Epstein, "European military influences," 137–148. Warren Schiff, "The Influence of the German Armed Forces and War Industry on Argentina, 1880–1914," *Hispanic American Historical Review*, 52 (Aug. 1972): 436.

89　Haggard's annual report for 1912 on Brazil. CP 10286. Bourne and Watt, part I, D, vol. 9.

90　H.S. Ferns, *Britain and Argentina in the Nineteenth Century* (Oxford: Clarendon Press, 1960), 392–396. Platt, *Finance, Trade, and Politics*, ch. 6.

91　Tower's annual report for 1912 on Argentina. CP 5066. Bourne and Watt, part I, D, vol. 9, paragraph 53.

92　Haggard's annual report for 1912 on Brazil. CP 10286. Bourne and Watt, part I, D, vol. 9.

93　R.J. Kennedy's annual report for 1911 on Uruguay. CP 5009. Bourne and Watt, part I, D, vol. 9.

94　Report by H. Gaisford on German Schools, Appendix II, of Tower's annual report for 1913. CP 10379. Bourne and Watt, part I, D, vol. 9.

95　Luebke, *Germans in Brazil*, 47–53.

96　Charles Jones, *International Business in the Twentieth Century: The Rise and Fall of a Cosmopolitan Bourgeoisie* (New York: New York University Press, 1987). Also, Ridings, *Business Interest Groups*.

97　Colin Lewis notes that Daniel Gowland, a large investor in railways in the 1860s, was also the president of the local British Chamber of Commerce. Lewis, *British Railways in Argentina*, 19.

98　Tower's annual report for 1912 on Argentina. CP 5066. Bourne and Watt, part I, D, vol. 9, paragraph 10.

99　Tower's annual report for 1913 on Argentina. CP 10379. Bourne and Watt, part I, D, vol. 9, paragraphs 21–22.

100　David Rock, *Argentina 1516–1987: From Spanish Colonization to Alfonsín* (Berkeley: University of California Press, 1987), 162.

101　Scobie, *Revolution on the Pampas*, ch. 3.

102　Arthur L. Holder (ed.) *Activities of the British Community in Argentina during the Great War, 1914–1919* (Buenos Aires: The British Society in the Argentine Republic, 1920), ch. II.

103　Newton, *German Buenos Aires*, 28.

104 Jones, *International Business*, 27–28.

105 Speech by H.H. Leng of Leng, Roberts & Co. at meeting of British business leaders to consider forming a Chamber of Commerce, quoted in the *Herald*, 2 July 1913.

106 Meeting of 1 July 1913, reported in the *Herald* and the *Standard* of 2 July 1913.

107 Minutes of Executive Committee, British Chamber of Commerce in the Argentine Republic, Buenos Aires, meetings of 23 Sept., 14 Oct., 21 Oct., and 20 Nov. 1913; 19 May, 16 June, and 4 Aug. 1914 (hereafter Executive Committee).

108 Minutes of Council, British Chamber of Commerce in the Argentine Republic, Buenos Aires, meeting of 2 June 1914 (hereafter Council).

109 Executive Committee, 4 Aug. 1914.

110 Mira Wilkins, *The Emergence of Multinational Enterprise: American Business Abroad from the Colonial Era to 1914* (Cambridge, MA: Harvard University Press, 1970), 191.

111 Bradford Perkins, *The Great Rapprochement: England and the United States, 1895–1914* (New York: Atheneum, 1968), 126–127.

112 Tower to FO No. 78 of 10 Mar. 1914, No. 15129 of 6 Apr. 1914; also Norman to FO No. 143 of 6 May 1914, No. 24427 of 2 June 1914. FO 368/925.

113 Kennedy's annual report for 1911 on Uruguay. CP 5009. Bourne and Watt, part I, D, vol. 9, paragraph 25.

114 Warren G. Kneer, *Great Britain and the Caribbean, 1901–1913: A Study in Anglo-American Relations*. Michigan State University Press, 1975. 221–224; Anne Orde, *The Eclipse of Great Britain: The United States and British Imperial Decline, 1895–1956*. New York: St Martin's Press, 1996, 33–34.

115 *Buenos Aires Herald*, 2 Jan. 1914, 7.

116 Report for the year 1911 on the Trade of the Consular District of Buenos Ayres. No. 5029, P.P. 1912, xciv, Cd. 6005–202.

117 *Buenos Aires Herald*, 30 Jan. 1914, 8, 11; quote from *Financial Times* in the *Buenos Aires Herald*, 13 Feb. 1914, 8.

118 Tower's annual report for 1912 on Argentina. CP 5066. Bourne and Watt, part I, D, vol. 9.

119 Tower's annual report for 1913 on Argentina, CP 10379. Bourne and Watt, part I, D, vol. 9.

120 Tower's annual report for 1911 on Argentina. CP 10009. FO 118/305.

121 Bradford Perkins, *The Great Rapprochement: England and the United States, 1895–1914* (New York: Atheneum, 1968), 160.

122 Tower's annual report for 1913 on Argentina. CP 10379. Bourne and Watt, part I, D, vol. 9.

123 Alan Sykes, *Tariff Reform in British Politics, 1903–1913* (Oxford: Clarendon Press, 1979) ch. 7.

124 P.A.R. Calvert, "Great Britain and the New World, 1905–1914," in Hinsley, British Foreign Policy, 385–88; Platt, *Finance, Trade and Politics*, 318–333; Miller, *Britain and Latin America*, ch. 3.

125 Platt, *Finance, Trade and Politics*, 50–53.
126 Holger Herwig, *Germany's Vision of Empire in Venezuela, 1871–1914* (Princeton: Princeton University Press, 1986), ch. 3.
127 Zara Steiner, *The Foreign Office and Foreign Policy, 1898–1914* (Cambridge: Cambridge University Press, 1969) 173–85; Ferguson, *The Pity of War*, ch. 3. Platt, "Economic Imperialism and the Businessman," 306; Ephraim Maisel, "The Formation of the Department of Overseas Trade, 1919–26," *Journal of Contemporary History*, 24, 1 (January 1989): 169–170.
128 For the anti-German biases of the Foreign Office clerks and undersecretaries, see Steiner, *The Foreign Office*, ch. 3.
129 Consul General O'Sullivan-Beare in Rio de Janeiro to FO, No. 21329 of 25 Apr. 1914. FO 368/940.
130 F.J.X. Homer, "Foreign Trade and Foreign Policy: The British Department of Overseas Trade, 1916–1922" (PhD dissertation, University of Virginia, 1971), 43–49.
131 Victor Wellesley, "Notes, Comments, and Suggestions on the Working of the New System of Commercial Attachés," 19 Sept. 1910. Bourne, Watt and Partridge, part II, K, vol. 1, 11.
132 Executive Committee, 29 Jan. 1914.
133 Victor Wellesley, "Notes, Comments, and Suggestions on the Working of the New System of Commercial Attachés," 19 Sept. 1910. Bourne, Watt and Partridge, part II, K, vol. 1, 23.
134 For instance, the two scenarios that the Trade with the Enemy (TWTE) sub-committee of the Committee for Imperial Defence looked into were wars where Germany and Britain opposed each other – one between two alliances of European states, the other between the British and German Empires. TWTE sub-committee report, part 1. CAB 16/18A.
135 Many historians have described differences among politicans and between the Foreign Office, Admiralty and War Office. See David French, *British Economic and Strategic Planning 1905–1915* (London: George Allen & Unwin, 1982); Nicholas d'Ombrain, *War Machinery and High Policy: Defence Administration in Peacetime Britain, 1902–1914* (London: Oxford University Press, 1973); Offer, *The First World War*.
136 John W. Coogan, *The End of Neutrality: The United States, Britain, and Maritime Rights, 1899–1915* (Ithaca: Cornell University Press, 1981) chs 5–6.
137 Coogan, *The End of Neutrality*, ch. 7; also Viscount Grey of Fallodon, *Twenty-Five Years, 1892–1916*, vol. 2 (New York: Frederick A. Stokes Co., 1925), 105–109.
138 Nicholas d'Ombrain has explained that the CID, despite not living up to its initial promise to integrate the Admiralty and War Office planning staffs and to make a full review of military policy, was "a useful organ of interdepartmental administration" that dealt with "relatively trivial, though useful, affairs." To people in the British government and armed services, planning for a campaign against German trade fit this description as both trivial and useful. d'Ombrain, *War Machinery*, 17.

139 Letter from Hankey to Lord Onslow, 29 July 1911. CAB 17/89. On Hankey's advocacy of economic warfare as Britain's primary weapon of war, see Lord Hankey, *The Supreme Command 1914–1918* (Volume One) (London: George Allen & Unwin, 1961), ch. 8–9.

140 The CID did compile information on imports of "certain important raw materials into Germany." Large amounts of Argentine wool, hides, skins, and linseed flowed into Germany, while Brazil supplied much rubber. TWTE supplementary papers 1912. CAB 16/18B.

141 Minutes of the 4th meeting of the sub-committee on 29 Jan. 1912, 71–77. CAB 16/18A.

142 Board of Trade memo "The Wool Trade and Germany" of 7 Feb. 1912, in Appendix XVI of the TWTE sub-committee report, "Report and Proceedings of the Standing Sub-Committee of the Committee of Imperial Defence on Trading with the Enemy 1912." CAB 16/18A.

143 Report of a sub-conference convened in accordance with the conclusions reached at the sixth meeting of the TWTE sub-committee, printed for the CID on 2 Apr. 1912. CAB 16/18B.

144 Offer, *The First World War*, 289.

145 TWTE sub-committee report, part I. CAB 16/18A.

146 On the naval arms race, see Paul Kennedy, *The Rise and Fall of British Naval Mastery* (London, 1976).

147 TWTE sub-committee report, part I. CAB 16/18A.

148 Arthur J. Marder, *From the Dreadnought to Scapa Flow: The Royal Navy in the Fisher Era, 1904–1919. Volume I: The Road to War, 1904–1914* (London: Oxford University Press, 1961).

149 Marder, *From the Dreadnought*, 358–366. French, *British Economic and Strategic Planning*, 57–73.

150 Offer, *The First World War*, 4, 225–229.

151 Avner Offer, "Morality and Admiralty: 'Jacky' Fisher, Economic Warfare and the Laws of War," *Journal of Contemporary History*, 23 (1988): 99–119.

152 Memo by Captain Webb of 11 Oct. 1913, in reply to the First Lord's minute of 18 Aug. 1913. ADM 137/2864.

153 War Staff paper of 30 Oct. 1913 on "Admiralty Responsibilities Regarding National Commerce in War." ADM 137/2864.

154 Undated memo "Proposals for initiating work in the Trade Branch"; also unsigned memo of 22 Oct. 1913 summarizing principles of trade protection and organization of the Trade Branch. ADM 137/2864.

155 Marder, *From the Dreadnought*, 58–66.

156 Slade memo for M. Borden entitled 'Imperial Defense', written on 16 Sept. 1912. Box MRF 39/3, Slade Papers, National Maritime Museum, Greenwich.

157 Bryan Ranft, calling the Admiralty plans to station cruisers along trade routes "an incredibly naive solution" to the threat of German cruisers, has questioned whether any number of British cruisers thus stationed could have succeeded in repulsing attacks on merchant ships. He believes that the Admiralty, blinded by its love of the offensive, too easily rejected the need to plan for convoys.

See Ranft, "The Protection of British Seaborne Trade and the Development of Systematic Planning for War, 1860–1906," *Technical Change and British Naval Policy, 1860–1939*, ed. Ranft (London: Hodder & Stoughton, 1977), 1–22.

158   War Staff paper of 30 Oct. 1913 on "Admiralty Responsibilities regarding National Commerce in War." ADM 137/2864.

159   Hurd, *The Merchant Navy*, vol. 1, 120, 124.

160   Simon G. Hanson, *Argentine Meat and the British Market: Chapters in the History of the Argentine Meat Industry* (Stanford: Stanford University Press, 1938), 48–51.

161   Paul Kennedy, *The Rise of the Anglo-German Antagonism 1860–1914* (London: George Allen & Unwin, 1980), 301–302.

162   On the inevitable flaws of Victorian era statistics on world trade, see D.C.M. Platt, "Problems in the Interpretation of Foreign Trade Statistics before 1914," *Journal of Latin American Studies*, 3, 2 (1971), 119–130.

163   Kennedy, *The Rise of the Anglo-German Antagonism*, 251. R.J.S. Hoffman has a good examination of British newspapers in his *Great Britain and the German Trade Rivalry* (Philadelphia: University of Pennsylvania Press, 1933).

164   F.A. Kirkpatrick, *South America and the War: Being the substance of a course of lectures delivered in the University of London, King's College under the Tooke Trust in the Lent Term* (Cambridge: Cambridge University Press, 1918) 30–33.

165   Searle, *The Quest for National Efficiency*, 57.

2 "What sort of patriotism is this?" Demanding changes to the British war, August 1914–December 1915

1   *Buenos Aires Herald*, 7 Aug. 1914, 27.

2   *Hansard*, 9 Sept. 1914, 4th series, vol. 66, 584.

3   "Notes on the Co-ordination of the War Arrangements for Trade Restrictions, &c.," printed for the CID in Jan. 1915. CAB 17/117.

4   Secret draft report of 25 Feb. 1915 from the "Interdepartmental Committee on Trade with the Enemy." CAB 17/117.

5   John Coogan, *The End of Neutrality: The United States, Britain, and Maritime Rights, 1899–1915* (Ithaca: Cornell University Press, 1981) ch. 8; Marsden, "The Blockade," in Hinsley (ed.) *British Foreign Policy*, 492–493.

6   Offer, *The First World War*, 228–229.

7   *Buenos Aires Herald*, 14 Aug. 1914, 34.

8   Marder, *From the Dreadnought*, 328–340.

9   *Buenos Aires Herald*, 14 Aug. 1914, 34.

10   Hurd, *The Merchant Navy*, vol. 1, 140.

11   Hurd, *The Merchant Navy*, vol. 1, 152–170.

12   *Buenos Aires Herald*, 14 Aug. 1914, 34. Hurd, *The Merchant Navy*, vol. 1, 244–249.

13   Hurd, *The Merchant Navy*, vol. 1, 238.

14   Hurd, *The Merchant Navy*, vol. 1, 239. C.E. Fayle, *The War and the Shipping Industry* (London: Oxford University Press, 1927), 66–67.

15   *Buenos Aires Herald*, 11 Sept. 1914, 12.

16   Tower to FO No. 211 Pol., 21 Nov. 1914. FO 118/335.

17   Hurd, *The Merchant Navy*, vol. 1, ch. 3.

18   Tower to FTD No. 15, 6 Feb. 1916. FO 118/390. Innes to FO No. 27 Com'l, 28 Sept. 1915. FO 505/358. Minute of 5 May 1915. FO No. 31691, 18 Mar. 1915. FO 368/1233. Robertson to FO No. 25, 16 Oct. 1914. FO 6–313, 16 Oct. 1914. FO 368/941.

19   H.H. Slater on 3 Jul. 1915 to Northern Assurance Co., in FO to Tower No. 57, 11 Aug. 1915. FO 118/350.

20   *Buenos Aires Herald*, 23 Oct. 1914, 24.

21   Robertson's No. 19 of 23 Apr. 1915. CP 10896/26. Bourne and Watt, part II, D, vol. 1.

22   FO to Tower No. 7 Pol., 29 Jul. 1914. FO 118/332.

23   Tower to FO No. 131 Pol., 17 Aug. 1914. FO 118/334.

24   Tower to FO No. 211 Pol., 21 Nov. 1914. FO 118/335.

25   Tower to FO No. 215, 29 Nov. 1914. FO 118/335.

26   Tower to FO No. 222, 4 Dec. 1914. FO 118/335.

27   *Buenos Aires Herald*, 16 Oct. 1914, 29.

28   Tower to FO No. 185 Pol., 17 Oct. 1914. FO118/335.

29   Tower to FO No. 188 Pol., 22 Oct. 1914. FO 118/335; also, *Buenos Aires Herald*, 23 Oct. 1914, 11.

30   Hurd, *The Merchant Navy*, vol. 1, 209.

31   Hurd, *The Merchant Navy*, vol. 1, 177.

32   Executive Committee, 30 Oct. 1914. Also, Tower to FO tel. No. 31 Com'l, 29 Oct. 1914. FO 118/337.

33   *Review of the River Plate*, 8 Oct. 1915, in Tower to FO No. 315, 8 Oct. 1915. FO 118/357.

34   Executive Committee, 30 Oct. 1914. Also, Tower to FO No. 280 Com'l, 2 Nov. 1914. FO 118/337.

35   Note from Vice-Consul Robinson at Santos, 3 Sept. 1915, in Atlee to FO No. 52, 9 Sept. 1915, CP No. 148344. ADM 137/2833.

36   Tower to FO No. 148 Pol, 28 Aug. 1914. FO 118/335.

37   Mackie to Tower, 7 Oct. 1914. FO 118/342.

38   Tower to FO tel. No. 31 Com'l, 29 Oct. 1914. FO 118/337.

39   Mackie to Tower, 7 Oct. 1914, in Tower to FO No. 268 Com'l, 16 Oct. 1914, FO No. 71594, 16 Nov. 1914. FO 368/928.

40   Dickson to Tower No. 41, 14 Oct. 1914. FO 118/342.

41   Correspondence about Harrison Line, letter from Norman Hill to Captain Webb on 2 Dec. 1914. ADM 137/2828.

42   Memo of 21 Jan. 1915 entitled "Transfer of British Ships to Neutral Flags." ADM 137/2917.

43   BT (Marine Dept.) to FO, 15 Feb. 1915, FO No. 18303 of 16 Feb. 1915. FO 368/1202.

44 Robertson to FO No. 25, 16 Oct. 1914, FO No. 60313 of 16 Oct. 1914. FO 368/941.

45 Royal Mail to FO, 16 Mar. 1915, and Hurst minute, 23 Mar. 1915, FO No. 31691 of 18 Mar. 1915. FO 368/1232.

46 Llewellyn-Smith to FO, 5 May 1915, FO No. 31691 of 18 Mar. 1915. FO 368/1232.

47 Minute by Cave (Contraband Committee) on 19 May 1915, FO No. 31691 of 18 Mar. 1915. FO 368/1232.

48 Peel to FO No. 55, 1 Sept. 1915, FO No. 148318 of 11 Oct. 1915. FO 833/18.

49 Correspondence about the Harrison Line. ADM 137/2828.

50 Innes to FO tel. No. 19 Com'l, 29 Oct. 1914, FO No. 64970 of 30 Oct. 1914. FO 368/1165.

51 FO to the Larrinaga, Lynzan and Maciver lines, FO No. 66356 of 3 Nov. 1914. FO 368/1165.

52 MacIver to FO, 10 Nov. 1914, FO No. 69881 of 11 Nov. 1914. FO 368/1165.

53 Innes tel. No. 62 Com'l, 14 Nov. 1914, FO No. 71248 of 15 Nov. 1914. FO 368/1165.

54 MacIver to FO, 2 Dec. 1914, FO No. 78310 of 3 Dec. 1914. FO 368/1165.

55 FO to Innes tel. No. 1 Com'l, 2 Jan. 1915. FO 118/350.

56 Norman to Innes tel., 4 Aug. 1914. FO 505/355.

57 Copy of Mackie's letter, in Norman to FO No. 119 Com'l, 7 Aug. 1914, FO No. 47736 of 9 Sept 1914. FO 368/926.

58 Mackie to Tower, 22 Sept. 1914, in Tower to FO No. 163 Com'l, 24 Sept. 1914, FO No. 60998 of 19 Oct 1914. FO 368/926.

59 FO to Mackie tel. No. 2 (drafted by Eyre Crowe), 9 Aug. 1914. FO 368/926.

60 FO to Mackie tel. No. 4, 15 Aug. 1914. FO 368/926.

61 Mackie to Tower, 22 Sept. 1914, in Tower to FO No. 163 Com'l, 24 Sept. 1914, FO No. 60998 of 19 Oct 1914. FO 368/926.

62 Letter from Hoult & Co., 9 Oct. 1914, FO No. 58140 of 10 Oct. 1914. FO 368/926.

63 ADM to FO, 24 Nov. 1914, FO No. 75021 of 25 Nov. 1914. Also, BT to FO, FO No. 86442 of 24 Dec. 1914. FO 368/926.

64 FO to Innes tel. No. 46 Treaty, 9 Dec. 1914. FO 505/355.

65 Innes to FO tel. No. 50 Treaty, 10 Dec. 1914. FO 505/355.

66 Innes to FO No. 22, 16 July 1915. FO 505/355.

67 Copies of Bank Black Lists from 18 Jun. 1915 to 11 Apr. 1919, entitled the "Finance lists of persons and firms whose transactions it is undesirable to facilitate or finance." FO 902/39.

68 Confidential letters from Rio de Janeiro branch to Home Office on 24 Aug., 1 Sept., 13 Oct., and 28 Oct. 1914. D 11/8, BOLSA.

69 Confidential letters from Buenos Aires to London on 20 Aug. and 5 Sept. 1914. D35/17, BOLSA.

70 Confidential telegrams from London to Buenos Aires on 11 Aug. and 24 Aug. 1914. D1/29, BOLSA.

71 Letter of 14 Jan. 1915. D1/29, BOLSA.

72 Letter from Buenos Aires to branches on 8 Feb. 1915, passing along Thurburn's letter of 14 Jan. D 6/17, BOLSA.
73 Letter of 4 Feb. 1915. D 1/29, BOLSA.
74 Private from Dey to Thurburn, 26 Feb. 1915. D 76/1, BOLSA.
75 Private from Harry Scott in Buenos Aires to Thurburn, 11 Mar. 1915. D 76/2, BOLSA.
76 Private from Harry Scott to Thurburn, 7 Jul. and 7 Sept. 1915. D 76/2, BOLSA.
77 FO 368/1205, Letter from Hope Gibson to Tower, in Tower to FO No. 279 Com'l, 1 Oct. 1915, FO No. 163811 of 3 Nov. 1915. Also, Parliamentary Council Sir A. Thring to FO, 1 Dec. 1915, FO No. 182849, 2 Dec. 1915. FO 368/1205.
78 *Buenos Aires Herald*, 4 Sept. 1914, 32.
79 Tower to FO No. 72 Com'l, 11 Mar. 1915. FO 118/355.
80 Mackie to FO No. 51, 14 Aug. 1914, FO No. 47806 of 9 Sept. 1914. FO 368/928.
81 Tower to FO No. 51 Com'l, 25 Feb. 1915, FO No. 33408 of 22 Mar. 1915. Also, Tower to FO No. 161 Com'l, 12 Jun. 1915, FO No. 94049 of 13 Jul. 1915. FO 368/1203.
82 WTD to FO, 2 Sept. 1915, FO No. 124793 of 3 Sept. 1915. FO 368/1203.
83 Letter by William Giles of Buenos Aires on 12 Oct. 1914, in the *Buenos Aires Herald*, 16 Oct. 1914, 24.
84 Letter from Alex Fraser on 16 Oct. 1914, in the *Buenos Aires Herald*, 23 Oct. 1914, 12.
85 Letter from FO to Glyn of Liebig, 29 Jan. 1915, FO No. 7425 of 20 Jan. 1915. FO 368/1201.
86 Letter from Glyn to FO, 1 Feb. 1915, FO No. 12582 of 2 Feb. 1915. FO 368/1201.
87 Filliter to Tower, 24 June 1915. FO 118/365.
88 Agnes H. Hicks, *The Story of the Forestal* (London: The Forestal Land, Timber and Railways Co., Ltd, 1956), ch. IV.
89 Letter from Ogilvie of Forestal Land, Timber & Railways Co. Ltd, 2 Feb. 1915, FO No. 12879 of 3 Feb. 1915. FO 368/1201.
90 FO to Forestal, 10 Feb. 1915, FO No. 12879 of 3 Feb. 1915. FO 368/1201.
91 Letter from Ernest Callard in London to FO, 10 May 1915, FO No. 58173 of 11 May 1915. Also, Tower to FO No. 185 Com'l, 7 Jul. 1915, FO No. 106183 of 3 Aug. 1915. FO 368/1201.
92 Letter from Forestal to FO, 25 May 1915, FO No. 66652 of 26 May. FO 368/1201.
93 Letter from Slater to FO, 26 Aug. 1915, FO No. 141992 of 1 Oct. FO 368/1201.
94 Letter from Knight to H.H. Slater of Buenos Aires, who passed it on to Tower, in Tower to FO No. 348 Com'l, 16 Nov. 1915, FO No. 193325 of 17 December. FO 368/1205.
95 Minute by B.C. Newton, 16 Oct. 1915, FO No. 149522 of 13 Oct. FO 368/1201.
96 FO to Tower No. 123 Com'l, 13 Dec. 1915, FO No. 193325 of 17 Dec. FO 368/1205.

97   Dickson to Tower, 27 Sept. 1914. FO 118/342.
98   *Buenos Aires Herald*, 21 Aug. 1914, 9.
99   *Buenos Aires Herald*, 21 Aug. 1914, 27.
100   Article from 20 Dec. 1915 sent to the Admiralty by Lamport & Holt Ltd, 20 Jan. 1916. ADM 137/2828.
101   Robertson's minute of sometime between 22–24 Aug. 1915, FO No. 116028 of 20 Aug. 1915. FO 368/1234.
102   Letter by H.E. Powell-Jones, in the *Buenos Aires Herald*, 7 Aug. 1914, 28.
103   *Buenos Aires Herald*, 25 Sept. 1914, 32.
104   Executive Committee, 30 Oct. 1914.
105   Executive Committee, 7 Dec. 1914.
106   Executive Committee, 28 Jan. 1915.
107   Column by Connon Thomson of Buenos Aires, written on 22 Aug. 1914, printed in the *Buenos Aires Herald*, 28 Aug. 1914, 15.
108   Executive Commmittee, 9 Oct. 1914.
109   Tower to FO No. 320 Com'l, 24 Dec. 1914. FO 118/337.
110   Tower to FO No. 320 Com'l, 24 Dec. 1914, FO No. 10092 of 27 Jan. 1915. FO 368/1202.
111   Tower to FO No. 320 Com'l, 24 Dec. 1914, FO No. 10092 of 27 Jan. 1915. FO 368/1202.
112   Executive Committee, 28 Jan. 1915.
113   Executive Committee, 3 May 1915.
114   Executive Committee special meetings, 16 and 19 June 1915. Also, Tower to FO No. 175 Com'l, 25 Jun. 1915, quoted in Tower to FO No. 257 Com'l, 14 Sept. 1915, FO No. 148298. FO 833/18.
115   Innes to various, 26 Oct. 1914. FO 505/361.
116   Letter from Powell-Jones to Tower, 4 Sept. 1915, in Tower to FO No. 280 Com'l, 4 Sept. 1915, FO No. 143923 of 4 Oct. FO 368/1205.
117   Executive Committee, 29 Nov. 1915.
118   Letter to ADM Trade Section, 9 Nov. 1915, Executive Committee, 5 Nov. 1915.
119   Luebke, *Germans in Brazil*, ch. 3.

3 The British government redefines Germanness

1   BT Com'l Dept. to FO, BT No. 15826 of 19 Jun. 1915. BT 12/100.
2   Chamber of Commerce letter, 23 Jun. 1915, in Tower to FO No. 175, 25 Jun. 1915, FO No. 102085 of 27 Jul. 1915. FO 368/1205.
3   Malkin's minute, 7 Aug. 1915, FO No. 102085 of 27 Jul. 1915. FO 368/1205.
4   Letter from FO to BT, 11 Aug. 1915, FO No. 102076 of 27 Jul. 1915. FO 368/1205.
5   Minute by Villiers, 18 Sept. 1915, FO No. 125276 of 4 Sept. 1915. FO 368/1205.
6   Minute by Villiers in Tower to FO No. 246 Com'l, 11 Aug. 1915. FO No. 126857 of 7 Sept. 1915. FO 368/1205.

7   Newton's memo of 20 Sept. 1915, FO No. 139228. FO 833/18.
8   Paper No. 2 in agenda for first meeting of the WTAC on 29 Sept. 1915. CAB 39/2.
9   Kenneth Rose, *The Later Cecils* (London: Weidenfeld & Nicolson, 1975), 150. Viscount Cecil, *A Great Experiment* (New York: Oxford University Press, 1941), 16–17.
10 Cecil, *A Great Experiment*, 30.
11 Letter from Cecil to G.M.Trevelyan, 19 Aug. 1935. Gascoyne-Cecil papers, Add. Ms. 51195, British Library.
12 Grey of Fallodon, *Twenty-Five Years*, vol. II, 113. Calvert, "Great Britain and the New World, 1905–1914," in Hinsley, *British Foreign Policy*.
13 David Cecil, *The Cecils of Hatfield House: An English Ruling Family* (Boston: Houghton Mifflin Co., 1973), 295.
14 Rose, *The Later Cecils*, 145.
15 Cecil minute of 19 Jul. 1915, in Gascoyne-Cecil papers, Add Ms. 51105, British Library. Also in papers of Lord Edward Grey, FO 800/95.
16 Cecil, *A Great Experiment*, 44.
17 For example, see Cecil's contribution to debates in the House of Commons on 2 Nov. 1915. *Hansard*, vol. 75, 579–626.
18 Letter from Leo Chiozza Money to Lloyd George, 13 Dec. 1915. David Lloyd George papers, D/12/1/21, House of Lords Record Office.
19 Offer, "Morality and Admiralty." Clive Parry, "Foreign Policy and International Law," in Hinsley, *British Foreign Policy*.
20 Førland, "The History of Economic Warfare," 153.
21 Tower to FO No. 257 Com'l, 14 Sept. 1915, FO No. 148298 of 11 Oct. 1915. FO 833/18.
22 Innes to FO No. 26 Com'l, 28 Sept. 1915, FO No. 154264 of 20 Oct. 1915. FO 833/18.
23 Innes to FO No. 26 Com'l, 28 Sept. 1915, FO No. 154264 of 20 Oct. 1915. FO 833/18. Also, Innes to FO No. 91 tel., 25 Sept. 1915, FO No. 138926 of 26 Sept. 1915. CAB 39/74.
24 Innes to FO No. 26 Com'l, 28 Sept. 1915, FO No. 154264 of 20 Oct. 1915. FO 833/18.
25 Memo by Robertson on the suggested prohibition of trading with the enemy in neutral countries, 23 Sept. 1915. CAB 39/74.
26 "Memorandum by Mr Nugent on certain Aspects of the Proposal to extend the Prohibition of Trading with the Enemy to Neutral Countries," 2. FO No. 152742 of 18 Oct. 1915. FO 833/18 and CAB 39/74.
27 Two memos entitled "Trade with the Enemy in relation to South American Trade" and "South American Trade." CAB 39/74.
28 Minutes of 5th meeting of the sub-committee, 12 Nov. 1915. CAB 39/74.
29 Minutes of 6th meeting of the sub-committee, 19 Nov. 1915. CAB 39/74.
30 Minutes of 6th meeting of the sub-committee, 19 Nov. 1915. CAB 39/74.
31 "Notes of Interview with Mr Worthington," minutes of 4th meeting of the sub-committee, 20 Oct. 1915. CAB 39/74.

32 Testimony by Mr Fountain, minutes of 8th meeting of the sub-committee, 29 Nov. 1915. CAB 39/74.

33 "Draft Report of the Sub-Committee appointed to consider the definition of 'enemy'." CAB 39/74.

34 Minutes of 6th meeting of the sub-committee, 19 Nov. 1915. CAB 39/74.

35 Minutes of 6th meeting of the sub-committee, 19 Nov. 1915. CAB 39/74.

36 "Report on Enemy Trading, Administration." CAB 39/74.

37 "Note on Black Lists in USA" CAB 39/108.

38 GBLC meeting, 16 Nov. 1915. TS 14/21.

39 "Report on Enemy Trading, Administration." CAB 39/74.

40 Minutes of 8th meeting of the sub-committee, 29 Nov. 1915. CAB 39/74.

41 Minutes of the 11th meeting of the WTAC, 9 Dec. 1915. CAB 39/12. Ephraim Maisel mistakenly argues that the genesis of the FTD did not occur until August 1916, in "The Formation of the Department of Overseas Trade, 1919–26," 24, 1 (Jan. 1989): 171–172.

42 Clipping from 3 Jan. 1916 edition of *The East Anglian Daily Times*, Worthington-Evans Papers, box c. 937, Bodleian Library. An identical article ran in *The Times* on 3 Jan. 1916, 7b.

43 *Evening Standard*, 3 Jan. 1916. Worthington-Evans Papers, box c. 937, Bodleian Library.

44 *North Star*, 4 Jan. 1916. Worthington-Evans Papers, box c. 937, Bodleian Library.

45 *Glasgow News*, 5 Jan. 1916. Worthington-Evans Papers, box c. 937, Bodleian Library.

46 *Hansard*, vol. 76, 2318–2358.

47 *Hansard*, vol. 76, 1883–1893.

48 Trevor Wilson, *The Downfall of the Liberal Party* (London: Collins, 1966) 79. John McDermott, "Trading with the Enemy: British Business and the Law During the First World War," *Canadian Journal of History/Annales canadiennes d'histoire* XXXII, Aug. 1997, 201–220.

49 Mr Rawlinson, *Hansard*, 13 Dec. 1915, vol. 76, 1893.

50 *Hansard*, 13 Dec. 1915, vol. 76, 1898–1901.

51 On these committees, see Trevor Wilson, *The Myriad Faces of War*, 207–211.

52 McDermott, "Trading with the Enemy: British Business and the Law During the First World War."

53 Memo on 'Effect of the Statutory List on the Conduct of the War', 14 Nov. 1916. FO 833/18.

54 Explanation of the FTD practices by Nugent to FO Central Registry, 12 Apr. 1916, No. 36736 of 17 Apr. 1916. FO 833/16.

55 *Glasgow News*, 5 Jan 1916; and *North Star*, 4 Jan 1916. Worthington-Evans Papers, Box c. 937, Bodleian Library.

56 Sir John Simon, *Hansard*, 13 Dec. 1915, vol. 76, 2194–2195.

57 Undated memo (probably of September or early October 1915) by H.B. Butler. FO 833/17.

58 30 Dec. 1915, No. 11135. FO 833/16.

59 Minutes of GBLC, 13 Jan., 25 Jan., and 27 Jan. 1916. TS 14/22.
60 Minutes of GBLC, 15 Feb. 1916, TS 14/22.
61 Minute by Butler telling of meeting with the Controller and with Penson of the WTID, 28 Mar. 1916, No. 29899. FO 833/16. Also, in minutes of GBLC, 28 Mar. 1916. TS 14/22.

4 The "ceaseless vigil": compiling the Statutory Blacklist

1   *Buenos Aires Herald*, 19 May 1916, 31.
2   Translation of article from the *Deutsche La Plata Zeitung* of 29 Mar. 1916, in Tower to FTD No. 68, 29 Mar. 1916. FO 118/390.
3   Article in the Times of Argentina, quoted in Tower to FTD No. 23, 1 Feb. 1916, No. 12815/2. FO 118/381.
4   *Buenos Aires Herald*, 7 Jan. 1916, 25.
5   *Buenos Aires Herald*, 14 Jan. 1916, 11.
6   *Buenos Aires Herald*, 7 Jan. 1916, 25.
7   Holder (ed.) *Activities of the British Community*, 240, 319, 344.
8   Holder (ed.) *Activities of the British Community*, ch. II.
9   *The Times* (London), 25 Jan. 1916, 8e.
10 *Buenos Aires Herald*, 28 Jan. 1916, 27.
11 *Buenos Aires Herald*, 4 Feb. 1916, 25.
12 *Buenos Aires Herald*, 24 Mar. 1916, 11; 21 Apr. 1916, 7.
13 Meeting of Tues. 18 Jan. 1916, Council minutes, pp. 48–49.
14 Worthington-Evans of 1 Apr. 1916 in reply to de Chair's of 27 Mar. 1916, No. 53595 of 21 Mar. 1916. FO 368/1495.
15 Peel to de Bunsen, 25 May 1916. Box 14, MB/IV/e, de Bunsen papers, Bodleian Library.
16 *Board of Trade Journal*, 92 (1916): 848–50.
17 *Buenos Aires Herald*, 21 Apr. 1916, 7.
18 H.W. Carless-Davis, "History of the Blockade. Emergency Departments," ch. 2. BT 60/2/1.
19 'Suggested rules for drawing up Statutory Black List,' No. 11932 of 13 Jan. 1916. FO 833/16.
20 Circular from Grey, No. 177982/15 of 2 Dec. 1915. FO 833/18.
21 Tower to FTD No. 5, 6 Jan. 1916. FO 118/390.
22 Tower to British Chamber of Commerce, 13 Jan. 1916. FO 118/416.
23 Tower to British Chamber of Commerce, 30 Jan. 1916. FO 118/416.
24 Tower to British Chamber of Commerce, 31 Jan. 1916. FO 118/416.
25 Tower to FTD No. 17, 12 Feb. 1916. FO 118/390.
26 Meeting of 21 Feb. 1916, Council.
27 *Buenos Aires Herald*, 11 Feb. 1916, 25.
28 *Buenos Aires Herald*, 11 Feb. 1916, 30.
29 *Buenos Aires Herald*, 12 May 1916, 9.
30 Letters from to Harry Scott in Buenos Aires to Thurburn in London, 13 Mar. 1916 and 15 Jul. 1916, D76/2, BOLSA.

31 Letter from Dey to Thurburn, 22 Jul. 1916, D76/3, BOLSA.
32 Tower to Innes, 1 Feb. 1916. FO 118/416.
33 Tower to FTD No. 284, 27 Jul. 1916. FO 118/391.
34 Tower to Powell-Jones, 25 Feb. 1916. FO 118/416.
35 Tower to FTD No. 417, 30 Sept. 1916, No. 89262 of 8 Nov. 1916, paragraph 91. FO 833/16.
36 Tower to FTD No. 288, 1 Aug. 1916. FO 118/391.
37 Tower to FTD No. 548, 13 Dec. 1916. FO 118/392.
38 Tower to FTD No. 142, 11 Mar. 1917. FO 118/432.
39 Undated letter sent by Tower to FO, and letter of 26 Jan. 1916. FO 118/405.
40 Memo by R.T. Nugent on a uniform doctrine to construct the Statutory List, No. 30279 of 25 Mar. 1916. FO 833/16.
41 Tower to FTD No. 15, 6 Feb. 1916. FO 118/390.
42 See D.C.M. Platt on British sources in South America, in Peter Walne (ed.), *A Guide to Manuscript Sources for the History of Latin America and the Caribbean in the British Isles* (Oxford: Oxford University Press, 1973).
43 Tower to FTD draft memo, 23 Feb. 1916. FO 118/390.
44 Circular from Grey to representatives in the Americas, No. 52963/50 of 1 July 1916. FO 833/16.
45 Tower to Peel, 28 Mar. 1916. FO 118/416.
46 Innes to Tower, 2 Feb. and 8 Feb. 1916. FO 118/405.
47 Letter to Admiralty on 9 Nov. 1915, Executive Committee, 8 Nov. 1915.
48 Tower to FTD No. 109, 26 Apr. 1916. FO 118/390.
49 Confidential memorandum from Murature to Tower on 11 May 1916. FO 118/394. Translation, which is quoted here, was sent from Tower to the FTD in his No. 136 of 12 May 1916. FO 118/390.
50 Promemoria to the Argentine Government from the British Legation, 7 Jun. 1916. FO 118/394.
51 *Buenos Aires Herald*, 28 Apr. 1916, 11.
52 Tower to British Chamber of Commerce, 31 Jan. 1916. FO 118/416.
53 Translations of articles of 28 Jun. 1916 from *La Nación* and *La Prensa*, Tower to FTD No. 237, 29 Jun. 1916. FO 118/391.
54 "La Constitucion Nacional y las 'listas negras'," in Tower to FTD No. 244, 6 Jul. 1916. FO 118/391.
55 Tower to FTD No. 265, 22 Jul. 1916. FO 118/391.
56 Tower to FTD No. 290, 2 Aug. 1916. FO 118/391. Townley's remarks are in Tower No. 417 of 30 Sept. 1916, FO 89262 of 8 Nov. 1916. FO 833/16.
57 Tower to FTD No. 277, 25 Jul. 1916. FO 118/391.
58 Ritchie Ovendale, *Anglo-American Relations in the Twentieth Century* (New York: St Martin's Press, 1998), 9–17; Anne Orde, *The Eclipse of Great Britain*, ch. 2.
59 Kathleen Burk, *Britain, America and the Sinews of War, 1914–1918* (Boston: George Allen & Unwin, 1985).
60 Bell, *A History of the Blockade*, 233.
61 CP 165341, Bourne and Watt, part II, H, vol. 6, 239–247.

62   Bell, *A History of the Blockade*, 316.

63   Thomas A. Bailey, "The United States and the Blacklist during the Great War," *The Journal of Modern History*, vi (March 1934), 22–23.

64   Grey to Spring-Rice No. 1446 Com'l, 10 Oct. 1916, CP 204227, Bourne and Watt, part II, H, vol. 7.

65   Grey to Barclay No. 184 FTD, 14 Nov. 1916, No. 88325 of 3 Nov. 1916. FO 833/16.

66   Memo by Stringer, Annex F, No. 98245 of 18 Dec. 1916, CP 10618. FO 833/16.

67   Grey to Spring-Rice tel. No. 296, No. 43896 of 13 Apr. 1915, Bourne and Watt, part II, H, vol. 5, 82.

68   For example, on the US protest in 31 July 1916, and the text of Grey's reply of 10 Oct. 1916, *The Times*, Wed., Nov. 15, 1916.

69   Bailey, "The United States and the Blacklist," 25; David Stevenson, *The First World War and International Politics* (Oxford: Oxford University Press, 1988), 69–72.

70   Translation of Braz's address in Peel to FO No. 54 of 16 May, No. 116083 of 11 Jun. 1917. FO 371/2901.

71   Tower No. 417 of 30 Sept. 1916, FO 89262, 9 Nov. 1916. FO 833/16.

72   Tower to FTD No. 315, 13 Aug. 1916. FO 118/391.

73   Tower to FTD No. 279, 25 Jul. 1916. FO 118/391.

74   Tower to FTD No. 323, 16 Aug. 1916. FO 118/391.

75   Tower to FTD No. 328, 17 Aug. 1916. FO 118/391.

76   Tower to FTD No. 181, 1 June 1916. FO 118/390.

77   Article of 11 Sept. 1916 in the *Diario*, in Tower to FTD No. 378, 12 Sept. 1916. Also, Tower to FTD No. 384 of 14 Sept. 1816. FO 118/391.

78   Tower to FTD No. 377, 30 Jun. 1917, No. 140701 of 22 Aug. 1917 (FTD No. 52963). FO 833/17.

79   Promemoria to the Argentine Government from Tower, 7 Jun. 1916. FO 118/394.

80   Tower to FTD No. 402, 13 Jul. 1917. FO 118/433.

81   Tower to FTD No. 218, 15 Jun. 1916. FO 118/390.

82   Tower to FTD No. 392, 7 Jul. 1917. FO 118/433.

83   Tower to FTD No. 619, 1 Nov. 1917. FO 118/433.

84   Tower to FTD No. 105, 22 Feb 1917. FO 118/432.

85   Tower MS, "Argentina: Notes for H.R.H. The Prince of Wales' Visit 1925," written in June 1925.

86   Tower to FTD No. 368, 26 Jun. 1917. FO 118/433.

87   Tower to FTD No. 130, 10 May 1916. FO 118/390.

88   Tower to FTD No. 417, 30 Sept. 1916, No. 89262 of 8 Nov. 1916, paragraph 17. FO 833/16.

89   Tower to FTD No. 44, 19 Jan. 1917. FO 118/432.

90   Tower to FTD No. 67, 29 Mar. 1916. FO 118/390.

91   Tower to FTD No. 100, 19 Apr. 1916. FO 118/390.

92   Tower to FTD No. 158, 22 May 1916. FO 118/390.

93   Tower to FO No. 244 Com'l, 12 July 1916, No. 154255 of 7 Aug. 1916. FO 368/1479.
94   Tower to FTD No. 417, 30 Sept. 1916, No. 89262 of 8 Nov. 1916, paragraph 16. FO 833/16.
95   Tower to FTD No. 247, 7 Jul. 1916. FO 118/391.
96   Tower to FTD No. 15, 8 Jan. 1917. FO 118/432.
97   Tower to FTD No. 118, 1 May 1916. FO 118/390.
98   Tower to FTD No. 293, 18 May 1917. FO 118/432.
99   Tower to FTD No. 169, 29 May 1916. FO 118/390.
100 Innes to FTD No. 42, 28 Aug. 1916. FO 505/359.
101 Tower to Hope Gibson, 13 Mar. 1916. FO 118/416.
102 Tower to FTD No. 319, 14 Aug. 1916. FO 118/391.
103 Tower to Innes, 21 Feb. 1916. FO 118/416.
104 Tower to FTD No. 30, 25 Feb. 1916. FO 118/390.
105 Tower to FTD No. 371, 8 Sept. 1916. FO 118/391.
106 Tower to FTD No. 411, 27 Sept. 1916; Tower to FTD No. 490, 10 Nov. 1916. FO 118/392.
107 Tower to FTD No. 457, 17 Oct. 1916. FO 118/392.
108 Tower to FTD No. 88, 11 Feb. 1917. FO 118/432.
109 Enclosure 8 (15404/50) of circular from Grey to representatives in the Americas, No. 52963/50 of 1 Jul. 1916. FO 833/16.
110 See c. 4216, c. 8830, and c. 8154. BT 11/13.
111 Recommendations of the Economic Conference of the Allies' at Paris on 14–17 June 1916. Parliamentary Paper Cd. 8271 of 1916.
112 BT to FTD, No. 21300 of 7 Aug. 1916. BT 12/122.
113 Tower to FTD No. 267, 2 May 1917. FO 118/432.
114 See Tower to FTD No. 426, 24 July 1917; No. 494, 24 Aug. 1917; No. 617, 1 Nov. 1917; and No. 679, 4 Dec. 1917. FO 118/433.
115 Tower to FTD No. 591, 16 Oct. 1917. FO 118/433.
116 Butler's report, 14 Nov. 1916. FO 833/18.
117 Tower to Stronge in Santiago, 2 Mar. 1916. FO 118/416.
118 Memo by Stringer on the work of the FTD, No. 98245 of 18 Dec. 1916, CP 10618. FO 833/16.

5 Fighting a "constructive" war

1   For instance, *The Times* on 14 Apr. 1916, p. 7; Cecil, "Why Mail Censorship is vital to Britain" (London: Jas. Truscott & Son, Ltd, 1916); Cecil, "Censorship and Trade," "Black List and Blockade," and "The Mails as a German War Weapon. Memorandum on the Censorship of Mails carried by Neutral Ships," (London: Eyre & Spottiswoode, Ltd, 1916).
2   No. 49351 of 1 Jun. 1916. FO 833/16.
3   No. 48719 of 29 May 1916. FO 833/16.
4   Newton's despatch to HM Representatives in the Americas, No. 52963/50 of 1 Jul. 1916. FO 833/16.

5   Memo by Butler, 14 Nov. 1916. FO 833/18.
6   W. Spens on 14 May 1917, No. 125385 of 17 May 1917, CP 10052. FO 833/16;
    "Memorandum on Trade War" by E. M. Pollock, No. 132255 of 27 Jun. 1917.
    FO 833/18.
7   Memo by Nugent on "Statement of Functions of the Foreign Trade Depart-
    ment," No. 11135 of 30 Dec. 1915. Also, No. 36736 of 12 Apr. 1916. FO
    833/16.
8   Tornquist, *Desarrollo Económico*, 136, 142.
9   Copy of cipher telegram of 21 Feb. 1916, in annex A of memo by Stringer
    describing the work fo the department. No. 10618, 18 Dec. 1916. FO 833/16.
10 Tower to Chamber of Commerce, 25 Feb. 1916. FO 118/416.
11 Council, 24 Feb. 1916.
12 Tower to FTD No. 105, 24 Apr. 1916. FO 118/390.
13 Tower to FTD No. 121, 1 May 1916. FO 118/390.
14 Council, 18 May 1916.
15 *The Times* (London), 29 Mar. 1916, 7a.
16 Executive Committee, 29 May 1916.
17 Council, 17 Aug. 1916, 29 Aug. 1916, 6 Sept. 1916.
18 Memorandum on "After War Trade" to Percy Ashley, Board of Trade, 31 Oct.
    1916, in Executive Committee minutes, 30 Oct. 1916.
19 Executive Committee, 4 June 1917.
20 Tower to FTD No. 417, 30 Sept. 1916, No. 89262 of 8 Nov. 1916. FO 833/16.
21 Tower to FTD No. 417, 30 Sept. 1916, No. 89262 of 8 Nov. 1916. FO 833/16.
22 Executive Committee, 2 May 1916.
23 Executive Committee, 11 Dec. 1916.
24 Executive Committee, 5 Feb. 1917.
25 Nugent memo of 29 May 1916, No. 49351. FO 883/16.
26 Kathleen Burk (ed.) *War and the State: The Transformation of British Govern-
    ment, 1914–1919* (London: George Allen & Unwin, 1982); L. Margaret Barnett,
    British Food Policy During the First World War (Boston: George Allen &
    Unwin, 1985).
27 Marsden, "The Blockade," in Hinsley, *British Foreign Policy*, 510–514.
28 Steiner, "The Foreign Office and the War," in Hinsley, *British Foreign Policy*,
    522. Also, McDermott, "Total War and the Merchant State," 70. For criticism
    of the press for being overly critical of the economic campaign's ineffective-
    ness, see Bell, *A History of the Blockade*, 161–165.
29 Cecil to Grey on a proposal he submitted to Asquith, with Grey's reactions, 12
    Jan. 1916. FO 800/96.
30 Emmott to Grey, 18 Feb. 1916. FO 800/102.
31 Steiner, "The Foreign Office and the War," 521.
32 Roberta M. Warman, "The Erosion of Foreign Office Influence in the Making
    of Foreign Policy, 1916–1918," *The Historical Journal*, vol. 15, No.1, Mar.
    1972, 133–135; K.G. Robbins, "Foreign policy, Government structure and
    public opinion," in Hinsley, *British Foreign Policy*, 541.
33 Parmelee, *Blockade and Sea Power*, 86–87.

34   Cecil, *A Great Experiment*, 46.
35   Steiner, "The Foreign Office and the War."
36   Parmelee, *Blockade and Sea Power*, 86. Steiner, "The Foreign Office and the War," 520–521, 527.
37   Bell, *A History of the Blockade*, 71–72.
38   On the operations of the WTID, see J.R.H. Weaver, *Henry William Carless Davis 1874–1928, A Memoir* (London: Constable and Company Ltd, 1933), 38.
39   Letter from Nugent to Worthington-Evans, 19 Dec. 1915. FO 833/17.
40   No. 11135 of 30 Dec. 1915. FO 833/16.
41   Minute by Nugent on 24 Feb. 1916, No. 21557 of 28 Feb. 1916. FO 833/16.
42   Fountain to Nugent, 13 May 1916 and 10 Jun. 1916, No. 15775. BT 12/122.
43   Letters from BT to FTD, 10 Mar 1916, No. 4818; and 21 Mar. 1916, No. 6186. BT 12/122.
44   From BT to FTD, 27 Apr. 1916, No. 11840. BT 12/122.
45   Steiner, "The Foreign Office and the War," 522.
46   Correspondence of Jan. 1915. ADM 137/2867.
47   Fountain to Liddell, 3 Aug. 1915. BT 12/109.
48   ADM 137/2862.
49   Letter from Houlder Bros., 17 Feb. 1916. In ADM 137/2913.
50   Worthington-Evans testimony to Faringdon Committee, 21 Feb. 1917. BT 60/1/3.
51   FTD memo in reply to Runciman's letter to Lord Hardinge. No. 84465, 18 Oct. 1916. FO 833/16.
52   Nugent's minute of 24 Feb. 1916, No. 21557 of 28 Feb. 1916. FO 833/16.
53   Minute by M.D. Peterson, in Tower to FTD No. 417, 30 Sept. 1916, No. 89262 of 8 Nov. 1916. FO 833/16.
54   R.P.T. Davenport-Hines, *Dudley Docker: The Life and Times of a Trade Warrior* (Cambridge: Cambridge University Press, 1984), 112.
55   No. 107599 of 2 Feb. 1917. FO 833/16.
56   Memo by Stringer on the work of the FTD, No. 98245 of 18 Dec. 1916. FO 833/16.
57   Memo by Stringer on the work of the FTD, No. 98245 of 18 Dec. 1916, CP 10618. FO 833/16.
58   Copy of letter from Runciman to Hardinge on 9 Oct. 1916, in memo by Townley, No. 84465 of 18 Oct. 1916. FO 833/16.
59   Hilda Runciman to Grey, 8 Jun. 1916. FO 800/89.
60   Copy of the Crowe report of 10 Aug. 1916 is found, among other places, in FO 505/367.
61   Crowe report of 10 Aug. 1916, 1–3. FO 505/367.
62   Crowe report of 10 Aug. 1916, 8. FO 505/367.
63   On the division between the diplomatic and consular services, see D.C.M. Platt, *The Cinderella Service: British Consuls since 1825* (Hamden, CT: Archon Books, 1971).
64   Crowe report of 10 Aug. 1916, 11. FO 505/367.
65   Runciman to Grey, 29 Aug. 1916. FO 800/89.

66　Grey to Drummond, 2 Sept. 1916. FO 800/89.

67　Drummond to Runciman, 4 Sept. 1916. FO 800/89.

68　From Hardinge to Rennell Rodd in Italy, 25 Oct. 1916, ff. 315–20, Vol. 26, Hardinge of Penshurst papers, Cambridge University Library. Also, see Steiner, "The Foreign Office and the War," 521.

69　Copy of letter from Runciman to Hardinge on 9 Oct. 1916, in memo by Townley, No. 84465 of 18 Oct. 1916. FO 833/16.

70　Cecil to Asquith, 27 Oct. 1916. Vol. 17, 120, Asquith Papers, Bodleian Library.

71　Copy of Cecil to Milner of 27 Oct. 1916, enclosed in Cecil to Asquith, 27 Oct. 1916. Vol. 17, 121–123, Asquith Papers, Bodleian Library.

72　D.C. Watt, *Succeeding John Bull: America in Britain's Place, 1900–1975* (Cambridge: Cambridge University Press, 1984), 32–35.

73　J.A. Salter, *Allied Shipping Control: An Experiment in International Administration* (Oxford: Clarendon Press, 1921) ch. 4.

74　Steiner, "The Foreign Office and the War," 524.

75　Quoted in Rose, *The Later Cecils*, 152.

76　Robert E. Bunselmeyer, *The Cost of the War, 1914–1919: British Economic War Aims and the Origins of Reparation* (Hamden, CT: Archon Books, 1975) 27–33.

77　Private from Townley at FTD to Innes, 28 Nov. 1916. FO 505/367.

78　Tornquist, *El Desarrollo Económico*, 136.

79　Letter from Tower to Chamber of Commerce, Executive Committee meeting, Mon. 23 Oct. 1916.

80　Tower to FTD No. 29, 7 Feb. 1919; and Tower to FTD No. 34, 13 Feb. 1919. FO 118/507.

81　Letter from the "Sucesion Diego Buchanan" to Chalkley on 19 Jun. 1917, in Tower to FTD No. 364, 25 Jun. 1917. FO 118/433.

82　Letter from Wilson Bros. to Innes, 19 July 1917. FO 505/367.

83　Executive Committee, 16 July 1917.

84　Memorandum on "After War Trade," Executive Committee, 30 Oct. 1916.

85　Gordon Ross, *Argentina and Uruguay* (London: Methuen & Co. Ltd, 1917), 104–122.

86　Executive Committee, 13 Nov. 1916.

87　Executive Committee, 8 Jan. 1917. Tower to FTD No. 186, 29 Mar. 1917. FO 118/432.

88　Council letter to Tower on 18 Jan. 1917. Council, 18 Jan. 1917.

89　Council letter to Tower on 30 Mar. 1917. Council, 29 Mar. 1917.

90　Innes to FO No. 6 Com'l, 24 Jan. 1918. FO 505/367.

91　Tower to FTD No. 229, 19 Apr. 1917. FO 118/432.

92　Enclosed "White List" in Tower to FTD No. 121, 1 May 1916. FO 118/390.

93　Tower to FTD No. 417, 30 Sept. 1916, paras. 49–57. FO 833/16.

94　Chamber to Percy Ashley of BT Committee on Commercial and Industrial Policy, 28 Nov. 1916. Executive Committee, 27 Nov. 1916.

95　FTD memo by Stringer describing the work of the department, No. 10618, 18 Dec. 1916, FO 833/16.

96   Executive Committee, 5 Mar. 1917.
97   Council, Mar. 12, 1917.
98   Executive Committee, 19 Mar. 1917, and 26 Mar. 1917.
99   Council, 16 Apr. 1917.
100 Council, 7 May 1917.
101 "Commercial Information System: Notes of an explanation of 'Form K' given to a meeting of Secretaries of Chambers of Commerce," June 1917. FO 118/425.
102 Memo from Pollock, 18 Apr. 1917, No. 227493 of 30 Apr. 1919. FO 833/17.
103 Circular from Pollock, No. 125841/General of 14 July 1917. FO 833/17.
104 Memo from Campbell, in letter from Macleay to Tower, 12 May 1917. FO 118/425.
105 Tower to FTD No. 498, 25 Aug. 1917; Tower to FTD No. 593, 17 Oct. 1917. FO 118/433.
106 FTD to Tower No. 10, 8 Jan. 1918, as noted in Tower to FTD No. 222, 13 Apr. 1918. FO 118/468.
107 Stevenson, *The First World War and International Politics*, 106.
108 Macleay to Tower, 12 May 1917. FO 118/425.
109 Executive Committee, 22 Oct. 1917.
110 Report of the sub-committee on the federation of manufacturers in particular industries for the promotion of their joint interests in relation to their export trade, 1917. BT 60/1/3.
111 Executive Committee, 28 May 1917.
112 Council, 15 Feb. 1917. Executive Committee, 26 Feb. 1917.
113 Testimony by Sir Eyre Crowe on 13 Feb. 1917. BT 60/1/3.
114 "Brief of evidence to be given on behalf of the Board of Trade." BT 60/1/3.
115 FO to Treasury, No. 27420 of 24 Mar. 1917; and letter from Clark to Llewellyn-Smith, 29 Mar. 1917. BT 60/1/3.
116 List of Committees of 1916, Ms. 14,477/5. Association of British Chambers of Commerce, Guildhall.
117 Davenport-Hines, *Dudley Docker*, 135–136.
118 "Memorandum by the Board of Trade and the Foreign Office with respect to the Future Organisation of Commercial Intelligence," House of Commons Sessional Papers, P.P. 1917, Cd. 8715.
119 Private and Confidential letter from Macleay to Tower, 1 May 1917. FO 118/425.
120 Council, 19 July 1917.
121 Minutes of the War Cabinet, 15 Aug. 1917, paragraph 10 and appendix II (Memo G.T.-1707). CAB 23/3.
122 "Memorandum by the Board of Trade and the Foreign Office with respect to the Future Organisation of Commercial Intelligence," House of Commons Sessional Papers, P.P. 1917, Cd. 8715. On the War Cabinet decision, see meeting 216, 15 Aug. 1917. CAB 23/3.
123 Milner to Bonar Law, 17 Oct. 1916. Bonar Law Papers, 53/4/9, House of Lords Record Office.

124 Steel-Maitland to Bonar Law, 19 July 1917. Bonar Law Papers, 82/2/10.
125 Steel-Maitland to Bonar Law, 17 Sept. 1917. Bonar Law Papers, 82/4/15.
126 Homer, "Foreign Trade and Foreign Policy," 141–51.
127 Homer, "Foreign Trade and Foreign Policy," 154–61.
128 Correspondence between Cecil, Steel-Maitland and Pollock from 7–13 December 1917, No. 228078 of 26 May 1919. FO 833/17.
129 Steel-Maitland to Lord Robert Cecil, 12 Nov. 1917. BT 60/1/1.
130 Steel-Maitland to F.M. Box in Leeds, 10 Dec. 1917. BT 60/1/1.
131 Report for the War Cabinet on the work of the FTD, 14 Mar. 1919, No. 224067 of 18 Mar. 1919. FO 833/17.
132 FO 118/508.
133 FTD-Development of British Interests in South and Central America. BT 13/85/E35466.
134 Steel-Maitland to Cecil, 28 May 1918. Cecil Add. Ms., 51071B.
135 Eyre Crowe to Cecil, 6 Sept. 1918. Cecil Add. Ms. 51094.
136 Executive committee, 8 July 1918.
137 DOT to Tower No. 1, 18 June 1918. FO 118/470.

6 Cloaks, Turks, the Octopus, and other undesirables: travails of the trade warriors in South America

1 Tower to FTD No. 284, 12 May 1917. FO 118/432.
2 Memo by H.B. Butler on 16 Nov. 1916, 88325, FO 833/16.
3 *The Times*, Tues. May 8, 1917, p. 12.
4 Nugent's memo, agreed to by Butler, No. 30279 of 25 Mar. 1916. FO 833/16.
5 "Effects of S/L on contracts," No. 24334 of 9 Mar. 1916. FO 833/16.
6 Circular despatch from Grey to HMRR in the Americas, No. 52963/50 of 1 Jul. 1916. FO 833/16.
7 "Replies to Enquiries as to fulfilling Contracts with Firms on the Statutory List," Enclosure 7 in Circular from Grey to HMRR in the Americas, No. 52963/50 of 1 Jul. 1916. FO 833/16.
8 Innes to FTD No. 42, 28 Aug. 1916. FO 505/359.
9 Tower to FTD No. 248, 10 Jul. 1916; and Tower to FTD No. 268, 23 Jul. 1916. FO 118/391.
10 Chalkley's No. 17 of 5 Sept. 1916, in Tower to FTD No. 368, 7 Sept. 1916. FO 118/391.
11 Dickson's of 20 Sept. 1916, in Tower to FTD No. 398, 21 Sept. 1916. FO 118/391.
12 Tower to FTD No. 187, 29 Mar. 1917. FO 118/432.
13 Tower to FTD No. 438, 31 July 1917. FO 118/433.
14 Kirkpatrick, *South America and the War*, 37.
15 Tower No. 377 of 30 June 1917, No. 140701 of 22 Aug. 1917, FO 833/17.
16 Innes to FTD No. 42, 28 Aug. 1916. FO 505/359.

17 Tower to FTD No. 547, 17 Sept. 1917. FO 118/433.
18 Tower private to Ronald Macleay (Deputy Controller of the FTD under Pollock), 21 Jul. 1917. FO 118/433.
19 Miller, *Britain and Latin America*, 182. Kirkpatrick, *South America and the War*, ch. I.
20 Tower to FTD No. 284, 12 May 1917. FO 118/433.
21 No. 110156, 16 Feb. 1917. FO 833/18.
22 Copy of letter from Crowe to Spring-Rice, in FTD to Innes No. 26, 26 Mar. 1917, No. 110156. FO 505/360.
23 Telegram from Townley to War Department No. 1058, 3 May 1917; FTD to Spring-Rice Tel. No. 86, 18 May 1917. In FTD No. 125385, 17 May 1917, FO 833/16.
24 Gerald D. Feldman, "War Aims, State Intervention, and Business Leadership in Germany: The Case of Hugo Stinnes," in Roger Chickering and Stig Förster (eds), *Great War, Total War*, 349–367. Fritz Fischer, *Germany's Aims in the First World War* (New York: W.W. Norton, 1967); Holger H. Herwig, *The First World War: Germany and Austria-Hungary 1914–1918* (London: Arnold, 1997) 314; Roger Chickering, *Imperial Germany and the Great War, 1914–1918*, 2nd edn (Cambridge: Cambridge University Press, 2004).
25 Example of such communications between Tower and Consul General Bayley in New York City, in Tower to FTD No. 387, 6 July 1917. FO 118/433.
26 Circular from FTD No. 139660/50, 18 Sept. 1917. FO 833/17.
27 Complaint from E. Woodward, the agent of Chadwick Weir & Co. Ltd, in Tower to FTD No. 388, 6 Jul. 1917. FO 118/433.
28 Letter from M.I.I.C. in Rio de Janeiro, 22 Jun. 1917, sent from WTID to ADM Trade Division on 8 Aug. 1917. ADM 137/2834.
29 Tower private to Ronald Macleay (Deputy Controller of the FTD under Pollock), 21 Jul. 1917. FO 118/433.
30 FO tel circular, 10 Nov. 1917; and Innes to FTD tel No. 218, 12 Nov. 1917. FO 505/360.
31 Innes to FTD No. 113, 5 Dec. 1917. FO 118/478.
32 War Cabinet meeting 191, 20 July 1917. CAB 23/3.
33 Comments by Cecil on Curzon's memo to the War Cabinet "Memorandum on Economic Offensive," 20 Sept. 1917. FO 800/214.
34 Undated memo likely by Pollock, 68b–d. Ms. Eng. hist. c. 943, Hanworth (Pollock) papers, Bodleian Library.
35 War Cabinet meeting 32, 11 Jan. 1917. CAB 23/1.
36 Carl Parrini, *Heir to Empire: United States Economic Diplomacy, 1916–1923* (Pittsburgh: University of Pittsburgh Press, 1969) especially chs 1–2; Burton I. Kaufman, *Efficiency and Expansion: Foreign Trade Organization in the Wilson Administration, 1913–1921* (Westport, CT and London: Greenwood Press, 1974).
37 Robert Mayer, "The Origins of the American Banking Empire in Latin America: Frank A. Vanderlip and the National City Bank." *Journal of Interamerican Studies and World Affairs*, vol. 15, no. 1, Feb. 1973. 60–76.

38 Joseph S. Tulchin, *Argentina and the United States: A Conflicted Relationship* (Boston: Twayne Publishers, 1990) 35.

39 For example, see correspondence of US Vice Consul W.H. Lawrence in Santos, to US Consul-General A.L.M. Gottschalk in Rio de Janeiro, in Atlee to FO No. 15 Com'l, 16 May 1917, No. 126282 of 26 Jun. 1917. FO 368/1708.

40 Emily Rosenberg, *World War I and the Growth of United States Predominance in Latin America* (New York and London: Garland Publishing, 1987), 54.

41 US Vice Consul W.H. Lawrence in Santos, to US Consul-General A.L.M. Gottschalk in Rio de Janeiro, in Atlee to FO No. 15 Com'l, 16 May 1917, No. 126282 of 26 Jun. 1917. FO 368/1708.

42 US Vice Consul W.H. Lawrence in Santos, to US Consul-General A.L.M. Gottschalk in Rio de Janeiro, in Atlee to FO No. 15 Com'l, 16 May 1917, No. 126282 of 26 Jun. 1917. FO 368/1708.

43 Rosenberg, *World War I*, 33; Kaufman, *Efficiency and Expansion*.

44 Unsigned report by someone appointed by the Department of Information in Oct. 1917 to travel to Argentina. INF 4/6.

45 Innes to FTD No. 115, 19 Dec. 1917. FO 505/360.

46 Tower to FTD No. 38, 18 Jan. 1918. FO 118/468.

47 Executive Committee, 4 June 1917.

48 Executive Committee, 11 June 1917.

49 Rory Miller, "Latin American Manufacturing and the First World War: an exploratory essay." *World Development* 9 (1981): 707–716.

50 Tower to FTD No. 703, 18 Dec. 1917. FO 118/433. Also, Tower to FTD No. 9, 4 Jan. 1918. FO 118/468.

51 Tower to FTD No. 546, 16 Sept. 1917, and Tower to FTD No. 692, 13 Dec. 1917. FO 118/433.

52 Tower to FTD No. 458, 3 Aug. 1917. FO 118/433.

53 Council, 15 Nov. 1917.

54 Tower to FTD No. 703, 18 Dec. 1917; and Tower to FTD No. 719, 26 Dec. 1917. FO 118/433.

55 Council, 17 Jan. 1918.

56 Executive Committee, 12 Nov. 1918.

57 Executive Committee, 4 Feb. 1918.

58 Tower to FTD No. 703, 18 Dec. 1917. FO 118/433.

59 Council, 17 Jan. 1918.

60 Chamber of Commerce to Tower, 26 Mar. 1918. FO 118/481.

61 Tower to FTD No. 213, 9 Apr. 1918. FO 118/468. Copy of letter of 3 Apr. 1918 from Tower to the Chamber of Commerce, in memo of 1 Jun. 1918 from Chalkley to Kerr, in Tower to FTD No. 358, 8 Jul. 1918. FO 118/469.

62 Council, 18 Apr. 1918.

63 Powell-Jones to Chalkley on 6 Mar. 1918, with the figures related to the FO by telegram on 7 Mar. and mail on 9 Mar. FO 118/480.

64 Tower to FTD, No. 283, 9 May 1918. FO 118/468.

65 Council, 1 July 1918.

66 Council, 18 July 1918.

67 Council, 24 Jan. 1918.

68 See reports by Wool Committee (headed by Gibson) and by Electrical Committee, Council, 20 Dec. 1917 and 17 Jan. 1918.

69 Tower to FTD No. 39 of 18 Jan. 1918. FO 118/468.

70 Powell-Jones to Chalkley on 6 Mar. 1918, with the figures related to the FO by telegram on 7 Mar. and mail on 9 Mar. FO 118/480. Also, see Tower to FTD No. 500 of 8 Oct. 1918. FO 118/469.

71 Tower to FTD No. 432 of 26 Aug. 1918. FO 118/468.

72 Tower to FTD No. 89 of 16 Feb. 1918. FO 118/468.

73 Tower to FTD No. 428 of 23 Aug. 1918. FO 118/469.

74 British Chamber of Commerce in the Argentine Republic, Annual report for year ended 30 June 1918.

75 Tower to FTD No. 56, 23 Jan. 1918. FO 118/468.

76 INF 4/6. Innes similarly requested "full responsibility to make immediate alterations" to make the Statutory List program more effective in Uruguay. Innes to FO tel. No. 79, 26 Mar. 1918. FO 505/367.

77 Tower to FTD No. 367, 14 Jul. 1918. FO 118/469.

78 Tower to Chamber of Commerce, Executive Committee, 10 June 1918.

79 Tower to FTD No. 109, 22 Feb. 1918. FO 118/468.

80 Telegram to HM ministers in South America from FO, 27 Mar. 1918, attached in No. 174609 of 29 Mar. 1918. FO 833/17.

81 Tower to FTD No. 340, 19 Jun. 1918. FO 118/469.

82 Tower to FTD No. 335, 17 Jun. 1918. FO 118/469.

83 Tower to FTD No. 281, 6 May 1918. FO 118/468.

84 Circular from Pollock to HM Representatives in Latin America, 28 Feb. 1918, attached in No. 174609 of 29 Mar. 1918. FO 833/17.

85 Tower to FTD No. 208, 4 Apr. 1918; and Tower to FTD No. 234, 19 Apr. 1918. FO 118/468.

86 See minutes of meeting of 25 Mar. 1918, in No. 174609 of 29 Mar. 1918. FO 833/17.

87 Council, 16 May 1918.

88 Executive Committee, 29 Apr. 1918. Tower to FTD No. 326, 17 Jun. 1918. FO 118/469.

89 Council, 26 Aug. 1918.

90 Memorandum of 1 June 1918 from Chalkley to Kerr of the de Bunsen mission, in Tower to FTD No. 358, 8 July 1918. FO 118/469.

91 Executive Committee, 3 Sept. 1918.

92 Council, 26 Aug. 1918.

93 Council, 22 Aug. 1918.

94 Tower to FTD No. 546, 16 Nov. 1918. FO 118/469.

95 Rosenberg, *World War I*, 54–55.

96 Tower private to Macleay, 21 Jul. 1917. FO 118/433.

97 Minute of 9 Oct. 1918 on the WTID weekly bulletin No. 157 of 3 Oct. 1918. ADM 137/2919.

98 Joslin, *A Century of Banking*, 234.

99   Council, 7 Mar. 1918.
100 Letter from B. Dolby of the Rosario branch of the London and Brazilian Bank, 7 May 1918. G 21/4, BOLSA.
101 Cain and Hopkins, *Volume II*, 149, follow Gravil, *The Anglo-Argentine Connection*, and Rosenberg, *World War I*, ch. 3.
102 Balfour to the Cabinet, 16 Apr. 1918. FO 800/200.
103 Letter from de Bunsen to his wife, Berta, on 28 May 1918. De Bunsen papers, Box 10, MB/I/rr, Bodleian Library.
104 Explained de Bunsen in an interview with a Reuters correspondent on 7 Oct 1918. De Bunsen papers, Box 11, MB/II/e.
105 Letter from de Bunsen to Berta on 28 May 1918. De Bunsen papers, Box 10, MB/I/rr.
106 Letter from de Bunsen to Berta on 2 June 1918. De Bunsen papers, Box 10, MB/I/rr.
107 De Bunsen diary while on Mission to South America, 10 May 1918. De Bunsen papers, Box 12, MB/III, a.
108 Letter from Powell-Jones to de Bunsen on 11 June 1918. De Bunsen papers, Box 11, MB/I/e.
109 Letter from Dey to Thurburn, private, 5 June 1918, D 76/3, BOLSA.
110 Letter from de Bunsen to Berta, 5 May 1918. De Bunsen papers, Box 10, MB/I/rr. Letter from de Bunsen to Balfour, 18 Sept. 1918. De Bunsen papers, Box 11, MB/II/e.
111 Couyoumdjian, *Chile y Gran Bretaña*, 145–147.
112 Couyoumdjian, *Chile y Gran Bretaña*, 235–238.
113 Letter from de Bunsen to Berta, 30 June 1918. De Bunsen papers, Box 10, MB/I/rr.
114 Kirkpatrick, *South America and the War*, 38.
115 Memorandum from Textile Committee, Council, 12 Mar. 1917.
116 Tower to FTD No. 325, 2 June 1917. FO 118/433. Tower to FTD No. 503, 8 Oct. 1918. FO 118/469.
117 Memorandum from Textile Committee, Council, 12 Mar. 1917.
118 Tower to FTD No. 152, 15 Mar. 1917. FO 118/432.
119 Textile Committee to Chalkley on 16 Jan. 1918, in Tower to FTD No. 54, 22 Jan. 1918. FO 118/468.
120 FTD to Tower No. 145, 8 Apr 1918, No. 174859/2. FO 118/460.
121 Tower to FTD No. 296, 20 May 1918. FO 118/468.
122 Tower to FTD No. 301, 25 May 1918. FO 118/469.
123 Council, 29 June 1918.
124 Hardware and Machinery Committee resolution, Council, 29 June 1918. Also, Tower to FTD No. 392, 23 July 1918. FO 118/469.
125 Council, 18 July 1918.
126 Council, 22 Aug. 1918.
127 Tower to FTD No. 503, 8 Oct. 1918. FO 118/469.
128 Tower to FTD No. 7, 9 Jan. 1919. FO 118/507.
129 Council, 17 Oct. 1918.

130 Tower to FTD tel No. 794, 26 Dec. 1918. ADM 137/2919.
131 Bell, *A History of the Blockade*, ch. 3.
132 *Buenos Aires Herald*, 31 Mar. 1916, 28.
133 Tower to FTD No. 90, 11 Apr. 1916. FO 118/390.
134 Tower to FTD No. 62, 24 Mar. 1916. FO 118/390.
135 Tower to FTD, No. 89262, 30 Sept. 1916, FO 833/16.
136 Tower to FTD No. 251, 12 July 1916. FO 118/391.
137 For example, the "Estancia La Pelada," the "Explotacion de campos y montes del Rio Bermejo," and the "Belga Americana." Tower to FTD No. 239, 23 Apr. 1917, and Tower to FTD No. 259, 1 May 1917. FO 118/432.
138 Tower to FTD No. 10, 5 Jan. 1917. FO 118/432.
139 Tower to FTD No. 468, 9 Aug. 1917. FO 118/433.
140 Tower to FO No. 140 Com'l, 30 Mar. 1916, No. 80318 of 28 Apr. 1916. Letter from Powell-Jones of the Chamber of Commerce of 24 May, in Tower to FO No. 202, 26 May 1916, No. 125796 of 29 Jun. 1916. FO 368/1478.
141 Tower to FTD No. 333, 22 Aug. 1916. FO 118/391.
142 Tower to FTD No. 46, 20 Jan. 1917. FO 118/432.
143 Tower to FTD No. 158, 17 Mar. 1917. FO 118/432.
144 Tower to FTD No. 633, 9 Nov. 1917. FO 118/433.
145 "First Report of the Royal Commission on Wheat Supplies," P.P. 1921., xviii, Cmd. 1544, appendix 5 and appendix 7.
146 Footnote, appendix 31, final Report of the Royal Commission on Wheat Supplies, 1921., Cmd. 1544, xviii.
147 Tower to FTD No. 231, 28 June 1916. FO 118/390.
148 Tower to FTD No. 417, 30 Sept. 1917. FO 118/391.
149 Tower to FTD No. 37, 15 Jan. 1918. FO 118/468.
150 "First Report of the Royal Commission on Wheat Supplies," P.P. 1921., xviii, Cmd. 1544, appendix 31.
151 Tower to FTD No. 65, 30 Jan. 1918. FO 118/468.
152 Tower to FTD No. 83, 14 Feb. 1918. FO 118/468.
153 Tower to FTD No. 537, 8 Nov. 1918. FO 118/469.
154 Tower to FTD No. 568, 2 Dec. 1918. FO 118/469.
155 On the 1917 wheat purchase, Tower to FTD No. 377, 30 June 1917, para. 40. FTD 140701, 22 Aug. 1917, 52963. FO 833/17.
156 Tower to FTD No. 403, 7 Aug. 1918; Tower to FTD No. 472, 18 Sept. 1918. FO 118/469.
157 Report by the British Chamber of Commerce, in Tower to FTD No. 114, 25 Feb. 1918. FO 118/468.
158 Tower to FTD No. 423, 16 Aug. 1918. FO 118/469.
159 Tower to FTD No. 472, 18 Sept. 1918. FO 118/469.
160 WTID weekly bulletin No. 135, 13 Jun. 1918. ADM 137/2919.
161 Peel to FO Pol No. 23, 25 Mar. 1918. No. 77130 of 1 May. FO 371/3166.
162 15 Mar. 1916. FO 505/359.
163 British Chamber of Commerce in Uruguay to Innes, 16 Feb. 1917. FO 505/367.

164   FO 505/360.
165   Innes No. 15 FTD of 27 Feb. 1918, Innes No. 11 Com'l of 12 Mar. 1918, and
      Innes No. 13 Com'l of 25 Mar. 1918. FO 505/367.
166   From Peek Bros & Winch, Ltd to Innes, 28 Feb. 1918; Innes to Peek, 25 Apr.
      1918; Peek to Innes, 2 July 1918; Innes to Peek, 7 Sept. 1918; Peek to Innes,
      20 Sept. 1918. FO 505/367.
167   Tower to FTD No. 347, 21 June 1918. FO 118/469.

7 How the economic war shaped South American
engagement in the world war

1   For a focus on interamerican relations, see Rosenberg, *World War I*, ch. 1. For
    the impact of pro-Allied thought and anti-German feelings, see Martin, *Latin
    America and the War*.
2   David Rock, *Politics in Argentina, 1890–1930: The Rise and Fall of Radical-
    ism* (Cambridge: Cambridge University Press, 1975), 63–66.
3   INF 4/6.
4   De Bunsen diary while on Mission to South America, 1 June 1918. De Bunsen
    papers, Box 12, MB/III, a.
5   Albert, *South America*, 246–255.
6   Tulchin, *Argentina and the United States*, 38.
7   Rock, *Politics in Argentina*, 134–142.
8   Alejandro Bendaña, *British Capital and Argentine Dependence, 1816–1914*
    (New York: Garland Publishing, 1988), ch. IV. Also, Lewis, *British Railways
    in Argentina*, 79–86, 97–123.
9   Letter from E.S. Jones in Buenos Aires to George R. Clerk in the FO, 5 Feb.
    1917. No. 53708, 13 Mar. 1917. FO 368/1690.
10 FTD memorandum, FTD 110156, 16 Feb. 1917. FO 833/18.
11 Minute of War Cabinet meeting, 4 Dec. 1917. 290A. CAB 23/4.
12 Martin, *Latin America and the War*, 212–215.
13 Newton, *German Buenos Aires*, 49.
14 Dickson to FO No. 146, 26 Oct. 1917. FO 118/438.
15 Ricardo Weinmann, *Argentina en la Primera Guerra Mundial: Neutralidad,
    transicion politica y continuismo economico* (Buenos Aires: Editorial Biblos,
    1994), Part III; Luis C. Alan Lascano, *Yrigoyen y la Guerra Mundial* (Buenos
    Aires: Editorial Korrigan, 1974).
16 Maria Monserrat Llairo and Raimundo Siepe, *Argentina en Europa: Yrigoyen
    y la Sociedad de las Naciones (1918–1920)* (Buenos Aires: Ediciones Macchi,
    1997). Also, Raimundo Siepe, *Yrigoyen, la Primera Guerra Mundial y las
    relaciones económicas* (Buenos Aires: Centro Editor de América Latina, 1992),
    9–10.
17 Tower to FTD No. 75, 5 Feb. 1918. FO 118/468.
18 Tower to FTD No. 328, 17 Aug. 1916. FO 118/391. Also, Tower to FTD No.
    443, 11 Oct. 1916. FO 118/392.
19 Tulchin, *Argentina and the United States*, 36.

20 Tower to FTD No. 107, 23 Feb. 1917; No. 108, 23 Feb. 1917; No. 140, 10 Mar. 1917; No. 142, 11 Mar. 1917; No. 149, 14 Mar. 1917. FO 118/432.

21 Tower to FTD No. 360, 23 June 1917. FO 118/433.

22 Tower to FTD No. 508, 31 Aug. 1917. FO 118/433.

23 Avner Offer highlights the importance of international sources of food for the United Kingdom during the war, but he focuses attention solely on the Dominions and the United States and expressly admits that his "agrarian interpretation" of the war fails to examine "non-Anglo suppliers" like Argentina. Offer, *The First World War*, 7.

24 Tower to FO tel No. 194 Com'l, 2 June 1916, No. 106489 of 3 June 1916. FO 368/1479.

25 From War Office Contracts Dept. to FO, 16 June 1916, No. 117498 of 19 June 1916. FO 368/1479.

26 Copy of Treasury letter to the Board of Agriculture, 24 Jun. 1916, No. 122631 of 26 June 1916. Tower explained these conditions to Dr Becu, the Minister of Foreign Affairs, as noted in Tower to FO tel No. 394, 26 Oct. 1916, No. 215299 of 27 Oct. 1916. FO 368/1479.

27 Tower to FO tel No. 194 Com'l, 2 Jun. 1916, No. 106489 of 3 Jun. 1916. Copy of Treasury to Board of Agriculture, 24 Jun. 1916, No. 122631 of 26 Jun. 1916. FO 368/1479.

28 Undated (probably late 1916) memo entitled "List of German Steamers in Neutral Ports," in ADM 137/2914. A French list in the same Admiralty file, entitled "Liste des Batiments Allemans et Autrichiens réfugiés dans les Ports Neutres," lists 19 German ships in Argentine ports with a gross tonnage of 79,900 tons.

29 From Board of Agriculture to Treasury on 7 July 1916, in Treasury to FO, 20 July 1916, No. 141658 of 21 July 1916. FO 368/1479.

30 Tower to FO No. 244 Com'l, 12 Jul. 1916, No. 154255 of 7 Aug. 1916. FO 368/1479.

31 Tower to FO No. 346 Com'l, 9 Nov. 1916, No. 247559 of 7 Dec. 1916. FO 368/1479.

32 Royal Commission on Wheat Supplies to FO, 28 Dec. 1916, No. 263542 of 29 Dec. 1916. FO 368/1479.

33 Tower to FO tel No. 124 Com'l, 27 Mar. 1917, and FO to Tower tel No. 107 of 28 Mar. 1917, No. 64894 of 28 Mar. 1917. FO 368/1690.

34 Albert, *South America*, 74.

35 Tower to FO No. 86 Com'l, 30 Mar. 1917, No. 91025 of 4 May 1917. FO 368/1690.

36 Tower to FO No. 128, 29 Mar. 1917, and minutes from the Foreign Office, No. 66522 of 30 Mar. 1917. FO 368/1690.

37 Memoranda from BT to War Office about meat, 2 Feb. 1917, Folder No. E31325. BT 13/74/E31640.

38 Tower to FO tel No. 128 Com'l, 29 Mar. 1917, and minutes by various officials in the Foreign Office through 7 Apr., No. 66522 of 30 Mar. 1917. FO 368/1690.

39   FO to Tower tel No. 123, 5 Apr. 1917, No. 71374 of 5 Apr. 1917. Note from
      William Morley-Alderson to FO, 12 Apr. 1917, No. 76968 of 14 Apr. 1917.
      Royal Commission on Wheat Supplies to FO, sent from FO to Tower tel No.
      180, 5 May 1917, No. 91900 of 5 May 1917. FO 368/1690. Also, ADM Intel-
      ligence Division to FO, No. 115664 of 11 Jun. 1917. FO 368/1691.

40   Tower to FO No. 233 Com'l, 11 Jun. 1917, No. 139071 of 14 July 1917. FO
      368/1691.

41   Tower to FO tel No. 160 Com'l, 19 Apr. 1917, No. 80942 of 20 Apr. 1917.
      FO 368/1690.

42   Tower to FO tel No. 21 Com'l, 19 May 1917, and Crowe's minute of 21 May,
      No. 101671 of 20 May 1917. FO 368/1691.

43   Tower to FO tel No. 424, 4 Oct. 1917, No. 191831 of 5 Oct. 1917. FO 368/1691.

44   "First Report of the Royal Commission on Wheat Supplies," P.P. 1921., xviii,
      Cmd. 1544, appendix 5, 27.

45   Gravil, *The Anglo-Argentine Connection*, 126.

46   Carl Solberg, *The Prairies and the Pampas: Agrarian Policy in Canada and
      Argentina, 1880–1930* (Stanford: Stanford University Press, 1987), 156–164.

47   Hew Strachan, *Financing the First World War* (Oxford: Oxford University
      Press, 2004), 216.

48   Albert, *South America*, 66–67.

49   H.S. Ferns, "Argentina: Part of an Informal Empire?" in Alistair Hennessy and
      John King (eds) *The Land that England Lost*, 50.

50   Sir Reginald Tower, "Argentina: Notes for H.R.H. The Prince of Wales' Visit
      1925," written in June 1925, 119–120. Mss. 813, University of London Library.

51   Rock, *Politics in Argentina*, 106–109.

52   Kirkpatrick, *South America and the War*, 57–65.

53   Tower, "Argentina: Notes for H.R.H.," 101.

54   "First Report of the Royal Commission on Wheat Supplies," P.P. 1921., xviii,
      Cmd. 1544, appendix 5.

55   Unsigned report by someone appointed by the Department of Information in
      Oct. 1917 to travel to Argentina. INF 4/6.

56   De Bunsen to Balfour, 13 June 1918. FO 800/200

57   Tower to FTD No. 360 of 9 July 1918. FO 118/469.

58   Sir Reginald Tower, "Argentina: Notes for H.R.H. The Prince of Wales' Visit
      1925," written in June 1925, 225–227. Mss. 813, University of London Library.

59   Tower to FTD No. 388, 20 July 1918. FO 118/469.

60   Tower to FTD No. 193, 27 Mar. 1918. FO 118/468.

61   Ross, *Argentina and Uruguay*, ch. II.

62   Copy of the US note verbale of Nov. 1916, in Peel to FO No. 16 Com'l of 16
      Feb. 1917, No. 73355 of 8 Apr. 1917. FO 368/1705.

63   Hambloch's report included in Peel to FO No. 4 Com'l, 17 Jan. 1917, No.
      78173 of 16 Apr. 1917. FO 368/1707.

64   See Miller, *Britain and Latin America*, 106–107.

65   Memo from FTD to BT on the relationship between the two departments, No.
      84465 of 18 Oct. 1916, No. 84465. Also, memo dealing with work of the FTD,
      No. 98245 of 18 Dec. 1916. FO 833/16.

66 Joslin, *A Century of Banking in Latin America*, 158; Albert, *South America*, 86.
67 Peel to FO tel No. 247 Pol., 27 May 1918, No. 94538 of 28 May 1918. FO 371/3167.
68 Minutes of meeting of 4 Nov. 1915. CAB 39/7.
69 Slade tells of this General Staff paper in the 43rd meeting of the WTAC, 27 Jul. 1916. CAB 39/32.
70 Memo from Hambloch of 25 Sept. 1916, enclosed in Peel to FO No. 112 Com'l, 28 Sept. 1916, No. 211014 of 21 Oct. 1916. FO 368/1495.
71 Letter from Wysard to Tufton of 10 Aug. 1916, No. 158665 of 12 Aug. 1916. From BT to FO, 27 Sept. 1916, No. 193017 of 28 Sept. 1916. FO 368/1496.
72 Copy of letter to Marconi from their representative in Rio de Janeiro, 28 Dec. 1915, in letter from Marconi Wireless Telegraph Co. Ltd. to FO on 17 Jan. 1916, No. 10728 of 18 Jan. 1916. FO 368/1494.
73 Minutes by Villiers, Tufton and Percy on 12 Sept., Crowe on 13 Sept., on Peel to FO No. 78 Com'l, 9 Aug. 1916, No. 176941 of 6 Sept. 1916. FO 368/1494.
74 Letter from Rothschild to FO, 25 Oct. 1916, No. 214537 of 26 Oct. 1916. FO 371/2640.
75 Memo to the War Committee of 23 Nov. 1916, No. 231061 of 17 Nov. 1916. FO 371/2640.
76 Minutes of War Committee meeting #139, 24 Nov. 1916. CAB 22/74.
77 Memo dealing with work of the FTD, No. 98245 of 18 Dec. 1916. FO 833/16.
78 FO to Peel No. 53 Pol., 26 Jan. 1917, No. 19822 of 25 Jan. 1917. FO 371/2900.
79 De Bunsen's minute on 28 Feb. 1917, No. 43559 of 27 Feb. 1917. FO 368/1706.
80 Peel to FO tel. No. 54, 31 Jan. 1917, No. 25732 of 2 Feb. 1917. FO 371/2900.
81 Peel to FO tel. No. 117, 26 Feb. 1917, No. 43982 of 27 Feb. 1917. FO 368/1706.
82 Villiers minute on 7 June 1917, Peel to FO No. 52, 12 May 1917. No. 112645 of 6 June 1917. FO 368/1705.
83 Peel to FO tel No. 119, 27 Feb. 1917, No. 44250 of 28 Feb. 1917. FO 368/1706.
84 Winston Fritsch, *External Constraints on Economic Policy in Brazil, 1889–1930* (Pittsburgh: University of Pittsburgh Press, 1988), 48–52.
85 ADM to FO, 19 July 1917, No. 143208 of 20 July 1917. FO 371/2901.
86 Hirst to Sperling, 17 May 1918, No. 92256 of 24 May 1918. FO 371/3168.
87 Memo from the Director of Military Intelligence of 19 Jul. 1917 (memo 0141/130, M.I.2), No. 142811 of 20 Jul 1917. FO 371/2901.
88 Martin, *Latin America and the War*, 82.
89 Peel to FO No. 106, 17 Nov. 1917, enclosed in Peel to Innes, 4 Dec. 1917. FO 505/360.
90 Minutes by Sperling on 24 Nov. 1917, H.G.K. on 28 Nov., Sperling on 3 Dec., No. 223156 of 23 Nov. 1917. FO 371/2900.
91 Peel to FO No. 121, 27 Dec. 1917, enclosed in Peel to Innes, 7 Jan. 1918. FO 505/360.
92 Peel to FO No. 23, 25 Mar. 1918, No. 77130 of 1 May 1918. FO 371/3167.
93 Peel to FO tel No. 595, 22 Nov. 1917, No. 223156 of 23 Nov. 1917. FO 371/2900.
94 Peel to FO No. 23, 25 Mar. 1918, No. 77130 of 1 May 1918. FO 371/3167.

95   For example, see the successful lawsuit brought by Zeizing against W.H. Walters for the refusal of the latter to deliver goods simply because Zeizing was on the British Statutory List. WTID weekly bulletin No. 142, 1 Aug. 1918. There is some indication that at the end of 1918, German firms had just begun what might have eventually become a rash of such lawsuits for breach of contract. Letter from Holmberg, Bech & Cia in Rio de Janeiro to Transmarina Co. of Stockholm, Daily Summary of Information No. 733, 5 Oct. 1918. ADM 137/2919.

96   Hirst memo of 17 May 1918, Percy memo of 22 May, minute by Peterson of 29 May, No. 92256 of 24 May 1918. FO 371/3168.

97   Luebke, *Germans in Brazil*, 193–196.

98   Steven Topik, *The Political Economy of the Brazilian State, 1889–1930* (Austin: University of Texas Press, 1987), 74. Fritsch, *External Constraints*, 49–52. Jeffrey J. Safford, *Wilsonian Maritime Diplomacy, 1913–1921* (New Brunswick, NJ: Rutgers University Press, 1978), 149.

99   O'Driscoll to Isaacs of Marconi Co., 18 Aug. 1917. Enclosure in Isaac to FO, 2 Oct. 1917. No. 190438, 3 Oct. 1917. FO 368/1705.

100 Peel to FO tel No. 148, 31 Mar. 1918, No. 64280 of 11 Apr. 1918. FO 371/3167.

101 Memo by Kerr, 8 Apr. 1918, No. 64280 of 11 Apr. 1918. FO 371/3167.

102 Memo by Crichton-Stuart, 8 Apr. 1918, No. 64280 of 11 Apr. 1918. FO 371/3167.

103 Peel to FO tel No. 168, 11 Apr. 1918, No. 65282 of 13 Apr. 1918. FO 371/3167.

104 From censors, D.S.I. No. U.S.A.E01214 of 12 Apr. 1918, a copy of the letter of 27 Feb. 1918, No. 65282 of 13 Apr. 1918. FO 371/3167.

105 FTD to Peel tel No. 205, 29 Apr. 1918, No. 65282 of 13 Apr. 1918. FO 371/3167.

106 Crichton-Stuart on 16 Apr. 1918, No. 65282 of 13 Apr. 1918. FO 371/3167.

107 Memo of 14 May 1918, No. 85430 of 14 May 1918. FO 371/3167.

108 Letter from de Bunsen to Balfour, 9 May 1918. De Bunsen papers, Box 11, MB/II/e.

109 Letter from de Bunsen to Balfour, 29 May 1918. From the original draft of the Parliamentary Paper (Cmd. 12) of May 1919 about the mission. This original draft was 54 pages, while the final published version was only 31, a result of much censorship of sensitive topics related to the economic war. Original draft is found in de Bunsen papers, Box 16, MB/V/b.

110 De Bunsen mission from Montevideo to FO tel No. 16, 24 May 1918, No. 106107 of 14 June 1918. FO 371/3167.

111 Peel to FO tel No. 247, 27 May 1918, No. 94538 of 28 May 1918. FO 371/3167.

112 FO to the Royal Commission on Wheat Supplies, 24 Jun. 1918, No. 109016 of 19 Jun. 1918. FO 371/3167.

113 Peel to FO tel No. 260, 3 Jun. 1918, No. 98629 of 4 June 1918. FO 371/3167.

114 Peel to FO tel. No. 303, 22 Jun. 1918, No. 111521 of 24 June 1918. FO 371/3167.

115 Minute by Sperling on the meeting of the inter-departmental committee, No. 115465 of 1 July 1918. FO 371/3167.

116 Peel to FTD tel No. 345, 15 July 1918, No. 124230 of 16 July 1918. FO 371/3167.
117 Peel to FO tel No. 65, 18 July 1918, No. 149318 of 30 Aug. 1918. Elliot minute of 17 July 1918, No. 116560 of 2 July 1918. FO 371/3167.
118 Pollock to Peel tel, No. 228041, 23 May 1919. FO 833/17.
119 Report by M.I.1.c. in Bahia on 20 Feb. 1918, sent from WTID to FO on 18 Apr. 1918, FO No. 69046 of 19 Apr. 1918. FO 368/1888.
120 Trade Division memo "German firms in Brazil," 22 Apr. 1918. ADM 137/2919
121 Minute by Sperling on the meeting of the inter-departmental committee, 12 June 1918, No. 106107 of 14 June 1918. Minute by Spens, 16 July 1918, No. 119253 of 8 July 1918. FO 371/3167.
122 Isaacs to FO, 2 Oct. 1917. No. 190438 of 3 Oct. 1917. FO 368/1705.
123 Hambloch to DOT No. 14, 24 Mar. 1918, FO No. 81604 of 30 May 1918. FO 368/2073.
124 Innes to FO No. 21, 11 Apr. 1918, No. 87870 of 17 May 1918. FO 371/3432.
125 Martin, *Latin America and the War*, 369–370.
126 Innes to FO No. 26, 18 May 1918. No. 116498, 2 July 1918. FO 371/3432.
127 Gerardo Caetano and José Rilla, *Historia Contemporánea del Uruguay, de la Colonia al Siglo XXI* (Montevideo: CLAEH, Editorial Fin de Siglo, 2005), 137–146.
128 Innes tel. No. 95, 9 Apr. 1918. No. 63959, 11 Apr. 1918. FO 371/3432.
129 Innes tel. No. 127, 11 May 1918. No. 84693, 13 May 1918. FO 371/3432.
130 Innes to FO No. 26, 18 May 1918. No. 116498, 2 July 1918. FO 371/3432.
131 Ross, *Argentina and Uruguay*, 60.
132 Juan A. Oddone, "The Formation of Modern Uruguay, *c.*1870–1930," in Bethell, Leslie (ed.) *The Cambridge History of Latin America, Vol. V, c.1870 to 1930* (Cambridge: Cambridge University Press, 1986), 464–470; Peter Winn, "British Informal Empire in Uruguay in the Nineteenth Century," *Past and Present 76* (1976): 125–126; Peter Winn, *Inglaterra y la Tierra Purpúrea* (Montevideo: Facultad de Humanidades y Ciencias Sociales, 1997), ch. 1.
133 Innes to FO No. 41 Com'l, 5 Jun. 1914, FO No. 29113 of 29 Jun. 1914. FO 368/1164.
134 Winn, "British Informal Empire in Uruguay," 100–126.
135 Innes to FTD No. 22, 22 Mar. 1917. FO 505/367.
136 Complaints by Mallet to DOT tel No. 75, 29 July 1919. FO 505/376.
137 Tonnage levels quoted in FO to Innes tel No. 69, 20 Apr. 1917. Number of ships is in FO tel No. 160, 4 Oct. 1917. FO 505/368.
138 Innes to FO tel No. 130, 3 July 1917. FO 505/368.
139 During the same five-year spans, meat products comprised 24 percent and 38 percent of the net value of Uruguayan exports. M.H.J. Finch, *A Political Economy of Uruguay since 1870* (New York: St Martin's Press, 1981), 129.
140 'First Report of the Royal Commission on Wheat Supplies', P.P. 1921., xviii, Cmd. 1544, appendix 5.
141 FO 505/368.
142 Finch, *A Political Economy of Uruguay*, 137.

143 See chapter "Yankees, War, and Trusts," in Peter H. Smith, *Politics and Beef in Argentina: Patterns of Conflict and Change* (New York and London: Columbia University Press, 1969).
144 Hanson, *Argentine Meat and the British Market*, 201n.
145 Report by Dr Spencer Low, a frigorifico inspector, in Innes to FO No. 30, 19 Oct. 1916, No. 229063 of 14 Nov. 1916. FO 368/1659.
146 BT to FO, 9 Dec. 1916, No. 250157 of 11 Dec. 1916. FO 368/1659.
147 Ministry of Shipping to FO on 18 Oct. 1917, enclosing letter from Consul-General J. Barboza Terra to Maclay of the Ministry of Shipping on 11 Oct., No. 200256 of 19 Oct. 1917. Uruguayan Legation to FO on 18 Oct. 1917, No. 201554 of 20 Oct. 1917. FO 368/1847.
148 Innes to FO tel No. 223, 18 Nov. 1917, No. 220641 of 19 Nov. 1917. FO 368/1847.
149 Ministry of Shipping to FO, 1 Dec. 1917, No. 229440 of 3 Dec. 1917. FO 368/1847.
150 Innes to FO No. 84, 24 Dec. 1917, No. 21052 of 2 Feb. 1918. FO 368/2027.
151 Innes to FO No. 16, 30 Jun. 1915, No. 102506 of 27 Jul. 1915. FO 368/1457.
152 See his regular, weekly reports on wool and hide exports to the US, in FO 505/358 and FO 505/359.
153 Innes to FTD No. 42, 28 Aug. 1916. FO 505/359.
154 Innes to FO tel No. 91, 10 May 1916, No. 89059 of 11 May 1916. FO 368/1659.
155 Innes to FTD No. 6, 8 Jan. 1917. FO 118/478.
156 Innes to FTD No. 113, 5 Dec. 1917. FO 118/478.
157 Innes, "Memorandum on the Reform of Birtish Companies and the Development of British Trade in Uruguay," given to Follett Holt of the de Bunsen mission, 5 June 1918. FO 505/367.
158 Innes to FTD tel No. 79, 26 Mar. 1918. FO 505/367.
159 Innes to FTD No. 97, 23 Oct. 1917. FO 118/478.
160 Innes to FTD No. 20, 28 Mar. 1918. FO 505/367.
161 Innes to FO tel No. 176, 6 Oct. 1917. FO 505/368.
162 Letters from de Bunsen to Balfour, 30 June 1918 and 17 July 1918. De Bunsen papers, Box 16, MB/V/b. For more on Chilean resistance to the Statutory List, see Couyoumdjian, *Chile y Gran Bretaña*, ch. VII.

8 Attempting to bring Greater Britain into the post-war

1 Margaret MacMillan, *Paris 1919* (New York: Random House, 2001), 159–160.
2 Chalkley to DOT No. 2, 3 Jan. 1919. FO 118/508.
3 DOT No. 18894, 8 Mar. 1919, No. 37801 of 10 Mar. FO 368/2050.
4 E. Lloyd Rolfe, *Report on Brazil's Trade & Industry in 1918, with Special Reference to the State of São Paulo. Hints & Information for Manufacturers & Merchants* (São Paulo: British Chamber of Commerce of São Paulo & Southern Brazil, 1919).
5 Pollock, "Effects produced by the Statutory List policy in Latin America, 1916–18," 19 Dec. 1918. FO 118/507.

6   Memo of 11 Nov. 1918, No. 207663 of 5 Nov. 1918. FO 833/17.
7   Memorandum to the Chancellor of the Exchequer asking for an annual subsidy, Council minutes, 15 Feb. 1917.
8   Report of the British Chamber of Commerce, in Tower to FTD No. 114, 25 Feb. 1918. FO 118/468.
9   Pollock, "Memorandum on Trade War," No. 132255 of 27 Jun. 1917. FO 833/18.
10 Council, 21 Nov. 1918.
11 Information from the IAC, Council, 19 Dec. 1918.
12 Executive Committee, 3 Jan. 1919.
13 Tower to FTD No. 12, 15 Jan. 1919. FO 118/507.
14 *The Times*, Sat., 21 Dec. 1918, p. 15.
15 FTD to Tower No. 9, 30 Jan. 1919, No. 216564/2. FO 118/507.
16 Tower to FTD No. 44, 10 Mar. 1919. FO 118/507. Also, Executive Committee, 7 Feb. 1919.
17 Executive Committee, 31 Jan. 1919.
18 Executive Committee, 31 Jan. 1919 and 14 Feb. 1919.
19 Pollock to Hankey, 14 Mar. 1919, No. 224067 of 18 Mar. 1919. FO 833/17.
20 Various minutes, No. 227955 of 19 May 1919. FO 833/17.
21 Telegram to Buenos Aires, No. 228041 of 23 May 1919. FO 833/17.
22 No. 227602, 3 May 1919. FO 833/17.
23 Kelly, *The Ruling Few*, 120.
24 See correspondence in BT 60/1/4.
25 Minutes on suggestion that the FTD should cease to exist as separate Dept. after 31 May 1919. No. 227955, 19 May 1919. FO 833/17.
26 No. 104928 of 17 July 1919. FO 368/2051.
27 FTD to Tower No. 388, 31 Oct. 1918, No. 205584/2 of 19 Dec. 1918. FO 118/461.
28 Hambloch memo of 16 Apr. 1919, in Peel to FO No. 13, 17 Apr. 1919. No. 72308 of 12 May 1919. FO 368/2073.
29 Executive Committee, 21 Feb. 1919.
30 Executive Committee, 5 Apr. 1919.
31 Executive Committee, 21 Mar. 1919.
32 This paragraph is based largely on B.W.E. Alford, *Britain in the World Economy since 1880* (London: Longman, 1996). Also, see Keith Grieves, *Sir Eric Geddes: Business and Government in War and Peace* (Manchester: Manchester University Press, 1989), ch. 5.
33 A.J.P. Taylor, *English History 1914–1945* (New York and Oxford: Oxford University Press, 1965), 130 (n.2), 139.
34 John Turner, "The Politics of 'Organised Business' in the First World War," *Businessmen and Politics: Studies of Business Activity in British Politics, 1900–1945*, ed. Turner (London and Exeter, NH: Heinemann, 1984).
35 Andrew Marrison, *British Business and Protection 1903–1932* (Oxford: Clarendon Press, 1996), 316–317.
36 Memo in Innes to FO No. 59, 30 Dec. 1918, and Wellesley minute on 12 Feb. 1919, No. 20779 of 6 Feb. 1919. FO 368/2226.

37   Ministry of Shipping to FO, 27 Feb. 1919, No. 32631 of 28 Feb. 1919. FO
      368/2226.
38   Steel-Maitland, "Reform and development of consular and commercial diplo-
      matic service," Mar. 1919. CP 11758. In Watt and Bourne, part II, K, vol. 1.
39   Steel-Maitland to Bonar Law, 17 Jan. 1919. Bonar Law papers, 102/1/20.
40   A. Geddes to Bonar Law, 5 May 1919. Bonar Law Papers, 97/3/5.
41   Homer, "Foreign Trade and Foreign Policy," 170–179. Also, Steel-Maitland to
      Bonar Law, 23 June 1919 and 13 July 1919. Bonar Law Papers, 97/4/21 and
      97/5/17.
42   D.O.T. to FO No. 85900, sending cable of 22 Aug. 1919, FO No. 123100 of
      1 Sept. 1919. FO 368/2074.
43   Executive Committee, 5 Sept. 1919.
44   Weaver, *Henry William Carless Davis*, 43.
45   Executive Committee, 14 Nov. 1919.
46   See G.H. Bennett, *British Foreign Policy during the Curzon Period, 1919–24*
      (New York: St Martin's Press, 1995).
47   Kelly, *The Ruling Few*, 203–209. Watt, *Succeeding John Bull*, 48.
48   DOT circular of 18 Aug. 1919, 68759/F/19. FO 118/507.
49   DOT circular of 17 Nov. 1919, 93245/F/19. FO 118/507.
50   Chalkley to DOT No. 123, 9 Oct. 1919. FO 118/508.
51   Circular 27657/F./20 to Chalkley, 16 Apr. 1920. FO 118/521.
52   11 Apr. 1921. BT 60/2/5.
53   20 Sept. 1921. Ms. 14,487, vol. 1 of the Committee Meetings of the Foreign
      and Colonial Affairs Committee of the Executive Council. Association of
      British Chamber of Commerce, Guildhall.
54   Homer, "Foreign Trade and Foreign Policy," 203.
55   Homer, "Foreign Trade and Foreign Policy," 220–223.
56   Kathleen Burk, "The Treasury: from Impotence to Power," in Burk (ed.) *War
      and the State*; Alford, *Britain in the World Economy*, ch. 4; Cain and Hopkins,
      Vol. II, 56–57; Taylor, *English History*, 129–130.
57   7th meeting of the Economic Mission to Argentina and Brazil, 25 July 1929,
      DOT 26538/1930. BT 60/26/2.
58   Meeting of 28 Mar. 1928. Ms. 16,508/1 London Chamber of Commerce,
      Argentine and Uruguay Section, Guildhall.
59   Chalkley to DOT No. 3, 8 Jan. 1920. FO 118/525.
60   BT 60/31/1.
61   Minutes of J. Tilley from conversation with Sir Herbert Gibson, 21 Sept. 1919.
      FO 800/152.
62   Mallet to DOT No. 3, 3 Dec. 1919, enclosing Chalkley's report. FO 118/507.
63   Innes to DOT No. 14, 27 Apr. 1919. FO 505/376.
64   Hambloch to DOT No. 14, 24 Mar. 1919, No. 81604 of 30 May 1919. FO
      368/2073.
65   See warning given by Butler to Ashley against including such statements in
      DOT funding appeals to the Treasury, 23 Mar. 1918. BT 13/85/E35466.
66   Chalkley to DOT No. 38, 28 Apr. 1919. FO 118/508.

67　Tower to FO No. 373, 23 Dec. 1918, No. 16026 of 29 Jan. 1919. FO 368/2050.
68　Chalkley to DOT No. 4, 8 Jan. 1919. FO 118/508.
69　DOT memo of 5 Feb. 1919, in circular to Innes No. 6, 11 Feb. 1919, DOT 643/LA. FO 505/377.
70　Kirkpatrick, *South America and the War*, 40.
71　Newton, *The 'Nazi Menace' in Argentina*, 21–23.
72　WTID weekly bulletin No. 173, 13 Mar. 1919. ADM 137/2919.
73　Mackie to FO tel No. 43, 31 Oct. 1919, No. 147556 of 1 Nov. 1919. FO 368/2051.
74　Chalkley's report on the quarter ending 31 Sept. 1920, in Chalkley to DOT No. 184 (A), 22 Oct. 1920. FO 118/525.
75　Chalkley to DOT No. 200 (A), 5 Nov. 1920. FO 118/525.
76　White's No. 58, 29 Aug. 1919, in Peel to FO No. 25, 11 Sept. 1919, No. 141113 of 14 Oct. 1919. FO 368/2074.
77　Mayer, "The Origins of the American Banking Empire in Latin America," 71.
78　Meeting of 10 Apr. 1923, Ms. 16,508/1, London Chamber of Commerce – Argentine & Uruguay Section, Guildhall.
79　Chalkley to DOT(B) No. 395/S.F.86, 14 Nov. 1923. FO 118/558.
80　British Chamber of Commerce in the Argentine Republic to Chalkley, 25 Mar. 1924. FO 118/565.
81　Hambloch to DOT No. 14, 24 Mar. 1919, No. 81604 of 30 May 1919. FO 368/2073.
82　Peel to FTD tel No. 156, 5 July 1919, and reply to Peel from M.D. Peterson on 15 July, FO No. 98803 of 7 July 1919. FO 368/2074.
83　FO No. 127557 of 11 Sept. 1919. FO 368/2074.
84　Minute by A. Duff Cooper, on letter from D.O.T. No. 115319 of 13 Aug. 1919. FO 368/2074.
85　Greenhill, "The Brazilian Coffee Trade," 227–230.
86　Tower to FTD No. 36, 15 Feb. 1919. FO 118/507.
87　Hoover memo "on German and Austrian trading in South America," 22 January 1919, in S.L. Bane and R.H. Lutz (eds), *The Blockade of Germany after the Armistice 1918–1919* (Stanford: Stanford University Press, 1942), 56–57.
88　Gravil, *The Anglo-Argentine Connection*, 121.
89　No. 88164 of 13 June 1919. FO 368/2051.
90　Dan Morgan, *Merchants of Grain* (New York: The Viking Press, 1979), 38–40.
91　FO to BT, 29 Mar. 1930, A1911/77/51 (DOT 26538/1930). BT 60/26/2.
92　Solberg, *The Prairies and the Pampas*, 143.
93　Greenhill, "Investment group, free-standing company or multinational?"
94　Newton, *The 'Nazi Menace'*, 24–27.
95　For the argument that Germans assimilated well, see Luebke, *Germans in Brazil*, 202–209. For the separatist view, see Hilton, *Hitler's Secret War*. For a more ambiguous, although generally separatist, view of Germans in Argentina, see Newton, *The 'Nazi Menace'*, 3.
96　Newton, *German Buenos Aires*, chs. 8–9; and Newton, *The 'Nazi Menace'*, chs 2, 4, 10.

97   Newton, *The 'Nazi Menace'*, ch. 10.
98   Hilton, *Hitler's Secret War*, 30, 37–38, 227, 293.
99   Barton, "Struggling Against Decline," 258.
100   Max Paul Friedman, *Nazis & Good Neighbors: The United States Campaign Against the Germans of Latin America in World War II* (Cambridge: Cambridge University Press, 2003). Knight, "Latin America," in Wm. Roger Louis (ed.) *Oxford History of the British Empire*, Vol. IV, 636.
101   Circular letter of 23 Sept. 1919, approved in Council, 18 Sept. 1919.
102   Circular letter of 17 Oct. 1919, approved in Council, 16 Oct. 1919.
103   Letter from British Chamber of Commerce in Brazil to British Chamber of Commerce in the Argentine Republic, 27 May 1920, in Council, 24 June 1920.
104   Kelly, *The Ruling Few*, 129.
105   Paul B. Goodwin, "Anglo-Argentine Commercial Relations: A Private Sector View, 1922–43." *Hispanic American Historical Review* 61:1 (1981): 29–51.
106   Barton, "Struggling Against Decline," 236.
107   Sir Hubert Llewellyn-Smith, *The Board of Trade* (London and New York: G.P. Putnam's Sons Ltd.), 82–83.

Conclusion: remembering the Great War in South America

1   Translation of article of 12 Apr. 1919 in Tower to FTD No. 54, 25 Apr. 1919. FO 118/507.
2   Tower to FTD No. 50, 5 Apr. 1919. FO 118/507.
3   Marion Siney, "British Official Histories of the Blockade of the Central Powers during the First World War," *American Historical Review*, 68, no. 2 (1963): 395 (note).
4   Inside front cover of FO 833/18.
5   Carless Davis's "History of the Blockade: Emergency Departments" is in BT 60/2/1. On the history of the books by Davis, Arnold-Forster, and Bell, see Siney, "British Official Histories," 392–401.
6   Medlicott, *The Economic Blockade*, 2: ch. IV. On US paternalism toward Latin America, see Friedman, *Nazis and Good Neighbors*.
7   Holder, *Activities of the British Community in Argentina*, 415.
8   Tower, "Argentina," 110–111.
9   Millington-Drake to J.C.C. Davidson, 17 Mar. 1938. Davidson Papers, folder 258, House of Lords Record Office.
10   Wm. Roger Louis, *Great Britain and Germany's Lost Colonies, 1914–1919* (Oxford: Clarendon Press, 1967), ch. 1. For criticism of Cain and Hopkins' use of the phrase "scramble for Latin America," see Knight, "Britain and Latin America," in Wm. Roger Louis, *Oxford History of the British Empire, Vol. III*, 139–142.
11   S.J. Hurwitz, *State Intervention in Great Britain: A Study of Economic Control and Social Response, 1914–1918* (New York: AMS Press, 1949). Keith Grieves, "Lloyd George and the Management of the British War Economy," in Chickering et al., *Great War, Total War*, 369–387. For a strong rejection of

the idea that improvisation ended up working well for Britain, see Ferguson, *The Pity of War*, ch. 9.

12 Correlli Barnett, *The Collapse of British Power* (London: Eyre Methuen, 1972), 93.

13 Joseph S. Tulchin, *The Aftermath of War: World War I and U.S. Policy Toward Latin America* (New York: New York University Press, 1971), 30–37. On the British "official mind" in the 1920s, see B.J.C. McKercher (ed.) *Anglo-American Relations in the 1920s: The Struggle for Supremacy* (Basingstoke: Macmillan, 1991), 11. John E. Moser, *Twisting the Lion's Tail: Anglophobia in the United States, 1921–48* (Basingstoke: Macmillan, 1999). Ritchie Ovendale, *Anglo-American Relations in the Twentieth Century* (New York: St Martin's Press, 1998), ch. 2. Watt, *Succeeding John Bull*, ch. 3.

14 Goodwin, "Anglo-Argentine Commercial Relations," 47.

15 For contemporary examples of the difficulty of maintaining financial and commercial embargos and blacklists, the lessons of the US treatment of North Korea and Iran are particularly appropriate. On the difficulty of tracking international transactions in a globalized world, see Steven R. Weisman, "The Ripples of Punishing One Bank," *New York Times*, 3 July 2007, C1, describing the blacklisting of the Banco Delta Asia for its holding of North Korean funds. Also, Steven R. Weisman, "Lack of ID Data Impedes U.N. Sanctions Against Iran," *New York Times*, 17 Sept. 2007, A3, on the difficulty of starting up sanctions on Iranian businesses and officials due to lack of sufficient information about the targeted companies; as the US government acknowledged to Weisman, "A mistake, like blocking travel or freezing the assets of the wrong entities, could produce a backlash." On the attempts, and failures, of a great power attempting to persuade its allies to join an economic war, see Steven R. Weisman, "Pressed by US, European Banks Limit Iran Deals," *New York Times*, 22 May 2006, A1; and Mark Landler, "Germany's Commercial Ties with Iran Prove Hard to Cut," *New York Times*, 21 Sept. 2007, A7.

16 Alan Knight, "Latin America," in Brown and Louis (eds) *The Oxford History of the British Empire, Vol IV*, 622–642; Miller, *Britain and Latin America*, 202.

Bibliography

Archives and personal papers

Foreign Office (FO), Board of Trade (BT), Admiralty (ADM), Cabinet (CAB), and other official papers, at the Public Record Office, Kew.

British Chamber of Commerce in the Argentine Republic, Buenos Aires, Argentina.

Association of British Chambers of Commerce and London Chamber of Commerce, Guildhall.

Private papers of Maurice de Bunsen, Viscount Hanworth (Pollock), Laming Worthington-Evans, at the Bodleian Library, Oxford.

Private papers of Lord Hardinge of Penshurst, at Cambridge University Library, Cambridge.

Private papers of Andrew Bonar Law, J.C.C. Davidson, David Lloyd George, at the House of Lords Record Office, London.

Private papers of Viscount Cecil of Chelwood, at the British Library, London.

Private papers of Admiral Edmond Slade at the National Maritime Museum, Greenwich.

Papers of various London-based South American banks, in Bank of London and South America Business Archives (BOLSA), Library of University College, London.

Manuscript by Sir Reginald Tower, "Argentina: Notes for HRH The Prince of Wales' Visit 1925", written in June 1925, in University of London Library, Senate House, London.

Periodical and serial sources cited

Board of Trade Journal

Bourne, Kenneth and D. Cameron Watt (eds), *British Documents on Foreign Affairs – Reports and Papers from the Foreign Office Confidential Print*. Frederick, MD: University Publications of America, various dates.

Buenos Aires Herald

Hansard

House of Commons Sessional Papers

The Times (London)

Secondary sources

Abel, C. and Lewis, C. (eds), *Latin America: Economic Imperialism and the State.* London: Athlone, 1985.

Albert, Bill, *South America and the First World War: The Impact of the War on Brazil, Argentina, Peru and Chile.* Cambridge: Cambridge University Press, 1988.

Alford, B.W.E., *Britain in the World Economy since 1880.* London: Longman, 1996.

Anderson, Benedict, *Imagined Communities: Reflections on the Origin and Spread of Nationalism.* London: Verso, 1991.

Armitage, David, "Greater Britain: A Useful Category of Historical Analysis?" *American Historical Review*, 104:2 (Apr. 1999): 427–445.

Arnold-Forster, W. *The Blockade, 1914–1919: Before the Armistice – and After.* Oxford: Clarendon Press, 1939.

Bailey, Thomas A., "The United States and the Blacklist during the Great War." *Journal of Modern History*, vi (March 1934).

Bailey, T.A., *The Policy of the United States Toward the Neutrals, 1917–1918.* Baltimore: The Johns Hopkins Press, 1942.

Bane, Suda Lorena and Ralph Haswell Lutz (eds), *The Blockade of Germany after the Armistice 1918–1919. Selected Documents of the Supreme Economic Council, Superior Blackade Council, Americal Relief Administration, and other Wartime Organisations.* Stanford: Stanford University Press, 2001.

Barclay, Glen, *Struggle for a Continent: The Diplomatic History of South America, 1917–1945.* London: Sidgwick & Jackson, 1971.

Barnett, Correlli, *The Collapse of British Power.* London: Eyre Methuen, 1972.

Barnett, L. Margaret, *British Food Policy During the First World War.* Boston: George Allen & Unwin, 1985.

Barton, Jonathan R., "Struggling Against Decline: British Business in Chile, 1919–33." *Journal of Latin American Studies*, 32 (2000): 235–264.

Bayly, C.A., *The Birth of the Modern World 1780–1914: Global Connections and Comparisons.* Oxford: Blackwell, 2004.

Bayly, C.A. et. al., "AHR Conversation: On Transnational History." *American Historical Review*, 111 (2006): 1441–1464.

Bell, A.C., *A History of the Blockade of Germany and of the Countries Associated with Her in the Great War, Austria-Hungary, Bulgaria, and Turkey, 1914–1918.* London: HMSO, 1961 [1937].

Bendaña, Alejandro, *British Capital and Argentine Dependence, 1816–1914.* NY: Garland Publishing, 1988.

Bennett, G.H., *British Foreign Policy during the Curzon Period, 1919–24.* New York: St Martin's Press, 1995.

Bethell, Leslie (ed.), *The Cambridge History of Latin America, Volume IV, c.1870 to 1930.* Cambridge: Cambridge University Press, 1986.

Boemeke, Manfred R., Roger Chickering and Stig Förster, *Anticipating Total War: The German and American Experiences, 1871–1914.* Cambridge: German Historical Institute and Cambridge University Press, 1999.

Bordo, Michael D., Alan M. Taylor, and Jeffrey G. Williamson (eds), *Globalization in Historical Perspective*. Chicago and London: University of Chicago Press, National Bureau of Economic Research, 2003.

Bryce, James, *South America: Observations and Impressions* (revised edition). New York: Macmillan, 1917.

Bulmer-Thomas, Victor, *The Economic History of Latin America since Independence*. Cambridge: Cambridge University Press, 1994.

Bunselmeyer, Robert E., *The Cost of the War, 1914–1919: British Economic War Aims and the Origins of Reparation*. Hamden, CT: Archon Books, 1975.

Burk, Kathleen (ed.), *War and the State: The Transformation of British Government, 1914–1919*. London: George Allen & Unwin, 1982.

Burk, Kathleen (ed.), *Britain, America and the Sinews of War, 1914–1918*. Boston: George Allen & Unwin, 1985.

Caetano, Gerardo and José Rilla, *Historia Contemporánea del Uruguay, de la Colonia al Siglo XXI*. Montevideo: CLAEH, Editorial Fin de Siglo, 2005.

Cain, P.J. and A.G. Hopkins, *British Imperialism: Innovation and Expansion, 1688–1914*. London: Longman, 1993.

Cain, P.J. and A.G. Hopkins, *British Imperialism: Crisis and Deconstruction 1914–1990*. London: Longman, 1993.

Cain, P.J. and A.G. Hopkins, *British Imperialism, 1688–2000* (2nd edn). Harlow, England: Longman, 2002.

Cecil, David, *The Cecils of Hatfield House: An English Ruling Family*. Boston: Houghton Mifflin Co., 1973.

Cecil, Hugh and Peter Liddle (eds), *Facing Armageddon: The First World War Experienced*. London: Leo Cooper, 1996.

Cecil of Chelwood, Viscount (Lord Robert), *A Great Experiment*. New York: Oxford University Press, 1941.

Chapman, S.D., "British-based Investment Groups before 1914." *Economic History Review*, 2nd series, 38:2 (May 1985): 230–251.

Chapman, S.D., "The Free-Standing Company, 1870–1914: an important Type of British Foreign Direct Investment." *Economic History Review*, 2nd series, 41:2 (May 1988).

Chickering, Roger, *Imperial Germany and the Great War, 1914–1918* (2nd edn). Cambridge: Cambridge University Press, 2004.

Chickering, Roger and Stig Förster (eds), *Great War, Total War: Combat and Mobilization on the Western Front, 1914–1918*. Cambridge: German Historical Institute and Cambridge University Press, 2000.

Chickering, Roger and Stig Förster (eds), *The Shadows of Total War: Europe, East Asia, and the United States*. Cambridge: German Historical Institute and Cambridge University Press, 2003.

Consett, M.W.W.P., *The Triumph of Unarmed Forces*. New York: Brentano's, 1923.

Coogan, John W., *The End of Neutrality: The United States, Britain, and Maritime Rights, 1899–1915*. Ithaca: Cornell University Press, 1981.

Couyoumdjian, Juan Ricardo, *Chile y Gran Bretaña Durante la Primera Guerra Mundial y la Postguerra, 1914–1921*. Santiago, Chile: Editorial Andres Bello, 1986.

Di Tella, G. and D.C.M. Platt, *The Political Economy of Argentina, 1880–1914*. London: Macmillan, 1986.

d'Ombrain, Nicholas, *War Machinery and High Policy: Defence Administration in Peacetime Britain, 1902–1914*. London: Oxford University Press, 1973.

Davenport-Hines, R.P.T., *Dudley Docker: The Life and Times of a Trade Warrior*. Cambridge: Cambridge University Press, 1984.

Edelstein, M., *Overseas Investment in the Age of High Imperialism in the United Kingdom, 1850–1914*. London: Methuen, 1982.

Egerton, George, *Great Britain and the Creation of the League of Nations*. Chapel Hill: University of North Carolina Press, 1978.

Epstein, Fritz T., "European military influences in Latin America." Unpublished, Library of Congress mss., 1941.

Farrar, Marjorie Milbank, *Conflict and Compromise: The Strategy, Politics and Diplomacy of the French Blockade, 1914–1918*. The Hague: Martinus Nijhoff, 1974.

Fayle, C.E., *The War and the Shipping Industry*. London: Oxford University Press, 1927.

Ferguson, Niall, *The Pity of War*. New York: Basic Books, 1999.

Ferns, H.S., *Britain and Argentina in the Nineteenth Century*. Oxford: Clarendon Press, 1960.

Ferns, H.S., "Argentina: Part of an Informal Empire?" in Alistair Hennessy and John King (eds), *The Land that England Lost: Argentina and Britain, a Special Relationship*. London: British Academic Press, 1992, 50.

Ferns, H.S., "Britain's Informal Empire in Argentina, 1806–1914." *Past and Present*, 4 (1963).

Finch, M.H.J., *A Political Economy of Uruguay since 1870*. New York: St Martin's Press, 1981.

Fischer, Fritz, *Germany's Aims in the First World War*. New York: W.W. Norton, 1967.

Forbes, I.L.D., "German Informal Imperialism in South America before 1914," *Economic History Review*, 2nd series, vol XXXI (1978), 384–398.

Ford, A.G., *The Gold Standard, 1880–1914: Britain and Argentina*. Oxford: Clarendon Press, 1962.

Førland, Tor Egil, "The History of Economic Warfare: International Law, Effectiveness, Strategies," *Journal of Peace Research*, 30:2 (1993).

French, David, *British Economic and Strategic Planning 1905–1915*. London: George Allen & Unwin, 1982.

Frieden, Jeffry, *Global Capitalism: Its Fall and Rise in the Twentieth Century*. New York and London: W.W. Norton & Co., 2006.

Friedman, Max Paul, *Nazis and Good Neighbors: The United States Campaign Against the Germans of Latin America in World War II*. Cambridge: Cambridge University Press, 2003.

Fritsch, Winston, *External Constraints on Economic Policy in Brazil, 1889–1930*. Pittsburgh: University of Pittsburgh Press, 1988.

Gallagher, John and Ronald Robinson, "The Imperialism of Free Trade". *Economic History Review*, 2nd series, 6:1 (1953).

Goñi Demarchi, Carlos A., José Nicolás Scala, and Germán W. Berraondo, *Yrigoyen y la Gran Guerra: Aspectos Desconocidos de una Gesta Ignorada*. Buenos Aires: Ediciones Ciudad Argentina, 1998.

Goodwin, Paul B., "Anglo-Argentine Commercial Relations: A Private Sector View, 1922–43." *Hispanic American Historical Review*, 61:1 (1981): 29–51.

Graham, Richard, "A British Industry in Brazil: Rio Flour Mills, 1886–1920." *Business History*, 8:1 (January 1966).

Graham, Richard, *Britain and the Onset of Modernization in Brazil, 1850–1914*. Cambridge: Cambridge University Press, 1968.

Graham, Richard (ed.), *The Idea of Race in Latin America, 1870–1940*. Austin: University of Texas Press, 1990.

Gravil, Roger, *The Anglo-Argentine Connection, 1900–1939*. Boulder and London: Westview Press, 1985.

Greenhill, Robert G., "Investment Group, Free-standing Company or Multinational? Brazilian Warrant: 1909–52." *Business History*, 37:1 (January 1995): 86.

Grey of Fallodon, Edward, *Twenty-Five Years, 1892–1916* (2 vols). New York: Frederick A. Stokes Co., 1925.

Grieves, Keith, *Sir Eric Geddes: Business and Government in War and Peace*. Manchester: Manchester University Press, 1989.

Guichard, Lieut Louis, *The Naval Blockade 1914–1918*, translated by Christopher R. Turner. New York: D. Appleton & Co., 1930.

Hankey, Lord, *The Supreme Command 1914–1918* (2 vols). London: George Allen & Unwin, 1961.

Hanson, Simon G., *Argentine Meat and the British Market: Chapters in the History of the Argentine Meat Industry*. Stanford: Stanford University Press, 1938.

Hardach, Gerd, *The First World War, 1914–1918*. Berkeley and Los Angeles: University of California Press, 1977.

Hennessy, Alistair and John King (eds), *The Land that England Lost: Argentina and Britain, a Special Relationship*. London: British Academic Press, 1992.

Herwig, Holger H., *Germany's Vision of Empire in Venezuela, 1871–1914*. Princeton: Princeton University Press, 1986.

Herwig, Holger H., *The First World War: Germany and Austria-Hungary 1914–1918*. London: Arnold, 1997.

Hicks, Agnes H., *The Story of the Forestal*. London: The Forestal Land, Timber and Railways Co. Ltd, 1956.

Hilton, Stanley E., *Brazil and the Great Powers, 1930–1939: The Politics of Trade Rivalry*. Austin and London: University of Texas Press, 1975.

Hilton, Stanley E., *Hitler's Secret War in South America, 1939–1945: German Military Espionage and Allied Counterespionage in Brazil*. Baton Rouge: Louisiana State University Press, 1999.

Hinsley, F.H. (ed.), *British Foreign Policy Under Sir Edward Grey*. Cambridge: Cambridge University Press, 1977.

Hobsbawm, Eric and Terence Ranger (eds), *The Invention of Tradition*. Cambridge: Cambridge University Press, 1992.

Hoffman, Ross J.S., *Great Britain and the German Trade Rivalry*. Philadelphia: University of Pennsylvania Press, 1933.

Holder, Arthur L. (ed.), *Activities of the British Community in Argentina during the Great War, 1914–1919*. Buenos Aires: The British Society in the Argentine Republic, 1920.

Homer, F.J.X., "Foreign Trade and Foreign Policy: The British Department of Overseas Trade, 1916–1922." Dissertation, University of Virginia, 1971.

Hopkins, A.G., "Informal Empire in Argentina: an Alternative View", *Journal of Latin American Studies*, 26 (1994).

Hurd, Archibald, *The Merchant Navy* (3 vols). New York: Longmans, Green & Co., 1921.

Hurwitz, S.J., *State Intervention in Great Britain: A Study of Economic Control and Social Response, 1914–1918*. New York: AMS Press, 1949.

Jones, Charles, *International Business in the Twentieth Century: The Rise and Fall of a Cosmopolitan Bourgeoisie*. New York: New York University Press, 1987.

Jones, Geoffrey, *Merchants to Multinationals: British Trading Companies in the Nineteenth and Twentieth Centuries*. Oxford: Oxford University Press, 2000.

Joslin, David, *A Century of Banking in Latin America: To Commemorate the Centenary in 1962 of The Bank of London & South America Limited*. London: Oxford University Press, 1963.

Kaufman, Burton I., *Efficiency and Expansion: Foreign Trade Organization in the Wilson Administration, 1913–1921*. (Westport, CT and London: Greenwood Press, 1974.

Keegan, John, *The First World War*. New York: New York: Knopf, 1998.

Kelly, Sir David, *The Ruling Few, or the Human Background to Diplomacy*. London: Hollis & Carter, 1952.

Kennedy, Paul, *The Rise and Fall of British Naval Mastery*. London: Allen Lane, 1976.

Kennedy, Paul, *The Rise of the Anglo-German Antagonism 1860–1914*. London: George Allen & Unwin, 1980.

Kennedy, Paul, *Strategy and Diplomacy*. London: Fontana Press, 1984.

Kirkpatrick, Frederick A., *South America and the War: Being the substance of a course of lectures delivered in the University of London, King's College under the Tooke Trust in the Lent Term*. Cambridge: Cambridge University Press, 1918.

Kneer, Warren G., *Great Britain and the Caribbean, 1901–1913: A Study in Anglo-American Relations*. Michigan: Michigan State University Press, 1975.

Lascano, Luis C. Alan, *Yrigoyen y la Guerra Mundial*. Buenos Aires: Editorial Korrigan, 1974.

Lewis, Colin, *British Railways in Argentina 1857–1914*. London: Athlone, 1983.

Llairo, Maria Monserrat and Raimundo Siepe, *Argentina en Europa: Yrigoyen y la Sociedad de las Naciones (1918–1920)*. Buenos Aires: Ediciones Macchi, 1997.

Louis, Wm. Roger, *Great Britain and Germany's Lost Colonies, 1914–1919*. Oxford: Clarendon Press, 1967.

Louis, Wm. Roger and Porter, Andrew, *The Oxford History of the British Empire. Vol. III: The Nineteenth Century*. Oxford and New York: Oxford University Press, 1999.

Louis, Wm. Roger and Brown, Judith, *The Oxford History of the British Empire. Vol. IV: The Twentieth Century*. Oxford and New York: Oxford University Press, 1999.

Louis, Wm. Roger and Winks, Robin, *The Oxford History of the British Empire. Vol. V: Historiography*. Oxford and New York: Oxford University Press, 1999.

Luebke, Frederick C., *Germans in Brazil: A Comparative History of Cultural Conflict During World War I*. Baton Rouge and London: Louisiana State University Press, 1987.

Maack, Reinhard, "The Germans of South Brazil: A German View." *The Quarterly Journal of Inter-American Relations*. v. 1, 3 (1939): 5–23.

MacMillan, Margaret, *Paris 1919*. New York: Random House, 2001.

Maisel, Ephraim, "The Formation of the Department of Overseas Trade, 1919–26." *Journal of Contemporary History*. 24:1 (Jan. 1989): 169–190.

Manchester, Alan K., *British Preeminence in Brazil. Its Rise and Decline. A Study in European Expansion*. Chapel Hill: The University of North Carolina Press, 1933.

Marder, Arthur J., *From the Dreadnought to Scapa Flow: The Royal Navy in the Fisher Era, 1904–1919. Volume I: The Road to War, 1904–1914*. London: Oxford University Press, 1961.

Marrison, Andrew, *British Business and Protection 1903–1932*. Oxford: Clarendon Press, 1996.

Martin, Percy Alvin, *Latin America and the War*. Baltimore: Johns Hopkins University Press, 1925.

Marwick, Arthur, *The Deluge: British Society and the First World War*. New York and London: W.W. Norton & Co., 1965.

Mayer, Robert, "The Origins of the American Banking Empire in Latin America: Frank A. Vanderlip and the National City Bank." *Journal of Interamerican Studies and World Affairs*, 15:1 (Feb. 1973): 60–76.

McDermott, John, "Total War and the Merchant State: Aspects of British Economic Warfare against Germany, 1914–16." *Canadian Journal of History* XXI (April 1986): 61–76.

McDermott, John, "Trading with the Enemy: British Business and the Law During the First World War," *Canadian Journal of History/Annales canadiennes d'histoire*, XXXII (Aug. 1997): 201–220.

McKercher, B.J.C. (ed.), *Anglo-American Relations in the 1920s: The Struggle for Supremacy*. Basingstoke and London: Macmillan, 1991.

Medlicott, W.N., *The Economic Blockade* (2 vols). London: HMSO and Longmans, Green & Co., 1952–59.

Miller, Rory, Britain and Latin America in the Nineteenth and Twentieth Centuries. London: Longman, 1993.

Miller, Rory, "Latin American Manufacturing and the First World War: An Exploratory Essay." *World Development*, 9, no. 8 (1981): 707–716.

Morgan, Dan, *Merchants of Grain*. New York: The Viking Press, 1979.

Moser, John E., *Twisting the Lion's Tail: Anglophobia in the United States, 1921–48*. Basingstoke: Macmillan, 1999.

Newton, Ronald C., *German Buenos Aires, 1900–1933: Social Change and Cultural Crisis*. Austin and London: University of Texas Press, 1977.

Newton, Ronald C., *The 'Nazi Menace' in Argentina, 1931–1947*. Stanford: Stanford University Press, 1992.

Nunn, Frederick M., *Yesterday's Soldiers: European Military Professionalism in South America, 1890–1940*. Lincoln and London: University of Nebraska Press, 1983.

Offer, Avner, "Morality and Admiralty: 'Jacky' Fisher, Economic Warfare and the Laws of War," *Journal of Contemporary History*, 23 (1988): 99–119.

Offer, Avner, *The First World War: An Agrarian Interpretation*. Oxford: Clarendon Press, 1989.

Orde, Anne, *The Eclipse of Great Britain: The United States and British Imperial Decline, 1895–1956*. New York: St Martin's Press, 1996.

Osborne, Eric, *Britain's Economic Blockade of Germany, 1914–1919*. London and New York: Frank Cass, 2004.

Osterhammel, Jurgen and Niels P. Petersson, *Globalization: A Short History*. Princeton: Princeton University Press, 2005.

Ovendale, Ritchie, *Anglo-American Relations in the Twentieth Century*. New York: St Martin's Press, 1998.

Parmelee, Maurice, *Blockade and Sea Power: The Blockade, 1914–1919, and its Significance for a World State*. New York: Thomas Y. Crowell Co., 1924.

Parrini, Carl, *Heir to Empire: United States Economic Diplomacy, 1916–1923*. Pittsburgh: University of Pittsburgh Press, 1969.

Perkins, Bradford, *The Great Rapprochement: England and the United States, 1895–1914*. New York: Atheneum, 1968.

Pinsdorf, Marion K., *German-Speaking Entrepreneurs: Builders of Business in Brazil*. New York, Bern, Frankfurt-am-Main and Paris: Peter Lang, 1990.

Platt, D.C.M., *Finance, Trade, and Politics in British Foreign Policy, 1815–1914*. Oxford: Clarendon Press, 1968.

Platt, D.C.M., *The Cinderella Service: British Consuls since 1825*. Hamden, Conn: Archon Books, 1971.

Platt, D.C.M., "Problems in the Interpretation of Foreign Trade Statistics before 1914," *Journal of Latin American Studies*, 3:2 (1971), 119–130.

Platt, D.C.M., "Economic Imperialism and the Businessman: Britain and Latin America before 1914," in Roger Owen and Bob Sutcliffe (eds), *Studies in the Theory of Imperialism*. London: Longman, 1972.

Platt, D.C.M., *Latin America and British Trade 1806–1914*. New York: Harper & Row, 1972.

Platt, D.C.M. (ed.), *Business Imperialism, 1840–1930: An Inquiry Based on British Experience in Latin America*. Oxford: Clarendon Press, 1977.

Proudman, Mark F., "The Most Important History: The *American Historical Review* and Our English Past," *The Journal of the Historical Society*, VI:2 (June 2006).

Ranft, Bryan (ed.), *Technical Change and British Naval Policy, 1860–1939*. London: Hodder & Stoughton, 1977.

Reber, Vera Blinn, *British Mercantile Houses in Buenos Aires, 1810–1880*. Cambridge, MA: Harvard University Press, 1979.

Ridings, Eugene, *Business Interest Groups in Nineteenth-Century Brazil*. Cambridge: Cambridge University Press, 1994.

Rippy, J.F., *British Investments in Latin America, 1822–1949: a Case Study of Private Enterprise in Retarded Regions*. Minneapolis: University of Minnesota Press, 1959.

Roche, Jean, *La Colonisation Allemande et Le Rio Grande do Sul*. Paris: Institut des Hautes Études de l'Amérique Latine, 1959.

Rock, David, *Politics in Argentina, 1890–1930: The Rise and Fall of Radicalism*. Cambridge: Cambridge University Press, 1975.

Rock, David, *Argentina 1516–1987: From Spanish Colonization to Alfonsín*. Berkeley: University of California Press, 1987.

Rolfe, E. Lloyd, *Report on Brazil's Trade & Industry in 1918, with Special Reference to the State of São Paulo. Hints & Information for Manufacturers & Merchants*. São Paulo: British Chamber of Commerce of São Paulo and Southern Brazil, 1919.

Rose, Kenneth, *The Later Cecils*. London: Weidenfeld & Nicolson, 1975.

Rosenberg, Emily S., *World War I and the Growth of United States Predominance in Latin America*. New York and London: Garland Publishing, 1987.

Ross, Gordon, *Argentina and Uruguay*. London: Methuen & Co. Ltd, 1917.

Rothwell, V.H., *British War Aims and Peace Diplomacy, 1914–1918*. Oxford: Clarendon Press, 1971.

Safford, Jeffrey J., *Wilsonian Maritime Diplomacy, 1913–1921*. New Brunswick, NJ: Rutgers University Press, 1978.

Salter, J.A., *Allied Shipping Control: An Experiment in International Administration*. Oxford: Clarendon Press, 1921.

Schiff, Warren, "The Influence of the German Armed Forces and War Industry on Argentina, 1880–1914." *Hispanic American Historical Review*, 52 (Aug. 1972).

Scobie, James R., *Revolution on the Pampas: A Social History of Argentine Wheat, 1860–1910*. Austin: University of Texas Press, 1964.

Searle, G.R., *The Quest for National Efficiency: A Study in British Politics and Political Thought, 1899–1914*. Berkeley and Los Angeles: University of California Press, 1971.

Siepe, Raimundo, *Yrigoyen, la Primera Guerra Mundial y las relaciones económicas*. Buenos Aires: Centro Editor de América Latina, 1992.

Siney, Marion, "British Official Histories of the Blockade of the Central Powers during the First World War." *American Historical Review* 68:2 (Jan. 1963): 392–401.

Siney, Marion, *The Allied Blockade of Germany, 1914–1916*. Westport, CT: Greenwood Press, 1973 [1957].

Smith, Sir Hubert Llewellyn, *The Board of Trade*. London and New York: G.P. Putnam's Sons Ltd, 1928.

Smith, Peter H., *Politics and Beef in Argentina: Patterns of Conflict and Change*. NY and London: Columbia University Press, 1969.

Solberg, Carl, *The Prairies and the Pampas: Agrarian Policy in Canada and Argentina, 1880–1930*. Stanford: Stanford University Press, 1987.

Steiner, Zara, *The Foreign Office and Foreign Policy, 1898–1914*. Cambridge: Cambridge University Press, 1969.

Stevenson, David, *The First World War and International Politics*. Oxford: Oxford University Press, 1988.

Stevenson, David, *Cataclysm: The First World War as Political Tragedy*. New York: Basic Books, 2004.

Stone, Irving, "British Long-term Investment in Latin America: 1865–1913." *Business History Review*, 42:3 (Autumn 1968): 311–339.

Stone, Irving, "British Direct and Portfolio Investment before 1914." *Journal of Economic History*, 37:3 (September 1977).

Strachan, Hew, *The First World War. Vol. 1: To Arms*. Oxford: Oxford University Press, 2001.

Strachan, Hew, *Financing the First World War*. Oxford: Oxford University Press, 2004.

Sykes, Alan, *Tariff Reform in British Politics, 1903–1913*. Oxford: Clarendon Press, 1979.

Taylor, A.J.P., *English History 1914–1945*. New York and Oxford: Oxford University Press, 1965.

Thompson, Andrew, "Informal Empire? An Exploration in the History of Anglo-Argentine Relations, 1810–1914." *Journal of Latin American Studies* (1992).

Thompson, Andrew, *Imperial Britain: The Empire in British Politics c.1880–1932*. London: Longman, 2000.

Tobler, Hans Werner and Peter Waldmann, "German Colonies in South America: A New Germany in the Cono Sur?" *Journal of Interamerican Studies and World Affairs*, 22:2 (May 1980): 227–245.

Topik, Steven, *The Political Economy of the Brazilian State, 1889–1930*. Austin: University of Texas Press, 1987.

Tornquist, Ernesto, & Cia, *El Desarrollo Económico de la República Argentina en los ultimos cinquenta años*. Buenos Aires: Tornquist, 1920.

Tulchin, Joseph S., *The Aftermath of War: World War I and U.S. Policy Toward Latin America*. New York: New York University Press, 1971.

Tulchin, Joseph S., *Argentina and the United States: A Conflicted Relationship*. Boston: Twayne Publishers, 1990.

Turner, John (ed.), *Businessmen and Politics: Studies of Business Activity in British Politics, 1900–1945*. London and Exeter, NH: Heinemann, 1984.

Vincent, Paul, *The Politics of Hunger: The Allied Blockade of Germany, 1915–1919*. Athens, OH and London: Ohio University Press, 1985.

Walne, Peter (ed.), *A Guide to Manuscript Sources for the History of Latin America and the Caribbean in the British Isles*. Oxford: Oxford University Press, 1973.

Warman, Roberta M., "The Erosion of Foreign Office Influence in the Making of Foreign Policy, 1916–1918." *The Historical Journal*, 15:1 (Mar. 1972): 133–159.

Watson, N.L., *The Argentine as a Market: A report to the Electors to the Gartside Scholarships on the Results of a Tour in the Argentine in 1906–7*. Manchester: Manchester University Press, 1908.

Watt, D.C., *Succeeding John Bull: America in Britain's Place, 1900–1975*. Cambridge: Cambridge University Press, 1984.

Weaver, Frederick S., *Latin America in the World Economy: Mercantile Colonialism to Global Capitalism*. Boulder, CO: Westview Press, 2000.

Weaver, J.R.H., *Henry William Carless Davis 1874–1928, A Memoir*. London: Constable and Company Ltd, 1933.

Weinmann, Ricardo, *Argentina en la Primera Guerra Mundial: Neutralidad, transicion politica y continuismo economico*. Buenos Aires: Editorial Biblos, 1994.

Wilkins, Mira, *The Emergence of Multinational Enterprise: American Business Abroad from the Colonial Era to 1914*. Cambridge, MA: Harvard University Press, 1970.

Wilson, Trevor, *The Downfall of the Liberal Party*. London: Collins, 1966.

Wilson, Trevor, *The Myriad Faces of War: Britain and the Great War, 1914–1918*. Cambridge: Polity Press, 1986.

Winn, Peter, "British Informal Empire in Uruguay in the Nineteenth Century." *Past and Present*, 76 (1976): 100–126.

Winn, Peter, *Inglaterra y la Tierra Purpúrea*. Montevideo: Facultad de Humanidades y Ciencias Sociales, 1997.

Young, George F.W., *The Germans in Chile: Immigration and Colonization, 1849–1914*. New York: Center for Migration Studies, 1974.

Index